CW01630613

AB

JAMES D.J. BROWN

Cracking the Crab

Russian Espionage Against Japan, from Peter the Great to Richard Sorge

HURST & COMPANY, LONDON

First published in the United Kingdom in 2025 by
C. Hurst & Co. (Publishers) Ltd.,
New Wing, Somerset House, Strand, London, WC2R 1LA
© James D.J. Brown, 2025
All rights reserved.

The right of James D.J. Brown to be identified as the author of this publication is asserted by him in accordance with the Copyright, Designs and Patents Act, 1988.

A Cataloguing-in-Publication data record for this book is available from the British Library.

ISBN: 9781805263036

This book is printed using paper from registered sustainable and managed sources.

www.hurstpublishers.com

CONTENTS

INTRODUCTION

Name a Russian spy, any Russian spy. There is no shortage of possible answers. Some will think of Kim Philby and the other members of the Cambridge Five who spied for Moscow against the United Kingdom during the Second World War. In the United States, memorable cases include Julius and Ethel Rosenberg, who passed nuclear secrets to the Soviets during the 1940s, and Aldrich Ames, the CIA officer who betrayed dozens of US agents until his arrest in 1994. A more recent example is Anna Chapman, the Russian "illegal" who, after being detained by the FBI in 2010, was returned to Russia in a spy swap and began a career as a glamour model.

What about examples related to Japan? Japan has been a rival of Russia since the Meiji Restoration of 1868, which thrust it into the modern era. The countries engaged in large-scale military combat on three occasions in the 20th century: during the Russo-Japanese War of 1904–5, at Nomonhan/Khalkhin Gol in 1939, and in August 1945 as Japan's Kwantung Army vainly resisted the Soviet invasion of Manchuria. During the Cold War, they remained adversaries, with Japan becoming the United States' main hub for power projection in East Asia. Japan's emergence as a technological superpower also made it an attractive target for industrial espionage.

Yet, while Japan has long been a logical target for Moscow's intelligence agencies, few Russian/Soviet spies or the operations they were involved in have gained public attention. The exception is Richard Sorge. This hard-drinking, womanising, motorcycle-crashing Soviet spy penetrated the German embassy in Tokyo during the 1930s and, via his network of Japanese agents, gathered crucial intelligence on Japan's military strategy. A cinematic figure, Sorge has been the subject of countless books and films, with each generation seeming to discover his story anew. Ozaki Hotsumi, who was Sorge's most important source and was executed alongside him in 1944, is also a well-known name in Japan and became the focus of a popular play.

But surely there is more to the history of Russian/Soviet espionage against Japan than Sorge? Indeed there is. In fact, there is more than can be addressed in a single volume. This book therefore covers only the earlier period, from first encounters in the 18th century to the end of the Second World War in 1945. It charts the most prominent operations, explains their underlying objectives, and describes what techniques were used. It also analyses the impact of these operations on Japan's development as a political and security actor.

Espionage is defined broadly here. There are plenty of cases in this book of traditional spying—that is, the stealing of political and military secrets. However, influence operations are also featured, as are many other types of state-approved skulduggery.

This focus on the untold story of Moscow's spying against Japan enables comparisons with intelligence activities in other regions. Furthermore, since espionage (like warfare) is the continuation of politics by other means, this history is an opportunity to view the countries' bilateral relations through a new lens. Usually the story of Japan-Russia relations is told with reference to the countries' simmering territorial dispute, which, to this day, has prevented the signing of a peace treaty. Here, instead of mist-shrouded islands, the central characters are intelligence officers and their agents.

Over the centuries, Japan has often been a hard target for espionage due to its history of national isolationism, suspicion of foreigners (especially Russians), and insular political elite. However, if this tough exterior can be breached, there is a soft inner layer where information controls are lacking, and intelligence collection is relatively straightforward. This is what Richard Sorge meant when he said that "Japan is like a crab."[1] This history of Russian espionage against Japan shows that Russia has often been successful in cracking Japan's outer shell and feasting upon the abundance of intelligence material within.

While this book is a work of history, many of the vulnerabilities identified remain as evident in modern-day Japan as they were in previous centuries. This volume therefore concludes with a textbook account of how to spy on Japan, identifying long-standing weaknesses in Japan's information security and the means to exploit them. This is intended to be instructive to Japanese policymakers. At a time when Japan is facing intensified espionage activity from a hostile Russia, as well as from China, it is imperative that the Japanese authorities enhance their historically weak counterintelligence capabilities.

1

THE FIRST "RUSSIAN SPY" IN JAPAN (1771)

The Japanese knew him as Hanbengoro. Commander of the Russian supply-ship the *Sviatoi Petr i Sviatoi Pavel* (St Peter and St Paul), Hanbengoro—as we shall call him for the time being—made his unexpected arrival at Sakinohama on the east coast of Shikoku in July 1771. This was the period of Japanese *sakoku*, or national isolation. Under this policy, which was introduced by the Tokugawa shogunate during the 1630s, Japan renounced most engagement with the outside world. Trade was rejected, foreigners turned away, and Japanese subjects prohibited from going abroad. The only exception for Europeans was the permission granted for the Dutch to conduct trade through Nagasaki. This too was highly circumscribed, since the Dutch traders were confined to the tiny artificial island of Dejima, and their opportunities to interact with Japanese society and to gather information about it were carefully restricted.

Since most Japanese were denied the opportunity to ever meet a European, it is no surprise that the denizens of rural Shikoku in 1771 regarded the arrival of Hanbengoro and his disparate crew with wonder (and a degree of exaggeration). One local samurai recorded in his diary that the ship was "thirty fathoms" in length. Having observed the foreigners on board, he estimated that "the adult male height is three metres and a quarter, the women are two and a half metres, the 15–16-year-old males around one and a half metres high." "Their noses are hooked and at least four inches long" and "their faces were red, and their bodies white."[1] Such reports were not unusual in *sakoku*-era Japan. Of the Dutch, it was said that they had no heels and that, when they urinated, they raised one leg like dogs.[2]

In his interactions with the Japanese, Hanbengoro made use of a crew member by the name of Bocharov, who had learned Japanese from a castaway who, after being shipwrecked on Kamchatka, had been employed by the Russians to teach Japanese in Siberia. Regrettably, Hanbengoro reported that "it turned out that Bocharov had forgotten most part, and remembered only a few compliments, with which he regaled the Japanese."[3] This was far from the last time that Russian attempts to gather information from the Japanese were hindered by the language barrier.

Despite this obstacle, Hanbengoro was able to communicate that he and his men were in distress on account of their ship having run out of food. The local authorities took pity and supplied them with all the food, water, and fuel they required, including, according to Hanbengoro's account, "eight hogs" and "six casks of a very agreeable kind of wine."[4] The *Sviatoi Petr i Sviatoi Pavel* was therefore able to set sail again and, after another stop in Satsuma province, left Japanese waters.[5] Their next port of call was Formosa (Taiwan), where, in true imperialist style, the crew responded to the killing of three of their party by massacring hundreds of locals and burning their village. Finally, in September 1771, the *Sviatoi Petr i Sviatoi Pavel* concluded its voyage by limping into the port of Macao, whereupon a fifth of those onboard promptly died, possibly from overeating following the prolonged period of enforced frugality.[6]

The *Sviatoi Petr i Sviatoi Pavel*'s visit highlights the extremely isolated nature of Japan during the *sakoku* period. It is also a reminder of the perils of European seafaring during the late 18th century, both for the voyagers and for those they encountered. Yet, Hanbengoro's story would initially seem to have little to do with the history of Russian spying on Japan. That would indeed be the case were it not for one curious letter that he left behind.

Dated 20 July 1771, this missive was handed to an official of Lord Shimazu, *daimyō* (feudal lord) of Satsuma, who then sent it to the Dutch in Nagasaki for translation. It was found to include the following remarkable confession:

> Caught in a storm for several days, battling the sea, we were driven to the territories of Japan for a second time. Thanks to your kindness we received your country's help. I am extremely sorry that I cannot meet you. I am expressing my fidelity in this letter. Having received orders from Russia to reconnoiter [Japanese] strongholds, I sailed this year with two galiots and one frigate from Kamchatka to the Japanese shores and cruised along them. We were supposed to assemble in one place. I have heard the notion expressed with certainty that next year raids will be made on the territories of Matsumae [Hokkaido] and on neighboring islands. We made a survey of these regions in latitude 41°38'N. Thereupon we constructed fortifications on the so-called Kuril islands, near Kamchatka, and stored military supplies and the like. ... Speaking secretly, I hope you will send ships from your country [Japan] to ward off that harm [Russia's alleged designs on Japan].[7]

In short, Hanbengoro not only admitted that Russia was spying on Japan and planning to attack in 1772, he also urged the Japanese to make a preventative strike. For good measure, he even provided a map of Kamchatka.

For many Japanese, Hanbengoro was thus a hero. In his abundant gratitude for Japanese aid, which had saved his life and that of his crew, Hanbengoro had provided forewarning of Russia's aggressive intentions, thus enabling Japan to prepare to defend itself. As one Japanese historian in the 20th century described Hanbengoro, "Even though his name was handed down incorrectly, he has for a long time been one of the important figures in modern Japanese foreign relations."[8] The history of Russian espionage against Japan therefore begins with a Russian spy who betrayed his motherland after having been overwhelmed by a sense of obligation instilled by Japanese *omotenashi* (hospitality).

* * *

There is only one small problem with this heart-warming tale. It is largely false. Hanbengoro was not a Russian spy. Indeed, he was not Russian at all. His real name was Maurice Benyovszky, and he lived a life of such incredible adventure that it bears a striking resemblance to that of Harry Flashman, the roguish hero of George MacDonald Fraser's celebrated novels.[9]

It is necessary to be careful in recounting the life of Benyovszky, since his own memoirs are unreliable. In fact, one reviewer wrote of them that "there is very little in them that is not 'romantic embellishment.'"[10] However, in his entertaining biography, Andrew Drummond sifts the fact from the fiction.[11]

Drummond reports that Maurice Benyovszky was a Hungarian who was born in 1746. After a family dispute and a short jail sentence for "various imprudent acts," Benyovszky left for Poland aged 22 to fight as a mercenary against Imperial Russia. Captured in May 1769, he escaped but was seized again after being betrayed by a Dutch sea captain who had agreed to smuggle Benyovszky out of the country from St Petersburg.[12] This time, Benyovszky and a group of fellow captives, who were mostly Russians who had fallen foul of Empress Catherine, were transported to Okhotsk in the Russian Far East, a journey that lasted a full eight months. From there, the prisoners were loaded onto the *Sviatoi Petr i Sviatoi Pavel* for the journey to Bol'sheretsk on Kamchatka. The ship was almost lost en route due to storms and drunkenness but ultimately arrived at the southern tip of Kamchatka, the captives' place of final exile, in September 1770.[13]

Safely installed at Bol'sheretsk, Benyovszky quickly set about ingratiating himself with Grigorii Nilov, commander of Kamchatka, who was described by near-contemporaries as "poorly literate, broken by paralysis and eternally drunk."[14] Captain Nilov was also a poor judge of character, for he soon invested utter confidence in Benyovszky and appointed him tutor to his son. This trust was misplaced, because, on 7 May 1771, taking advantage of the inebriation of the local guards, Benyovszky led a band of around 70 followers in open revolt. After murdering the unfortunate Nilov and looting government property, including many furs, the escapees took possession of the *Sviatoi Petr i Sviatoi Pavel* and set sail for freedom.[15]

In Benyovszky's own telling, he also made off with the commander's daughter, Afanasia Nilova. She is described as "a girl of perhaps 15 or 16 years of age who had fallen head over heels in love with the dashing Benyovszky. Her mother had pushed the star-struck girl into Benyovszky's bed and had, in all but name, married the girl off."[16] She was taken aboard the stolen ship dressed as a boy and the crew named her Achilles. As Benyovszky wrote in his memoirs, "Her figure in this dress was charming, and she certainly had as much courage as it is possible for a woman to have."[17] In reality, Afanasia Nilova's presence on the ship was one of Benyovszky's flights of fancy, since, while Captain Nilov did have a daughter, he had only brought his son with him to Bol'sheretsk.[18] This was just as well for the young Afanasia, since Benyovszky already had a wife and child in Hungary. In his memoirs, Benyovszky arranges for the girl to conveniently die off on arrival in Macao.

One issue that seems not to have been an invention was the state of privation suffered by Benyovszky and his followers. Benyovszky reports that, in desperation at having run out of food onboard the *Sviatoi Petr i Sviatoi Pavel*, he came up with the idea of using their cargo of furs by "boiling some skins of beavers, and seasoning them with whale oil." Meanwhile, Benyovszky was informed by another crew member "that several of the associates had washed their shoes and half boots, and that, at the instant he was speaking, there were more than twenty pair in the pot."[19] It was this privation that drove Benyovszky to visit Japan. In his telling, he informed his men "that my intention was to sail for Japan, and, there make a descent near a town, from which we would carry off as many women as we could seize, together with cattle and grain."[20]

Benyovszky's life after Japan does not overly concern us here, but, suffice to say, it was not dull. Highlights included betraying his shipmates in Macao, persuading the French government to fund an expedition to Madagascar during which he claims to have been crowned king, and engaging in money-making schemes in the fledgling United States. A return to Madagascar in 1785 ended less happily when he was shot dead by French troops at the age of 39. Given the fantastical nature of Benyovszky's adventures, it is little surprise that his memoirs proved a popular success and were adapted into plays and an opera.[21] Even Alexander Pushkin, the great Russian poet, owned a copy of the French edition.[22]

Returning to the infamous letter, it seems likely that Benyovszky was motivated by a desire for revenge on his Russian captors, as well as an eagerness to ingratiate himself with the Japanese. It is also probable that he alone was responsible for it, since most of his crew was Russian and, no matter what their differences with the regime of Catherine the

Great, it is unlikely they would have welcomed Benyovszky's attempt to incite Japan into attacking their motherland.

There can be no doubt that Benyovzsky's claims about Russia's hostile intentions towards Japan at this time were without foundation. As we have seen, Benyovzsky and his crew were certainly not under orders to reconnoitre Japan's coastal defences. There is also no truth to his assertion that the Russian authorities were planning raids on Hokkaidō in 1772 or that Russian fortifications had been constructed on the Kuril Islands. In fact, as we shall see, in the second half of the 18th century, Russia was only dimly aware of Japan's existence. Moreover, rather than amassing forces in Kamchatka for a southbound invasion, Russia's settlements in the North Pacific were clinging on for survival. As Donald Keene memorably puts it,

> Far from planning aggressive moves against Japan, the Russians had all they could do to hold together their Pacific empire, which had never consisted of much more than a wretched colony in Kamchatka (where vodka was the most plentiful commodity), a handful of traders in the Kuriles and a string of tiny outposts in America, sometimes marked by such revealing names as Massacre Bay.[23]

Bol'sheretsk itself was far from an imposing fortress. According to the journal of Captain James Cook, whose third voyage visited Kamchatka in 1779, Bol'sheretsk consisted of little more than 30 houses, plus "one publick-house for selling brandy, and one distillery."[24] Moreover, the governor of Kamchatka reported that, in terms of military strength, "his total command of 398 men was underarmed, underfed, and ill clothed, and that he could neither fortify nor defend his position."[25]

Despite not being an intelligence mission (and certainly not being the vanguard of an invading army), the voyage of the *Sviatoi Petr i Sviatoi Pavel* did inadvertently provide an opportunity to add to the Russian government's understanding of Japan, because some of the crew was finally able to return to Russia. Their information was potentially valuable since the *Sviatoi Petr i Sviatoi Pavel* had explored more of Japan than any previous Russian vessel. However, while the Japanese assumed that Benyovszky's visit must have considerably deepened Russian knowledge of Japanese waters, in reality, while "a journal and chart of the cruise were taken back to Russia, they never got beyond the file on the Kamchatka uprising."[26] As so often, serviceable intelligence was wasted due to bureaucratic failings of analysis and distribution.

The main impact of Benyovszky's visit was therefore not on the Russian side, but on the Japanese. This is because many Japanese took the Hungarian adventurer's fabricated claims at face value. Indeed, Benyovszky's visit is recorded in several Japanese historical texts, with reports such as that "Hanbengoro repaired to Nagasaki, and through the Hollanders informed our country of Russia's sinister designs."[27] It is surprising that the Japanese were so easily convinced that a Russian officer would so readily betray his country's plans to a potential adversary. George Lensen accounts for this credulity by explaining that "the Japanese concept of gratitude and obligation to one who has saved one's life—and well it may have seemed that the Japanese supplies did so—is such that a confession like Benyovszky's would be conceivable."[28] John Harrison, for his part, puts it down to the "xenophobic temper" roiling Japan at that time, meaning that the Japanese were ready to credit almost any tale about malicious foreign schemes.[29] Another possibility is that Benyovszky was believed because his claims chimed with ancient Japanese prophecies that "The time will be, when a people will come from the north, and conquer Japan."[30]

Whatever the reason, Benyovszky's small work of disinformation had a remarkably large effect on Japanese thinking. Indeed, it encouraged the emergence of a whole class of scholarship, of which the most prominent contributors were Kudō Heisuke (1738–1800), Honda Toshiaki (1744–1821), and Hayashi Shihei (1754–1793).[31] These writers pointed to the supposed military threat from Russia and demanded that the Tokugawa Bakufu (Japan's military regency) introduce several reforms, including by strengthening the country's coastal defences. For this reason, Benyovszky's letter of warning has been described as Japan's "first piece of national defense literature."[32] This is little exaggeration since, prior to this time, Japan had scarcely known the fear of a foreign attack, and defence planning had focused exclusively on internal warfare. Despite being a maritime country, at the time of Benyovszky's visit, Japan possessed not a single warship, and its coastal defences consisted of little more than a few naval batteries around Nagasaki.[33] As well as urging for the entire coastline of Japan to be fortified, these strategists called for the rapid colonisation of Ezo (Hokkaidō), since, were it to be seized by Russia, only the narrow Tsugaru Strait would separate Japan from a seemingly aggressive northern neighbour.[34]

Interestingly, while the Dutch themselves were far from persuaded of the truth of Benyovszky's claims,[35] they were happy to stoke Japanese suspicions. In doing so, they were motivated by a desire to maintain their status as the sole Europeans with the right to trade with Japan. For instance, Hayashi Shihei's belief in Russian plans to occupy Ezo seems to have derived from a meeting with a Dutchman by the name of Aaron Westvert in 1780.[36] Kudō Heisuke was also warned by the Dutch in Nagasaki about Russia's creeping advance.[37] Moreover, fears about Russian ambitions were compounded by Dutch reports that the Russians were using shipwrecked Japanese to teach themselves the Japanese language. This prompted anguish that "Japan's secrets are being revealed to the foreigners!"[38]

As much as being worried about a supposed Russian threat, the Bakufu police state was alarmed by the domestic fervour that followed Benyovszky's visit. After publication of his *Kaikoku Heidan* (*Military Discussions for a Maritime Nation*) in 1791, Hayashi Shihei was imprisoned and the printing blocks for the book destroyed. Matsudaira Sadanobu, the principal adviser to the Shōgun who had ordered Hayashi's arrest, accused the author of having "written strange and absurd stories about the risk of foreign invasion based on mere hearsay or groundless conjecture; that he had agitated the people, and that he had described points of strategic importance and inserted maps in his book."[39] Hayashi survived his imprisonment but died one year later "of chagrin."[40]

Yet, while condemning the messenger, the Bakufu quietly took the message to heart. Influenced by Kudō Heisuke's *A Study of Red Ainu Reports* of 1781 (with "Red Ainu" meaning Russians), Tanuma Okitsugu, a powerful counselor to the Shōgun, ordered the Matsumae clan, to whom control over Ezo had been devolved, to submit a report on the security situation in the north. Dissatisfied by the vague response, Tanuma dispatched a research team to Ezo in 1785–6.[41]

However, rather than discovering signs of Russian encroachment, the most that was discovered was "one miserable party of 'Red Ainu'," who were scraping an existence on Urup, an island in the central part of the Kuril chain.[42]

Despite the lack of evidence of Russian hostile intentions, the Bakufu proceeded to raise funds for coastal defences by extracting more resources from the *daimyō* and by debasing the currency.[43] Lingering fear of Russia also prompted responsibility for Ezo to be taken from the Matsumae clan and for the island to be placed under the direct control of the shogunate in 1799. This same security concern encouraged the Bakufu's eventual colonisation of Ezo on the basis that the island was "the key of the Northern Gate," and that military colonisation was the surest means of keeping this frontier closed to Russian ambitions.[44] Prior to the 19th century, the Japanese government had already claimed Ezo, yet, as John Harrison puts it, "had never really explored, governed, or exploited the area."[45] Indeed, in *Tales of the West* (*Seiiki Monogatari*), which was published in 1798, Honda Toshiaki despaired that some of his contemporary Japanese "go so far as to claim that Ezo is a foreign country, declaring that the inhabitants, unlike other human beings, have only one eye, in the middle of their foreheads, and that it flashes like lightning!"[46]

Of course, not all these changes in Japanese policy can be attributed to Benyovszky's influence. Even without the Hungarian adventurer's malicious missive, sooner or later Japan's leaders would have turned their attention to their northern border. Still, the fears inspired by Benyovszky's note, which were gladly fanned by the Dutch, undoubtedly had a lasting impact on Japan. Indeed, Donald Keene acknowledges Benyovszky's visit as one "of the two major outside stimuli to Japan of the late eighteenth century."[47] The other—Russia's repatriation of the castaway Daikokuya Kōdayū in 1792—is discussed in chapter 2.

The history of Russian spying on Japan therefore begins unexpectedly, with Russia as the victim, rather than the perpetrator, of intrigue. At a time when Russia was not engaged in spying on Japan, Benyovszky dripped poison into the ears of the Japanese about Russia's intentions. The suspicion this provoked was to become a recurring feature of Japanese attitudes towards their northern neighbour.

2

EXPLORERS AND CASTAWAYS OF THE 18TH CENTURY

Since Benyovszky was a fraud, what is the reality of Russian spying on Japan before diplomatic relations were established in 1855? The short answer is that these efforts were rather modest. In Russia's multi-volume history of its foreign intelligence service, which was published in the name of SVR (foreign intelligence) director Evgenii Primakov, Japan does not get a serious mention until chapter 27, when the focus is on the years immediately preceding the Russo-Japanese War (1904–5).[1] There is nothing of any substance about Japan during the 18th or the vast majority of the 19th century. This is not the case with other countries. In fact, Russian intelligence activities towards not only European states, but several others, including Brazil, receive significant attention in this official volume before Japan makes a single appearance. Gregory Afinogenov has also demonstrated that the history of Russian spying on China goes back to the 17th century.[2]

One reason for Russia's slow start in conducting intelligence operations against Japan is the comparatively late establishment of diplomatic relations. Then, as now, one of the functions of a country's overseas legations was to provide hubs for intelligence gathering. This is a point made explicitly in Primakov's volume, where it is noted that, in the early 18th century, "in international practice, the concepts of 'diplomat' and 'intelligence officer' were synonymous and meant, in fact, the same thing: a spy."[3] The fact that official relations between Russia and Japan were not established until the Treaty of Shimoda of 1855 thus restricted Russia's opportunities for intelligence gathering in Edo-era Japan.

A second point is that *sakoku*-era Japan was an exceptionally hard target for intelligence gathering. This included the Dutch in Nagasaki, who spent most of their time effectively imprisoned in their compound on Dejima, which "measured only eighty-two common paces in width and two hundred and thirty-six in main length."[4] When no Dutch ships were present, Dejima was populated by only the Dutch factor and a few companions. Yet, to the paranoid shogunate even this handful of bored Europeans was a serious threat. The tiny island was therefore surrounded by fencing, and the small stone bridge that connected Dejima with Nagasaki was always guarded. Ordinary Japanese were not permitted to visit, though an exception was made for prostitutes.[5] One Dutch sea captain describes "feeling that we were criminals who had been imprisoned in some sort of institution."[6] If this was the situation for the privileged Dutch, consider how much more difficult it was for other outsiders to pierce the secrecy of the Tokugawa police state.

All the same, during the 18th and first half of the 19th century, the Russian authorities did make periodic efforts to enhance their knowledge of Japan. For the most part, these activities were more in the nature of exploration than espionage. This remained necessary because, as John Harrison notes, "until as late as the mid-nineteenth century the state of European cartographic knowledge regarding the northern frontier of Japan—including on such basic issues as whether Ezo and Sakhalin were islands—'was one of muddled ignorance'."[7] As well as determining the precise nature of Japan's borders, Russia's other chief goal was to open commercial relations. However, such was the suspicious nature of the Tokugawa shogunate that even Russia's unconcealed efforts to enhance knowledge of Japan and to develop ties were often seen as spying. In a sense, since everything in *sakoku* Japan was a secret, all external efforts to learn about it were espionage.

Intelligence gained from Dembei and via China

While Benyovszky was seen as the first Russian spy in Japan, he cannot be credited as the person to mark the start of Russia-Japan relations.

That honour goes to Dembei, a Japanese merchant clerk from Ōsaka. Dembei was travelling from his home city to Edo on a coastal freighter in the winter of 1695 when his ship was driven eastward into the open sea by a typhoon. Since Japanese shipping was not made for ocean voyages, Dembei's vessel was tossed around helplessly for 28 weeks before finally making landfall on Kamchatka, where Dembei and the rest of the crew were taken captive by the local Kamchadals. The fate of Dembei's shipmates is unclear, though it is suggested that some died at sea while others were poisoned by the pungent diet of "rotting fish and roots" on which they were forced to survive on Kamchatka.[8] In any case, Dembei was the only Japanese still present when Vladimir Atlasov, the famous Russian explorer, arrived in 1699.

Struggling with mutual incomprehension, Atlasov had difficulty discerning Dembei's nationality. He thought he looked like a Greek on account of being "lean, [with] small moustaches and black hair," but he ultimately decided that he was from India.[9] This is likely because Atlasov did not even know of Japan's existence. Despite this confusion, Atlasov rcognised Dembei's potential as a source of first-hand information about foreign lands and took him with him, first to Yakutsk, then to Moscow, where they arrived in 1701. It was only in the Russian capital that the long-suffering Dembei was finally identified as Japanese.[10]

Just as Atlasov hoped, Dembei proved an excellent source of knowledge. He provided his hosts, including Peter the Great, with Russia's first information about Japan. As George Lensen recounts,

> Dembei described Japan as a civilised country with walled cities and sturdy buildings, rich in gold and silver, and with internal commerce well developed, a country whose prosperous people worshipped images like those of China and who, though they lived at peace with their neighbors, had firearms.[11]

He also revealed aspects of Japan's isolation, explaining that the Japanese did not travel abroad and that their ships were restricted to the size and design required for coastal trade. He added that the Germans (he meant the Dutch) were permitted to trade at Nagasaki.[12]

Just as significant as the accurate information provided by Dembei were the omissions, exaggerations, and miscommunications. First,

Dembei's boasting of Japan's supposed riches gave the Russians an inflated idea of Japan's natural wealth. Second, while Dembei noted that the Japanese did not venture abroad, he seems not to have explained that foreign ships were barred from Japan's shores. In fact, his mention of the German/Dutch commerce at Nagasaki encouraged the view that trading relations with Japan could be opened. Third, Dembei gave the impression that Japan was part of the Eurasian landmass. This resulted from a confusion over vocabulary. When asked about China ("*Kitai*" in Russian), Dembei believed his hosts were enquiring about Akita, and replied that he had travelled there by land, as well as by sea. As a result, the Russians concluded that Japan was connected to the Eurasian continent via a land bridge.[13]

Dembei's arrival was therefore the start of both Russian understanding and misunderstanding of its insular Asian neighbour. In particular, Dembei's information encouraged a miscomprehension of Japan's *sakoku* policy. As we shall see, for decades to come Russian leaders never accepted the earnestness of Japan's desire to be left alone and continued to believe that relations could be opened if only persistence were shown. At the start of the 19th century, this misapprehension was to result in Russian indignation and a desire for revenge when her efforts to negotiate commercial relations were conclusively rebuffed.

That was to come later. In the short term, the main consequence of Dembei's appearance was to generate desire in the Russian court for additional information about Japan. Peter the Great, who reigned from 1682 to 1725, had a keen interest in intelligence, and his widespread reforms extended to the intelligence field. These changes included the creation of an "explicit division between public and secret knowledge, funneling different types of intellectual production into different bureaucratic structures—public knowledge through the Imperial Academy of Sciences, secret knowledge into the College of Foreign Affairs, among others." Severe punishments were also introduced to promote information security, including the threat of "death or eternal galley slavery for such crimes as 'secretly carrying off College letters or documents for evil purposes'."[14]

Regarding Japan, after meeting Dembei, Peter the Great ordered that work begin to "investigate the route to Japan, clarify the state of

Japanese defences, the range of Japanese goods available and the demand for Russian goods."[15] He also commanded that Dembei be taught Russian and be assigned students to whom he was to teach written and spoken Japanese. This was the origin of Japanese language teaching in Russia, though a school was not formally established until 1736. Dembei was originally promised that he would be permitted to return to Japan. However, he was ultimately deemed too valuable as a source of knowledge. His request to return to his homeland was rejected by Peter the Great in 1710 and he was ordered to convert to Christianity, taking the name Gavriil Bogdanov. Indeed, impressed by the information gained from Dembei, the Russian authorities commanded that when further Japanese ships were wrecked on Russian shores one crew member should be sent to the capital.[16] Consequently, after Dembei, there followed a stream of Japanese castaways, though the information they provided added little to what Dembei had already explained. Donald Keene describes them as "pathetic but colourless sailors, at first bewildered by the unfamiliar society which they had accidentally entered, and then swallowed up by it, almost without a trace."[17] As well as their rough argot making them less than ideal language teachers, these castaways further inflated the expectations of "their hosts with stories of Japan's great wealth of precious metals, costly materials, and foodstuffs."[18]

The other main source of Russian information about Japan during the first decades of the 18th century was China. Whereas Russia's first consulate in Japan did not open until 1860, Russia had a settled presence in Beijing from 1715, when the Russian Ecclesiastical Mission was established. As well as its religious duties, the Mission functioned as a hub for intelligence gathering (not to mention, according to Gregory Afinogenov, as a den "of unceasing drunkenness, violence, and sexual misconduct").[19]

Additionally, there were regular trade caravans that slowly trudged across the Eurasian steppe. The leaders of these expeditions were tasked with tracking down Oriental *curios* by their acquisitive masters, but they were also assigned intelligence duties. For instance, when Ivan-Lorents Lange joined the embassy to the Chinese capital in 1719, he was ordered to gather as much information as possible about Japan, especially regarding trade relations. He was not able to clarify the exact location of the Japanese islands, but he did report back that the Dutch earned great profits from their commerce with the Japanese and that such trade would be possible for Russia too as soon as access to the Amur River was secured. Drawing on his Chinese sources, Lange added considerable detail, covering not only trade, but also military matters. As George Lensen recounts, Lange reported that:

> trade was permitted to the Dutch only, that it consisted in the exchange of tawed skins from Batavia for Japanese gold, silver, and porcelains, and that it was limited to four or five Dutch vessels a year. Lange described how the Japanese forced the Dutch to disarm and to remain within the confines of a special fortress, and how, when they were permitted to visit the city, they must first trample on a cross to give evidence that they would not propagate the Christian faith. He added that the Japanese were no more versed in military matters than the Chinese, had but a few small vessels, and relied primarily on arrows rather than firearms.[20]

In the 1750s, China was also the source of some early maps of Japan. These were procured by Eremei Vladykin, a geodesist accompanying the 1752–5 caravan to China. With the help of students at the Russian Ecclesiastical Mission, Vladykin obtained maps from the Beijing Palace Library, which he and his assistant spent "day and night" frantically copying. These reproductions, which were presented to the Russian Senate in 1756, included three maps of the Amur region, featuring both Korea and parts of the Japanese archipelago.[21]

The first Russian voyages to Japan

The material gleaned from both the earliest castaways and China whetted the Russian leadership's appetite for more information about Japan. Yet, to gain real understanding of this land of fabled riches, Russians needed to set foot on Japanese shores. Thus began over a century of sporadic efforts to open relations with Japan.

Since the Amur River remained under Chinese control until the mid-19th century, Russia's early voyages to Japan all proceeded from the north, beginning in Kamchatka, then following the stepping stones of the Kuril chain all the way to Hokkaidō. In 1713, the

Cossack Ivan Kozyrevskii toured the three northernmost Kuril Islands and received information from the local inhabitants, as well as from a captured Japanese sailor, about the rest of the Kuril chain, of which there are 21 principal islands.[22] Most importantly, Kozyrevskii discovered that Hokkaidō is separated from Japan's main island by a strait.[23] In fact, despite not proceeding beyond the northernmost islands, Kozyrevskii's map of the Kurils was far more accurate than anything possessed by Japan's Tokugawa government at the time.[24] Kozyrevskii also learned about the main Japanese islands, reporting that politics was structured around a system of "separate landowners" (the *daimyō*), and that there existed "a great potentate like a patriarch," who the Japanese revere "like a god."[25]

Seven years later, in 1719, Ivan Evreinov and Fedor Luzhin, two geodesists with the Russian Naval Academy, were dispatched on a secret mission by Peter the Great. The ostensible goal was to establish whether the Asian and American continents were joined, though their real task was "to explore the Kuril Islands and to collect detailed information about Japan."[26] George Lensen speculates that the reason for the secrecy was Peter's hope that the islands were rich with gold and silver. In any case, little progress was made, because Evreinov and Luzhin were unable to proceed beyond the northern islands of the Kuril chain before their ship was swept into the open sea by a storm. The two geodesists made it back to Russia with their lives but delivered no new information about Japan.[27]

The first Russian mission that succeeded in going beyond the Kurils did not take place until 1738–9. The lead ship of this expedition was commanded by Captain Martin Spanberg, a Dane, and the other ships were overseen by Lieutenant William Walton, an Englishman, and Midshipman Aleksei Shelting, the son of a Dutch seaman.[28] Spanberg's instructions were to conduct a basic mission of exploration. He was ordered to chart the Kuril Islands, then press on in search of Japan. On discovering the main Japanese islands, Spanberg was to establish friendly relations and was told that under no circumstances should he seize Japanese vessels or engage in other hostile acts. At the same time, he was tasked with investigating the conditions in Japan and reporting back on the nature of its ports. If his ships were attacked, he was to peacefully withdraw.[29]

During the summer of 1738, none of the expedition's three ships made it as far as the Japanese main islands. Trying again the next year, they finally made the long-awaited breakthrough. On 27 June 1739, Spanberg's ship, the *Arkhangel Mikhail*, reached the shores of what was then Mutsu Province in the northeast of Honshū.[30] This was the first recorded case of a Russian vessel penetrating the main islands of Japan. Spanberg remarked that the "coasts were rocky and covered with great forests." He also noted "four large villages with stone buildings and around them were fields of ample grain."[31] The *Arkhangel Mikhail* was approached by local fishing boats, and we have an account of the first ever trade between Russia and Japan, with the Russian ship purchasing "rice, pickled cucumbers and large fresh radishes, leaf tobacco and broad-leaved and other vegetables."[32] Spanberg also welcomed a group of Japanese dignitaries aboard the *Arkhangel Mikhail*, although communication proved difficult, since the Ainu interpreters Spanberg had brought were found unable to speak Japanese.[33]

Spanberg remained cautious and did not send any men ashore. The honour of becoming the first Russians to set foot on the main Japanese islands therefore fell to the sailors of the *Sviatoi Gavriil* under the command of William Walton. The *Sviatoi Gavriil* had become separated from the *Arkhangel Mikhail* and ventured further south, making landfall in Awa Province in what is now Chiba Prefecture on 30 June 1739. Displaying greater boldness than the expedition's commander, Walton sent ashore a landing party led by a second mate named Lev Kazimirov. As well as obtaining fresh water, "Kazimirov was invited into Japanese houses and regaled with wine, rice, fruit, and various delicacies," while the locals marvelled at the Russians' red wavy hair, long noses, and eyes that were the colour of sharks.[34] While the local Japanese were happy to entertain these unexpected guests, they did not report back to the Bakufu authorities on these friendly exchanges, thereby suggesting they were more fearful of their repressive rulers than of the supposed threat of outsiders.[35]

The Russian expedition's return journey to Kamchatka was not an easy one, with 13 sailors falling ill and dying on the *Arkhangel Mikhail*, and the last of the expedition's ships, the *Nadezhda* under the command of Shelting, not making it back to Bol'sheretsk until early September.[36] Still, Spanberg's mission had been a success. His ships had not only identified the location of, but had actually visited, the main Japanese island of Honshū.

The only problem with this impressive achievement was that the Russian authorities refused to believe that Spanberg and Walton had really been in Japan. The issue was that the intelligence delivered by Spanberg contradicted the established opinion of the Russian Admiralty. Specifically, Spanberg's charts placed Japan 11 to 12 degrees west of where the country was supposed to be.[37] It was therefore concluded that Spanberg's expedition had mistakenly visited Korea.[38] It was only in 1746, some seven years later, that the Admiralty reluctantly conceded that Walton and Spanberg had indeed been in Japan.[39] Spanberg's mission is therefore another example in the history of intelligence of good information being disregarded because it conflicts with entrenched assumptions.

Much of the initial impetus for exploring Japan had come from the hyperactive Peter the Great following his meeting with Dembei in 1702. This interest was maintained under Peter's immediate successors, yet, by the mid-18th century, the central authorities' attention had drifted. At this time, initiatives by Russian regional leaders took greater prominence.

The first regional mission of significance was the expedition to the Kurils of 1766–9 under the command of the Cossack leader Chernyi. The initiative for this mission had come from Governor Soimonov of Siberia, who instructed his subordinates on Kamchatka to increase the collection of tribute from the Ainu on the Kuril Islands, and to explore the possibility of establishing commercial relations with Japan. In pursuit of these objectives, the Bol'sheretsk Command sent out Chernyi with clear instructions. He was explicitly banned from mistreating the local population of the Kuril Islands, and, when seeking to establish a tributary relationship over them, Chernyi was told to use no force but to persuade them through evidence of Russia's good conduct. Meanwhile, with respect to information, Chernyi was told to report back on "the way of life and standard of living of the Kurilians and on the type of weapons which they used." In addition, Chernyi was instructed "to gather as much information as possible about the activities of the Japanese, if they came to these islands, and bring back samples of Japanese products."[40]

The Russian regional authorities were thus looking to softly extend influence over the Kuril chain and to put out feelers about trade with Japan. However, they erred in their selection of an expedition leader, for Chernyi proved a blackguard. During the voyage to Etorofu (known as Iturup in Russian), Chernyi treated both his crew and the local Ainu with severity, causing the latter to abandon their hunting grounds and flee from Russian influence. When some Ainu were recaptured, they were bound so tightly that one of them died and his body was tossed into the sea.[41] Meanwhile, Chernyi "made the most of his good fortune, and immersed himself in wine and women, while fugitives and oarsmen toiled for him under the constant threat of his whip."[42]

Chernyi's personal focus was on terrorising the Ainu and enriching himself, but he did not altogether neglect intelligence-gathering duties. His logbook, although it did not contain a map, provided the first detailed geographical description of the northern and central Kuril Islands as far as Etorofu. Chernyi also reported that several small Japanese ships, with a crew of around 20, made visits to Akkeshi (northeast Hokkaidō) and Kunashiri (the most southerly of the main Kuril Islands) to conduct trade for two to three months each year. He was even able to describe the main Japanese products as including "wine, tobacco leaves, cereals, swords, knives, axes, and kettles."[43] After returning to Kamchatka, Chernyi was called to Irkutsk to provide further information in person but died of smallpox before being able to testify.[44] Still, through his written report, Chernyi inspired the idea that trade with the Japanese could be established by sending vessels to northeastern Hokkaidō.

The Secret Voyage

Just a few years after Chernyi's tyrannical campaign, the regional authorities in Siberia sought to follow up his findings. This time, the key figures were Governor Bril of Irkutsk (who gave the initial orders in 1772) and Matvei Bem, the new commander of Kamchatka (whose job it was to see the plan implemented). What followed is described by George Lensen as the "Secret Voyage," and it has a much better claim to being the first Russian spy mission to Japan than Maurice Benyovszky's disingenuous visit in 1771.[45]

There are several features of the Secret Voyage that make it noteworthy. The first is that it was a public-private partnership. Since the central authorities had lost interest in funding further missions after Spanberg's voyage of 1738–9, Bem arranged for the Secret Voyage to be financed by Siberian merchants. In return, Bem promised—without St Petersburg's authorisation—that these merchants would be granted a temporary monopoly over the fur trade on the Kurils and that other Russian vessels would be prevented from visiting the islands.

The Secret Voyage was similarly hybrid in its combination of commercial and military objectives. The main aim remained economic since the Russian settlements on Kamchatka still required a more reliable source of supplies than the overland route through Siberia. To this end, Bem ordered that, as well as further exploring the Kuril chain, the leaders of the Secret Voyage were to sow various crops on the island of Urup (the fourth major Kuril Island from Hokkaidō) as a test of agricultural potential. They were also instructed to research the islands' mineral resources. After that, the Secret Voyage was to press on to Hokkaidō, where the expedition's leaders were "to inquire whether the Japanese might not like, for the sake of mutual trade, to make a treaty."[46] Showing his capitalist instincts, Bem added that, were trade possible, Russian products should be sold for the greatest possible price, while efforts should be made to reduce the cost of the Japanese goods. Mindful of the susceptibility of Kamchatka residents to the bottle, he added that no alcohol was to be purchased ("except for one bucket to be tasted in Russia"), and there were to be no sales of firearms.[47]

As for the expedition's military objectives, these were not of an aggressive nature but were still to be concealed from the Japanese. As well as conducting the agricultural trial on Urup, expedition leaders were to construct a small fortress on the island. Afterwards, when reaching Matmai (Hokkaidō), they were to present themselves as merchants—despite their ship being a man-of-war—and to keep all weapons and ammunition out of sight. Only after gaining the trust of the Japanese were they to gather intelligence. Specifically, according to George Lensen's account:

> the Russians were to gather detailed information about the extent of the Japanese Empire, about its cities, economy, and way of life. They

> were to find out what foreigners came to trade with them by sea and land, whether the Japanese had any seagoing vessels of their own and if so, where did they sail? They were to obtain data on Japanese military forces, training, fortifications, and weapons and, if possible, to acquire Japanese maps.[48]

In addition to the prescribed secrecy, another feature of the mission was the plan to use Ainu as intermediaries. To this end, the Ainu were to be given gifts to persuade them to overcome misgivings engendered by Chernyi's mistreatment and to get them to travel with the Russians to Matmai (Hokkaidō). It was hoped that the presence of the familiar Ainu would reduce Japanese distrust of the Russians.[49] This use of border communities as go-betweens and for intelligence gathering was a common tactic for Russia. For instance, Gregory Afinogenov details how the Russian Empire used indigenous border groups, such as Evenki hunters, Khalkha Mongols, and Buriats, as "brokers and spies, messengers and translators" with which to gather information on Qing China.[50]

The Secret Voyage was thus well-organised. Indeed, the crew included not only a secretary and first-aid man, but also a "sober corporal," who could be relied upon to step in whenever someone fell victim to inebriation.[51] However, as detailed as Bem's plans were, the hostile weather of the North Pacific did its best to blow the voyage off course.

By 1774, two years after Governor Bril of Irkutsk had given his initial instructions, Matvei Bem, in his capacity as commander of Kamchatka, had secured the agreement of Pavel Lebedev-Lastochkin, a merchant from Yakutsk, to finance the Secret Voyage. Supplies were purchased and sent by ship from Okhotsk to Kamchatka, yet the vessel sank and the investment was lost. Lebedev-Lastochkin was reluctant to commit further funds, yet he was persuaded to do so alongside Grigorii Shelikhov, another merchant, who later became famous as the founder of the Russian colonies in America. These investors purchased the *Sviatoi Nikolai*, a small gunboat, which set sail from Kamchatka on 5 July 1775, under the command of a Siberian nobleman named Ivan Antipin. However, after reaching Urup, the *Sviatoi Nikolai* was wrecked in a storm, leaving some crew stranded on the island, while others struggled back to Bol'sheretsk on *bidarkas*, a type of small boat made of skins stretched over a wooden frame.[52]

Despite this second shipwreck, the Secret Voyage was not abandoned. Shelikhov withdrew his support to concentrate on the Americas, yet Lebedev-Lastochkin, having doubled down on his investment, was determined to see some return. To this end, another ship—the brigantine *Natalia*—was dispatched in September 1777 under the leadership of Navigator Mikhail Petuchkov and Dmitrii Shabalin. Shabalin was an Irkutsk trader who initially joined the expedition as an interpreter but ultimately became its leader. After wintering on Urup, Shabalin led a small party to Etorofu and Kunashiri in the summer of 1778, then on to Notkome (Nokkamapu), a small settlement in the northeast corner of Hokkaidō. There, Shabalin met Araida Daihachi, a Matsumae official, to whom he submitted the request to open trading relations. Araida replied that he lacked the authority to respond but promised to pass the request to the lord of Matsumae, who, in turn, would submit a report to the shogunate. Araida therefore asked that the Russians return the following summer for an official response. In the meantime, Araida agreed that goods could be exchanged in the harbour of Kunashiri Island.[53]

Encouraged by the start of informal trade and the invitation to visit again next year, Shabalin and Antipin, who had remained on Urup, returned to Russia confident they were on the verge of establishing formal trade relations with Japan. Lebedev-Lastochkin, who must have been relieved that his persistence in backing the Secret Voyage was finally paying off, arranged for the *Natalia* to be loaded with a fresh cargo of tradable goods. The ship was hurriedly dispatched back to Urup in September 1778, ready to meet the Japanese at the first opportunity in 1779.

However, the Russians were in for a long wait. When the next summer came, Shabalin and Antipin proceeded to Etorofu and Kunashiri. Finding no Japanese there, they went on to Notkome on Hokkaidō, only to be told that the envoys of the lord of Matsumae had been delayed by bad weather. It seemed the Russians would have to return again the next summer, but, after a wait of several weeks, on 16 September 1779, the Matsumae officials finally arrived bearing Japan's official answer. Its contents came as a shock. The message from the lord of Matsumae was that "foreign trade is limited exclusively to the port of Nagasaki, and as it is not permitted at all in other places, no matter how much you would ask, permission will not be given. In the future to cross the sea and come here will be of no use whatsoever."[54] In case the message was not clear enough, the Japanese also returned the letter and gifts that the Russians had presented during their visit the previous year.

The Secret Voyage did have some notable achievements. It was the first time Russian representatives conducted formal negotiations with Japanese counterparts. Unlike Spanberg and Walton, who only spent a few days in the company of Japanese in 1739, Shabalin, Antipin, and other members of the Secret Voyage spent several weeks on Hokkaidō in 1778 and 1779. They were also able to learn more from the Japanese since their language skills were better. As noted, Shabalin initially joined the Secret Voyage as an interpreter. Antipin had also studied Japanese in Irkutsk.[55]

Taking advantage of their enhanced access, Shabalin and Antipin verified the information about Japanese political geography that Ivan Kozyrevskii had received from the Ainu when visiting the Kuril Islands in 1713. This included the names of Japan's main settlements and the details of their *daimyō*. They were also able to report that the Japanese were not interested in certain fine fabrics, which were similar to their own, but were attracted by other materials, including leather boots.[56] Additionally, the expedition's leaders catalogued Japanese procedures and etiquette, information that was useful for the future conduct of diplomacy. For instance, Shabalin recorded the formal procession by the Matsumae officials, describing that "The commanders each carried two swords whose hilts were gilded silver. The other Japanese each had one sword, and on their arrival knelt and bowed politely in their manner."[57] Furthermore, he described the Japanese officials, including details of their "long black satin caftans" and their hairstyles, "which were shaved right up to the middle as smoothly as if there had never been hair there, leaving a small part of hair at the back, which was caught up and oiled, and bent forward over the shaved patch."[58] Shabalin also remarks on the *ume* and *shōga* (plum and ginger) that they were given to eat, thus showing that some aspects of Japanese cuisine have changed little in two and a half centuries.

These findings were, however, slim pickings for an expensive expedition that had been seven years in the making. As well as failing in its overt goal of securing a trade agreement with Japan, it was unable to fulfil its clandestine objectives, since no meaningful intelligence on Japanese military forces and weapons was obtained. This was because the expedition was prevented from proceeding beyond the most northeasterly point of Hokkaidō, which was itself still a distant outpost of Japan and not yet under the direct control of the shogunate. The first explicit and well-organised Russian effort to gather secret information on Japan was therefore a disappointment.

Daikokuya Kōdayū and Adam Laxman

There then came a lull in Russian efforts to discover more about Japan. This was not only because of the disappointment of the Secret Voyage. It was also because Catherine the Great, who reigned from 1762 to 1796, never shared Peter the Great's passion for learning about Japan. She was also preoccupied with events in Europe, including the Russo-Turkish War (1787–92), the Russo-Swedish War (1788–90), and the French Revolution (from 1789). Consequently, no new expeditions to Japan were undertaken for over a decade after the Secret Voyage, and Russia's Japanese language skills atrophied. While in 1760 the language school in Irkutsk had seven Japanese instructors and 15 pupils, by the 1780s all the native Japanese teachers were dead, there were only three pupils, and state funding had ended.[59] This decline in Russian interest in Japan might have continued had it not been for the arrival of Daikokuya Kōdayū.

As with the castaways who preceded him, Kōdayū ended up in Russia after a storm.[60] In early 1783, he was aboard the *Shinshō Maru*, a Japanese transport ship, which was carrying rice along the coast of Suruga Province (modern-day Shizuoka Prefecture) when high winds damaged the vessel and swept it out into the ocean. They spent eight months at sea, with Kōdayū and the 16 other crew members surviving by eating their cargo and drinking rainwater. At last, they made landfall on the desolate island of Amchitka, one of the Aleutians, where they remained for four years. It was only in 1787 that Kōdayū and the remaining crew—eight had already died—made it to Kamchatka, where another three perished. It was thus only six Japanese castaways, including Kōdayū, who were transported to Irkutsk, where they arrived in February 1789.[61]

Kōdayū was markedly different from the Japanese castaways who had preceded him in Russia. Far from being "pathetic but colourless," Kōdayū "was a lively and intelligent person."[62] This was confirmed by Jean-Baptiste Barthélemy de Lesseps, a French explorer, who met Kōdayū on Kamchatka in 1788. He describes him as having "a very distinguished superiority" over his Japanese companions, since Kōdayū was a merchant and the others, sailors. Moreover, "He is possessed of great penetration, and apprehends with admirable readiness every thing you are desirous to communicate." De Lesseps noted that "He employs no concealment or reserve, but tells with the utmost frankness what he thinks of every one."[63]

Kōdayū's vivacity and intelligence were significant because, on arrival in Irkutsk, he befriended Erik Laxman, a Finnish polymath who had been living in Russia since 1762. The two came up with a plan to send a new expedition to Japan with the purpose of both returning the Japanese castaways and trying again to establish trade relations. To this end, Laxman took Kōdayū with him to St Petersburg in January 1791. In the capital, Laxman drew up a formal proposal for the new voyage. Kōdayū was also granted an audience with Catherine the Great at which the Japanese castaway, who was still getting used to court etiquette, "licked" her hand.[64]

Despite this solicitousness, Catherine the Great was unconvinced, telling Kōdayū that "there is no persistent desire to trade on our part and you can act, therefore, just as you wish."[65] Still, in September 1791, she decreed that Laxman's plan be implemented. Leadership of the expedition was assigned to Lieutenant Adam Laxman, the 26-year-old son of Erik, and command of the brigantine *Ekaterina*, which was selected for the voyage, was given to Navigator Grigorii Lovtsov. Erik Laxman thought Lovtsov "almost completely ignorant" but he was judged "more sober" than the alternatives.[66] The rest of the party of 40 included three Japanese castaways, including Kōdayū, as well as the interpreter Tugolukov and Dmitrii Shabalin, who had led the Secret Voyage.

Intriguingly, Laxman was not the only one to recognise Kōdayū's potential. Through their broader intelligence network, the Russians learned that both the Dutch and the British were eager to get their hands on him. The Dutch were aiming to ingratiate themselves further with the Japanese by returning their castaway. Additionally, they may have been seeking to stymie Russian attempts to open trade with Japan and thereby maintain their monopoly. As for the British, they were then preparing George Macartney's mission, which famously took the British envoy to Beijing in 1793. As well as the goal of opening Chinese ports to British commerce, London had hopes of initiating trade with other Asian countries, including Japan. There was the added aim of checking the spread of Russian influence. The British authorities, including ambassador Charles Whitworth in St Petersburg, therefore sought opportunities to abduct Kōdayū and hand him over to Macartney. However, apprised of the British plans, the Russians were able to prevent Kōdayū's capture.[67]

Having dodged foreign chicanery, Adam Laxman and his crew put to sea in the *Ekaterina* in September 1792, arriving one month later in Nemuro, close to where the Secret Voyage had visited 13 years earlier. There, Laxman told local officials of his plan to deliver the castaways to Edo, the *de facto* Japanese capital, but initially kept quiet about his hopes of opening trade relations. Given the lateness of the season, he also stated his desire to spend the winter in that northeast corner of Hokkaidō.

When Laxman's message was communicated, first to the town of Matsumae, then to Edo, it created a panic, with the lord of Matsumae telling the shogunate, "As we are dealing here with foreigners, it is difficult to calculate what intentions they nurse in their heart."[68] Eventually it was decided that, since the priority was to keep the Russians away from Edo, Laxman's party would be permitted to travel to Matsumae on the northern side of the Tsugaru Strait that divides Hokkaidō from Honshū. Accepting this compromise, the *Ekaterina* set sail from Nemuro in June 1793, and, missing its intended destination of Edomo due to fog, arrived at Hakodate, from where Laxman travelled overland to Matsumae. Reaching the regional capital at the end of July, Laxman was greeted with considerable ceremony. He handed over Kōdayū and one other castaway (the third man had died in Nemuro), and, in return, was gifted substantial supplies, including 100 sacks of rice, 20 boxes of tobacco, and six barrels of salted goat meat.[69]

More significantly, Laxman was granted an official certificate, which has come to be known as the Nagasaki Permit. In the Russian understanding, this was "an imperial certificate with the mark of their sovereign, on which they could authorise free passage to Nangasaki [Nagasaki], where at a future date the Russians could proceed with the certificate in order to conclude a treaty and agreement if the Russian side had the intention to do so."[70] In short, in the Russian view, Laxman had succeeded in laying the groundwork for the official opening of relations with Japan.

As we shall see in the next chapter, the granting of the Nagasaki Permit proved a contentious moment that ultimately led to a serious downturn in Russo-Japanese relations. However, Laxman's expedition was also a turning point in Russian understanding of *sakoku* Japan. If the Secret Voyage was a small step forward from Spanberg and Walton's achievement, Laxman's embassy was a major stride. Rather than remaining in an isolated corner of Hokkaidō, Laxman and his companions spent time in both Hakodate and the regional capital of Matsumae. Additionally, since the last stage of his journey was conducted overland, Laxman supplemented his charting of Japan's coastal areas with direct observations of inland areas, something that no Russian expedition had previously managed. Furthermore, as well as holding talks with Matsumae representatives, as the Secret Voyage had done, Laxman interacted with higher-ranking Edo officials.

The information that Laxman communicated back to Russia featured much of geographic interest. As well as reporting the details of the voyage from Nemuro to Hakodate, Laxman's expedition carried out a further survey of the Kurils on their return journey to Okhotsk. Profiting from the time spent in the interior of Hokkaidō, Laxman also returned with "many plans and sketches of the places he visited, which often capture their topography in considerable detail."[71] Additionally, when waiting in Nemuro, Laxman managed to copy a Japanese map of Ezo (Hokkaidō) that also featured Sakhalin Island. Such cartographic knowledge became extremely valuable, especially as the Bakufu authorities banned Japanese maps from being given to foreigners."[72] It was this interdiction that led to the famous Siebold Incident in 1828–9, when German physician Philipp Franz von Siebold was arrested on suspicion of espionage after being accused of attempting to take maps of northern Japan out of the country. Von Siebold was eventually expelled from Japan. Takahashi Sakuzaemon, the court astronomer from whom von Siebold had obtained the maps, was less fortunate. He was imprisoned and had his teeth smashed to prevent him from committing suicide by biting off his tongue. Sentenced to death, Takahashi died in prison before it could be carried out.[73] As we shall see in chapter 3, von Siebold was also accused of spying for Russia.

Returning to Laxman, he also offered observations on Japanese military capabilities, including the mixture of modern and traditional features. He described soldiers "with firearms, which they held sloping on their right shoulder. In their left hands they had a lighted wick, and from their left shoulders hung a bow and quiver."[74] He also confirmed previous reports about the limitations of Japanese shipping, noting that the vessels were not designed for the open sea and did not have cannons.[75] Other information related to Japanese agriculture ("the Japanese do not use four-legged animals for food") and transport infrastructure ("bridges similar to those in China" and "The road everywhere ... had evidently cost a great deal of work").[76]

Above all, Laxman's information was beneficial in giving Russia its first real insight into Japanese politics and society. As David Wells explains, in Laxman's "unmediated account of the operation of Japanese diplomacy ... He gives details of the names and positions of the officials he meets, and paints a picture of a highly complex, sophisticated and wealthy society, clearly worthy of a high level of respect in the future dealings that he hopes to pursue."[77] More broadly, Laxman communicated his experience of Japanese culture, including his observations of funeral rites and New Year celebrations. Indeed, Laxman's description of Setsubun, in which the new season is marked by scattering beans and shouting "*oni wa soto! fuku wa uchi!*" ("Devils out! Fortune in!"), will be familiar to residents of modern-day Japan.[78]

For the most part, Laxman acquired his information openly. He simply asked the officials in Nemuro to lend him the map of Japan to copy, and, in return, he provided them with those of his charts of interest to them. There was, however, one small piece of espionage. Every day while the crew of the *Ekaterina* waited in Nemuro to discover if they would be permitted to proceed to Edo, Laxman sent Tugolukov, the ship's interpreter, to spend time with the Japanese officials. This was partly to help Tugolukov to improve his Japanese, but also, as Laxman explains, "I was always seeking through the interpreter to find out the disposition and thoughts of the Japanese regarding the Russian people."[79]

This tactic proved useful, as the Russians found out about the efforts of the Dutch to inflame Japanese fears of their northern neighbour. Specifically, on 21 February 1793, Tugolukov reported to Laxman

> that he had secretly learned from the Edo officials, one of whom had served in Nagasaki for nine years, that the Japanese had been told by the Dutch a long time ago that the Russians cruelly and barbarously mistreated all foreigners, who happened to come to their country, and that the letter which they [the Russians] had now brought concerning the humanitarian and amicable motivation of the expedition, therefore, was received with mistrust.[80]

This was valuable intelligence, since it reinforced the importance of demonstrating to the Japanese that Kōdayū and the other castaways had been well-treated in Russia. It was also an indication that the Dutch in Nagasaki could be expected to sabotage third countries' efforts to open relations with Japan.

Whether the product of Dutch intrigue or the legacy of Benyovszky's warning of 1771, there is no doubt that, at the time of Laxman's arrival, the Japanese viewed the Russians with suspicion. Honda Toshiaki, the author of *Tales of the West* and a contemporary of Laxman, writes of the case of Simeon Drohevitch Izuyosov. This Russian man spent eight years on the islands of Etorofu and Kunashiri up to 1792. When questioned by Matsumae officials and asked to leave, Izuyosov explained that he was under threat of persecution in Russia, and that, "Rather than be driven from here, I would prefer that you cut off my head."[81] Given the number of political exiles in Catherine the Great's Russia, this is a credible explanation, yet Honda rushed to the conclusion that Izuyosov "was a Russian spy who had been selected for his heroism, conspicuous even in Russia, to keep watch on the government and people of Japan."[82] Honda also feared that Russia had already sent spies to Japan disguised as crew members on Dutch ships. He panicked that "They may even have come to Edo, visited the castle, and examined conditions."[83]

Despite the intensity of local suspicions, Laxman was able to considerably improve Russia's image in Japanese eyes. This occurred rapidly as prejudice gave way in the face of first-hand knowledge and personal relationships. The Japanese also proved as eager to learn about Russia as Laxman's expedition was to learn about Japan. Indeed, the Japanese are reported to have sent spies to keep watch on Laxman in Nemuro.[84] After being returned to the care of the Japanese authorities, Kōdayū was also intensively grilled for everything he had discovered during his years in Russia. The result was a multi-volume report that featured not only information on the Russian military and shipping but also such minor items as "billiards, umbrellas, chess, tiles, glass, soap and many other subjects."[85] Donald Keene describes this testimony as "the most comprehensive picture of a European nation yet obtained in Japan."[86] On the whole, Kōdayū and the other surviving castaway created a favourable impression by describing their admiration for Russia and their gratitude for their return. However, they also provoked alarm when they declared, with considerable exaggeration, that the Russians already knew "everything without exception" about Japan.[87]

The reality, as we have seen, is that Russian knowledge remained seriously limited prior to Laxman's expedition. What is more, even though Laxman's voyage was fruitful in deepening Russian understanding of Japan and seeming to lay the foundations for a trade agreement, it did not maximise its potential as an intelligence-gathering mission. The main obstacle was the Bakufu's obsessive secrecy. Had the *Ekaterina* been permitted to proceed to Edo, Laxman would have gained insight into the centre of Japanese political power. However, Edo officials had rejected this out of hand, telling Laxman that, if the Russians insisted on handing over the castaways at Edo, it would be better that they should not return the Japanese at all.[88]

Additionally, the Bakufu took further measures to limit Laxman's access to information. When at Nemuro, the Russians were permitted to talk with both Matsumae and Edo officials, but instructions were given to prevent them from speaking with locals. In particular, Laxman describes that it was difficult to acquire any information from the Ainu, "since the Japanese employed all their efforts to keep them from us so that we could not learn anything from them."[89] All the same, Laxman did come to understand that the Ainu "harbour a hatred towards the Japanese, for their cruelty towards them, and had often rebelled."[90]

Such restrictions became only tighter as Laxman's expedition moved south. At Hakodate, they were permitted to explore the local countryside in the company of Matsumae officials but were barred from making visits to the town, even to wash clothes at the shoreline.[91] When arriving at Matsumae, Laxman noted that the roads had been cleared of all ordinary people, albeit that he could see them crowded into houses along the route to catch a glimpse of the rare foreigners.[92] Furthermore, the accommodation provided for Laxman in Matsumae was designed to prevent him from gaining any unauthorised insight into Japan's society. While the rooms were comfortable and equipped in Western style, "In front of the house there was a garden and around it a low fence, which had been topped with a striped white and blue curtain, so that the city and people beyond were hidden from the Russian view."[93] Additionally, just in case the Russians should slip out or anyone should slip in, the house was surrounded by sixty guards.[94]

The Bakufu police state was therefore a virtual "denied area" for intelligence collection.[95] However, Laxman did not exploit all the opportunities available to him. Most notably, he refused the Japanese authorities' request that the Russians travel all the way from Nemuro to Matsumae by road. This demand was presumably made because the Japanese feared that, if Laxman travelled by sea, the *Ekaterina*, despite being prohibited from doing so, might head directly for Edo. Laxman rejected the overland route as being too slow, which is why the Russians travelled as far as Hakodate by sea. The overland journey, over 700km in length, would have been arduous. However, in traversing the entire width of Hokkaidō, even under the watchful eye of accompanying officials, Laxman would have gained much additional insight into *sakoku* Japan. What is more, when the Edo officials finally relented and agreed to the Russians making most of the trip by sea, Laxman refused the offer of a Japanese under-officer to join them aboard. Such an individual would undoubtedly have reported back all he learned about the Russians and their ship, but it also would have provided Laxman with an opportunity to extract information from a serving Japanese officer free of the presence of his superiors.[96]

In summary, while not pushing the envelope, Laxman's expedition of 1792–3 was an important milestone in Russia's understanding of Japan. In addition to returning with the copy of a Japanese map, as well as various other charts and sketches, Laxman added to Russia's knowledge of Japanese diplomatic practices and learned of Dutch attempts to provoke Japanese hostility towards Russia. He also expanded Russian appreciation of Japanese culture and society and brought home samples of Japanese goods and scientific specimens. This is not to mention the Nagasaki Permit, whose significance is discussed in the next chapter.

These are impressive achievements for a voyage led by a 26-year-old lieutenant. However, while Laxman was promoted, the Russian central authorities undervalued the information with which he returned. Catherine the Great, who was never a fulsome supporter of the expedition, wrote to a French correspondent:

> And what kind of a story is that about the Japanese castaway! He was shipwrecked and sent back home again. And that is all there is to it. Laxman's son accompanied him and returned with knicknacks which were exhibited to us this year in the Tsarskoe Selo and for which I wouldn't give ten sous. Let anybody, who so wishes, trade there, but not I.[97]

Laxman's report did receive attention by the Academy of Sciences in January 1794, but, with the empress taking such a dismissive attitude, it soon "gathered dust in the Siberian archives."[98] No public account of the expedition was published until 1805,[99] and, more importantly, it was over a decade before an attempt was made to use the Nagasaki Permit.

3

CAPTIVES AND THE OPENING OF JAPAN

While chapter 2 charted Russian intelligence-gathering efforts during the 18th century, this chapter addresses the first half of the 19th century, up to and including the arrival in Japan of Vice-Admiral Evfimii Putyatin in 1853 and his successful negotiation of the Treaty of Shimoda (1855) that finally established official relations between the empires of Russia and Japan. Since the first half of the 19th century was still the *sakoku* era, Russian opportunities for intelligence collection remained limited. The focus of this chapter is therefore as much on the shogunate's efforts to prevent Russia from learning Japanese secrets as it is on deliberate attempts at spying. Recounting the history of this period through the intelligence lens is also an opportunity to revisit Russia's role in the opening of Japan.

Rezanov and Krusenstern are denied

The 18th century ended positively with Laxman returning to Russia with the Nagasaki Permit, which, it was believed, was as good as a promise that Japan would open commercial relations with Russia. Given this optimistic interpretation, it is surprising that St Petersburg did not follow up more rapidly. As it was, it was a full 11 years before a Russian ship finally arrived in the waters around Nagasaki. This fateful delay was partly caused by Catherine the Great's disdainful attitude towards the results of Laxman's expedition. Furthermore, after the death of Catherine in 1796, there followed a period of political instability that culminated in the assassination of Catherine's successor, Paul I, in March 1801. It was therefore some time before the next tsar, Alexander I, approved a new mission to Japan.

The man appointed to lead this expedition was Nikolai Rezanov, the head of the Russian-American Company, a commercial entity not dissimilar to the British and Dutch East India Companies. Rezanov owed his position to his marriage to the 14-year-old daughter of Grigorii Shelikhov, who had been a backer of the Secret Voyage to Japan of 1777–9 before withdrawing to concentrate on the Americas. Shelikhov founded the firm that became the Russian-American Company, and, on Shelikhov's death in 1795, Rezanov became the majority shareholder.[1]

The involvement of the Russian-American Company was not the only difference between Rezanov's voyage and that of Laxman. While Laxman had been a humble lieutenant, Rezanov was an official ambassador with the title of Chamberlain of His Imperial Highness and Knight of St Anna First Class. Additionally, while Laxman had set forth from Okhotsk, Rezanov's expedition to Japan was part of the famous round-the-world voyage of the *Nadezhda* under the command of Adam Johann von Krusenstern.[2] Having departed Kronstadt (near St Petersburg) in summer 1803, the *Nadezhda* crossed the Atlantic and rounded Cape Horn. The ship then headed north to resupply at Kamchatka, before sailing to Nagasaki, where it arrived in September 1804.

One thing that the expeditions of Rezanov and Laxman did have in common was that they both used the return of Japanese castaways as the pretext for visiting Japan. In Rezanov's case, four Japanese were selected for repatriation. These men had been aboard a transport ship that had been swept out into the ocean by a storm in 1793. Eventually discovered on the Aleutian Islands in 1795, they were taken to Russia, where they spent the next eight years.[3] What these Japanese sailors had expected to be a short trip along Japan's shores therefore turned into a decade-long odyssey, including a semi-circumnavigation of the globe. This does not appear to have been a happy experience, since relations between Krusenstern's crew and these Japanese never became friendly, with one officer describing the castaways as "ugly people who guzzle like hedgehogs and have a lot of pretentions."[4]

There was little attempt, however, to disguise the real purpose of the voyage. According to an article in the contemporary Russian press:

> The expedition of Rezanov will go to Japan in order to open and establish commercial relations for Russia with these islands, where the industry and ignorance of the people are equally surprising, where some skills have reached a degree of perfection unknown to us, but where reason is still in the cradle.[5]

Aside from this primary objective, Rezanov's voyage was assigned intelligence responsibilities. Minister of Commerce Count Nikolai Rumyantsev requested that Rezanov engage in

> the gathering of information about Sakhalin—whether it belonged to China or Japan, and how it could be reached for the establishment of trade; investigation of what the Japanese knew about the Amur Estuary; what the relations were between Japan, China, and Korea; whether the Liu Ch'iu [Ryūkyū] Islands belonged to Japan—and if independent, to try to reach them and establish commercial relations.[6]

Furthermore, there were hopes of deepening Russian knowledge of Japan itself. During the six months the *Nadezhda* was expected to spend in Japan, Captain Krusenstern anticipated "that many liberties would be allowed us ... by the opportunity we should have of acquiring some information on this little known country."[7] In Krusenstern's view, intelligence about Japan was sorely needed because "the only Europeans competent to impart any knowledge concerning it, have, during the last two hundred years, made a rule not to publish any thing."[8] He is, of course, referring to the Dutch.

> They have never even published a decent map of the situation of Firando [Hirado] and Nangasaky [Nagasaki] ... I cannot help attributing this reserve of the Dutch to a ridiculous, mean, and at all events a very useless policy, contrary to the spirit of a philosophical age, and unbecoming a republican government.[9]

The arrival of the *Nadezhda* in 1804 was expected to change all this, yet it ended in anger and frustration. The Russians did spend over half a year in Japan, but they were ultimately turned away with a message from the shogunate that "it is our government's will not to open this place; do not come again in vain. You must sail home quickly."[10] To this was added that, if the Russians discovered further Japanese castaways on their territory, they should not attempt to return them, but hand them over to the Dutch.

This alone was a major setback. Despite the high status of the expedition and their possession of a document they believed to amount to a promise of trade, Rezanov achieved just as little as the Secret Voyage. The outcome was also worse than Laxman's mission, since that had at least generated goodwill and raised the prospect of a future treaty. Now, the door had been conclusively slammed shut on Russia's hopes.

What made the situation worse was that Rezanov, his pride bruised, decided to take revenge. In a letter of February 1806, Rezanov informed Tsar Alexander I of his intention to "build ships and set out next year to destroy their settlements on Matmai [Hokkaidō], to push them from Sakhalin, and ravage their coasts. By cutting off their supply of fish and depriving 200,000 people of their food we will force them to open up trade with us."[11]

Rezanov also planned to kidnap several Japanese, including a priest. His idea was for these Japanese to be taken back to Okhotsk, where, treated with kindness and ministered to by their own holy man, they would form a favourable impression of Russia. As George Lensen explains, "After a year, the Japanese were to be sent back to their homeland to tell their countrymen of the good treatment they had experienced and to inspire them with confidence in the Russians!"[12] This plan to brainwash Japanese captives bears a resemblance to Moscow's treatment of thousands of Japanese internees, who were detained by the Soviet Union after the Second World War and subjected to political re-education. Rezanov did not anticipate repatriating all the Japanese. Instead, just as the Soviet Union used Japanese internees as forced labourers, so Rezanov anticipated transporting Japanese prisoners to work in the settlements of the Russian-American Company.[13]

Rezanov knew full well that his course of action was not guaranteed to receive support in St Petersburg. He therefore acted without waiting for authorisation, telling the tsar in his letter that he would rather be punished "as a criminal for taking action without your command" than "let time pass in vain."[14] Moreover, Rezanov "commanded that the expedition be cloaked in secrecy, all concerned being made to sign a promise not to reveal anything."[15] He also made sure to distance himself from the action. Rezanov did not join the raids but outsourced them to Nikolai Khvostov and Gavriil Davydov, a lieutenant and midshipman in the service of the Russian-American Company. Additionally, to absolve himself of responsibility should things go awry, Rezanov issued confusing orders on the eve of the raids then disappeared from Okhotsk.[16]

Fatefully, despite the lack of clarity in Rezanov's orders, Khvostov and Davydov decided to proceed. In October 1806, Khvostov, as commander of the *Iunona*, attacked a Japanese settlement on Sakhalin, burning houses, pillaging supplies, and carrying off four Japanese guards. The raiding party also stole the deity from a local temple, and, in its place, left a copper plaque that included the threat that, if Japan continued to deny Russia's demand for trade, "the Russians will lay waste the northern part of Japan."[17]

The destruction continued the next year. In June 1807, the *Iunona*, joined by the *Avos* under Davydov's command, arrived at Etorofu in the Kuril chain, where Japan had a garrison of over 300 soldiers, plus "five ladies and a sake brewer."[18] The Japanese sent negotiators, but these were attacked. An exchange of fire took place, following which the Russians, whose landing party consisted of fewer than 30 sailors, withdrew. However, the Russians returned after dark, and, catching the defenders unawares, forced the Japanese to abandon their fortress. Mamiya Rinzō, the famous Japanese explorer, who happened to be on Etorofu at the time, was shot in the buttocks as he fled for his life.[19]

After an orgy of celebratory drinking, Khvostov and Davydov's raiding party burnt everything they could find then departed. When the Japanese cautiously returned, they discovered two Russians who had been left behind in a drunken stupor. After being speared to death, these two men were decapitated, with their heads then salted and sent to Hakodate. Meanwhile, Khvostov and Davydov led further attacks against Japanese shipping and Sakhalin, before sailing back to Okhotsk, where they arrived at the end of July 1807.[20]

Believing they had successfully fulfilled their orders, Khvostov and Davydov might have expected a warm welcome. Instead, Captain Bukharin, the commandant of Okhotsk, arrested them for launching the raids without authority, though this may have been a pretext to seize the ships' plunder, which Bukharin himself estimated as worth 18,000 roubles.[21] Fearing they would die in prison before receiving a fair trial, Khvostov and Davydov escaped and headed on foot to Yakutsk, a journey of 500 miles. There, they were detained again but permitted to submit a petition to higher authorities. When informed of the case, Minister of Commerce Rumyantsev judged that the two officers should not be held accountable for the attacks. The Admiralty still court-martialled the men, but, on account of their subsequent good service in the war with Sweden (1808–9), Khvostov and Davydov avoided punishment.[22]

Having survived all this, Khvostov and Davydov ultimately fell victim to a heavy night out. When back in St Petersburg in October 1809, the two officers happened upon an old friend in the street and proceeded to enjoy a late night of eating and drinking. As many a reveller in St Petersburg has discovered, the bridges over the Neva open at night to permit shipping to pass. It is therefore easy to be trapped on the wrong side of the river. This was the situation in which Khvostov and Davydov found themselves. Instead of waiting for dawn, the two well-lubricated men decided to jump from one side of the bridge to the other with the assistance of a passing barge. However, instead of saving themselves a few hours, Khvostov and Davydov fell into the Neva and were drowned.[23]

Fate also brought an early, though less dramatic, end to Rezanov's life. After leaving Khvostov in Okhotsk in August 1806, Rezanov had planned to travel to St Petersburg. However, he fell ill en route and died in Krasnoyarsk in March 1807.[24]

As we saw previously, there had long been a fear in Japan of the supposed threat from the north. This had not been entirely dispelled by Laxman and now reached new levels of fervour. While the Russians had previously been referred to as "*aka-hito*" ("red people"), after Khvostov and Davydov's raids they were upgraded to "*aka-oni*" ("red devils").[25] We will see the implications of this shortly, but it is useful, firstly, to consider the reasons for the failure of Rezanov's expedition and the role played by deficient intelligence.

Despite the unequivocal rejection it eventually received, Rezanov's mission was not preordained to fail. Donald Keene argues that, in the late 18th century, the Bakufu was on the verge of abandoning *sakoku* and that opening Ezo (Hokkaidō) to trade was one of the options being seriously considered.[26] In fact, one of the Japanese interpreters had confided to Rezanov in Nagasaki the "profound secret" that "Two hundred of the 'highest dignitaries' had been summoned to Edo by the Shogun to consult upon the expediency of establishing trade relations with Russia."[27] The Russians also learned later that, when Rezanov had arrived, many Japanese had been delighted at the prospect of commercial relations and were dismayed by the disrespectful way in which the shogunate treated the Russian envoy. When it was discovered that Rezanov had died soon after leaving Japan, the rumour spread that shame had driven him to suicide.[28] Given this domestic political situation, it is possible that Russia could have achieved earlier success in opening Japan had Rezanov persisted with diplomacy rather than giving the order to burn bridges.

German physician Philipp Franz von Siebold, who became a noted expert on Japan, argued that the shogunate ultimately decided to reject Rezanov's offer of trade because of Russia's lack of understanding of certain important customs and etiquette. Above all, von Siebold judged that the Russians had erred in having Rezanov deliver an official letter that was "written in Japanese by a quasi-literate Japanese castaway" and lacked the necessary style and diplomatic language.[29] This made it possible for the vacillating shogunate to take the easy option and ignore the missive. Another error was Rezanov's reluctance to promptly surrender all arms on arrival in Nagasaki.[30]

These were clear mistakes, yet the instructions given to Rezanov ahead of his departure reveal that, by the start of the 19th century, St Petersburg did have a fair understanding of Japan's political system and the pitfalls to avoid when engaging with it. Minister of Commerce Rumyantsev had briefed Rezanov on the fact that real power lay with the *Kubō* (the shogun) and that the "spiritual emperor ... lives in splendor and esteem, but in utter insignificance, so that, having his own capital, he is forgotten and consequently you are by no means to seek access to him."[31] Rezanov was also told that he should stress to the emperor that he was not subservient to the pope, thereby presenting the Russians as more like the commercially focused Protestant Dutch than the proselytising Catholics of Spain and Portugal. Further advice was that Rezanov would gain respect if, when engaging with Japanese dignitaries, he was to remove his sword before being asked to do so.[32]

Rather than believing that they had made any diplomatic blunders, many on the Russian side attributed the failure of Rezanov's mission to sabotage, with fingers again pointed at the Dutch. Vasilii Golovnin, whom we shall meet properly in the next section, claimed that Dutch interpreters in Nagasaki had turned "everything to the advantage of the Dutch and had given the Japanese such an idea of Russia that they had dismissed Rezanov with an answer that would make the Russians think no more of sending ships."[33] The Dutch certainly had the motivation of maintaining their monopoly on European trade with Japan, through which they sold "trifling articles at a most exorbitant price."[34]

Also, there is the possibility that the waters of Nagasaki harbour were poisoned for Rezanov by one of the castaways he had brought back to Japan. During the long wait to be handed over to the Japanese authorities, this individual, named Okuda Tajūrō, had slit his own throat in a suicide attempt. Krusenstern claims that this was due to guilt for having spread lies about the Russians. Krusenstern specifies that, shortly after their arrival in Nagasaki, Tajūrō (as he is usually known) had passed a written statement to the local magistrates

> in which he not only complained of the cruel treatment his countrymen experienced in Russia, but described the Russians as the most bigotted of Christians, adding that several of them had been forced to embrace that religion, and that the object of this voyage was chiefly to make an attempt to introduce it into Japan.[35]

It remains a topic for speculation as to exactly why Rezanov's mission failed and to what extent better intelligence on Japanese politics and etiquette could have made a difference. It is almost certain, however, that the delay between Laxman's receipt of the Nagasaki Permit and Rezanov's voyage did not help. Indeed, when Rezanov at last arrived in 1804, one Bakufu official is quoted as saying, "[We had] waited for a Russian ship for four years since [we] gave the document. And then another eight years. [We] gave up on seeing Russian people again. Why did you not come [to Japan] during this period?"[36]

While failing to open Japan to trade, did Rezanov's expedition at least succeed in its intelligence tasks? Regarding regional knowledge, there was some progress. On leaving Nagasaki, Krusenstern sailed the *Nadezhda* through the Tsushima Strait and surveyed Japan's west coast. He then navigated La Pérouse Strait (Sōya Strait) between Sakhalin and Hokkaidō. These explorations permitted the drawing of more accurate maps.

Another step forward was that Krusenstern was able to report back on Japan's contemporary trade relations.

> The following is the intelligence, though indeed very incomplete, which I have been able to collect with regard to the Chinese trade. Twelve ships are permitted to come to Nangasaky annually from Ningpo [Ningbo] ... Their cargo consists chiefly of sugar, ivory, tin plates, lead, silk stuffs and tea.[37]

In his view, the junks serving this route were inefficient and the trade would be better handled by outside powers. In his opinion, "It would be very advantageous to any European nation that might be allowed to enjoy the carrying trade between Ningpo and Nangasaky."[38] Krusenstern added that "During the whole time of our stay here, we never witnessed the arrival of a single ship, either from Corea or the Likeo [Ryukyu] islands, notwithstanding their vicinity; and all intercourse between these countries and Japan is said to have ceased for some time past."[39]

One matter that Krusenstern was unable to settle was whether Sakhalin was an island. Indeed, he remained confused about some basic aspects of regional geography. Under his captaincy, the *Nadezhda* wasted much time searching for the island of Karafuto that was believed to lie between Ezo (Hokkaidō) and Sakhalin.[40] Karafuto is, in fact, simply the Japanese name for Sakhalin.

However, while the *Nadezhda's* voyage was not able to answer all questions about Japan's geography, it did considerably better on this score than on gathering intelligence about Japan's domestic affairs. Indeed, while Rezanov's mission surpassed Laxman's by spending half a year not on isolated Ezo but in bustling Nagasaki, the expedition added little to Russia's existing knowledge of conditions within Japan. As Krusenstern grumbles,

> the time of our stay here was literally a confinement, from which the ambassador was no more exempted, than the meanest sailor in the ship. It will therefore easily be seen, how impossible it was for those who continued on board, to obtain even the slightest information.[41]

These restrictions were more draconian than those applied to Laxman. During the first six weeks, none of the crew of the *Nadezhda* were permitted to go ashore, nor even to row about within a short distance of the ship. They were also surrounded by 32 guard boats. These Japanese watchmen therefore had the privilege of observing the Russian ambassador in "his habit of appearing on deck in a loose jacket and pissing off the side of the ship."[42] Only after the Russians pretended that Rezanov was suffering ill health were they reluctantly granted access to a confined bay where they could exercise. This place, at Kibachi, was only 100 paces in length and 40 in width. It was enclosed on the land side by a high bamboo wall and was overlooked by two watchtowers.[43]

Later, Rezanov and his officers were allowed to use a specially prepared house at Megasaki (also in Nagasaki), though this afforded little more comfort and no more insight into life in Japan. Located on a small peninsula, "the Russian Deshima," as Krusenstern called it, was surrounded by water on three sides, while fencing and locked doors prevented access to the land. While Rezanov and the other Russians strolled in a small fenced-in area, "Japanese men, women, and children, on the other side of the fence, peered at them as at animals in the zoo."[44] Subjected to months of such humiliation, one can imagine the proud Chamberlain of His Imperial Highness becoming increasingly frustrated and plotting his revenge.

When negotiations with officials dispatched from Edo did belatedly begin, these also provided the Russians with little opportunity to learn anything of their surroundings. Although the talks were conducted within the city, nearby buildings were curtained off to prevent the Russians from seeing anything unsanctioned. "Only here and there an inquisitive head, irresistibly propelled by curiosity, would pop through the drapes to stare at the foreigners."[45] Visits to the *Nadezhda* by Japanese officials proved similarly unenlightening since, when they were questioned by the Russians, they were found to be "extremely ignorant of the geography of their own islands, or at all events pretended to be so."[46]

In consequence of this strict confinement, Rezanov's mission added next to nothing to Russia's knowledge of Japanese politics and society. All Krusenstern could manage was a few disparaging remarks about the attire of the Japanese officials ("very similar to the female dress in Europe"), as well as about their absence of facial hair (since they "pluck out the hair with small pincers").[47] The only other noteworthy observations relate to the functioning of Japanese bureaucracy, with Krusenstern reporting on the tendency of Japanese officials not to do anything until it is approved by higher authorities, as well as noting their insistence on implementing rules to the letter, even when there is no logic in doing so.[48]

Since such crumbs do not amount to meaningful intelligence, Rezanov's mission must be judged as much a disappointment from the perspective of information gathering as it was with respect to opening Japan to trade. Rezanov and Krusenstern were not officially prisoners in Japan, yet the information they gained was as meagre as one might expect from someone consigned to jail. Ironically, the next step forward in uncovering the hidden realities of *sakoku* Japan was made by a Russian who really was a prisoner.

Golovnin's prison notebook

The Japanese authorities were understandably alarmed by the attacks of Khvostov and Davydov in 1806–7. Not only did these represent an external threat, they also demonstrated the weakness of the shogunate, thereby encouraging domestic opposition. While waiting to see if the attacks would be renewed, the Bakufu ordered Japan's positions on Karafuto (Sakhalin), Etorofu, and Ezo (Hokkaidō) to be reinforced. John Harrison describes contemporary Japan as being "in a commotion, with war preparations being made at all important centers."[49] Japan's military leadership also sought their opportunity for revenge, and this finally arrived with the appearance of Vasilii Golovnin in May 1811.

Vasilii Golovnin was commander of the *Diana*, a sloop-of-war that is not to be confused with the eponymous frigate discussed later in this chapter. Golovnin's mission was not to open trade relations with Japan, a goal that had been temporarily shelved after Rezanov's rebuff, but to engage in naval reconnaissance around Sakhalin and the Southern Kuril Islands. Precisely how this task was intended to be accomplished remained vague, because Golovnin began his expedition without waiting for the arrival of detailed instructions from the Admiralty, which he anticipated taking several months.[50] One point that was clear, however, was that the *Diana* was supposed to avoid interactions with the Japanese. Indeed, Golovnin tried to avoid attracting attention by "sail[ing] without any flag in the neighborhood of the islands belonging to them."[51] Additionally, not expecting to set foot on Japanese territory, Golovnin was not as familiar with Russia's existing knowledge of Japanese politics and society as he could have been. He had brought a copy of Krusenstern's memoirs with him, yet he admits to not having read all of it by the time of his arrival in Japanese waters.[52]

Had Golovnin been more familiar with the extreme suspicion with which Rezanov and Krusenstern had been treated in Nagasaki, he may have proceeded more cautiously. As it was, when Golovnin discovered that much of the ship's supplies had been consumed by rats, he ordered the *Diana* to approach the Japanese fortress on Kunashiri. Despite initially being fired upon by cannon, Golovnin persisted with his attempts to secure supplies, and, on the morning of 23 July 1811, he headed ashore in a small boat along with two officers, four sailors, and an Ainu named Aleksei. The *Diana* was left under the command of his deputy, Petr Rikord. On the island, Golovnin and the seven others were taken prisoner by the Japanese and thus began a period of captivity that was to last two years, two months, and 26 days.[53]

Golovnin's own account of his imprisonment is a fascinating read. It includes the rough treatment he and his men received at first, with Golovnin himself bound so tightly around the neck that he fell unconscious, waking later with "blood flowing from my mouth and nose."[54] He also describes their forced trek across Hokkaidō to first Hakodate, then Matsumae, as well as their daring escape from prison and recapture. Finally, Golovnin recounts the process of their eventual release. This involved the crew of the *Diana* retaliating against the Japanese by seizing a merchant named Takadaya Kahei.[55] The Russian side also provided a formal assurance that the raids by Khvostov and Davydov had not been officially sanctioned. With the captives on each side released and Japan choosing to accept Russia's explanation for the earlier attacks, the Golovnin incident actually lightened the atmosphere in Russo-Japanese relations after the frictions that followed Rezanov's mission.

What primarily interests us here is that Golovnin's lengthy confinement in Japan provided an excellent opportunity to observe the inner workings of the hermit state that went far beyond the restricted access permitted to Laxman and Rezanov. As George Lensen puts it, "From the point of view of greater knowledge and better understanding between Russia and Japan, Golovnin's dismal prison proved to be a gilded cage."[56] Indeed, so rare and valuable was Golovnin's first-hand account that it continued to be consulted for several decades and was read by Commodore Matthew Perry's crew in preparation for their famous voyage to Japan in 1853.[57]

Part of the reason for Golovnin's unusually deep insight was that he and most of his companions successfully escaped and enjoyed several days of freedom during which they tramped across the Hokkaidō countryside. Yet, even when Golovnin and his men were under the control of the Japanese, their captors made little effort to hide anything from them. For example, Golovnin describes the unsettling experience of being led through an artillery battery near Hakodate:

> They sought to conceal nothing from us, even in their military works. From this we inferred that they doubtless intended to detain us prisoners for life, as in that case we could not turn to their disadvantage any knowledge we might collect respecting their system of fortification.[58]

This assumption was probably correct, at least initially. This is because, while the ordinary Japanese looked upon the Russians' plight with sympathy, more powerful individuals were less forgiving. The famous explorer Mamiya Rinzō, still smarting from the bullet in the backside he had received during Khvostov and Daydov's raid on Etorofu, declared to the authorities that Golovnin's arrival in Japan was not accidental, but that the Russians had "been sent thither for the express purpose of acting as spies."[59] These "spies" should therefore never be permitted to return home.

Another factor that contributed to Golovnin's success was his own character. Despite the considerable hardship he suffered during imprisonment, Golovnin developed a strong respect for Japanese civilisation. Describing an early stage in his confinement, Golovnin writes that "We now entertained a very good opinion of [the Japanese], and were persuaded that nothing but the inhuman conduct of our countrymen could have induced them to treat us with cruelty."[60]

As well as an open mind, Golovnin possessed good instincts for intelligence collection. Prior to his capture, Golovnin used local Ainu to gather information on the Japanese, including on the location of their cannons. To induce the Ainu to share such knowledge, the Russians gave them brandy, gunpowder, and tobacco.[61] This proved a bad deal, since the Japanese government later condemned "the Ainu, to forfeit their heads, on discovering that they had been sent by the Russians as spies to inspect the villages and fortresses of Japan." Fortunately, this sentence was not carried out, as the Japanese ultimately judged that the Ainu "had been compelled blindly to obey the orders of the Russians."[62]

Collecting information about a secretive foreign state is, of course, no use if it cannot be recalled and communicated. Golovnin therefore developed techniques to help him remember key information during the almost 27 months of his detention. He devised a system using threads from items of clothing. Whenever anything occurred that he particularly wished to record, he would tie a knot in a piece of thread, using different colours for each category of event. He explains: "Often did I count over these knots, and recall to my mind the events they served to denote."[63] Later, when the prisoners gained access to paper, Golovnin noted down his observations, but "wrote only half sentences and arbitrary signs, and mingled Russian, French, and English words together, in such a way that none but myself could decipher the manuscript."[64]

The information on Japan with which Golovnin ultimately returned to Russia covered a range of fields. In terms of the military, he and his men, as already noted, were able to observe Japanese artillery batteries. They were not impressed with what they saw. Golovnin explains that the fortress on Kunashiri was partly concealed by cloth and made to look more forbidding through the addition of painted embrasures, though this had been done "in so rough a style, that even at a considerable distance we could perceive the deception." He also judged the aim of the Japanese gunners to be poor.[65] Batteries elsewhere in Hokkaidō were inappropriately sited and poorly constructed.[66] Meanwhile, Golovnin's account of Japanese infantry, which emphasises the irregularity of their drill and their continued use of bows and arrows, as well as muskets, suggests that little progress had been achieved in the two decades since Laxman's visit.[67]

Separately, through conversations with various officials, Golovnin learned something of Japanese military strategy and that "one of their principal maxims of war was to allure the enemy as much as possible into the interior of their country, and then to surround him on every side with powerful armies."[68] He also discovered that the Japanese had contemplated retaliating against Russia following the raids of Khvostov and Davydov by sending three ships to destroy Okhotsk. To this, the Russians had responded that "we were sorry the Japanese had not sent thither thirty, or even three hundred ships instead of three, as we were certain none of them would ever have got back."[69] This was bluster, since accounts of Okhotsk at this time describe it as "grim, violent and desperate," and known more for "vodka, native whores and gluttonous feasting" than for its defensive capabilities.[70]

To this military intelligence, Golovnin added the political insight that Japan's *sakoku* policy did not have strong public backing, and that many Japanese were eager to engage in international trade. Indeed, it was this public eagerness that convinced the shogunate that extreme measures were required to prevent Japanese society from exposing itself to foreign influence.[71] Golovnin also reported that the Bakufu itself was not united, but "has split into two factions. One of them seeks to avert danger by having no relations whatsoever with Russia: while the other on the contrary sees all the security for the Japanese empire in commercial relations with Russia."[72] This knowledge revived Russian hopes that a trade agreement with Japan might be possible after all.

Lastly, Golovnin's account of Japanese society is one of the most valuable of the pre-Meiji era. This includes issues of etiquette and hierarchy, but also observations on architecture and cuisine. As noted, Golovnin formed a generally positive impression of Japan, though there were exceptions. He concluded that ordinary Japanese "excel our most crafty European courtiers in the practice of falsehood and deceit."[73] He also criticised Japanese people's "well-known cowardice."[74] This he attributed to the fact "that peace had sapped Japan of vital military strength, that the Japanese lacked daring, fearlessness, bravery, and manliness."[75]

The Japanese were, not surprisingly, also eager to learn all they could from their "guests." The interpreter Uebara Kumajirō was sent to spend six hours each day with the prisoners. While the Russians initially welcomed the distraction, they soon tired of the endless questions, which ranged from "what number of cannon was planted round the imperial palace" to "what kind of birds are found in the neighborhood of St. Petersburg." At one point the Russians became so exasperated by the interminable questioning that they complained, "we had rather they would put an end to our existence at once than torture us in the way they did."[76]

Despite this outburst, the Russians were mostly willing to answer honestly. There were, however, areas where disinformation was judged appropriate. For instance, rather than reveal that the *Diana* had been engaged in a naval reconnaissance, Golovnin claimed that they were sailing from the eastern end of the Russian Empire to St Petersburg but had been pushed off course by unfavourable winds.[77] Moreover, when quizzed on Russia's military strength in the Pacific, the Russians exaggerated liberally. "They increased the number of fortresses and the amount of garrisons in Siberia and distributed at pleasure numerous fleets in the harbors of Okhotsk, in Kamchatka, and on the northwestern coast of America."[78]

Crucial for the prospect of their release, Golovnin also concealed the extent of his acquaintance with Khvostov and Davydov. When asked to translate a proclamation left behind on Sakhalin by Khvostov in which the lieutenant claimed the island as Russian, Golovnin misrepresented key phrases to avoid the impression that Khvostov was operating under official orders.[79] Whether the Japanese really believed this or not, the claim that Khvostov and Davydov were acting without authorisation was a convenient pretext to justify the Russian prisoners' release.

The other reason why the Golovnin incident is of relevance is because it features the first instance of a Russian officer attempting to defect whilst in Japan. It is therefore an early forerunner of the cases of Viktor Belenko, who flew his MiG-25 (Foxbat) jet to Hakodate airport (Hokkaidō) and asked to defect to the West in September 1976, and Stanislav Levchenko, a KGB officer stationed in Tokyo who defected in October 1979. Within Golovnin's staff, the attempted defector was Ensign Fedor F. Mur.

Assuming that their imprisonment in Japan would be permanent, Mur decided to ingratiate himself with his captors. As a German, he had already changed his homeland once when entering Russian service and taking a Russian wife. It seems he thought he could do so again. He therefore began to inform on his fellow inmates. As Golovnin relates, Mur "explained [to the Japanese] the object of our voyage, and minutely described the situation of eastern Russia, and the political relations between France and Russia after the peace of Tilsit."[80] Incidentally, Mur also provided the Japanese with their first information about Napoleon, including his conquering of Holland, which the Dutch in Nagasaki had kept quiet about.[81] More to the point, Mur did not join his shipmates' escape attempt and told the Japanese afterwards that he had only initially consented to participate to "detect our plans, and, by disclosing them to the Japanese, perform a service to the magistrate."[82]

Mur assumed his actions would win the gratitude of the Japanese. Instead, the Japanese held his treachery in low regard and rejected his offers to work for them. It was explained to him that the Bakufu did not even trust Japanese who had spent any length of time in a foreign country. "'How then,' said they, 'can we venture to take a foreigner into our service…?'"[83]

Given the extent of Mur's perfidy, it might be assumed that Golovnin would seek retribution upon their return to Russia. On the contrary, showing a disposition markedly different from the vengeful Rezanov, Golovnin quickly forgave Mur and urged others to do the same. Despite this, "Some secrets of which he had made a written disclosure to the Japanese weighed upon his mind." Golovnin and his colleagues endeavoured to cheer him up but, ultimately, they were unable to prevent him from committing suicide by shooting himself in the chest during a hunting trip just weeks after their return. Golovnin therefore ends his account with an entreaty to "the reader not to condemn this unfortunate officer … [but to] shed a tear over the sad memory of this poor miserable youth."[84]

Sakhalin

As yet, little has been said about Russian-Japanese interactions on Sakhalin. This is because, despite Khvostov's brazen attempt to claim the island for Russia at the start of the century, by the 1850s Sakhalin (or Karafuto) remained without a Russian presence. Instead, the island was populated with Ainu communities, as well as Japanese settlements concentrated around Aniva Bay at Sakhalin's southern tip. This changed with an attempt by Russia to occupy the island in 1853. The decision was shaped by St Petersburg's increased interest in the Amur River. At the time, Russia was busy wresting control over this important waterway, whose outlet to the sea is shielded by Sakhalin Island, from the Qing Empire. Russian action was also encouraged by Gennadii Nevel'skoi's discovery in 1849 of the strait that now bears his name. This proved that Sakhalin is an island and that the Amur can be accessed from both north and south. In fact, according to Anton Chekhov's report from Sakhalin, Captain Nevel'skoi was not initially believed by the St Petersburg authorities, who "considered his conduct insolent and liable to punishment." He was only saved from being reduced to the ranks by the tsar's intercession.[85] Having finally accepted Sakhalin's insular status, Russia wisely kept this discovery secret. Consequently, during the Crimean War in 1855, Russian ships were able to escape through the strait when British forces thought they had blockaded them in what they regarded as the "Bay of Tartary."[86]

Struggling ashore on Sakhalin in October 1853, the small Russian contingent led by Nevel'skoi declared to the bemused Ainu and Japanese that their intentions were peaceful and that their occupation of the island was merely to prevent its seizure by the United States. The Russians established their own settlement, the Murav'evskii Post, then Nevel'skoi departed before winter, leaving the expedition under the command of Nikolai Busse.[87] There followed several awkward months during which the Russians and Japanese lived cheek by jowl. This provided opportunities for cultural education. For instance, one

Russian officer, when inspecting a Japanese mountain shrine, was surprised to come across an unfamiliar trinity. Inside, he discovered "an erect gilded phallus, flanked by a phallus of stone and a phallus of wood, pointing at the sky."[88]

For the most part, the Russian and Japanese soldiers eyed each other warily. In particular, the isolated Russians were nervous about a possible Japanese attack. To understand Japanese intentions, Busse entertained Japanese at his house and plied guests with tea and rum until some of them became "embarrassingly familiar."[89] The Russians also made use of the local Ainu. In Busse's words, "I wanted to attach some Ainu to myself in order to find out from him about the country and to teach him Russian."[90] In this, he quickly succeeded, as Ainu began to visit him every day. Indeed, "One Ainu had secretly joined Busse and stayed in his attic."[91]

Through these contacts, Busse learned that, "In secret, almost all of the Ainu who came to visit me inveighed against the Japanese, saying ... the Japanese is bad, the Japanese beats the Ainu, the Russian is kind and good."[92] The Ainu also informed Busse that the Japanese were planning to send reinforcements in the spring and that these would surround and eliminate the Russian forces. Moreover, they alleged that the Japanese were plotting to arrange a great banquet on Sakhalin to which the Russians would be invited. After getting the Russians drunk, the Japanese would murder them.[93]

While this seemed vital intelligence, the Russians began to distrust their Ainu sources. Busse gained the impression that "the Ainu love to deceive one, and therefore it is difficult to learn anything reliable from them about the country."[94] He also feared that any criticism he made of the Japanese would be reported back to them by the Ainu. Furthermore, when Busse confronted the Japanese with the claim that they were plotting to attack the Russians, "They [the Japanese] declared that not only were the Ainu allegations untrue, but that the Ainu had told them the same thing about Russian intentions toward them."[95] It seems that, finding themselves squeezed between two expanding empires, the Ainu had adopted the tactic of offering to serve both the Russians and Japanese while simultaneously seeking to provoke conflict between them.

Ultimately, this initial Russian occupation of Sakhalin ended abruptly when Russian forces were withdrawn in June 1854. Part of the reason was the outbreak of the Crimean War, which left Russian outposts vulnerable to attacks by British and French warships. Another factor was that the occupation of Sakhalin was opposed by Vice-Admiral Evfimii Putyatin, who worried that Russia's uninvited presence might complicate broader negotiations with the Japanese. It is to these talks that we now turn.

Relations are finally opened

As with the voyage that brought Nikolai Rezanov to Nagasaki in 1804, Putyatin's arrival in August 1853 was the culmination of a much longer expedition. After setting sail from Kronstadt in October 1852, the *Pallada*, Putyatin's three-masted frigate, visited Portsmouth and Cape Town, before stopping at Singapore and Hong Kong. However, Japan was always the main objective. That was where the *Pallada*'s crew "would pursue its unofficial goal, the most important, top-secret mission. This mission was to open up Japan."[96] This ambition had been revived by the knowledge that the United States was preparing a similar expedition under Commodore Matthew Perry. Onboard the *Pallada*, Vice-Admiral Putyatin was joined by Iosif Goshkevich, who was to become Russia's first consul in Japan. Another officer was Ivan Goncharov, who later found fame with the novel *Oblomov*. As Putyatin's secretary, Goncharov's role was to write an account of the voyage, which was published as *The Frigate Pallada* in 1858.[97] It is from this that we have the most detailed account of the Russians' visit to Nagasaki.

Putyatin was issued with "Secret Instructions" to gather information about everything he observed.[98] However, on arriving in Nagasaki, Putyatin and his men were once again treated as virtual captives. Goncharov describes "an oppressive feeling as if going into prison."[99] During the three months they spent moored outside Nagasaki's harbour, no members of the expedition were permitted to spend the night onshore. Moreover, when Goncharov and other officers were finally allowed to set foot in the city to attend a ceremonial dinner, they found, as Laxman and Rezanov had before them, that "Buildings along their path were covered up lest they prove of reconnaissance value."[100] Even basic information was off-limits. When Goncharov asked one of his Japanese interlocutors how many inhabitants there were in Nagasaki, he received the response: "Sometimes there are less, and sometimes more."[101] Exasperated, he jokes that he has experienced nothing aside from Japanese food: "I know intimately Japanese pigs, elk, even crayfish..., but so far I have learned nothing about Japan."[102]

This was an exaggeration, for the Russians were able to make some observations from the deck of the *Pallada* and thanks to daily visits by Japanese officials. Specifically, the *Pallada*'s crew confirmed assumptions about Japanese military weakness. The artillery batteries close to the harbour were screened from view, but, as Goncharov describes, "A breeze began to blow and the curtains fluttered open revealing cannon: in one place three, all with broken gun-carriages, in another, one with no carriage at all. How frightening! Our gunners suspect that these batteries may also contain wooden guns."[103] Further to these casual observations, Putyatin ordered a special study of Nagasaki's fortifications. This found that the port was defended by 38 batteries and 137 guns. However, due to the guns' poor placement, "These shores would not have withstood an attack from the sea by the most insignificant power."[104]

Goncharov also mocks the Japanese infantry.

> Soldiers! You couldn't imagine anything less like our conception of soldiers. They were so old they could barely stand on their feet, and their eyesight was poor. Their grey pigtails of three hairs wouldn't lie flat on their heads but stuck up in the air, while their bald patches shone like copper.[105]

He concludes, "In the present moment [Japan] can be opened at once; it is so weak that it cannot withstand any war."[106]

Elsewhere, Goncharov expressed contempt for the "utter childishness" of Japan's seclusion policy and described its politics as the "arbitrary laws of its anthill."[107] He was also far from complimentary about Japanese officials, saying of them: "Could these be corpses that arose from thousand-year old tombs and gathered for a summit?"[108] Goncharov was not aware that the Japanese were equally unimpressed by him, referring to him as the "pot-bellied barbarian."[109]

Although Goncharov's account is more travelogue than intelligence report, it proved enormously influential within Russia. Not only was *The Frigate Pallada* "greedily read by our entire public," the section on Japan was used for training Russian officers.[110] This was unfortunate, because Goncharov's amusing account of his three months in Nagasaki harbour replaced Golovnin's much more insightful report of his two years on Hokkaidō as the leading source of Russian knowledge about 19th-century Japan. George Lensen argues that this had serious security consequences, since "the popularity of Goncharov's writings contributed no doubt to the unfortunate failure of the Russians in later years to take the Japanese seriously."[111]

Although a disappointment in terms of intelligence gathering, Putyatin's voyage proved a triumph with respect to its main objective. After a frustrating wait at Nagasaki, Putyatin departed Japan to collect supplies and information. The latter was especially important given gathering tensions in Europe, which ultimately led to declarations of war against Russia by Great Britain and France in March 1854 and the start of the Crimean War. Having switched from the ageing *Pallada* to a newly constructed frigate named the *Diana*, Putyatin returned to Japanese shores, reaching Shimoda on the Izu peninsula in December 1854.

Just two months later, on 7 February 1855, the Treaty of Peace and Friendship (the Shimoda Treaty) was signed at Chōraku-ji, a small temple overlooking Shimoda's pretty harbour. This established official relations between the empires and permitted a Russian consul to take up post from 1856. The countries' border was drawn between Etorofu and Urup, while the status of Sakhalin was left to be decided at a later date.[112] Crucially, the Treaty of Shimoda opened the ports of Shimoda, Hakodate, and Nagasaki to Russian vessels. In the follow-up Treaty of Edo (1858), these rights were clarified. Russia was granted access to the ports of Hakodate, Nagasaki, Kanagawa, Hyōgo, and a further port to be specified later. Shimoda was removed from the list, as the harbour there was judged unsafe. With the opening of these five ports, the Treaty of Edo affirmed that "Trade between Russians and Japanese shall be carried out freely, according to mutual agreements." A further provision stated that "All rights and privileges, which may subsequently be accorded to other nations, shall at the same time be extended to the Russians, without further negotiations." Lastly, the treaty granted extraterritoriality, providing reassurance that "Russians staying in Japan permanently or temporarily, may live there with their families, following their own laws and customs."[113]

In short, more than a century and a half after Dembei's arrival had spurred Peter the Great's initial interest, Russia finally succeeded in securing access to Japan. This was a remarkable achievement. It came less than a year after Commodore Perry, on behalf of the United States, had concluded the Treaty of Kanagawa that put an end to Japan's *sakoku* era. Putyatin gained everything that had been granted to Perry plus more since the Treaty of Shimoda opened three ports, whereas the Treaty of Kanagawa only names Shimoda and Hakodate.

Putyatin's success is especially impressive given the disadvantages he had to contend with. The Russians had little of the muscle of the Americans. Perry arrived in Japan with four warships, including steam-powered frigates. He returned the next year with nine men-of-war, carrying almost a quarter of the total personnel of the US Navy.[114] By contrast, the *Pallada* was over 20 years old and decrepit. The *Diana*, to which Putyatin transferred before returning to Japan in 1854, was an improvement, but this was destroyed by a tsunami while the Russians were negotiating at Shimoda. The enterprising Russians constructed a new vessel, a schooner named the *Heda*, on which Putyatin and 40 others were able to sail back to Russia. This saved the Russian officers but gifted intelligence to the Japanese. By providing workmen to assist the Russians, Japan was able to learn modern shipbuilding techniques. This knowhow was used to construct six exact copies of the Russian schooner. For this reason, Mizuno Hironori, who served as a captain in the Russo-Japanese War, describes the Japanese workmen who helped build the *Heda* as "the fathers of the shipbuilding industry in modern Japan."[115]

Aside from his lack of military power, Putyatin had to overcome external attempts to sabotage the trade negotiations. The British sought to exacerbate Japanese fears of their northern neighbour, with Admiral Sir James Stirling telling the Bakufu that Russia was seeking to seize not only Sakhalin but Honshū as well.[116] Commodore Perry is also described as "Russophobic," and he ordered his men "to keep intelligence about the mission from the eyes and ears of the Russians."[117] He tried to thwart Putyatin's expedition by instructing Edward Cunningham, the American vice consul in Shanghai, not to sell the Russians any coal. Fortunately for Putyatin, Cunningham ignored the order and sold the Russians 50 tonnes.[118]

Lastly, Putyatin was not able to compensate for military weakness with a show of economic prowess. The Russian gifts included malachite clocks, thermometers, and samovars. By contrast, Perry's expedition brought a telegraph, a daguerreotype, and a steam engine. The Japanese officials unfavourably compared the Russians' "stinginess" with the Americans' "extravagance."[119]

This begs the question of how Putyatin was able to secure such a favourable treaty and whether any legerdemain was involved. Part of the explanation is simply wise diplomacy. Since Putyatin and Perry's expeditions reached Japan within months of each other, it is tempting to portray them as being in a race to open Japan. However, Edyta Bojanowska demonstrates that this was not the case.

> Based on the Ministry of the Navy's "secret instructions" ... Putiatin was instructed to let the Yankees do the heavy lifting and hover just close enough to profit from their actions, whether peaceful or violent. Should the Russians, contrary to expectations, overtake them, Putiatin was actually advised to postpone talks with the Japanese for as long as Perry's negotiations were in progress.[120]

In essence, Putyatin was to let the Americans barge in through the front door then slip in after them.

More intriguing is the part played by Philipp Franz von Siebold. Readers will recall that von Siebold was a German scientist who served as physician at the Dutch trading post at Dejima in Nagasaki from 1823. He was expelled from Japan in 1829 after being accused of spying for Russia by procuring Japanese maps and seeking to smuggle them out of the country.[121] Von Siebold returns to our attention here because of his central role in the planning and success of Putyatin's mission.

After his return to the Netherlands, von Siebold was appointed advisor to the Dutch king.[122] By the early 1850s, however, he had shifted his focus to assisting the Russian authorities. In 1851, he began to correspond with several Russian ambassadors, as well as with Governor General of Siberia Nikolai Murav'ev, who was later awarded the name Murav'ev-Amurskii for bringing the Amur River basin under Russian control. It was through these letters that von Siebold learned of Russia's plans for a new expedition to Japan. In return, he informed the Russians of what he had learned of Perry's voyage and he urged them to make haste, writing, "now that American and other maritime powers are looking towards Japan ... Russia needs to act quickly."[123] In early 1853, von Siebold also visited St Petersburg at the invitation of Count Karl Robert Nesselrode, Russian Minister of Foreign Affairs.

Using the knowledge he had amassed during six years in *sakoku* Japan, von Siebold provided important advice about how the Russians should engage with the Japanese. This included instructions on the language in which the official letter from Tsar Nicholas I should be written (French, not Japanese), as well as instructions that the Russian sovereign must distance himself as much as possible from Rezanov's expedition. Von Siebold added that Russia should seize Sakhalin if Japan refused to open relations and suggested that Putyatin counteract Japan's usual tactic of playing for time by setting a strict deadline for the talks. However, von Siebold's role went beyond that of a mere advisor. The official letters that were delivered to the Japanese authorities, the additional instructions issued to Putyatin before his arrival in Japan, and the Shimoda Treaty itself were all based on von Siebold's drafts. Von Siebold also took credit for the decision that the countries' official border should be drawn to the south of Urup.[124] According to Edgar Franz, it was von Siebold's assistance that was key in enabling the Russians to secure a treaty with Japan that went beyond what was achieved by the United States.[125]

Von Siebold was certainly essential to Putyatin's success, but is there any truth to the claim he was a Russian spy? There are certainly some causes for suspicion. First, the documents von Siebold acquired that led to his expulsion in 1829 included maps of Sakhalin, the Kurils, and Ezo—that is, precisely the areas of interest to Russia.[126] Second, von Siebold later became frustrated at the way he was treated in the Netherlands since his hopes of being appointed as an official envoy were not realised. Therefore, as Herbert Plutschow explains, "Disappointed about the way the Dutch government had treated him; von Siebold now turned his attention to Russia."[127] Indeed, von Siebold secured a promise from Ivan Likhachev, commander of the

Russian Pacific Fleet, that he would lobby his government in favour of von Siebold's appointment as Russian envoy to Japan.[128] This did not happen, but von Siebold was made a Knight of the Order of St Vladimir, 3rd Class, and a Knight of the Order of St Anne, 2nd Class with diamonds. Lastly, there are some indications that von Siebold was ideologically inclined to support Russia over her rivals. In one letter to Likhachev, von Siebold wrote that "England is a global factory. Her government must constantly seek new trading ports to satisfy the commercial zeal of her people. … America is also a freebooting commercial state."[129]

One can therefore manufacture a picture of a man who felt underappreciated at home, who disliked the capitalist Anglo-Saxons, and who saw cooperation with Russia as the route to personal advancement. These factors have motivated many Russian/Soviet spies. It is also notable that Commodore Perry refused to employ von Siebold for his mission to Japan because he suspected him of being a Russian agent.[130]

However, while the mistrust is understandable, the evidence for von Siebold being a Russian spy is not compelling. To begin with, the "secrets" that led to von Siebold's expulsion from Japan were only secrets by the paranoid standards of the Bakufu police state. In Enlightenment countries, the maps that von Siebold received were considered public knowledge. Also, the fact that many of the charts related to northern Japan does not mean they were procured on behalf of Russia. Instead, since this was the area about which geographical knowledge was least advanced, it is natural that these maps were of greatest interest to the inquisitive von Siebold. Lastly, there is no evidence of treachery or deception in the German doctor's actions. He was not employed by the Japanese or the Dutch at the time he was helping the Russians. As such, rather than being a Russian spy, it is more appropriate to categorise von Siebold as a devoted scholar, who became committed, as he said himself, "not to rest in helping Japan open up to the civilized world by peaceful means."[131] To this end, he was willing to offer his expertise to whichever power was most eager to listen. In the 1850s, this proved to be Russia.

Although von Siebold's involvement was above board, in other respects Putyatin's success did owe something to sneakiness. As noted, the central element of the Russian plan was to stand aside as

Perry's expedition strong-armed the Bakufu into making concessions, then step in and use the terms offered to the United States as the starting point for negotiations. However, this was only possible if the Russians had access to the US-Japan Treaty of Kanagawa, and the Japanese negotiators were not inclined to disclose the terms. The Russians' simple solution was to bribe Tatsunosuke, one of the Japanese interpreters, to provide a copy.[132] In this way, Putyatin learned exactly what had been granted to the United States and was able to press for more. The resulting similarities between the treaties caused one American observer to complain that the Shimoda Treaty "is copied from ours."[133]

Critical to Putyatin's success was also the ability to avoid British and French ships, which, if they found the Russian vessel, would have put an immediate end to the expedition. In this endeavour, the *Diana*'s crew was assisted by intelligence delivered by a former Japanese castaway who managed to get aboard the Russian frigate near Ōsaka Bay. This individual had, along with six others, been returned to Japan by a Russian ship, the *Kniaz Menshikov*, under the command of Shipmaster Lindenberg, in 1852. When Lindenberg had tried to hand over the castaways in Shimoda, the local authorities had refused, saying they lacked the necessary permission from Edo. Lindenberg therefore dropped off the Japanese at a small bay just five miles from Shimoda. It was in gratitude for this service that the castaway risked climbing aboard the *Diana* in November 1854. He passed on the valuable warning that the British squadron of Admiral Sir James Stirling had been in Nagasaki just one month earlier before moving away from Japanese waters to search for the Russians in the South China Sea.[134]

Lastly, the Russian party at Shimoda received the covert assistance of one other Japanese. This was Tachibana Kōsai, whose past included time as a Buddhist priest, as well as three stints in prison.[135] Tachibana helped Putyatin's expedition (presumably for a price) by teaching Japanese to Iosif Goshkevich. This might seem innocent enough, but the Bakufu was extremely suspicious of foreigners learning Japanese, believing that it facilitated spying. Indeed, even after the signing of the Shimoda Treaty, Japan insisted that all Russians seeking to study the language within the country must report this intention to the authorities.[136] The understanding of Japanese that Goshkevich gained from Tachibana helped during the negotiations at Shimoda. It was also beneficial for Goshkevich himself, who went on to serve as Russia's first consul in Japan from 1858.

In addition to the illicit language lessons, Tachibana engaged in "the selling of information about his country to foreigners."[137] He received money from the Russians to buy maps and books to which they were not permitted access. Since these were cheap, Tachibana spent the surplus on prostitutes.[138] However, when his work for the Russians was discovered, Tachibana risked execution. Fortunately for him, the Russians agreed to smuggle him out of the country. This was not easy, especially after the *Diana* was wrecked by the tsunami, forcing the Russians to live ashore. Their solution was to hide Tachibana. As Lensen recounts, "they disguised him in a black hemp wig and a Russian sailor suit and kept him surrounded by members of the crew." When the time came for departure, the Russians slipped Tachibana aboard in a crate.[139] Another account claims that Tachibana evaded a pre-departure inspection by concealing himself under a blanket and pretending to be a Russian sailor suffering from an infectious disease.[140]

After leaving Japan, Tachibana and Goshkevich worked together on the first proper Japanese-Russian dictionary, for which Goshkevich won the prestigious Demidov Prize.[141] Within Russia, Tachibana worked for the Ministry of Foreign Affairs and changed his name to Vladimir Iosifovich Yamatov. The patronymic was selected in honour of Goshkevich and the surname chosen in memory of his homeland, since "Yamato" is an ancient name for Japan.

One final point is that, aside from the assistance of these individuals, Putyatin's mission was helped by the shogunate's lack of intelligence on the weakness of Russia's position. After the *Pallada* was retired and the *Diana* destroyed, Russia had only four warships in the Pacific compared with 25 for the British and French.[142] Russian forces did manage to repulse a chaotic Anglo-French attack on Petropavlovsk, Kamchatka, in September 1854, but, with its resources committed to the Crimean War, St Petersburg decided to withdraw from many outposts in the Far East. Indeed, when British forces scouted the area in 1855, they found that Russian bases on Kamchatka and the Kurils had been evacuated and the fortifications destroyed. In Petropavlovsk in May 1855, the British reported "not a ship, gun, or person to be seen—nothing but empty embrasures and deserted houses."[143] As John Harrison concludes, "The Japanese could have driven a hard bargain in 1855 had they known all the facts."[144]

Overall then, Putyatin secured the Shimoda Treaty against the odds. His achievement was ultimately recognised, not only in Russia, but in Japan too, where he was awarded the Order of the Rising Sun in 1881. His demise, however, was less glorious than the great admiral deserved. He died in the bathtub of a French hotel in 1883.[145]

4

INFLUENCE IN JAPAN, INTRIGUE IN MANCHURIA AND KOREA

Russian intelligence activities towards Japan began comparatively late, since the absence of permanent representation within the country deprived Russia of a hub from which to conduct operations. Moreover, Japan's isolationist stance meant it was not a regional rival and therefore was a low intelligence priority. All this changed in the second half of the 19th century. With the Treaty of Shimoda in 1855, Russia was granted permission to dispatch consuls to Japan. The Russian-Chinese Treaties of Aigun (1858) and Peking (1860) also placed the Amur basin under Russian control and gave the Russian Empire a coastline on the Sea of Japan. Furthermore, the Meiji Restoration in 1868, which saw the end of the shogunate and the consolidation of political power under the emperor, led to Japan's embrace of Western-style imperialism and the corresponding attempt to establish a sphere of influence in neighbouring territories. The second half of the 19th century therefore witnessed the start of serious competition between the Russian and Japanese empires. This resulted in more Russian intelligence activity within Japan, as well as a considerable amount of intrigue in the struggle for influence over Korea and Manchuria.

Russian influence in Hakodate

The United States, under consul general Townsend Harris, established their legation in Shimoda in 1856, then, from 1859, in Edo. By contrast, until the 1870s, the home of Russia's permanent diplomatic representative to Japan was Hakodate. This was partly because Ezo, as Hokkaidō was still called, is closer to Russian ports. However, the decision to remain in Hakodate was also a means of maximising influence since, in the absence of other legations, the Russians could develop a dominant position.

Russia's first diplomatic representative to Japan was Iosif Goshkevich. Having arrived in Hakodate in October 1858, Goshkevich's priority was to oversee construction of a suitable consulate. He did this well. As one Russian visitor reported on arrival, "we can see only a single house of European architecture, our consul's house, which dominates the entire town, standing higher than everything else and looking more attractive."[1] French observer Victor de Mars agreed, writing that:

> The residence of the Muscovite envoy, placed at the summit of a mountain, dominates the village ... it looks like the place of some governor of the country.[2]

De Mars also remarked on Russia's extraordinary local influence.

> Of all the foreign languages which one hears in Hakodate, it is already the Russian language which is most widespread. Young Japanese, taught at the consulate, speak it with extreme facility, even write it, and become in a way natural missionaries in aid of Muscovite policy.[3]

The rapid expansion of Russian influence in Hakodate could just be seen as successful diplomacy, yet many saw something more ominous. The rumour spread that the consulate was so grand because it was to serve as the governor's residence after Russia had annexed Ezo (Hokkaidō).[4] De Mars also considered the Russians' "calculated absence" from the capital to be part of a shrewd strategy of infiltration, since concentrating resources at Hakodate "assures Russian propaganda facilities which it would not have elsewhere." Indeed, de Mars assessed that the local Japanese were "already more than half subjugated." He warned that the Russians would await the opportunity of a crisis, then step in to provide "protection."[5] Hodgson, the British consul, concurred, arguing that the Russian objective was to "make of Yezo a Russian Gibraltar."[6]

The Russians did not ultimately attempt to occupy Ezo, but they did briefly seize Tsushima in 1861. This was done on the pretext of protecting the island, which is strategically located between Japan and Korea, from occupation by the British. The Japanese were unconvinced and appealed to the British on the basis that one should "use barbarians to fight barbarians."[7] When two British warships arrived in August 1861, they found "a very complete naval depot including a hospital and workshop with the Russian flag flying on the hill above."[8] Despite the Russians having firmly established themselves, they backed down when faced by a direct challenge and withdrew all forces.

Orthodox spies?

Along with the start of Goshkevich's diplomatic mission in Hakodate in 1858 came the arrival of the Russian Orthodox Church. The first priest was already in his sixties and soon returned home. The task of planting the seed of Orthodox faith in Japan therefore fell to his successor, Father Nikolai (originally Ivan Kasatkin), who became synonymous with the Orthodox church in Japan. Indeed, the Orthodox cathedral in Tokyo is still commonly known as Nikolai-dō (Nikolai Cathedral), although its official name is the Holy Resurrection Cathedral.

When Nikolai arrived in Hakodate in June 1861, missionary activity was still banned, and Christianity regarded with considerable suspicion. This is not surprising given that opposition to proselytising had been a leading cause of the shogunate's embrace of the *sakoku* policy in the 17th century. Furthermore, since the tsar was the official head of the Russian Orthodox Church, there was fear that Orthodox priests would be used in the service of Russian political goals. This was not a far-fetched idea, as the Russian Ecclesiastical Mission in Beijing was used as a hub for intelligence collection from the 18th century.[9]

Reflecting on his first years in Hakodate, Nikolai wrote that "the Japanese of that day looked on foreigners as on animals, and on

Christianity as on a wicked sect, to which only arrant evil-doers and sorcerers can belong."[10] Ironically, it was the intensity of this suspicion that delivered Nikolai's first convert. During a visit to Goshkevich's house, Nikolai met a man who had been employed by the consul as a fencing instructor for his son. This was Sawabe Takuma, a samurai from Tosa (modern-day Kōchi prefecture) and cousin of the famous Sakamoto Ryōma, a leading advocate of the overthrow of the Bakufu.

On that day at the consul's home, Nikolai saw that Sawabe was eyeing him with hostility and asked why he was so angry. Sawabe replied: "You foreigners must all be killed. You have come here to spy on our country. And you with your preaching will hurt Japan most of all."[11] Nikolai asked if he was familiar with the church's teachings and Sawabe admitted he was not. Thereupon, Nikolai began to instruct him in the Orthodox faith and, in time, Sawabe was secretly baptised as Pavel (Paul).

The suspicions of Nikolai and his small flock did not diminish when the shogunate fell in 1868. Indeed, after Nikolai had secretly baptised ten more Japanese in 1872, he discovered that the ceremony had been attended by a police spy. Moreover, when work began in 1884 on the Holy Resurrection Cathedral in what had now become Tokyo, "rumors circulated that the Russians were building a fortress with cannons in the belfry, and suggestions were made that the building on the hill be surrounded with so high a wall that the imperial palace could not be seen from it or better still that the building be purchased and presented to the Emperor as a gift."[12] These fears swelled with the number of Orthodox believers in Japan, which reached 25,231 in 1900.[13]

Despite this deep distrust, there is no evidence that Nikolai engaged in espionage or sought to influence his converts for political objectives. True, many of the first to be baptised were social outcasts and opponents of the status quo, yet this is natural in the case of what was, for Japan, a new religion. Nikolai did submit at least one report to the Russian Ministry of Foreign Affairs, yet this covers religious affairs rather than any reporting of political matters.[14] This was in keeping with Nikolai's commitment that the Orthodox Church in Japan serve the Japanese people, and not Russia's political and security concerns. To this end, he endeavoured to make the Church as Japanese as possible.[15] He spent seven years studying the language and, until his death in 1912, maintained an active routine of translating the scriptures and other religious documents into Japanese.

The clearest demonstration that Nikolai's commitment was to the Orthodox faith and not the Russian state came ahead of the outbreak of the Russo-Japanese War in February 1904. At that time, Nikolai told his followers,

> And if an Imperial Proclamation of war is issued, your members must pray for the triumph of Japan, and when the Japanese army has conquered the Russian forces you must offer to God a prayer of thankfulness. This is the obligation laid on the Orthodox Christian in his native country.[16]

Saint Nikolai Yaponskii, as he came to be known after his canonisation, did not therefore serve the political or intelligence interests of the Russian state. However, the Orthodox Church in Japan did indirectly contribute to Russian espionage through the educational facilities it established, including a seminary in Tokyo. This was to train students for the priesthood, yet the Russian authorities used it for the cultivation of several future spies.

After the catastrophe of the Russo-Japanese War, the Russian military recognised the need for more intelligence personnel with advanced Japanese skills. This was best achieved by training intelligence officers from childhood. The original plan was to establish a specialist school in the Russian Far East, yet this was abandoned due to a lack of funding. Instead, it was decided that a better outcome could be achieved at a fraction of the cost by sending boys to the seminary in Tokyo.[17]

The first eight boys were dispatched to Tokyo at the end of 1906. However, the most noteworthy graduate arrived the next year. This was Vasilii Oshchepkov. Born in northern Sakhalin to a convict mother in December 1892, Oshchepkov became an orphan by age 12. After being sent to the Tokyo seminary in 1907, Oshchepkov excelled not only at Japanese but also at judo. These skills led to his acceptance at the Kōdōkan judo school, which was established in 1882 by Kanō Jigorō, the sport's founder. Oshchepkov went on to popularise judo in Russia and invented sambo, a Russian martial art that combines judo with other self-defence techniques.[18]

After Oshchepkov's return to Russia, he worked first as a non-commissioned officer in counterintelligence for the Tsarist military. Then, during the Russian Civil War (1917–22), he was employed as a translator by both the anti-Bolshevik forces of Admiral Kolchak and the Imperial Japanese Army, which had occupied parts of the Russian Far East. It was at this time, most likely in 1920, that Oshchepkov was recruited by the Bolshevik underground in Vladivostok, becoming "secret employee of Soviet military intelligence—agent 'DD'."[19]

The next year, Oshchepkov was sent back to his birthplace of Sakhalin, which was entirely under Japanese control between 1920 and 1925. Taking a film projector with him, Oshchepkov used the cover of screening films to the local population and Japanese soldiers. With his fluent Japanese, he developed close contacts with Japanese officers. In this way, he was able to send back detailed reports on the locations and weaponry of Japanese units, descriptions of Japan's economic activities, and biographies of senior Japanese officers.[20] After this success, Oshchepkov was dispatched to Japan in 1924, where he based himself first in Kōbe, then in Tokyo. In the capital, he became the Soviet military's first illegal station chief under the codename MONAKH (monk), a nod to his upbringing in the seminary.

In 1926, Oshchepkov was ordered back to the Soviet Union and spent a decade in various roles, including translator and judo instructor for the Red Army. However, Oshchepkov ultimately fell victim to the Great Terror. His fate was sealed by NKVD Order No. 00593, which was issued on 20 September 1937 by Nikolai I. Ezhov ("The Poison Dwarf"), who headed Stalin's secret police at this time. This order was targeted at "Harbinites," meaning Soviet citizens who had lived in Harbin, especially those who had worked on the Chinese Eastern Railway. Order No. 00593 alleged that

> the overwhelming majority of Harbinites who left for the Soviet Union are former White officers, police officers, gendarmes [meaning counterintelligence officers], and members of various émigré espionage-fascist organisations etc. The overwhelming majority are agents of Japanese intelligence, who, over the course of several years, have

> been sent to the Soviet Union for terrorist, diversionary, and espionage activities.[21]

This meant the end for Oshchepkov. Having lived in Harbin for two years and worked for both the Whites and the Japanese military, he was a prime target for liquidation.

Oshchepkov was arrested on 1 October 1937 and died nine days later of a heart attack.[22] This spared him from the torture, forced confession, and bullet to the back of the head that was the fate of others who had studied with Oshchepkov at the Tokyo seminary. This included his friend Trofim Yurkevich. Yurkevich also worked for Soviet military intelligence and had the codename "R." He was arrested in March 1938, confessed to spying for the Japanese, and was shot.[23]

As for Oshchepkov, he was officially pardoned in 1957 and his sporting legacy is now celebrated by the Russian authorities. A monument to Oshchepkov was unveiled in Vladivostok in 2016 and he has been honoured by President Vladimir Putin, himself a former spy and practitioner of sambo (as well as judo).[24]

The Tripartite Intervention

In the three decades following the establishment of diplomatic relations in 1855, the Russo-Japanese relationship remained unbalanced in Russia's favour. This was demonstrated by the Treaty of St Petersburg in 1875 that addressed the issue of Sakhalin, whose status had been left unsettled in the Treaty of Shimoda. The solution was to grant Russia sovereignty over the entirety of Sakhalin, while Japan gained possession of all the Kuril Islands, right up to Kamchatka. Although officially an exchange, many saw the agreement as disadvantageous to Japan, with some Japanese historians claiming the country had been "robbed" of Sakhalin, which was much more valuable than the Kurils.[25]

However, while Japan felt compelled to concede in the face of superior Russian strength in 1875, little more than a decade later the distribution of power had shifted significantly. By the 1890s, Japan had transformed itself into a competitor in Manchuria and Korea, and Russian decisionmakers had to employ all their wiles to prevent the expansion of Japanese power from taking place at Russia's expense. This "balance of intrigue," to use George Lensen's term, played out primarily in Korea, whose weak regime left a power vacuum which both China's decaying Qing dynasty and a rising Japan determined to fill. Recognising that power dynamics were moving in their favour, the Japanese government sought to initiate a conflict with China, with Foreign Minister Mutsu Munemitsu instructing his minister to China to "manufacture any kind of pretext to start a war."[26]

The argument used to justify Japan's efforts to dominate the Korean peninsula was, as Japan's chargé d'affaires in Beijing Komura Jutarō put it in June 1894, to "protect the country from falling a prey to the ambitious designs of Russia."[27] There were also longstanding claims that Russia was seeking a protectorate over Korea. Indeed, *The Times* of London alleged in 1888 that such a protectorate had already been established by means of a secret Russo-Korean treaty.[28]

In reality, Russia's contemporary strategic goals were more modest. These had been determined at a special meeting of Russia's most senior diplomats in May 1888. This established that the Korean peninsula, due to its strategic position, was indeed a leading priority. However, it was agreed that Russia should not annex Korea, since "She was a poor country of no commercial value and was too remote for effective defense."[29] Russia's goal was therefore not to seek territorial gains, but to prevent any single country from attaining dominance over Korea and to stop others from securing strategic gains elsewhere. These plans were challenged by Japan's victory in the Sino-Japanese War of 1894–5, which forced Russia into more proactive measures.

The best-known piece of intrigue in which Russia played a leading role at this time was the Tripartite Intervention of 1895. During the Sino-Japanese War, Japan's modernised armed forces delivered punishing victories over Qing China's outdated military. Japan was therefore able to impose a punitive peace. This came in the form of the Treaty of Shimonoseki of April 1895. This agreement demanded China's recognition of Korea's "independence," thereby removing Korea from China's sphere of influence. China was also required to pay Japan an indemnity of 200 million taels and to open four ports to Japanese commerce. Most controversial, however, was the treaty's requirement for China to permanently cede not only Formosa (Taiwan) and the neighbouring Pescadores (Penghu) Islands but also the Liaodong Peninsula that juts out from the northern shore of the Yellow Sea.

That the peace settlement should feature territorial concessions was expected, but the fact that these should include the Liaodong Peninsula was a surprise to St Petersburg. The peninsula's strategic position, just west of Korea and within striking distance of Beijing, offered Japan the opportunity to vastly increase its regional influence. The existence of Port Arthur (Lüshun) at the tip of the peninsula also gave Japan the chance to develop a prominent naval presence on the Asian mainland.

Determined to prevent the Liaodong Peninsula from falling under Japanese control, Russia, abetted by France and Germany, intervened to pressure Japan to relinquish this territorial gain. Facing the combined might of these three powers, Japan had no option but to accept a humiliating revision to the Treaty of Shimonoseki. This subsequent agreement, which was made in November 1895, saw Japan return the Liaodong Peninsula to China in exchange for an additional indemnity of 30 million taels. The diplomatic manoeuvre was completed in March 1898 when St Petersburg coerced the Chinese authorities to lease the peninsula to Russia for a period of 25 years.[30] As the century came to an end, it was therefore Russian warships anchored in Port Arthur's ice-free harbour, rather than those of the Imperial Japanese Navy.

The effectiveness of the Tripartite Intervention owed much to straightforward power politics. Russia, France, and Germany had 38 warships in East Asia with a total displacement of 95,000 tonnes, whereas Japan had 31 warships with a total displacement of only 57,000 tonnes.[31] In an unsubtle demonstration of this point, when the Treaty of Shimonoseki was signed at the Chinese port of Yantai on 8 May 1895, there were nine Russian warships present in the harbour that day, "all repainted in battle color in readiness for action."[32] The proposal for Japan to relinquish the Liaodong Peninsula was therefore an offer Tokyo could not refuse. However, while force was the foremost factor in the Tripartite Intervention, more stealthy techniques were involved in Russia's extraction of subsequent concessions from China.

In June 1896, Russia and China signed the Li-Lobanov Treaty (also known as the Alliance Treaty). Named after Chinese Viceroy Li Hung-chang and Russian Foreign Minister Aleksei Lobanov-Rostovskii, this secret agreement was Russia's principal response to Japan's victory in the Sino-Japanese War.[33] It provided China with a guarantee of its territorial integrity against the threat of future Japanese aggression, plus a loan with preferential terms to enable China to pay the war indemnity to Japan. However, these gains were purchased at a high price. Russia gained permission for its warships to use Chinese ports. Additionally, the treaty granted Russia a railway concession that enabled it to construct the Chinese Eastern Railway, which would traverse Manchuria, creating a more direct route between the cities of Chita and Vladivostok. Crucially, Russia also obtained extraterritorial jurisdiction and the permission to station troops in the railway zone. Consequently, this unequal treaty awarded Russia significant influence in Manchuria and laid the groundwork for the lease of the Liaodong Peninsula that followed less than two years later.

Why did China agree to terms that were so unfavourable to its own interests (as well as to those of Japan)? Beijing was certainly aware that the agreement was exploitative. Officials from the Tsungli Yamen, the office that handled foreign relations for the Qing dynasty, complained directly to St Petersburg, stating "Formerly Russia promised to unite in mutual aid, but now she acts like a bandit chieftain and the chief plotter of military action."[34]

Part of the reason the objections of officials were ignored is that, at each stage of the process, Russian "lucre had eased the way."[35] Firstly, bribery was involved in the creation of the Russo-Chinese Bank, whose role was to finance the payment of the indemnity as well as to provide capital for the construction of Russian railway infrastructure. Initially, the Chinese side insisted that the bank be Chinese. However, a one-million-franc bribe to China's representative in the talks was sufficient to secure agreement that it would be a Russo-Chinese joint-stock company.[36]

Even more significant were the bribes paid to Li Hung-chang himself. Li was the leading Chinese diplomat of the day.[37] Prior to agreeing the secret alliance with Russia, Li had negotiated the Treaty of

Shimonoseki to end the war with Japan. During those talks, he had narrowly survived an assassination attempt when a Japanese fanatic had shot him in the face as he was being carried back to his lodgings in Shimonoseki in a sedan chair. The bullet struck Li just below his left eye and the doctors were unable to remove it. Despite this, Li made no complaint and merely sent a note to his Japanese counterparts to apologise that he would be absent from the next day's talks. The Japanese officials were greatly impressed by the Chinese diplomat's fortitude and agreed to the unconditional armistice that Li had been seeking ahead of the finalisation of the treaty.[38]

By contrast, Li Hung-chang's actions in agreeing the secret alliance with Russia were far less heroic. To purchase the Chinese diplomat's compliance, St Petersburg established a special "Li Hung-chang Fund" to which was allocated up to three million roubles for "discretionary expenses."[39] Russia's financial hold over Li helped ensure that the agreement governing the reversion of the Liaodong Peninsula to Chinese control, for which Li was the chief negotiator, did not include a provision banning China from subsequently transferring the peninsula to another power, as Japan had initially insisted.[40] Li Hung-chang did not receive all the money promised him, ultimately pocketing only 609,109 roubles and 50 kopecks. Despite suspicions of his corruption, Li continued to work as a leading Chinese envoy. However, when he died in 1901, it was said that he was "missed by no one but the Russians."[41]

Through a mixture of diplomatic manoeuvring and straightforward bribery, Russia had ensured that Japan, despite its convincing victory over Qing China, would not gain territory on the Chinese mainland. However, in retrospect, the Tripartite Intervention represented a serious misjudgement by Russia. Above all, it contributed to the catastrophic Russo-Japanese War that broke out just six years after Russia gained control of the Liaodong Peninsula. This mishandling of the intervention was partly a failure of intelligence.

Although France and Germany were also involved, it was Russia that was the ringleader and the country most determined to deprive Japan of its territorial gains. Japanese fury intensified when St Petersburg proceeded so quickly to pressure China into conceding the lease to the Liaodong Peninsula. This was despite the fact that Foreign

Minister Lobanov-Rostovskii had assured Japan in November 1895 that Russia had no intention of acquiring the peninsula for itself.[42] The impact on public opinion was significant. As Hamada Kenji describes, "The full import of the renunciation of Liaotung, the overwhelming shame attendant upon this act, turned the nation into a writhing, cursing mob. It spat venom and hate and irreverent diatribes."[43] Much of this was directed at Japan's own leaders, yet there was also a burning desire for revenge against Russia. According to Commissioner for Foreign Affairs Asaina Kansui, who was a paid source of British Minister Ernest Satow, "if the Japanese people were polled, their voice would be for war unprepared as they were."[44] The government also "started a vigorous nationwide campaign, known as *Ga-Shin-Sho-Tan*—'Submit to any hardships to achieve revenge'" (or, more literally, "sleeping on firewood and licking bile").[45]

This outcome could have been avoided. If St Petersburg had known that it was Japan's intention to include the Liaodong Peninsula within the Shimonoseki Treaty, Russia, along with France and Germany, could have intervened earlier to dissuade Japan from enforcing this concession. The basic result would have been the same, yet the perception within Japan would have been very different. Psychologically, it is much worse to have gained and lost territory than never to have gained it at all. This was acknowledged at the time. Gustave Montebello, the French ambassador to St Petersburg, regretted that "one had let the moment pass when the Japanese had not yet revealed their intentions and it would have been possible, or at least easier, to limit their eventual pretensions."[46] The Japanese leadership was also frustrated that, during the Sino-Japanese conflict, Russia had only indicated that Korean independence should be preserved and had given no warning of its opposition to other territorial gains. As George Lensen explains, Japanese statesmen had "interpreted the silence as acquiescence to the permanent conquest of Chinese territory on the continent."[47]

To intervene earlier, Russia needed to know what peace conditions Japan was going to impose. Since these were being carefully guarded by Japanese foreign minister Mutsu Munemitsu, Russia's knowledge was dependent on its ability to tap unauthorised sources. Russian officers were in a good position to do so. In a diplomatic telegram sent in September 1894, British minister to Tokyo P.H. Le Poer Trench warned Foreign Secretary Lord Kimberley about the closeness of Russian military attachés Konstantin Vogak and A. Shvank to Japanese politicians and military officers. Trench reported that they "constantly called on the Japanese cabinet ministers and frequently visited the General Staff Department of the War Office. They were, 'on the most intimate and friendly terms' with Japanese army and navy officers."[48] Prime Minister Itō Hirobumi also asserted that "Hitrovo [the Russian Minister] spends a good deal of money on Japanese, some high official persons."[49] Assisted by these contacts, St Petersburg was well enough informed about Japanese military strength to know that they could launch the Tripartite Intervention without fear of an immediate armed response. This is because the Russian military knew that the Japanese army did not have sufficient cavalry and transport to advance against Russia at that time.[50]

However, more broadly, Russian intelligence during the Sino-Japanese War left much to be desired. Finance Minister Sergei Witte complained that it was difficult to formulate adequate policy because, as well as not knowing Japan's exact goals, Russia lacked precise information about how the war was progressing.[51] Russian Foreign Minister Lobanov-Rostovskii did eventually learn of Japan's intention to claim Formosa, but even this he learned from the British rather than from Russia's own sources in Japan. It therefore came as an unpleasant surprise when, just days before the Shimonoseki Treaty was signed, the Japanese Foreign Ministry finally informed Russia that the terms included the cession of the Liaodong Peninsula.[52]

Better intelligence would have helped Russia to handle the Tripartite Intervention more skilfully and to limit the backlash, yet the scale of Russia's failure should not be exaggerated. Other major countries were equally in the dark about Japan's plan to seize territory on the Chinese mainland. This was due to the obsessive secrecy of Foreign Minister Mutsu. Since he did not even share the draft peace treaty with Japanese cabinet ministers, even the most adept intelligence service would have struggled to learn its details.[53] Had Japan more clearly signalled its intentions to the great powers, the spike in tensions provoked by the Treaty of Shimonoseki could have been significantly reduced.

A Korean coup

Aside from Manchuria, the other main area of tension between the Russian and Japanese Empires was the Korean peninsula. With the Treaty of Shimonoseki forcing China to recognise Korea's independence, the door was opened to increased Japanese influence. For the time being, this was exercised, not through the imposition of a protectorate, but by efforts to control Korea's faction-ridden politics from behind the scenes.

At the end of the Sino-Japanese War in April 1895, Korea was still headed by King Gojong, who had been on the throne since 1864. He was a "weak and confused king who had no feeling for the prestige and dignity of his own office." This "personal ineptitude" left space for his official wife, Queen Min, to exert control over the court.[54] For Japan, this was a problem, since she was viewed as anti-Japanese and sympathetic to Russia.

In 1888, the Japanese had already tried to remove Queen Min by poisoning her birthday cake.[55] These efforts were renewed after the Sino-Japanese War, and she was eventually assassinated in October 1895. This occurred when troops of the Hullyeondae, a Japanese-trained Korean army regiment, attacked the imperial palace. The resulting confusion permitted Japanese civilian thugs (*sōshi*), who were acting under the orders of Japanese Minister to Korea Miura Gorō, to murder the queen. The scene was witnessed by Afanasii Seredin-Sabatin, a Russian advisor to the Korean king. He described how the attackers threw court ladies out of palace windows and dragged them by the hair through the mud. When Queen Min was finally identified by one of the assassins, "The killer threw her down, jumped on her breast three times with his shoes and then hacked her with his sword. Satisfied with their deed, the *sōshi* took the body of the queen to the lawn and burned her with kerosene."[56] According to a slightly different account, which was noted in the diary of British Minister to Japan Ernest Satow, "her head was cut off, which looks like a Japanese performance."[57] Miura was acting without Tokyo's approval and later described the assassination as a matter that he himself had "decided in the space of three puffs on a cigarette." He was sent back to Japan and arrested, but released when the court conveniently ruled that there was "insufficient" evidence.[58]

Following the queen's removal, the Korean court came under the control of pro-Japanese cabinet ministers. US Minister to Korea John Sill reported that "The king was a prisoner in his palace and was compelled to submit to various indignities by threats of bodily harm."[59] Seeing this as an unfavourable shift in the status quo, Russian officials were spurred into action.

Their response came on 11 February 1896. Early in the morning, at a time when the languid monarch was usually fast asleep, King Gojong and the crown prince were disguised as women and carried, "pale and trembling," out of the palace in closed sedan chairs. To reduce the guards' vigilance, in the days before the rescue several court ladies had been instructed to ride out from the palace at the same hour. On the eve of the escape, Russia had supplemented its forces in the Korean capital with several naval officers, plus over a hundred sailors and a Maxim gun. Ultimately, these forces were not required, since, by 7 am, the king and crown prince were safely ensconced in the Russian legation, where they remained for the next year.[60]

While the rescue operation was handled neatly, the consequences were messier. Freed of Japanese influence, King Gojong was emboldened to dismiss the Japanese-sponsored cabinet, leaving the outgoing ministers vulnerable to retribution. Just hours after the king's flight, the premier Kim Hong-jip and Minister of Agriculture Chung Pyong-ha were arrested by police, given a summary court martial, and decapitated. Their bodies were then thrown to an anti-Japanese mob.[61]

The Japanese leadership expressed grudging admiration for the skill with which the coup (for that was how they regarded it) had been carried out.[62] With the demise of the previous cabinet, Japan lost its preeminent position in Korea, while Russia was able to press its advantage. Under guard at the Russian legation in 1896, King Gojong was persuaded to grant exclusive rights to fell timber on the Korean side of the Yalu and Tumen Rivers to Yulii I. Briner, a Russian merchant based in Vladivostok. Based on the advice of Aleksandr M. Bezobrazov, a businessman and advocate of Russian expansion in East Asia, the Russian government purchased the project in 1898. These timber concessions came to be seen by Japan as a mechanism for Russia to covertly extend its influence over northern Korea. These suspicions were enhanced by the fact that "it was not unusual for work parties to include Russian soldiers in disguise, who steadily expanded the network of Russian camps, roads, and even telegraph poles in the region."[63]

The smuggling of the king to the safety of the Russian legation gave St Petersburg what it wanted by (at least in the short term) checking the spread of Japanese control over Korea. However, the Russian central authorities were not responsible for this intrigue. Foreign Minister Lobanov-Rostovskii was opposed to bold action, taking the view that, while the situation had taken an unfavourable turn, it was better to be patient than to risk a crisis with Japan. The main instigator was, therefore, not St Petersburg, but Aleksei Shpeier, Russia's chargé d'affaires in Seoul.

As Shpeier confessed to a French colleague:

> Since my arrival in Seoul … I was disagreeably surprised to see the state of affairs existing in Korea: on one hand a king without the strength to resist the unreasonable demands of his ministers, on the other hand ministers receiving their instructions from the legation of Japan. It seemed to me that such a situation could not be tolerated much longer and I looked for the means of remedying it. I thought that the simplest plan to adopt in order to knock the ministers from power would be to try to induce the king to leave his palace secretly and come to our legation. There, sheltered from all coercion, he could dismiss his ministers and freely form a new cabinet of his choice. I unbosomed myself of this scheme [*je me suis ouvert de ce projet*] to the king, but I found at first a certain hesitance on his part to venture on the undertaking. … To induce him to take a decision, it was necessary for me on different occasions to represent to him his situation in the darkest light and to persuade him that by remaining in his palace longer, he daily ran the risk of assassination. The king, as you know, has a great fear of death. Hence, he was responsive to my arguments and ended by adhering to my plan.[64]

Shpeier did telegraph his intentions to St Petersburg, but he then set the scheme in motion before receiving the reply that he should refrain from any provocations.[65] The result was that Russia ended up effecting a coup in Korea, eliminating a Japanese-sponsored government, and swinging the balance of influence on the peninsula in its own favour, yet without any of this being approved by St Petersburg.

* * *

As the century ended, Russia's position looked strong, with its ships moored in Port Arthur, its troops stationed at strategic points in Manchuria, and Korea akin to a co-protectorate. However, Russian intrigue had provoked a burning desire for revenge amongst the Japanese. Many Russian policymakers were blind to the threat, but not all. Finance Minister Sergei Witte strongly opposed Russia's seizure of Port Arthur and, when overruled by the tsar, lamented to Grand Duke Aleksandr Mikhailovich, "Remember this day, Your Imperial Highness, … You will see what terrible consequences this fateful step with have for Russia."[66]

5

ESPIONAGE AND THE RUSSO-JAPANESE WAR

During the second half of the 19th century, Russia, by means of several acts of intrigue, had maintained the upper hand over Japan in the struggle for influence in Korea and Manchuria. However, the tables were turned by Japan's historic victory in the Russo-Japanese War (1904–5). As we shall see, intelligence failings did contribute to Russia's defeat. Yet, ironically, this period of weakness in Russian intelligence was precisely when Japanese angst about Russian spies was at its most intense.

Spy scares in Tokyo

After the Tripartite Intervention (1895), there was serious anger towards Russia within Japan, but there was also chronic fear. This was driven by the Russian Empire's vast size and seemingly mighty army, but also by the belief that Russia was adept in its use of subterfuge. Oku Takenori describes Japanese society as afflicted by "*kyōrobyō*," meaning "fear of Russia sickness."[1] While this condition was aggravated by the Tripartite Intervention, its symptoms were already discernible during the so-called Ōtsu incident.

The Ōtsu incident was an assassination attempt against Tsesarevich Nicholas in May 1891 at Ōtsu, Shiga Prefecture, during the future tsar's official tour of Japan. Having been taken on a day trip to Lake

Biwa, Nicholas was returning to Kyoto when Tsuda Sanzō, one of the police escorts, suddenly attacked him with a sword. Nicholas was struck on the right side of the head and might have been killed had not his cousin fought off the assassin with a bamboo cane. Nicholas was not seriously wounded, though he was left with a permanent scar.[2] The outcome might have been very different had Tsuda used a Japanese *katana*, rather than an inferior, foreign-made sabre.[3]

The Japanese authorities were understandably alarmed by this attack on their foreign guest. More surprising was the histrionic response of the Japanese public. A 27-year-old woman called Hatakeyama Yūko committed suicide in front of the Kyoto Prefectural Office by slitting her own throat with a razor. She had become extremely agitated after the Ōtsu incident and left a suicide note addressed to Russian officials.[4] Elsewhere, in the village of Kaneyama in Yamagata Prefecture, the decision was taken to ban the use of the names Tsuda and Sanzō. It is unclear if this provision remains in effect. The public shock even silenced Tokyo's raucous red-light districts, where musical performances were temporarily banned.[5]

The intensity of this response speaks to the depths of Japanese fears of their northern neighbour. The reality of the royal visit was that it was a month-long jolly for the 22-year-old crown prince and his cousin. Like many young, male visitors in subsequent decades, Nicholas seems to have engaged in lively interactions with the Japanese female population. As he wrote approvingly in his diary, "Japanese erotica is more refined and subtle than the crude proffers of love on European streets. … The tea ceremony ends. … All that follows remains a secret."[6] Nicholas and his cousin also got tattoos in Japan, with the tsesarevich opting for the "image [on his right forearm] of a dragon with a black body, yellow horns, a red belly and green paws."[7]

Yet, while the young tourists were giving themselves over to hedonism, wild rumours swirled that Nicholas was really in Japan to spy on the country in preparation for a Russian invasion. Most imaginatively, it was whispered that the Russian crown prince had come to Japan to secretly return Saigō Takamori. Saigō was a samurai from the Satsuma domain (Kagoshima), who led the Satsuma rebellion (1877) against the new Meiji government and its reforms that rendered the samurai class obsolete. Saigō was wounded in the Battle of Shiroyama, the final battle of the war, and is believed to have then committed suicide. However, according to the rumours, Saigō had really escaped to Russia, where he had spent the next decade training the Russian military. He was now said to be hiding aboard Nicholas' ship, and, with Russian assistance, would soon lead a renewed uprising against the Meiji authorities. It was this belief that Nicholas was engaged in intrigue against Japan, as well as anger that the Russian crown prince had not immediately visited the emperor to pay his respects, that drove Tsuda to undertake the assassination attempt.[8]

In the years that followed 1891, this paranoia only intensified. This was not only the consequence of the Tripartite Intervention, but also a result of the continuing construction of the Trans-Siberian Railway, which would enable Russia to move troops into Northeast Asia with much greater speed. Russia was also seen as a hotbed of socialism and anarchism that could spread to other countries. Additionally, fears in Japan were heightened by Russian actions in China, especially the Amur anti-Chinese pogrom of July 1900. Occurring at the time of the Boxer Rebellion, this incident involved Russian forces killing between 3,000 and 20,000 Chinese civilians and throwing the corpses into the river. Ishimitsu Makiyo, a Japanese spy working in Manchuria at the time, reported that, "The massacred bodies of old and young, men and women were washed down the muddy waters of the Amur River like rafts."[9] This news encouraged the view in Japan that the Russians were a "merciless" ("*zannin*") people, at least when it came to dealing with East Asians.[10]

Therefore, well before the outbreak of the Russo-Japanese War, suspicions of Russia were deeply entrenched in Japan and there was a tendency to view all Russian officials as spies. When Minister of War Aleksei Kuropatkin visited Tokyo in June 1903, the Japanese press sizzled with allegations against the Russian general and those he met.[11] This belief that Russian officials were particularly adept at intrigue in Asia was not confined to the Japanese. Writing in 1905, US journalist Frederic William Unger alleges that:

> The Russian diplomat has all the softness and suavity of his Asiatic congeners; he can glide through their closest net of diplomacy with-

> out displaying an angle in his body; .... He is an adept in the art of bribery; has emissaries everywhere.[12]

There were few actual Russians in Japan at the dawn of the 20th century and even fewer once the war began in February 1904. For this reason, suspicions about a wave of Russian espionage were primarily directed not towards Russian nationals but towards fellow Japanese. So widespread did the accusations become that a new word, "*rotan*," was coined.[13] Meaning "Russian spy," "*rotan*" became one of the most popular "poison words" (*doku-go*) of the era.[14] It was such a damaging label that "Once named and criticised as a '*rotan*', even if you exhaust yourself with explanations, it is too late. Even intimate friends and acquaintances will not help you."[15]

Numerous Japanese were accused of being Russian agents during the first decade of the new century, but three stand out. These can be categorised as the first, the most high-profile, and the most tragic.

The first "*rotan*" was Osada Shūtō. Born in 1871 as the son of a Japanese diplomat, Osada became a scholar of French literature and a playwright. He taught at both Waseda University and the Military Staff College. Early in his career, he was briefly manager of the Imperial Hotel, where, four decades later, Soviet intelligence officer Richard Sorge would regularly prop up the bar. Osada was first accused of being a Russian spy shortly after Aleksei Kuropatkin's visit to Japan in 1903. It was alleged that Kuropatkin had taken the time to pay his respects at the grave of Osada's father, who had served as minister resident in Russia. Osada was also accused of secretly meeting Russian officials, and of working to divide Japan from Great Britain, with whom Japan had signed an alliance in 1902. The main architect of these accusations was Gondō Shinji, a journalist and the first editor-in-chief of Denpō Tsūshin-sha (Dentsu) when this modern-day communications and advertising colossus was founded in 1901. Osada sued Gondō but lost the case, leading many to conclude that the allegations were correct. His name blackened, Osada resigned from the Military Staff College. His enduring despair may have contributed to his early death in 1915.[16]

Osada's case brought the term "*rotan*" to public attention but more high-profile was Akiyama Teisuke. Akiyama founded the *Niroku Shimpō* in 1893. He used this newspaper to whip up public sentiment against the financial and political elite, and organised one of Japan's first major workers' rallies in 1901. The *Niroku Shimpō* was also Akiyama's springboard to parliament, to which he was elected in 1902.[17]

As with Osada, the allegations against Akiyama were animated by Kuropatkin's visit. It was claimed that the two went fishing together and that the newspaperman gave the Russian minister secret documents. Additionally, Akiyama was accused of regularly visiting the Russian embassy. It was claimed that he accepted money in return for publishing pro-Russian articles in his newspaper.[18] Matters came to a head on 23 March 1904, when Diet member Ogawa Gen'ichi, a supporter of Prime Minister Katsura Tarō, stood up in the chamber to warn that there may be a Russian agent amongst them and to propose an emergency motion to form a committee to investigate Akiyama. Less than a week later, a resolution was passed to demand Akiyama's resignation. He stepped down as a member of parliament on 29 March.[19]

Akiyama's enforced resignation was a major blow to his reputation, and the circulation of the *Niroku Shimpō* dropped precipitously. Nonetheless, Akiyama fared better than Osada. He remained politically influential for several decades and was even involved in creating Prime Minister Konoe Fumimaro's "New Order Movement" in 1940.[20]

The third, and most tragic, of the "*rotan*" was Maeda Seiji, who was stabbed to death in the street in August 1907 near Shibakōen, close to where Tokyo Tower now stands. Maeda had studied Russian at the Tokyo University of Foreign Studies and had taught Japanese at the Oriental Institute in Vladivostok. Suspicions of Maeda increased when he remained in Russia after the outbreak of the Russo-Japanese War. It was also reported that he had naturalised as a Russian citizen and had received an award from the Russian state. There were additionally the inevitable rumours that he was connected with Minister of War Aleksei Kuropatkin. When Maeda eventually returned to Japan in May 1907 to visit his family, he was greeted by the headline "The return of the Russian spy." Such inflammatory reporting may have contributed to his murder just a few weeks later. The newspapers were no more sympathetic after Maeda's demise, with one headline proclaiming "End of the road for a national traitor."[21]

None of these three individuals appears to have been a genuine Russian agent. In Osada Shūtō's case, the accusations were encouraged by his father's time spent serving as minister resident in Russia. Osada was also a critic of the Anglo-Japanese alliance. He had studied at the University of Cambridge but had been called "Jap" and made to feel unwelcome. Consequently, he appears to have favoured Russia as a partner for Japan, rather than Great Britain. As well as political considerations, the attacks on Osada may have been encouraged by his bohemian lifestyle. He began an affair with a geisha who worked at the Kōyōkan, a high-class members club and restaurant. Known as "*O-kinu*" ("the silken one"), this geisha came to live with Osada and his wife.[22] While Osada's political views and personal life inspired controversy (and perhaps some envy), there is nothing to support the claim he was a Russian spy.

There is a similar lack of evidence against Akiyama Teisuke, though it is easy to see why he was targeted. His populist newspaper's encouragement of worker activism was viewed as dangerous. Outspoken in his criticism of the Katsura government and a fierce opponent of the powerful Mitsui *zaibatsu* (financial conglomerate), Akiyama had plenty of powerful enemies. At a time of vicious competition between Japan's newspapers, rival publications to Akiyama's *Niroku Shimpō* were only too glad to join the criticism of their competitor's owner.[23]

As for Maeda Seiji, he did at least have a direct connection with Russia. It is also true that he (and his wife) took Russian citizenship, though the claim that he received a Russian award appears false. By teaching at the Oriental Institute in Vladivostok, Maeda may have contributed to the Japanese language skills of some Russians who went on to work in intelligence. However, there is no evidence that he actively spied against the country of his birth. By character, Maeda was bookish. He had little time for political matters or the military, but had a passion for literature and philosophy, and it was these scholarly interests that took him to Russia.[24]

Of these three "*rotan*," it is the Maeda case that leaves the most unanswered questions. His killer was not a nationalist fanatic, but a fellow graduate of the Tokyo University of Foreign Studies by the name of Imamura Katsutarō. Imamura had his own connections with Russia and had lived in Nikolaevsk. During the Russo-Japanese War, he too was accused of being a Russian spy. Oku Takenori reports that, after Maeda's return to Tokyo, Imamura and an associate attempted to entrap him in criminal behaviour. When this failed, it appears that Imamura decided to murder Maeda. One possibility is that Imamura wanted to clear all suspicions against himself by bringing down another suspected *rotan*. Imamura was immediately arrested but avoided the death penalty due to his seemingly patriotic motivations.[25]

The overall impression of this time is therefore of a still insular Japanese society in which any interactions with the outside world could be viewed with suspicion. This atmosphere became yet more overwrought as the outbreak of the Russo-Japanese War approached. In many cases, those hurling the accusations were driven by genuine fears about Japan's northern neighbour. In others, applying the label of *rotan* was simply a convenient way to dispose of a political enemy or of someone whose lifestyle failed to conform to the standards of Meiji-era Japan.

The reality of Russian intelligence on Japan

If the most high-profile accusations were false, what was the reality of Russian espionage prior to and during the Russo-Japanese War? Some have suggested that there really wasn't any. Soviet military expert Konstatin Zvonarev states dismissively that "the Russian army began and finished the war against Japan without intelligence at all, and, accordingly, without any knowledge of its adversary."[26] Others claim that, at the start of the conflict, the only books that Russia had about Japan were "about such marginal topics as geisha, teahouses, hairdos, and legends."[27]

There were certainly blind spots in Russian intelligence about Japan. There was also a damaging tendency to underestimate the Japanese. However, Russian intelligence on Japan was not quite the blank canvas that these two commentators suggest. In addition, Russia improved its intelligence capabilities during the conflict, and the lessons learned led to advances in Russian and Soviet intelligence on Japan in the decades to come.

The following overview of the reality of Russian intelligence on Japan at the time of the Russo-Japanese War is divided into four sections: Russian intelligence gathering within Japan; failures of military intelligence within the theatres of conflict; successes of military intelligence within the theatres of conflict; and signals intelligence.

Russian intelligence gathering within Japan

The primary form of Russian intelligence gathering within Japan prior to the war was not, as the rumours suggested, through Japanese *rotan* but rather through Russia's military attachés. These "shoulder-strapped diplomats" were attached to Russia's legation in Tokyo and were able to operate until diplomatic relations were broken off at the start of hostilities.[28] The attachés received some assistance from Russian consuls, as well as trade representatives who visited Japanese ports and reported back on the activities of Japanese naval vessels.[29] In the years prior to the war, the Priamur military headquarters in Vladivostok also sent young subalterns to Japan for two-to-three-month holidays. As well as learning about life in Japan, these junior officers were expected to collect intelligence on the Japanese armed forces. This did not prove terribly successful, since, as Evgeny Sergeev reports, "They could hardly speak Japanese and could not read the language; besides, they did not act as professionals but rather amateurishly."[30] The weight of responsibility for ascertaining Japan's strategic intentions and military strength therefore fell largely unshared upon the shoulders of the military attachés.

During the years prior to the Russo-Japanese War, three military attachés of the Russian army served in Tokyo. The first was Major General Nikolai I. Yanzhul, who was in post from 1896 to 1899. His successor was Colonel Gleb M. Vannovskii, who was, in turn, replaced by Lieutenant Colonel Vladimir K. Samoilov in 1903. Russia's naval attachés were, from 1897, Lieutenant Ivan I. Chagin, then, from 1899, Captain Second Rank Aleksandr I. Rusin.

All these military attachés found pre-war Japan a difficult operational environment, though some handled the challenge better than others. This inconsistent performance owed much to the low regard with which military intelligence was viewed by the General Staff. As Evgeny Sergeev explains in his study of contemporary Russian military intelligence (MI), "most officers originated from traditional Russian nobility regarded MI as a dishonest 'filthy' business inappropriate for a noble man."[31] This disdain resulted in little training in intelligence. Indeed, a course on secret intelligence was not introduced at the General Staff Academy until after the Russo-Japanese War.[32] A further weakness was nepotism, as evident in the case of Gleb Vannovskii, who owed his position to his uncle, former Minister of War Petr Vannovskii.[33]

To take each military attaché in turn, Nikolai Yanzhul was honest about his difficulties. These owed much to his lack of language skills, especially when it came to *kanji*. As he explained,

> Chinese hieroglyphs are the greatest impediment for military attachés ... This gibberish not only prevents them from examining any confidential paper they get, maybe quite accidentally, but also makes a military attaché fully and sadly dependent on the conscientiousness ... of Japanese translators.[34]

Yanzhul described his situation as "tragicomic," and lamented: "I am unable to recruit any civilians or officials as secret agents to gather data on the arms race in Japan. I have, therefore, to take trips about the country ... particularly with the purpose of checking accidental intelligence or speculations in the press and society."[35] Deeply frustrated, Yanzhul requested a six-month leave of absence, then never returned to Tokyo.[36]

Yanzhul was certainly not a major asset, but his replacement was worse. Gleb Vannovskii faced the same obstacles and concluded it was not even worth the effort to try. The General Staff in St Petersburg repeatedly complained about the scarcity of his intelligence reports.[37] In the first half of 1901, Vannovskii sent only four reports, whereas military attachés elsewhere submitted closer to 20. He also refused to provide the head of the Russian legation, Aleksandr Izvolskii, with assessments of the Japanese army.[38]

Vannovskii's indolence led to his recall in July 1902, yet his negative legacy endured. Despite having little insight into the Japanese military, Vannovskii still put forward judgments about its capabilities. These were based on his assumptions about the moral inferiority of the Japanese yet were taken seriously by some of the top brass on account of his family connections. Vannovskii did concede that "The Japanese army ... has already ceased to be an Asiatic horde."

However, he maintained that "Decades or even hundreds of years will have passed before the Japanese army adopts the moral principles of European troops and can compete with the weakest of them on equal terms." He added, "against such an army a powerful cavalry detachment, armed with artillery, in fast-moving and energetic partisan-style actions will have sure and decisive successes."[39] Such overconfidence was widespread on the Russian side and caused decision-makers to fail to take seriously more accurate intelligence assessments.

By contrast, the third of the Russian army attachés did considerably better. Vladimir Samoilov also found the intelligence environment arduous and complained in May 1903 that "Everything that concerns the numerical strength of the army in Japan is a big secret, and you can only get any information by chance."[40] At the same time, Samoilov had the benefit of knowing Japanese. On arriving in Tokyo, he quickly learned that the dismissive attitude that prevailed in St Petersburg was mistaken, and he set about seeking more reliable information. Since Samoilov also struggled to recruit Japanese agents, he relied on third-party sources, including foreign commercial visitors to Japan as well as European and American reporters. Samoilov developed a close relationship with French military attaché Baron Charles Corvisaire. This was a natural partnership given the Franco-Russian Alliance of 1894. Through Corvisaire, Samoilov received information about the Japanese military's mobilisation schedules and learned of a secret plan to lay siege to Port Arthur. In thanks, Samoilov arranged for his French colleague to be awarded the Order of St Stanislaus (2nd class).[41]

Amalgamating intelligence from several sources, Samoilov reported back to St Petersburg on specific issues, including the combat readiness of Japanese divisions and the condition of military vehicles. In November 1903, he submitted a report warning that, in the event of conflict between Russia and Japan, "we will be defeated before the arrival of reinforcements." Moreover, "our fleet is definitely considered to be weaker than the Japanese."[42] Samoilov continued reporting until shortly before the start of hostilities, and, in a coded telegram on 13 January 1904, he warned: "Dangerous sign: strong excitement in the army, they are talking openly about imminent war."[43] With better resources, Samoilov's intelligence could have been even better. He was contacted by an anonymous source offering advance information on the manoeuvres of the Japanese fleet. However, lacking the finances to pay the informant, Samoilov missed out on information that could have revealed the Japanese fleet's preparations for the attack on Port Arthur on the night of 8–9 February 1904.[44]

Turning to Russia's naval attachés, their performance was more consistent and surpassed that of their army colleagues. This is partly because it is easier to assess an adversary's naval capabilities, as it is difficult for a country to hide its capital ships from public view. However, the superiority of Russian naval intelligence in Japan also owed much to the skill of Lieutenant Aleksandr Rusin, who was appointed naval attaché in 1899.

Evgeny Sergeev praises Rusin as "one of the most brilliant naval attachés in the history of imperial Russia."[45] In his regular memoranda to the Main Naval Staff, "Rusin commented on [Japan's] fitting out new warships, reshuffling naval forces, working out a schedule for mobilization and plans for attack against Russian naval fortresses."[46] Thanks to his efforts, by January 1904 the Russian navy's Digest of Naval Information about Foreign States contained a comprehensive listing of all Japan's naval vessels, including their tonnages and armaments, as well as lists of all flag officers.[47] Furthermore, Rusin acquired Japanese plans for an invasion of Korea and for an attack on Southern Manchuria that was intended to isolate Port Arthur.[48] As with Samoilov, Rusin clearly saw the start of hostilities approaching, reporting on 28 January 1904 that the Japanese naval and ground forces had been put on a full war footing.[49]

As with Samoilov, Rusin made use of the French connection by recruiting two French lieutenants, Jacques Boissier and Pierre Martini.[50] Rusin was also aided by Japanese national Takahashi Monsaku. Takahashi had studied Russian at the Nikolai-dō in Tokyo and had spent a year in Siberia.[51] Unlike those Japanese who were unfairly accused of being "*rotan*," the claims against Takahashi had considerable grounding.

Takahashi was employed by the Russian naval attaché to provide translations of Japanese documents, yet his activities went further. He also cultivated sources in Yokosuka and Maizuru, two important naval bases.[52] The Japanese authorities were, however, watching Takahashi, and he was arrested for violating the Military Secrets Protection Law. During the trial, Takahashi admitted he had engaged in the activities of which he was accused yet insisted he had not known he was handling military secrets. The court rejected this explanation but, because Takahashi was merely a facilitator, he was sentenced to only eight years in prison.[53]

Despite the glowing appraisal that modern-day experts give to Rusin's intelligence work, the contemporary Russian authorities were far less appreciative. According to Igor' Bunich, "Rusin's reports ... were simply filed away in the archives of the Main Naval Staff without any practical response."[54] Part of the reason was because Rusin's warnings ran counter to Vannovskii's dismissive comments about Japan's capabilities. Indeed, when Rusin accurately predicted how Japan would conduct its attack against Russian positions in Manchuria, Vannovskii mocked his naval colleague, saying "Only a mariner may believe that, on besieging such a fortress as Port Arthur, the Japanese will advance further to Mukden."[55]

Overall, except for Yanzhul's floundering and Vannovskii's ill-informed swagger, Russian military attachés in Japan prior to the outbreak of the Russo-Japanese War did a creditable job. Both Samoilov and Rusin gave clear indications of Japan's likely plan of attack and warned in January 1904 that Japan was readying itself for immediate conflict. That the Staff marginalised their reports was not their fault. However, while the attachés did well in assessing Japan's intentions, their calculations of Japanese troop strength were far less impressive. Prior to the conflict, the War Ministry estimated that Russia might confront 120,000–160,000 Japanese troops in Manchuria, whereas, in reality, Japan deployed 442,000. Russian intelligence had miscalculated by a factor of three.[56]

With the start of the war, Russia's military attachés had to be withdrawn. However, Russian intelligence gathering within Japan did not cease. Early in the conflict, General Yakov Zhilinskii, who was head of Viceroy Evgenii Alekseev's headquarters, inquired of his staff "whether it is possible to obtain secret intelligence straight from Japan through spies or from the French Minister and the French attachés stationed in the country."[57] The French government, despite nominally being neutral, did assist the Russians during the conflict.

However, the main way in which Russia sought to collect intelligence within Japan during the war was through foreign nationals without government affiliation. Commercial travellers and journalists proved especially useful.

Details of one of these operations are recorded in a note sent in April 1904 from Colonel Aleksandr Nechvolodov, Russia's military representative in Korea, to the quartermaster general at the field headquarters of Russia's Manchurian Army. Nechvolodov reports that he has recruited three foreign nationals who will pose as merchants and be sent from China to spy on the Japanese. The three are listed as Jean Shaffangeune (French), Oscar Barbier (Swiss), and Otto Meier (German). They were instructed to telegraph information to trusted contacts in Europe. As Nechvolodov explains: "Telegrams are sent from Japan and Korea using conventional trade-related phrases, and from ports in China using a specially established cipher that agents know by heart." Having been received in Europe, these messages were telegraphed, first to St Petersburg, then to the Manchurian Army's field headquarters.[58]

The first jobs with which the three foreign agents were tasked were:

> a) to determine the composition and strength of the siege corps landing near Port Arthur, b) to find out exactly which units, other than the 1st Army, are advancing from Korea and in which direction, c) to monitor the organisation of the 4th Army, the timing of its landing, and the direction of its transports.

For this dangerous work behind Japanese lines, the agents were well compensated. Oscar Barbier received a salary of 1,300 roubles a month, plus 1,000 roubles for his supposed trading activities. For the first important piece of information delivered, he received 500 roubles, for the second, 1,000, for the third, 1,500, and so on. He was promised a further 2,000 roubles at the end of the war. A similar system was arranged for Shaffangeune and Meier.[59] For comparison, a junior Russian officer was paid 100 roubles a month.[60]

However, despite the resources expended, the quality of information delivered by these agents was disappointing and slow in arriving, not least because of the indirect way it was communicated.[61] In preparation for the arrival in East Asia of the Second Pacific Squadron (as the ships of the Baltic Fleet had been renamed), Nechvolodov sought to use his spies to provide insight into Japanese naval activity. To this end, Shaffangeune was dispatched to Batavia in the Dutch East Indies and Barbier to Macao. However, these missions were not productive, and Russian contact with the three agents was terminated in May 1905.[62]

More success was achieved by using the foreign correspondents who flocked to the Far East to report on the century's first major war. Some foreign journalists were engaged by the Russians simply as letter carriers. Others were directly employed for intelligence collection. These individuals were controlled by Colonel F.E. Ogorodnikov, Russia's military attaché in China, as well as by Aleksandr I. Pavlov, who established the branch of Russia's intelligence service in China known as "the Shanghai Service." Those employed by the Russians included: "James F.J. Archbald (*Collier's Weekly*, New York), Bennet Burleigh (*Daily Telegraph*, London), Baron Thomas T. Ward (Associated Press and *Chicago Daily News*), MacDermid (Reuters and Associated Press)."[63] Their greatest asset, however, was Jean C. Balais.

Balais was a correspondent for a French newspaper, *L'Illustration*, who arrived in Tokyo in June 1904.[64] Working for Aleksandr Pavlov, Balais was especially valuable because of his fluent Japanese. Using these language skills and his status as a journalist, Balais obtained information from the Japanese Foreign Ministry and military. According to historian Dmitrii Pavlov, Balais "became acquainted with the head of the diplomatic chancellery of General Hasegawa, the commander of the Japanese expeditionary corps, and was able to discover Japan's 'military programme' for Korea from the general and officers on his staff."[65] As early as August 1904, Balais warned that Japan would attack Mukden at the start of 1905. The French journalist's reports also included information on the types of arms and vessels used by Japan, the number of Japanese deserters, and descriptions of the personal relationships between Japanese commanders.[66] Added to this, in a development with parallels to Richard Sorge's actions in Tokyo in 1941, Balais informed his Russian handlers that Japan did not intend to attack the Russian Far East in early 1905.[67] This should have enabled Russia to concentrate its forces on the defence of Mukden. However, Balais was ignored and General Kuropatkin dispatched 12 infantry battalions and 35 cavalry companies to defend Vladivostok, thereby contributing to Russia's defeat at Mukden in March 1905.[68] Mukden also marked the end of Jean Balais's career as a Russian spy. Since the intelligence fiasco that accompanied the defeat (described shortly) risked Balais's exposure by the Japanese authorities, he was hurriedly withdrawn from Tokyo.

Seeking to compensate for Balais's loss, in April 1905 Russian headquarters developed a plan to install another spy under journalistic cover in Japan. This time, instead of recruiting a foreign correspondent, they decided to send one of their own. The person selected was Lieutenant Subbotich of the 11th East Siberian Rifle Regiment. Subbotich was to pose as a Serbian journalist named Marinkovic. According to Lieutenant Colonel Aleksandr Vineken, who reported on the operation to the Quartermaster-General, Subbotich was ideal on account of "His military education, non-Russian origin, perfect command of the German and French languages, [and] ties of kinship in the Serbian ruling elite."[69] Subbotich was to be funded lavishly "to let him stay in the best inns and get together with 'intellectual circles of society' without attracting the attention of the Japanese police."[70] It is also recorded that Subbotich was to relay intelligence from Japan via Leonid Davydov, a member of the governing board of the Russo-Chinese Bank in Beijing.[71] However, while we have these initial details, no further information is available on whether Subbotich's mission was successful or not.

While it is not known whether Subbotich was captured by the Japanese, some Russian agents were. One was H.B. Collins. Collins was a British national of Portuguese descent who was born in Hong Kong. He moved to Yokohama when young and apparently worked as a jockey at the Japanese Imperial court.[72] He later moved to Shanghai, then Port Arthur, where he married a Russian national. In June 1904, Collins was recruited by Russia's military representative in China, Colonel Ogorodnikov, who encouraged him to return to Yokohama. Back in Japan, Collins reported on Japanese troop deployments, noting their size, destination, and purpose. This intelligence was sent in coded messages via Nagasaki to Colonel Ogorodnikov and Lieutenant General Konstantin Desino, another of Russia's military representatives in China. One of these communications was intercepted, leading to Collins's arrest in November 1904. At his trial, Collins admitted that he had agreed to spy for Russia but claimed he had simply taken the Russians' money and provided them with worthless information in return. He was nonetheless found guilty and given an 11-year prison sentence.[73]

Confusingly, there is another similar case to that of H.B. Collins. José Maria Guedes (or José Giddis or Joseph Goddes) was a commercial traveller who was born Portuguese but became a British national. He was the 22-year-old son of the owner of a Shanghai newspaper. Viewing the Russo-Japanese War as a business opportunity, Guedes contacted Russian officials, including Colonel Ogorodnikov, and volunteered to work for Russian intelligence in China. Referred to in Russian documents as "No. 1," Guedes provided useful information on Japanese troop deployments between April and December 1904. He also informed Russia about alleged Japanese plans to assassinate General Kuropatkin and other Russian commanders.[74] Furthermore, "It was Giddis who notified Ogorodnikov in advance that the Japanese were going to poison wells in the rear of the Manchurian armies."[75] However, Russian officials ultimately concluded that Guedes was also working for the Japanese and may have passed them plans of Port Arthur. He was arrested in Mukden in December 1904 and held for nearly a year.[76] He was finally released in November 1905, possibly following a request from the British government.

Lastly in this context, it is worth mentioning French military officer Alexandre Etienne Bougouin. Bougouin first visited Japan as part of France's second military mission (1872–80), which assisted with the military modernisation of early Meiji Japan. After the mission, Bougouin maintained his connection with Japan, first by serving as military attaché in Tokyo, then, from 1893, as founder of a company trading in military equipment.[77] In 1901, Bougouin was made an officer of the *Légion d'honneur* by his native France.[78]

By the time of the Russo-Japanese War, Bougouin had considerable status and decades of experience of Japan. During his time as a visiting instructor, he had taught many young officers who went on to become prominent figures in the Japanese military. Bougouin was accused of abusing these connections to obtain Japanese military secrets, which he passed on to French officials and newspapers. It was suspected that these were then handed over to France's Russian ally. Bougouin was arrested in 1905 and sentenced to 10 years in prison. He was, however, pardoned just six days after sentencing, most likely to avoid damaging relations with France.[79]

Failures of military intelligence within the theatres of conflict

Having considered Russian intelligence gathering within Japan, we now turn to military intelligence in the theatres of conflict, principally Korea and Manchuria. Starting with the failings, these were partly rooted in structural problems. Reforms of Russian military intelligence had been introduced between 1900 and 1903. These had seen responsibility for military intelligence handed primarily to the Second Directorate of the Quartermaster Service of the General Staff. A new Naval Strategic Directorate was also created. This may sound streamlined but, as Evgeny Sergeev explains, there remained much duplication and little coordination. This is because intelligence was also collected by the Main Engineer Department, the Main Artillery Department, the Main Department of Fortresses, and by individual military districts. Consequently, during the early stages of the war, "the vast majority of officers of intelligence sections operated almost autonomously."[80] At times, this lack of cooperation reached absurd levels. When one general was asked to share intelligence with colleagues, he replied bluntly: "No! I am not going to give you any information, or you may report it to higher staff before we would!"[81] This weak system of organisation also applied to the data itself, since the familiar categorisation of military intelligence into strategic, operational, and tactical was not established until midway through 1905.[82]

Compounding these difficulties were problems of institutional culture. In addition to nepotism and the disdain with which many senior officers regarded intelligence work, there was the issue of subordinates tailoring reports to superiors' wishes. General Staff Captain Aleksandr Svechin explains that:

> The intelligence officers at Kuropatkin's headquarters did their utmost not to find out the real strength of the Japanese armies, but to provide the higher commanders with confidence and fighting spirit.

> To this end, the assembled data were collated unilaterally—every finding on the adversary's numerical weakness was put forward, while opposing information suffered critical remarks and was removed to the back stage.[83]

It was also a major challenge to rapidly scale up intelligence resources, especially given their low levels before 1904. The total funds assigned to military intelligence in 1903 were a mere 56,590 roubles.[84] Human resources were equally sparse, with only 17 individuals assigned to work centrally on military intelligence for the army and 12 for the navy.[85] This is because most intelligence resources were directed internally towards monitoring the activities of the anarchist and socialist revolutionaries for which Russia was then notorious.

Funding was, of course, increased following the start of the conflict, but the earlier underinvestment took its toll. One area of persistent weakness was interpreters proficient in Japanese or Chinese. The Oriental Institute in Vladivostok did produce some skilled military interpreters, but these were far too few. Indeed, when it was established in 1899, the institute only accepted four officers per year.[86] The Russian military was therefore impeded, not only in its ability to read Japanese documents, but also (as explained later) in its efforts to recruit Chinese to spy on Japanese forces in Manchuria.

It takes a long time to train officers who are proficient in Japanese or Chinese. Less forgivable is that officers were often not provided with basic equipment, such as binoculars, that they required for reconnaissance.[87] The distribution of intelligence summaries was also hindered by a lack of printing machines. As Evgeny Sergeev reports, this was not at first deemed a serious problem as, "Amazingly, both [Admiral Evgenii] Alekseev and [General Aleksei] Kuropatkin supposed initially that it was useless to disseminate copies of summaries to lower ranking commanders."[88]

Given these institutional, attitudinal, and resource constraints, it is no surprise that Russian military intelligence struggled during the early stages of the war. On 30 March 1904, Major General Vladimir Kosagovskii of the Intelligence Section of Russia's Manchurian Army confided in his diary that "I have learned … that we are obtaining practically no information about our adversary and that we are in the process of setting up a wide network of intelligence agencies, although today we are completely blind."[89]

This impairment was evident in Russia's failure to observe signs that Japan was preparing to attack Port Arthur on the night of 8 February 1904. One month earlier, a Russian naval captain named Lebedev was approached by "a strange Briton," who told him "of the Japanese plan to descend on Russia in Port Arthur in the forthcoming weeks. The attack, added the visitor, would be unexpected, before war was formally declared by the Japanese government." The informant met the captain three times and provided him with a map. However, when Lebedev reported this intelligence to Admiral Alekseev, the Commander-in-Chief "ordered the captain not to spread false rumours and threatened him with a disciplinary arrest."[90]

Even after Japan had taken the final decision to attack, there remained the opportunity for some forewarning. On the morning of 7 February, the Japanese fleet captured two Russian cargo vessels. Had these ships been equipped with radios, they could have warned Port Arthur that the conflict had begun. In the afternoon of 8 February, the Russian gunboat the *Koreets*, which was trying to depart the Korean port of Chemulpo (Incheon), was fired upon by Japanese torpedo-boats and forced to retreat.[91] News of this did not reach Russian headquarters until after the main assault had been launched against Port Arthur later that night.

As such, the Russian fleet remained unprepared for the forthcoming attack. Indeed, the authorities were relaxed enough to permit a grand ball to be held at the Naval Club in Port Arthur on the evening of 8 February.[92] *Daily Telegraph* war correspondent Bennett Burleigh alleges that senior officers "drank with Moscovite disregard for immediate and ulterior consequences. Long before morning numbers were wildly drunk and making a bacchanalian revel of the night."[93] Whether this is exaggeration or not, the Russian defenders were certainly caught with their pants down. Even when Japanese torpedo-boats were sighted in the outer harbour, it was blithely assumed they were Russian boats.[94] Then, when the first shots were fired, the revellers assumed it was part of the festivities, and "The ball continued to the accompaniment of the orchestra and artillery fire.[95]

As explained later, the shock of the attack did spur improvements in Russian military intelligence. However, some areas of weakness endured throughout the conflict. One was in the recruitment and running of Chinese agents.

With much of the conflict playing out in Manchuria, the Russian General Staff recognised the value of employing Chinese for intelligence work. As well as being familiar with the geography and having the necessary language skills, Chinese operatives were less visible than a stereotypical fair-haired, blue-eyed Russian. The aim was to gather intelligence on the Japanese forces deployed to Port Arthur and other parts of Manchuria. However, there was also the need to clarify the intentions of China itself and its many powerful warlords. This is because, as Major General Kosagovskii put it, "China declared neutrality but the Celestial Empire sides with Japan by all means against the detestable Russians."[96]

On 23 February 1904, the Russian high command urged the recruitment of Chinese subjects. According to a special expense sheet of secret intelligence, "those agents and intelligence scouts employed from the local population ought to be paid from ten to 200 roubles for each message delivered to Russian command."[97] However, while the General Staff was quick to appreciate the value of Chinese agents, their actual employment and use proved far from easy.

Part of the problem was the aforementioned lack of language skills. However, even with sufficient Chinese speakers, Russia would have struggled to overcome the reluctance of most Chinese to work for Russian intelligence. There was the perception that Russia was losing the war, meaning that many Chinese did not want to board a sinking ship. Additionally, Japanese counterintelligence were known to often hang or bury alive those they suspected of spying for Russia.[98] The Russian side might have countered this by treating the locals with greater kindness. Instead, they mimicked Japanese tactics. Lieutenant Colonel Panov of the Intelligence Section of the Manchurian Army proposed in July 1904 that Russia compel Chinese to assist them by taking their family members hostage. He conceded that "This measure is perhaps cruel and unfair, but it should give the best results."[99]

Furthermore, even when they succeeded in recruitment, Russian military intelligence found that "Chinese agents are exceptionally transient and not at all interested in what they are doing, and, besides, there are very few of them."[100] Between April and October 1905,

Russia dispatched 885 Chinese agents to the Japanese rear, yet 797 (90%) failed to complete even one mission.[101] There was also the suspicion that many Chinese did not actually visit the areas to which they were sent and simply invented intelligence. The Russian military therefore began to require Chinese agents to present proof that they had really been close to Japanese positions by bringing back Japanese ammunition casings or documents. Soon, however, a trade in these artefacts had begun.[102]

To add professionalism, Russia established a special training school for Chinese spies in April 1905. Recruits were also given more specific instructions. Some Chinese agents were told to seek employment with the Japanese military, then, having worked for some time, to sneak back to Russian lines to report what they had learned. If direct employment was not possible, they were to visit establishments close to Japanese positions, such as brothels and opium dens, where they could cultivate contacts with Chinese who were in Japanese service. Arrangements were also made to ease identification of Russia's own Chinese agents, thus enabling them to cross Russian lines safely. One method was to embroider the character "*fu*" (meaning "happiness") into their left sleeve.[103] Another was to issue agents with pipes. As explained by Chief of Russian Rear Services Lieutenant General Nadarov: "each emissary of this kind is given a smoke pipe with engraved numbers on the metallic part: 001, 002, 003 etc."[104] Presumably, there was therefore a spy working for Russia during the Russo-Japanese War with the codename 007.

By 1905, a more formal system had therefore been established for training and managing Chinese agents. However, while 600 Chinese passed through the special spy school, the results remained meagre. Colonel Mikhail Kvetsinskii, Military Commissar for Mukden province, complained that trained Chinese agents "did not reveal any high pitch of intensity in spying in comparison with their untrained compatriots and, thus, did not warrant money to be wasted on their drill."[105] In July 1905, the school was ordered closed.

Unable to get what they wanted from Chinese recruits, the Russians had to do much reconnaissance work themselves, including creeping up on Japanese positions. Often this merely served as an opportunity for heroic self-sacrifice since 30–40% of officers and men taking part in such operations were lost.[106] In one memorable case, Vasilii Ryabov, a volunteer in the 284th Chembarskii Regiment, disguised himself as a Manchurian peasant, complete with false queue, and set off to gather intelligence behind enemy lines. Not speaking any Chinese, Ryabov was soon captured and executed, but his bravery impressed the Japanese, who left a note for the Russians expressing respect for this "Russian samurai."[107]

Another problem area was the attempted use of open-source intelligence for insight into Japanese intentions and actions. During the first months, Russian military intelligence did not have regular access to Japanese newspapers and specialist publications. What is more, only 11 Japanese-language translators were deployed with Russian forces during the war.[108] Even when a recent Japanese newspaper did find its way into the hands of someone who could read it, the Russians found little illumination. This is because the Japanese authorities were effective in preventing their media from publishing any information of benefit to the enemy.[109] This is common sense, but it was something the Russians failed to replicate. For instance, when, on 20 June 1904, the Pacific Fleet sought to break the blockade on Port Arthur and make a dash for Vladivostok, the *Novoe Krai* newspaper prepared a special edition to announce the departure.[110] The escape attempt had to be postponed and ultimately ended in failure.

The Russian General Staff was left to lament:

> At the time when our papers, not excluding government ones, published news with outstanding frankness and reprinted official dispatches on army composition, numerical strength and disposition, on mobilization in military districts, on logistics …, the Japanese press keeps absolute silence about everything relating to warfare, and the military censorship all over the Land of the Rising Sun prohibits referring to commanders by name, to say nothing of units and their manoeuvres. The Japanese Main Staff realized quite well that it was not enough to administer reconnaissance, one had also to hamper the adversary developing it.[111]

These are the main areas of persistent weakness that impeded Russian intelligence throughout the Russo-Japanese War, yet there were also specific fiascos. The first was the Dogger Bank incident, when the

Russian navy briefly went to war with the fishermen of Hull. On the night of 21 October 1904, Russia's Second Pacific Squadron, which was traversing the North Sea during the first part of its fateful voyage from the Baltic to the Straits of Tsushima, mistook a local British fishing fleet for Japanese torpedo boats and opened fire.[112] The crew of a trawler named the *Crane* suffered worst. "Young Joseph Alfred Smith was awoken by the fury of the firing. He ran up on deck to find his father and the third hand both headless and in a pool of blood."[113] In total, the Russians sank one fishing boat and damaged five others. They also hit some of their own vessels, including the *Aurora*. The ship's chaplain had his hand blown off and died later of blood-poisoning, making him the fleet's first casualty.[114]

The cause of this entire mess was a lack of Russian naval intelligence. St Petersburg was deeply concerned that the repurposed Baltic Fleet would be attacked during its 18,000-mile odyssey. Indeed, there was debate about whether the naval reinforcements should be sent at all. Admiral Zinovii Rozhestvenskii prophesised that "We shall complete our voyage … and find Port Arthur fallen and the Pacific Squadron perished."[115] It was therefore with foreboding that the Russian ships began their passage through the Baltic Sea. In the absence of accurate intelligence on Japanese activity beyond East Asia, rumours began to fly. According to one Russian crew member:

> Japanese spies were everywhere. They were watching upon each manoeuvre of our squadron with the aid of submarines, balloons and neutral cargo vessels. … Some people swore that they had observed the Japanese destroyers stationed secretly in Dutch and British seaports.[116]

There were even tall tales that the Japanese were hunting for the Russian ships while disguised as Turks, Malays, or even acrobats. Convinced that an attack was imminent, the Russian forces were on full alert, with gun crews sleeping in shifts beside their weapons.[117] So convinced were the Russians that they were surrounded by hostile torpedo-boats that, even long after the truth of the Dogger Bank incident was revealed, some continued to insist that the whole thing had been cleverly planned by Japan and Britain.[118] The reality, however, is that the Second Pacific Squadron had become so panicked that, as crewmembers peered into the night-time mist off the coast of England, they came to imagine Japanese ships all around. Some months earlier, Captain Hartling, a Russian officer, had been dispatched to Copenhagen to hire agents along the Baltic coastline to track suspect ship movements. Yet this intelligence network only added to Russia's paranoia, since Hartling's agents, either through the instigation of the Japanese or simply to justify their income, submitted wildly exaggerated reports of Japanese naval activity, reporting "sightings in quiet creeks, off islands, on the high seas, building to a crescendo and swamping the Russian Admiralty just as Rozhdestvenski's fleet approached the Skaw [the entry point to the North Sea]."[119]

As humiliating as the Dogger Bank incident was, it was less consequential than the second intelligence fiasco, Russia's surrender of Port Arthur. Despite the initial attack on its fleet in February, Russia had sustained relatively little damage and retained control of Port Arthur. However, from summer 1904, its forces, while protected by extensive fortifications, came under sustained attack. This siege lasted until 2 January 1905, when Port Arthur was surrendered to the Japanese, representing one of the most painful defeats in Russian military history. Debate continues about whether the surrender was premature, but there is little doubt that Russia's position was undermined by poor intelligence.[120]

Part of the problem was overconfidence, with General Kuropatkin boasting that Port Arthur could hold out against a 10-year siege.[121] General Anatolii Stessel', who was directly in command of Russian forces at Port Arthur, was also a poor leader. One modern expert describes him as "an inflated military manikin puffed up by his epaulettes."[122] A particular problem was Stessel''s disregard for intelligence. Colonel Sergei Rashevskii, who was among the defenders of Port Arthur, bemoaned in his diary:

> We have not yet learned which of the adversary's divisions is now operating against us at Port Arthur. Neither do we know anything of the numerical strength of troops besieging the fortress. In a word, we are totally unaware of the adversary's forces and intention.[123]

The Russians even lacked information about their own position. According to Rashevskii: "there is no one officer in his [Stessel''s] staff who knows the plan of the fortress, who is familiar with the new bastions, weaponry, roads, etc."[124] Indeed, the Japanese may have had a better understanding of the Russians' position than the Russians themselves. Tat'yana Soboleva recounts that, just ahead of the outbreak of the Russo-Japanese War, Russian fortification plans and cyphers were stolen from Port Arthur. This theft was allegedly conducted by Sidney Reilly, the legendary "ace of spies" who was an agent of British intelligence. Reilly then sold this information to the Japanese.[125] Separately, Japan succeeded in getting their agents, disguised as Chinese coolies, within Port Arthur. Once there, they "calculated mathematically all the heights and angles to be required for the deployment of howitzers to shoot at the troops and warships stationed at the fortress."[126]

Lastly, we turn to Russia's defeat at the Battle of Mukden (February to March 1905). This was an intelligence fiasco from beginning to end. We have already seen that the Russian command failed to act on Balais's report from Tokyo that Japan did not intend to attack the Russian Far East, thus missing the opportunity to transfer troops from Vladivostok to Mukden. Additionally, the Russians lacked detailed maps of the area around Mukden, since they "had not bothered to survey the area to the north" of Liaoyang as it was assumed the Japanese would never advance that far.[127] General Kuropatkin also underestimated Japanese strength, believing that many of their best officers had been killed during earlier battles. To make matters worse, the Russians lost track of the Japanese forces. They missed the landing of three reserve divisions in Manchuria and were taken by surprise when these units appeared at the frontline.[128] Once the fighting began, Japanese troops also had the good fortune of finding a copy of the Russians' battle plan on the body of a dead Russian staff officer.[129]

However, what really marks out the Battle of Mukden as an intelligence disaster is that, during their hasty retreat, the Russians abandoned several carriages containing secret documents, including maps, and codes, "information concerning secret agents abroad and their activities." These agents were not even protected by codenames, since, under the leadership of Admiral Alekseev, Russian spymasters in East Asia were instructed to refer to sources in reports by their real names. The precaution had at least been taken to refer to the French journalist Jean Balais as "'B' from Yokohama," yet, fearing his exposure, he was withdrawn from Japan, while contact with other agents was frozen, thus dealing a blow to Russia's HUMINT network.[130]

Successes of military intelligence within the theatres of conflict

Since the Russians lost the war, it is natural to focus on their intelligence failures. Yet there were successes too and several areas in which improvements were made during the conflict. One area of progress was Russia's extraction of intelligence from prisoners of war. Many Japanese officers committed suicide before capture, but this was less common among ordinary soldiers. To encourage their capture, the Russian military offered rewards of 300 roubles for an officer and 100 for a private.[131] Initially, Russian intelligence officers beat POWs in the hope of extracting information. This did not prove effective, and, in time, the authorities learned that "gentleness and cordiality towards the prisoners, especially playing on their pride, could achieve more than severity and intimidation."[132] Other than improved interrogations of POWs, Russian intelligence became better at drawing information from the material found in their possession, including soldiers' notebooks and personal letters.

As the war proceeded, Russia also began to conduct what the Soviets would call "active measures." The Russian high command assessed that Japan was winning the information war, both within China and beyond. To counteract this, in September 1904, the Russian military funded the launch of an English-language newspaper called *The China Review*, which would "communicate the events of the war in a truthful manner." This was supplemented by a Chinese-language publication called *Shengjingbao*.[133]

Russia's growing intelligence activities in the Far East were supplemented by information delivered from Europe, where Russia had established espionage networks. The military attaché to Berlin, Colonel Vadim Shebeko, successfully recruited a spy in the Krupp factory in Essen and was able to report on the munitions ordered by Japan. Shebeko warned on 7 December 1904 that a German cargo vessel, the *Sambia*, was transporting to Japan "326 field cannons and 93 mountain howitzers in addition to steel slabs." This should have enabled the Russian navy to intercept the freighter, yet they failed to do so.[134] Further intelligence came from the French government, which passed on updates about the progress of Japanese ships under construction in French shipyards. Less helpful was German Kaiser Wilhelm II. Obsessed with the purported "Yellow Peril," Wilhelm sent a bizarre warning to his cousin Tsar Nicholas II claiming there were "10,000 Japanese men in the plantations in South Mexico, all in Military Jackets with brass buttons."[135] Sensibly, St Petersburg ignored this.

In reviewing the better aspects of Russian intelligence, a few words are due about technical innovation. One such undertaking was the use of balloons for reconnaissance. After a demonstration was provided at the Peterhof Palace in August 1904, Nicholas II excitedly ordered the founding of the East Siberian Field Balloon Battalion. The Russian defenders of Port Arthur also tried to launch an improvised balloon that had been put together from silk clothing contributed by ladies of the garrison. Quite apart from the reconnaissance value, a balloon stitched together from women's undergarments might have helpfully distracted the Japanese attackers. Unfortunately, the attempt failed due to a lack of acid to make the hydrogen.[136]

Even bolder was the attempt to develop a helicopter. A prototype was put together by engineer Iosif Lippovskii in 1904. Remarkably, this was said to be capable of carrying a two-man crew, as well as 490kg of bombs. However, despite the project's apparent potential, it was not taken forward due to criticism from the famous Russian scientist Nikolai Zhukovskii.[137] Submarines, by contrast, were not only developed, but actually deployed by Russia during the war. The first of these, the *Dolphin*, was shipped to Vladivostok in 1903. The initial plan was to drag the submarines into positions at night from which they could attack enemy shipping. When this proved unworkable, the emphasis shifted to using them for reconnaissance. One submarine, the *Kasatka*, even succeeded in completing a seven-day reconnaissance mission along the Korean coastline.[138]

Lastly, the remaining examples of contemporary Russian success can best be related through the stories of three individuals. The first was David Livkin, who Evgeny Sergeev lauds as "the first Russian super-spy in the twentieth century."[139] A former Cossack, Livkin was highly educated and polyglot. Prior to the Russo-Japanese War, Livkin had already conducted secret missions in Egypt, Persia, and India in the guise of an Azeri merchant named Mohammed Gasanov. He had also cultivated a network of agents within the British Empire.[140] This experience proved useful when Livkin was dispatched on a secret mission within China in April 1904.

China was officially neutral during the Russo-Japanese War, but St Petersburg feared that China was simply waiting for the right moment to side with Japan. Needing to ascertain Chinese intentions, Russia dispatched several spies. Livkin's specific task was to infiltrate the camp of General Ma, a leading Chinese general whose troops were deployed to the west of Mukden. To achieve this, Livkin went in the guise of a Russian tea merchant called Popov. He and his assistants were initially treated with suspicion. However, helped by generous gift giving and Livkin's knowledge of Chinese customs, the Russian spy eventually befriended General Ma. In this way, Livkin learned that General Ma had received no secret instructions to cooperate with the Japanese. Livkin was also reassured that China would maintain its neutral status until the end of the war. Thanks to this, the Russian high command was able to redeploy troops away from Inner Mongolia.

Livkin was awarded the Golden Weapon for Bravery and the Order of St Vladimir. However, as with so many Russian spies, he did not to enjoy a happy retirement. Livkin suffered a head injury during the Battle of Mukden in March 1905, which left him unable to speak or move by himself. Demobilised from the military, he fell into penury. Although the tsar was petitioned for assistance, Livkin died in poverty before World War I.[141]

The second successful Russian spy was Leonid Davydov, official representative of the Russian Ministry of Finance in Beijing and board member of the Russo-Chinese Bank. Davydov had the rank of state councillor, and his staid appearance as a financial bureaucrat was useful cover for his intelligence activities. Davydov recruited the secretary of the Japanese military attaché in Chefoo (Yantai). His agents also set fire to Japanese ammunition dumps in Manchuria and attacked transport infrastructure.[142] Some information collected by Russian operatives in Japan was relayed via Davydov, including that gathered by Lieutenant Subbotich, who, as noted previously, was sent to Tokyo in April 1905 in the guise of a Serbian journalist.

The third notable individual was Aleksandr I. Pavlov, who established Russian intelligence's "Shanghai Service" in April 1904. Pavlov and his agents were active in many areas, including gathering information on Japan's activities in China. However, Pavlov's greatest impact was not in China but in Korea. Before Shanghai, Pavlov had served as Russian minister to Seoul. This ended with the start of the Russo-Japanese War, but, before departing Korea, Pavlov met a representative of King Gojong. This is the same monarch who had been smuggled out of the palace in February 1896 and given shelter in the Russian legation. The message passed to Pavlov was that the king remained willing to be "actively cooperative" with Russia. Pavlov passed on a secret code that the monarch could use to communicate with St Petersburg. In his subsequent secret communication, King Gojong bitterly complained about the behaviour of the Japanese in Korea during the war, including that "recently they blinded and then killed two Korean governors." Gojong also promised that he was "secretly preparing a general uprising" against the Japanese presence.[143]

Recognising Korea as fertile ground for anti-Japanese resistance, Pavlov's "Shanghai Service" organised and financed a Korean partisan movement. One key figure was Kim In-su (also known as Viktor Kim), who led a 3,000-strong independent cavalry division that the Russians arranged to operate in the north of Korea. There was also a group of 300 Korean insurgents who were tasked with sabotage. They were not always successful. In January 1905, several Koreans disguised as Japanese were caught and executed when they attempted to burn down Japanese food warehouses in Chemulpo (Incheon).[144] Pavlov's service also distributed anti-Japanese leaflets and cleverly used Japanese material back against them. In 1904, the Japanese distributed photographs of several dozen Koreans they had executed as Russian spies. The intention was to discourage cooperation with Japan's enemy. The loss of the agents was a blow, yet, instead of playing down the incident, Pavlov further publicised the photos to agitate public opinion against the Japanese.[145]

The work of the "Shanghai Service" came to an end in November 1905, when, following the end of the war and Japan's establishment of a protectorate over Korea, the service was dissolved. Rather than being rewarded for his work, Aleksandr Pavlov was accused of financial misdealing on account of a deficit in his organisation's budget. Scholars have suggested that the accusations were simply an attempt by the Russian military to direct blame for the loss of the war towards civilian administrators. Whatever the truth, Aleksandr Pavlov left public service in disgrace.[146]

Signals intelligence

Having considered Russian spies operating in Japan, as well as the successes and failures of Russian espionage in the theatres of conflict, we turn finally to signals intelligence. As it happens, Aleksandr Pavlov's "Shanghai Service" is a good place to start. Operating as a hub for Russian intelligence within East Asia, Pavlov's service was active in sending and receiving encrypted messages. Between April and December 1904 they dispatched more than 650 telegrams, and received a similar number. The "Shanghai Service" therefore offers interesting insight into the several types of encryption used by Russia at this time.

> For his correspondence with regular Russian consuls, Pavlov used a "naval" code, with "irregulars," a letter-based code, and agents and collaborators operating on secret missions in various locations in China, Korea, and South-East Asia were provided with special personal codes. Separate "diplomatic" codes were used for reports to the "top brass."[147]

The "Shanghai Service" also intercepted Japanese communications that were transmitted to Tokyo via China, with 350 Japanese telegrams being deciphered between April 1904 and March 1905. However, this source of intercepts dried up following the introduction of a new submarine cable between Japan and the United States, which reduced the need for transcontinental wire communication. "The Russian MI [military intelligence], thus, lost one of the most decisive channels of SIGINT in the course of the war."[148]

Another figure worth mentioning is Vice Admiral Stepan O. Makarov, who was assigned command of the Russian fleet at Port Arthur after the attack of 8 February 1904. In stark contrast to

General Stessel', Makarov was an inspiring leader. He advocated an active defence of Port Arthur that entailed his ships leaving harbour to seek engagement with the Japanese fleet. He would often lead these sallies himself. Aside from these leadership skills, Makarov was "a brilliant and innovative naval architect, inventor, tactician, and ship designer." His innovations included specialist mine-laying ships and the development of armour-piercing shells that came to be known as "Makarov tips." He also oversaw construction of the *Ermak*, the world's first polar icebreaker.[149]

Bringing this energy and inventiveness to SIGINT, soon after his arrival in Port Arthur on 7 March 1904, Makarov ordered a local station for signal intercepts to be established.[150] Later that month, when the Japanese resumed their bombardment of Port Arthur, "Makarov responded by jamming the cruiser's signals—perhaps the first recorded instance of radio-electronic combat."[151] This would surely have been just the start of Makarov's efforts. However, tragically for the Russian war effort, Makarov was killed little more than a month after his arrival. This occurred on 13 April 1904, when Makarov took to sea on the bridge of his flagship, the *Petropavlovsk*. Encountering Admiral Tōgo's main battle squadron, Makarov was forced to retreat. However, when reaching the entrance to Port Arthur, the *Petropavlovsk* struck a mine. "The resulting explosion ignited the forward magazine and burst the boilers, breaking the flagship's back immediately." Roughly 650 men were lost, including the admiral and his friend, the painter Vasilii V. Vereshchagin, among whose most famous works is *The Apotheosis of War*. French historian Girard Piouffe argues that, with the death of Makarov, Japan had already won the war, though they did not know it yet.[152]

The story of Makarov's role in the Russo-Japanese War is one of unrealised potential, yet, in another area of signals intelligence Russia did achieve considerable success. This was thanks to cooperation between Russia's secret police, the Okhrana, and a branch of the French police, La Direction de la Sûreté Générale. The Okhrana is best known for its tracking of socialist revolutionaries domestically. However, during the late 19th and early 20th centuries it also operated an outpost in the French capital. This *zagranichnaya okhranka*, as it was called, opened in 1883 at 97 Rue de Grenelle and continued to function until 1913. "At its peak the Paris bureau had about 40 detectives on its payroll and some 30 agents in Paris and elsewhere in Europe."[153] Its presence was welcomed by the French as a means of keeping control of the many Russian revolutionaries who had taken refuge in France. Interestingly, Petr Rachkovskii, who headed this Paris bureau from 1884 to 1902, is believed to have played a role in producing the *Protocols of the Elders of Zion*, the infamous forgery that describes a Jewish plot for global domination.[154]

At the time of the Russo-Japanese War, a prominent figure within the Okhrana's Paris operations was Ivan Manasevich-Manuilov. His job was to persuade French investors to continue providing loans to the Russian government. He also bribed French newspapers to ensure favourable coverage.[155] However, Manasevich-Manuilov's most significant contribution was to facilitate cooperation between the Russian and French *cabinets noires* (that is, government offices for the interception and decoding of messages) in the stealing and decrypting of Japanese communications.[156]

The Russians were already skilled in decoding messages, with Christopher Andrew describing St Petersburg's *cabinet noir* as "the world's leading SIGINT agency."[157] However, Russia needed help getting hold of Japanese telegrams, especially since Japan's embassy in St Petersburg was closed during the war. France provided this assistance by copying all correspondence between Tokyo and Japan's embassy in Paris. This still left the problem of decryption, yet Manasevich-Manuilov infiltrated an agent into the Japanese legation in the Hague. In return for 8,000–9,000 francs, this individual secretly photographed two large codebooks.[158] This enabled French and Russian officers to crack the Japanese diplomatic code. Commissaire Jacques-Paul-Marie Haverna, who was awarded the *Légion d'honneur* for his work on the project, boasted that they were able to decrypt 1,600 Japanese telegrams. This may have been an exaggeration, but the Russians and French were certainly able to read dozens of secret Japanese telegrams, including from Minister of Foreign Affairs Komura Jutarō.[159]

Further success was achieved when Colonel Akashi Motojirō visited the French capital. Akashi, who is one of the most famous spies in Japanese history, was officially working as Japan's military attaché to Sweden but his principal role was to operate espionage networks in Europe. However, even a highly regarded intelligence officer like Akashi was not above making mistakes. When in Paris in February 1905, Akashi left secret documents in his hotel room, thus enabling Manasevich-Manuilov to arrange for them to be photographed.[160] This apprised the Russians of the extent of Akashi's operations, which included providing weapons and financial support to Finnish nationalists and other revolutionary groups in Russia. Indeed, it is alleged that Akashi funded the demonstration in January 1905 that resulted in the Bloody Sunday massacre, when Russian troops opened fire on unarmed protesters.[161]

Not surprisingly, when it came to selecting a location for a peace conference to end the war, Russia favoured Paris. This could have been disastrous for Japan if they had agreed and continued to use the same code. This danger was avoided when US President Theodore Roosevelt's offer of mediation was accepted and the negotiations got under way in Portsmouth, New Hampshire. Even so, St Petersburg's *cabinet noir* assisted by decrypting correspondence between Washington and the US embassy in Russia.[162] In this way, Sergei Witte's negotiating team gained insight into the disposition of their mediator. Roosevelt was no admirer of Tsarist Russia, but, as Japanese military successes accumulated, he became concerned that an unchecked Japan could threaten US interests in the Pacific.[163] This helped inform the US president's decision to support St Petersburg's insistence that they should pay no indemnity. Witte also cultivated US public opinion by propagating the view that the Japanese were motivated by greed and that the Russians were not yet beaten. Japan's draft peace treaty proposals were also leaked to the US press, most likely by the Russian delegation.[164] This artfulness assisted Russia to secure a peace agreement which Witte heralded as "a victory of the feather over the sword."[165] By contrast, the terms were so distasteful to the Japanese public that it provoked the Hibiya Park riots, which lasted two days and caused 17 fatalities.[166]

* * *

There were certainly serious weaknesses in Russian intelligence prior to the start of the Russo-Japanese War. However, this chapter has shown that Russian intelligence on Japan was not as abject as some have suggested. Since good-quality information was available, if only sporadically, why was it that the Russian high command was caught so off guard? This mystified President Theodore Roosevelt, who wrote in the days after the attack on Port Arthur: "I cannot understand Russia having been caught so unprepared and supine."[167] It was obvious to others that a conflict was imminent. Indeed, German newspapers dispatched their war correspondents to East Asia a full three weeks before Japanese ships fired the first shots.[168]

The answer is that Japan was facing "a somnolent, incompetent, and lethargic enemy, inert in its supreme self-confidence."[169] That is to say that the Russian leadership, from Tsar Nicholas II down, was insensitive to the warning signs due to their hubristic assumption that an upstart like Japan would lack the gumption to begin a full-scale conflict against the Russian colossus. Prejudice and racism were undoubtedly a factor. Pavel M. Lessar, Russia's chargé in London, took the view that war with Japan would be "an easy business" and that "these dwarfs were quite out of their reckoning in thinking they would stand up against European troops."[170] Another Russian writer put it this way: "How can we consider as equal to ourselves people who cannot eat with our forks and who sit crossleggedly on mats! Those are not people—those are yellow-faced barbarians or simply reborn macacos!"[171] There was even a curious rumour that the Japanese were afflicted by a form of narcolepsy, meaning that "Japanese infantrymen might fall asleep quite unexpectedly to themselves, right in the heat of any battle!"[172]

This prejudice inclined the Russian leadership not to take seriously those intelligence reports that indicated that Japan's armed forces were increasingly modernised and were being readied for use. Had St Petersburg been more alert, Russia might not only have been prepared for the coming attack but might have averted the conflict entirely by engaging seriously with Japanese efforts to negotiate a pre-war delineation of spheres of influence. However, arrogance prevented Russia from treating Japan as an equal. The result was a humbling defeat.

In his study of Russian intelligence at the time of the Russo-Japanese War, Il'ya Derevyanko describes Russia as a boxer, stepping blindfolded into the ring.[173] This is an arresting image, but it is not quite right, since the danger was clearly visible if only the Russian leadership had cared to look. Instead, Russia, on the eve of this conflict, is better thought of as a faded former champion, much diminished in his capabilities but still too proud to take seriously the challenge of an upstart rival. Having been humiliated in the ring, this heavyweight was going to have to learn major lessons if he was to get his revenge.

6

BOLSHEVIK SPIES

St Petersburg was left with several intelligence lessons to learn from the failures of the Russo-Japanese War. In this chapter, we see that these lessons were learned well, resulting in wide-ranging reforms after 1905. Within just a few years of the ignominy of Dogger Bank, Port Arthur, and Mukden, Russia had developed an efficient and well-funded intelligence service. This inadvertently aided the Bolsheviks after their seizure of power in 1917 since, as Alex Marshall argues, the intelligence reforms made after the Russo-Japanese War initiated "developments that would ultimately culminate in the Soviet Union becoming one of the premier 'panoptic' surveillance states of the twentieth century."[1] These tools of espionage and political manipulation were used to considerable effect during the 1920s and 1930s against Japan to promote Soviet national interests and the cause of international communism.

Post-1905 reforms

As noted in chapter 5, Russia did make improvements to military intelligence during the Russo-Japanese War. In Evgeny Sergeev's assessment, "we may compare dilettantism at an early stage of 1904 with the professionalism in the last months of 1905."[2] However, systematic reform had to wait until the end of hostilities. On 14 September

1905, just nine days after the signing of the Treaty of Portsmouth, the Russian General Staff completed its review of intelligence during the war. Recommendations included more scrupulous planning of intelligence strategy in advance of any armed conflict, as well as better training for secret agents, including in oriental languages. The report also suggested that the Russian side learn from Japan's effective censorship of its own media and should devote more funding to local-language newspapers to influence foreign opinion. Further proposals emphasised the need to capture and interrogate prisoners of war more systematically, as well as to make better use of technology, including balloons, telephones, and wireless telegraphy.[3]

Proposed changes are often not implemented, yet, on this occasion, the reforms went beyond those suggested. On 5 May 1906, a major reorganisation took place, resulting in the creation of the 5th Section within the Main Directorate of the General Staff. This was designated the central organ for military intelligence and became the forerunner of the GRU. This avoided duplication and promoted professionalism. For example, a proper system of card indexes, complete with photographs and fingerprints, was created by 1910 to record individuals that the Main Directorate suspected of espionage.[4] Intelligence departments were also set up within the headquarters of all military districts and each was assigned a geographic focus. Responsibility for Japan, Korea, and part of Manchuria was assigned to the Priamurskii military district.[5] Additionally, funding improved dramatically. One expert estimates that spending on Russian military intelligence increased 1,600% between 1905 and 1911.[6]

Overall, these reforms brought about a rapid improvement in the effectiveness and reputation of Russian intelligence. As early as 1908, Chief of the German General Staff Helmut von Moltke (the younger) fretted that "the Russian intelligence machinery comprises a well-ordered, widely dispersed system, which has considerable funds."[7] It might be assumed that a key target for this revamped intelligence apparatus would be Japan. Yet the magnitude of defeat in the Russo-Japanese War prompted a reorientation of Russia's entire foreign policy away from the Far East and back towards Europe, especially the Balkans. Regarding Japan, the immediate priority became not revanchism but stability. As noted by Sergei Witte, Russia needed peace with Japan to rebuild its economy after the damage of both the war and the 1905 revolution.[8] The Japanese leadership was also open to warmer relations, since their war aims had been achieved and they needed time for economic recovery after being stretched to breaking point by the conflict. Paradoxically, the period after the Russo-Japanese War was therefore one of the least antagonistic in Russia-Japan relations. The two sides even agreed to a secret alliance, signed in the (recently renamed) Russian capital of Petrograd on 3 July 1916. However, while Japan was a low intelligence priority in the last years of tsarism, all this changed after 1917.

After the revolution

The Bolshevik Revolution of October 1917 threw Russia-Japan relations into a state of turmoil. Having toppled the Provisional Government at the end of October, the Bolsheviks, under Vladimir I. Lenin, signed an armistice with the Central Powers in December, thus ending Russia's involvement in the First World War. Russia's new leadership renounced previous diplomatic agreements, including the alliance with Japan, and published secret treaties. Additionally, the Bolsheviks repudiated the debts of the Tsarist and Provisional governments, including huge sums owed to Japan.

The Siberian Intervention

Japan did not passively observe these events, but became the largest contributor to what is known as the Siberian Intervention. Lasting between 1918 and 1922 (or 1925, if one includes Japan's occupation of northern Sakhalin), the Siberian Intervention was the attempt by allied powers—principally Britain, France, the United States, and Japan—to oppose the Bolshevik takeover. Japan, which was also seeking territorial gains, deployed more than 72,000 soldiers to Siberia and north Manchuria, representing one third of Japan's total active service personnel.[9] The area of Japanese occupation included all the Trans-Siberian Railway from Vladivostok to Irkutsk, as well as the Chinese Eastern Railway and the town of Nikolaevsk at the mouth of the Amur River.

Japan also lent selective support to the White forces. They explored cooperation with Admiral Aleksandr V. Kolchak, who established an anti-Bolshevik government in Irkutsk. More active assistance was given to another White leader, Grigorii M. Semenov, a Cossack ataman, who controlled territory in the Transbaikal region. Semenov was one of Japan's "principal puppets in Siberia."[10] He was given financing, arms, and promises that Japan would support his claims to the Kingdom of Mongolia. However, Semenov's forces became better known for cruelty and rapaciousness rather than for effective opposition to the Bolsheviks. Most notorious was Roman von Ungern-Sternberg, a subordinate of Semenov, who came to be known as the "Mad Baron." According to Richard Connaughton, "The Baron fed selected victims to his wolf pack, others were torn apart by horses, and to ring the change to satisfy his sadistic pleasures, some were burned alive at the stake."[11]

Such tactics did not endear the local population to the Whites or to their Japanese backers. Indeed, Japan's Siberian Intervention has been described as "a case-study in failure if ever there was one."[12] Evidently, the Whites failed to defeat the Bolsheviks. Admiral Kolchak was captured and executed in February 1920, his body dumped into a hole in the ice on the Ushakovka River.[13] Semenov fared somewhat better. As the Red Army advanced, the Japanese helped their man escape. Semenov eventually settled in Manchuria, where he lived under Japanese protection. It was only in 1945, following the Soviet invasion of Manchuria, that Semenov was captured and executed.[14]

The Siberian Intervention did not deliver to Japan any territory or the hoped-for sphere of economic influence. It also came at considerable cost. Japan is estimated to have allocated 600 million yen to the Siberian Intervention. Total Japanese combat deaths are recorded as 1,480, plus 600 who died of disease or exposure.[15] Several hundred of these fatalities were suffered during the Nikolaevsk massacre of 1920, when the entire Japanese garrison was wiped out by a band of Bolshevik-supporting partisans. Many Japanese were killed in the initial fighting, but 136 were taken prisoner, only to be murdered in cold blood when a relief expedition later approached. According to a contemporary account, "The bodies of all these unfortunate people had been dismembered and flung into the river."[16]

Insurrection in Japan

The Siberian Intervention embittered Russia-Japan relations. Soviet diplomat Adol'f A. Ioffe wrote: "All the hardships of the war of 1904–05 and the heavy bloodshed in that war did not rouse such indignation among the Russian people as exists to-day, after the Japanese intervention of recent years."[17] Lenin also regarded Japan as a threat. He described Japanese imperialism as characterised by "unheard of bestiality combining the most modern technical implements with downright Asiatic torture."[18] An added factor was that many White émigrés had taken refuge in Japan (including Fedor Morozov, who founded the famous Morozoff chocolate company). Yet, as well as viewing Japan as an enemy, the Bolsheviks increasingly looked to east Asia as an area of opportunity.

The Bolsheviks' expectation was that the Russian Revolution was just the start, and that a wave of uprisings would soon overwhelm other capitalist countries. In October 1918 Lenin declared that "The international revolution has come so close within the course of one week that we may count on its outbreak during the next few days."[19] Europe was seen as most promising following the creation of Soviet republics in Hungary and Bavaria in 1919. However, these fledgling regimes were quickly crushed. Moscow's ill-considered attempts to foment revolution in Germany in both 1921 and 1923 also failed. Consequently, the Bolsheviks' focus for the spread of revolution shifted from Europe to Asia.

Japan was viewed as especially promising. The Meiji Restoration of 1868 had encouraged the modernisation of Japan, kick-starting the industrialisation and formation of an urban working class, which, according to Marxist dogma, would inevitably lead to proletarian revolution. A higher level of economic and military development also made Japan a more attractive partner if it could be turned red. As Joseph Stalin, having become General Secretary of the Soviet Communist Party, told a Japanese newspaper in 1925, "An alliance between the Japanese and Soviet peoples would mark a decisive moment in the task of liberating the East. … Such a union would mark the beginning of the end for the great colonial powers, for world imperialism; and it would be invincible."[20]

There was therefore a strong incentive for the Bolsheviks to encourage revolution within Japan. Yet, even before they commenced doing so, Russia had already long served as a source of inspiration for Japanese radicals. Russian literature was exceptionally popular within Japan during the late 19th and early 20th centuries. Between 1868 and 1950, no fewer than 300 Russian writers were translated into Japanese.[21] This had political implications. As argued by Tatiana Linkhoeva, "Russian literature—its penetrating depiction of cultural homelessness and the suffering of commoners in the modern age—resonated with many people in Japan and contributed to the favorable reception of Russian revolutionary ideas among the Japanese reading public."[22] Further encouragement came with the Russian Revolution of 1905. It was one year later that the Japan Socialist Party was first founded, although it was banned within a year.

In many cases, Japanese were prompted to engage in benign activities, such as translating the works of Lev Tolstoi and Aleksandr Herzen. Yet some were inspired to copy the tactics of political terrorism that had become notorious in Tsarist Russia. Most prominent had been the assassination of Alexander II by Narodnaya Volya (People's Will) in 1881. Also notable were the assassinations of Minister of the Interior Vyacheslav K. Plehve in 1904 and Prime Minister Petr A. Stolypin in 1911.

Within Japan, a Nihilist Party of the Far East, which was modelled on Narodnaya Volya, was formed in 1882. However, it was not until 1910 that Russian-inspired political violence reached its apogee in Japan. This occurred with the High Treason Incident (*taigyaku jiken*), when a group of socialist anarchists, associated with the writer Kōtoku Shūsui, planned to assassinate Emperor Meiji by means of a bomb attack.[23] The plot was foiled, and, during the subsequent trial, it became clear that the group had been inspired by Russian revolutionaries. Kōtoku himself had well-established ties with Russian socialists and anarchists. He was a correspondent of Petr Kropotkin, who had asked Kōtoku in a 1907 letter to distribute his works of political agitation among Russian POWs still held in Japan after the Russo-Japanese War. Kanno Sugako, who was the only woman hanged for her role in the assassination attempt, admitted that her role models had been Vera Zasulich and Sofia Perovskaya, who themselves had been executed for their role in the killing of Tsar Alexander II in 1881.[24]

The High Treason Incident itself had a later echo since, in December 1923, in what is known as the Toranomon Incident, Nanba Daisuke, the son of a Diet member, attempted to assassinate Prince Regent Hirohito by firing a pistol at his carriage. The window shattered but Hirohito was uninjured. Following his arrest, Nanba confessed that he was seeking to avenge Kōtoku Shūsui. He also admitted to communist convictions and explained that he had been inspired by an article by Kawakami Hajime from 1921, in which the socialist author had emphasised the importance of terrorism in the success of the Russian Revolution.[25]

The excitement about Russia strengthened further after the October Revolution of 1917. According to anarchist Ōsugi Sakae, about whom we shall hear more shortly, "The second Russian Revolution made an enormously deep impression on the masses. The dispatches that appeared in the daily newspapers were read avidly and with great interest."[26] Enthusiasm was further fuelled by the unstable economic situation in Japan that was caused by inflation during World War I as well as by the post-war downturn. The result was an upsurge in unrest. Most prominent were the Rice Riots of July to September 1918, when high food prices led to hundreds of popular disturbances. There was also a big increase in labour activism, with more than 300 strikes between July and October 1919 alone.[27] Consequently, as the Bolsheviks sought to plant the seeds of revolution in Japan, they found they were working with fertile soil.

Prior to the establishment of official ties

The Bolsheviks did not have a base within Japan until the establishment of official relations in 1925. Prior to then, the Russian embassy in Tokyo remained in the hands of White officials. However, even before the signing of the Basic Convention, the Bolsheviks made efforts to gather intelligence on Japan and to incite revolutionary fervour.

In general, the Bolsheviks were quick to establish organs of state intelligence. On 20 December 1917, just six weeks after the October Revolution, the All-Russian Extraordinary Commission (Cheka) was set up under the leadership of Felix E. Dzerzhinskii. Its primary function was to eradicate domestic opposition, yet the Bolsheviks also emphasised international activities. Before the end of 1917, the People's Commissariat of Foreign Affairs (Narkomindel) had already been allocated two million roubles to promote international revolutionary movements.[28] As such, Narkomindel initially took on the role that was later performed by the Comintern. Additionally, in 1920, on the third anniversary of the Cheka's founding, Dzerzhinskii established a new Foreign Department (*Inostrannyi otdel* or INO) to run the organisation's foreign operations.

In Japan, the Bolsheviks' early priority was to gather intelligence on Japanese troop movements during the Siberian Intervention and to counteract Japanese spies in the Russian Far East. One notable figure was Aleksei N. Lutskii. Lutskii had been a staff-captain in the Russian Imperial Army. He served during the Russo-Japanese War and had begun to teach himself Japanese. After the conflict, the tsarist military dispatched him to Tokyo "for further study of Japanese customs, the Japanese language, and acquaintance with the organisation and methods of intelligence activities within Japan."[29] In Tokyo, Lutskii developed contacts with several Japanese officers. This proved useful because, after Lutskii had begun working for the Bolsheviks during the Civil War, one of these officers became a valuable source of information on Japanese intelligence activities within the Transbaikal and Maritime territories. Lutskii also began to handle intelligence and counterintelligence issues for the provisional government of Primor'e, a short-lived pro-Bolshevik authority based in Vladivostok. However, Lutskii's career as a spymaster was cut short when, in April 1920, he, along with fellow Bolsheviks Sergei G. Lazo and Vsevolod M. Sibirtsev, was captured by the Japanese. The exact circumstances of their deaths are debated but, according to the version propagated in the official history of Russian foreign intelligence, the three men were tortured by the Japanese, then burned alive in the firebox of a steam engine. The locomotive in which these martyrs of the revolution are said to have met their grisly end was preserved as a memorial in Ussuriisk, a city north of Vladivostok.[30]

Another prominent individual was Yakov Kh. Davtyan, the first head of the Cheka's INO, who placed considerable emphasis on establishing intelligence networks in the Far East. As he enthusiastically reported to Moscow in February 1923, "I have greatly developed our work ... We now have proper agents in Shanghai, Tianjin, Beijing, and Mukden. I'm putting in place a serious apparatus in Harbin. There is hope of penetrating Japanese intelligence." Moreover, he noted that, in Changchun, "Two people who will work for us are connected with the Japanese and the Russian White Guards."[31] Davtyan continued intelligence work after being replaced by Mikhail A. Trilisser as head of the INO, yet he increasingly found he did not have the stomach for it. Davtyan successfully transitioned from intelligence to diplomatic work, yet he fell victim to Stalin's Great Purge and was shot in July 1938.[32]

Japan's Siberian Intervention was certainly a threat to be monitored, yet it also represented an opportunity for the Bolsheviks. The intervention sent thousands of young soldiers far from home to fight in an unpopular conflict. What is more, most of the Japanese soldiers were from poor rural families. Many were aggrieved with their government after the Rice Riots of 1918, when they were forced to suppress protesting farmers whose plight they well understood.[33] Not surprisingly, many Japanese troops found appeal in the Bolsheviks' slogan of "peace, land, and bread." In December 1919, the head of the army's third section, Hoshino Shōzaburō, warned Prime Minister Hara Takashi that his troops were displaying worrying levels of sympathy for Bolshevik ideas. He urged that Japanese forces in Siberia be rotated frequently to reduce exposure to subversive ideology.[34] Seeking to exploit this situation, in 1922 the Bolsheviks set up a printing press in Chita and distributed propaganda leaflets to Japanese soldiers.[35] The aim was to hasten the end of the intervention but also to cultivate converts who would carry communism back with them to Japan.

The Bolsheviks also recognised the potential for Korea to be used to needle the Japanese. During Japan's Siberian Intervention, large numbers of Koreans were incorporated into pro-Bolshevik partisan groups where their knowledge of Japanese made them valuable as translators and informants.[36] The Bolsheviks also did their best to fan the flames of Korean resistance. In February 1921, the Korean People's Communist Party was formed in Khabarovsk, with its headquarters moved later to Chita.[37] This was in addition to the provisional government in Shanghai. German journalist Erich von Salzmann reported to the Japanese in September 1922 that, according to a Soviet diplomat named Rigin, "'the main object' of propaganda schools in Moscow, Tomsk, Omsk, Irkutsk and Tashkent was 'to stir up Korea against Japanese rule'."[38] The Japanese themselves estimated that, by the autumn of 1921, 150,000 Koreans in Manchuria and Siberia had fallen victim to "Bolshevik propaganda."[39] Furthermore, Moscow now provided generous financial support. In June 1920, Lenin issued 2 million roubles to Korean revolutionary Han Hyong-gwon to fund operations against the Japanese.[40] Additionally, a report sent by Korean militants to Commissar of Foreign Affairs Georgii V. Chicherin in October 1921 reveals that Moscow provided financing (5,300 Mexican dollars) to the Heroic Corps, a radical Korean nationalist group that sought to carry out terrorist attacks against the colonial authorities within Korea.[41]

Subversive activities within Japan remained difficult until the Soviet Union had an embassy, yet the Bolsheviks were still alive to opportunities during the early 1920s. One of these came with the Great Kantō Earthquake of September 1923, which left large sections of Tokyo in ruins and killed over 100,000. Despite its own financial troubles, the Soviet government allocated 200,000 roubles in gold for relief efforts and encouraged workers to provide further contributions. Emergency supplies were delivered via the *Lenin*, a steam ship, which arrived in Yokohama on 12 September, carrying "over 700,000 pounds of wheat, 180,000 pounds of rice, 100,000 pounds of fish and almost 800,000 pounds of other products."[42] Such aid was needed, yet the Japanese authorities quickly understood that the Soviets' motivations were more political than humanitarian, not least since the crew of the *Lenin* insisted that the supplies only be given to workers and that the Russians themselves must handle the distribution. The local authorities also complained that "the Russian representatives had made speeches that, it was feared, could lead to disturbances among the population."[43] Suspecting a Trojan horse, the Japanese turned the *Lenin* away.

After the establishment of official ties

Fear of communist penetration delayed the opening of official relations, meaning that, by the time the Soviet-Japan Basic Convention was signed in January 1925, the Soviet Union had already been recognised by most major powers, including Germany and France. The Bolsheviks worked hard to convince the Japanese that they had nothing to fear. In February 1920, Commissar of Foreign Affairs V. Chicherin reassured Japanese ambassadors that: "The Peoples of Russia cherish no aggressive desire against Japan. ... The Soviet government has no intention of interfering in the internal affairs of the Japanese people."[44]

In reality, right from the start, the Soviets saw an embassy in Tokyo as a forward base for its machinations. In an April 1925 speech to the Harbin Provincial Committee of the Communist Party, Viktor L. Kopp, who became the Soviet Union's first ambassador to Japan, confided that the Soviet-Japan Basic Convention would be "a mythical treaty ... merely giving us the possibility for the legal existence in the territory of Japan of the leading organ of the vanguard of the revolution." Kopp also spoke of "making use of Japan as a threat to America," and of his plans to establish socialist associations within Japan and to disseminate communist literature.[45]

The Russian embassy in Tokyo was finally handed over to the Soviets in 1925. Soviet consulates general followed in 1926 in Kōbe and Seoul, while consulates were opened in Hakodate, Otaru, Tsugaru, and Dairen.[46] This diplomatic infrastructure provided cover for the Soviets' "legal" intelligence officers, meaning spies with official cover and benefitting from diplomatic immunity. This contrasts with the "illegals" who conceal their status as state employees and often have elaborate "legends," including false name, citizenship, and background. The "legal" intelligence station within a country is known as the "*rezidentura*" and the head of its operations is the "*rezident*." Georgii S. Agabekov, who was *rezident* in Tehran before his defection in 1930, describes the hierarchy within Soviet embassies at the time:

> Theoretically the OGPU [as the Cheka was called from 1923] resident is subordinate to the ambassador, of whom he is officially the second secretary or something of the sort. But, in fact ... his authority often exceeds that of the ambassador. Greatly feared by his colleagues, even by the ambassador, he holds over their heads the perpetual fear of denunciation.[47]

In the case of the Soviet embassy in Tokyo, it took time for the "legal" *rezidentura* to become fully operational. According to the official history of the Russian foreign intelligence service, the Tokyo *rezidentura* began with just one officer and did not submit its first official report to the centre until January 1928. A second intelligence office was set up in the Soviet consulate in Hakodate.[48]

Despite its initially small scale, the Tokyo *rezidentura* made rapid progress. Its greatest success is reported to have been the running of a Japanese agent known as "Krotov," although the codenames "Kot" and "Kostya" were also used. "Krotov" is derived from the Russian word for "mole." The official history does not reveal if Krotov was ideological or mercenary, but it states that he was the *rezidentura*'s prize asset for more than a decade from the late 1920s. He is said to have been an employee of Japanese intelligence services, and, "thanks to his connections, he had access to practically all information of interest to Soviet intelligence at that time."[49] The documents he handed over included:

> annual mobilisation plans for military districts; plans for the redeployment of military units in Japan, Korea, and Manchuria; information about attitudes and political movements in the Imperial Army; cypher tables and books, not only from Japanese military intelligence, but also the United States, China, and Germany; Tokyo's air-defence plans; data on personnel changes in the Japanese military leadership; and details about the development of new types of weapon.[50]

Furthermore, Krotov is said to have passed on intelligence about the Japanese military plans "Otsu" and "Hei." These were plans for an attack on the Soviet Union which were prepared for implementation in 1932 after the seizure of Manchuria. Specifically, "In the first stage of military action against the USSR, it was planned to capture Nikol'sk-Ussuriiskii, Vladivostok, and Iman, then to launch attacks on Khabarovsk and Blagoveshchensk."[51]

The Krotov case also sheds light on how the OGPU ran their agents in Japan. Krotov was designated an agent of first-rank importance, so when Boris I. Gudz' took over as Tokyo *rezident* in 1933, he was ordered to do everything possible to make his life easier. Gudz' was also instructed not to use Krotov to recruit other Japanese. Meetings between handler and agent were conducted at night in isolated spots, such as beaches and parks, as well as once in a public toilet. When the Soviets wished to request a meeting, they would send a postcard to Krotov's home address with "greetings from Mr. Yamamoto." When someone other than the *rezident* was sent to meet Krotov, they would identify themselves by presenting one half of a torn ticket.[52]

Having faithfully photographed Japanese documents for the Soviets for many years, Krotov's behaviour suddenly changed. He began to request meetings in public places and "forgot" to photograph the most important sections of Japanese mobilisation plans. He also seemed under mental strain and turned up to one meeting drunk. Suspecting that Krotov had been discovered and that the Japanese were pressuring him to feed disinformation to the Soviets, the *rezidentura* cut ties, thus losing their best Japanese agent before Ozaki Hotsumi. No details are available about Krotov's subsequent fate.[53]

While the *rezidentura* in the embassy in Tokyo was the main station for "legal" intelligence operations in Japan after 1925, it was not the only one. A second hub was provided by the Soviet trade representative office. Moscow's justification for this second permanent delegation was that foreign trade was a state monopoly within the Soviet Union and supplementary government officials were needed to complete work that, in capitalist countries, would be done by private companies. With some reluctance, the Japanese government conceded to this request, and the Soviets' first trade representative arrived in Tokyo in December 1925. This was Yakov D. Yanson, who, as explained later, served as a Comintern agent and took an active role in organising left-wing agitation within Japan.[54]

Aside from benefitting from a permanent presence within Japan, Soviet operatives continued intelligence gathering against Japan elsewhere. For instance, when Chinese police controversially raided the Soviet embassy in Beijing in April 1927, secret documents were discovered that had been stolen from the British, Italian, and Japanese legations. According to the contemporary British ambassador to China, "those from Japanese [legation] are comprehensive and even include such details as seating arrangements at official dinners and record of conversations held between officials of Legation and visitors thereto."[55]

The opening of diplomatic relations in 1925 also meant that Japanese diplomats began to be stationed in Moscow. This offered further espionage opportunities. Some examples are revealed by Roman Kim, who began his career as an intelligence officer before becoming an influential writer of Soviet spy novels. Roman Kim was born in Vladivostok in 1899. Thanks to his father's friendship with Japanese diplomat Watanabe Rie (who was rumoured to be Japan's chief intelligence officer in the city), Kim was dispatched to Japan at age seven for his education. He thus learned fluent Japanese.[56] During the civil war, Kim was drafted into the White Army to serve in military intelligence, yet he soon switched to the Bolsheviks, for whom he worked as a spy in Japanese-occupied Vladivostok. After the Japanese withdrawal, Kim was ordered by Soviet intelligence to move to Moscow, where, after the establishment of diplomatic relations, he conducted operations against Japanese nationals. His cover job was as professor of Japanese literature at the Moscow Institute of Oriental Studies. Kim contributed to work directed at cracking Japanese codes, yet his most important contribution was in deception operations against Japanese military attachés in Moscow. "According to Kim's biographer Ivan Prosvetov, these operations were so successful that imperial Japan never had an accurate assessment of the Soviet military strength in the 1920s and 1930s."[57]

Kim was awarded the Order of the Red Star, yet this did not prevent his arrest in 1936 during Stalin's Great Terror on suspicion of conducting espionage for Japan. As Filip Kovacevic explains, after sustained torture, Kim confessed, not just to being a Japanese spy, but to being

> the Japanese station chief in the Soviet Union and an illegitimate son of the former Japanese foreign minister. Nothing could be further from the truth, and yet it was this outrageous lie that saved his life. He was set aside as a particularly valuable captive. By contrast, all the other counterintelligence officers from his unit, all of his superiors, and even the NKVD officer who had signed his arrest order, were shot.[58]

Kim remained in prison throughout the Second World War, but, so valued were his skills that, even when incarcerated, he was used to translate official Japanese documents. In December 1945, Kim was finally released and resumed his work in the area of influence operations against Japan. However, henceforth, he did so as the author of propagandistic novels. In *A Manuscript Found in Sunchon* (1951), Kim condemned post-war cooperation between US intelligence and former Japanese militarists. The main American character, who is given the name "Harshberger," is portrayed as a racist who murders underage girls during the Korean War. By contrast, the North Korean Communists are "courageous, humanistic, loyal, and patriotic."[59] The Soviet Ministry of Defence arranged for the novel to be published in Japan, where the Japanese Communist Party gave it a warm reception.[60]

It is evident that, starting in the 1920s, the Soviet Union viewed Japan as a prominent target for intelligence gathering and subversion. The response from the Japanese elite was, however, ambivalent. On one side were those who argued that the Bolsheviks' radical fervour was little more than a campaign strategy for seizing power and that, now that the revolution had been achieved, the Soviet Union would become an ordinary state with which Japan should engage. One prominent advocate of closer relations with the Soviet Union was Gotō Shinpei, who served as home minister, foreign minister, and mayor of Tokyo. Gotō saw the Bolshevik Revolution as a modernising development akin to the Meiji Restoration. An advocate of Pan-Asianism and an opponent of the Anglo-American powers, Gotō also welcomed the Bolsheviks' anti-Western tone. In his words, "Since communist Russia has stood for the cause of opposition to aggression and of coexistence and co-prosperity with other nations, there is no reason to fear bad effects from a rapprochement and to hesitate to open trade with the Soviets."[61] Gotō was so convinced of the benevolent nature of the Soviet state that he proposed a scheme for two million unemployed Japanese to be resettled in the Russian Far East. The project came to nothing but the territory discussed as the possible homeland for Japanese settlers was the area that later became the Soviet Union's (and now Russia's) Jewish Autonomous Region.[62]

By contrast, other Japanese leaders always viewed the Soviet Union as malevolent and considered its promotion of international communism to be a serious threat to Japan's *kokutai* (national body politic). Indeed, the communist threat was a key driver of Japan's notorious Peace Preservation Law, which was passed in April 1925, just months after the signing of the Basic Convention with the Soviet Union. When arguing for the Peace Preservation Law in the national Diet, Home Minister Wakatsuki Reijirō explicitly referred to the establishment of formal relations with the Soviet Union and warned of the "opportunities for extremist activists" that this created.[63] The law significantly restricted individual freedoms, with Article 1 stating that:

> Anyone who has formed a society with the objective of altering the national polity or the form of government or denying the system of private property, and anyone who has joined such a society with full knowledge of its object, shall be liable to imprisonment with or without hard labor for a term not exceeding ten years.[64]

In 1928, an amendment raised the maximum penalty from 10 years to death. Once again, the communist menace was invoked, with Prime Minister Tanaka Gi'ichi warning that Soviet operatives were already active within Japan and attempting to infiltrate the political system.[65] The Peace Preservation Law is therefore a notable instance of the threat of Soviet espionage having a marked impact on Japanese politics.

The Comintern

When considering Soviet penetration of Japan in the years after the Bolshevik Revolution, special attention must be given to the Communist International (Comintern). Founded in Moscow in March 1919, the Comintern's mission was "to build a 'world party' of communists dedicated to the armed overthrow of capitalist private property and its replacement by a system of collective ownership and production."[66] In theory, the Comintern was independent of Soviet government control. This was consistent with the organisation's claim to be promoting international revolution rather than the interests of the Soviet state. The pretence of independence was also important because it enabled Soviet diplomats to claim that the Comintern's activities did not violate the anti-subversion clause of the Soviet-Japan Basic Convention of 1925.[67]

This claim of autonomy was never convincing. At the time, the *North-China Daily News* wrote of the Comintern that it may be "technically true that the latter is not a Soviet Government organization; but in fact it might as well be said that the sun has nothing to do with the maggots it breeds in a dead dog as to pretend that the two are not inseparably linked."[68] This is an arresting image, yet, if anything, it underplays Moscow's role. This is because the Soviet state not only inspired communist parties around the world, but, in many cases, actively managed them.

The lack of true internationalism in the Comintern was apparent from its founding congress. This has been described as a "mostly fraudulent piece of Russian revolutionary theater," since it featured only five delegates from abroad.[69] The "Japanese" delegate was Comrade Rutgers, whose qualification was that he had once visited Japan.[70] The Executive Committee of the Communist International (ECCI) was dominated by Moscow, and "Foreign communists were called upon simply to ratify decisions previously taken by the Russian delegation."[71] Additionally, the ECCI dispatched representatives to member parties. Known as the "eyes of Moscow," these officials were assigned to "meddle" in overseas communist movements and reported back on their activities.[72] This manual control intensified after Joseph Stalin became General Secretary of the Soviet Communist Party in 1922. He made explicit his view that supporting international communism meant supporting the Soviet state, arguing that "an *internationalist* is one who is ready to defend the U.S.S.R. without reservation, without wavering, unconditionally."[73] Consequently, by the end of the 1920s, the Comintern had been "turned from a living political body into a dead mechanism which on the one hand is capable only of swallowing orders in Russian and on the other of regurgitating them in different languages."[74]

Just as Moscow's dominance was ingrained from the start, so was the Comintern's commitment to clandestine activity. This is apparent from the "Twenty-One Conditions," which, in 1920, specified the Comintern's rules for all member parties. Most controversial was condition 3, which stated that "Communists can place no faith in bourgeois legality" and that all communist parties must therefore employ illegal, as well as legal, means to promote revolutionary change. Further conditions required all members "to conduct vigorous and systematic propaganda in the army," as well as to implant communist cells within trade unions.[75]

Much of the covert activity was handled by the Comintern's Department of International Communications (*Otdel Mezhdunarodnoi Svyazi* or OMS). As well as allocating funding to communist parties, this department distributed propaganda, forged passports, and oversaw foreign espionage operations.[76] The OMS also conducted training, including at a secret school in Mytishchi, just outside Moscow, where foreign Comintern agents were instructed in the use of coded radio communications.[77]

Within Japan during the 1920s, the Comintern's primary mission was to establish a local Communist Party and to shape its development. Initially, the Comintern's operations in East Asia were conducted from Irkutsk, but, in May 1920, a Far Eastern Bureau was established in Shanghai with separate sections for China, Korea, and Japan. The first head was Vladimir D. Vilenskii-Sibiryakov, though he was soon replaced by Grigorii N. Voitinskii. Unable to have Comintern officers with official cover in Japan until 1925, the Far Eastern Bureau relied upon messengers, usually Koreans, to contact Japanese radicals.

The task of creating an illegal Communist Party within interwar Japan was not straightforward. In part, this was because of the well-resourced domestic security apparatus, especially the *Kenpeitai* (military police). The task was also made difficult by the fragmentary nature of radical left-wing politics. As noted previously, there was undoubtedly a degree of revolutionary fervour within Japan during the first decades of the 20th century. However, many of the most prominent figures were reform-minded socialists or anarchists, and thus not neatly aligned with Moscow. The Comintern's initial approach therefore became to court Japanese leftists of all stripes and, with time, to persuade them to abandon the "infantile sickness of anarcho-syndicalism" and to convert to Marxism-Leninism.[78]

In 1920, the Comintern ordered one of their Korean agents, Yi Chung-rim, who was a Meiji University student, to contact Japanese socialists Yamakawa Hitoshi and Sakai Toshihiko and convince them to visit Shanghai. However, since Yamakawa and Sakai were not yet familiar with the Comintern's representatives in the Far East, they were hesitant and declined the offer. Instead, they suggested that Yi contact Ōsugi Sakae, since they judged him sufficiently "reckless" to make the trip.[79]

Ōsugi was a noted anarchist who published several radical periodicals and translated the works of Kropotkin and Bakunin into Japanese. He was also involved in setting up the first Esperanto school in Japan. As befits the popular image of an anarchist, Ōsugi had a wild lifestyle. He was notorious for his drinking, gambling, and sexual appetite. In his autobiography, Ōsugi was open about his youthful addiction to masturbation ("Two or three times a day"), and he was expelled from cadet school for homosexual behaviour.[80] As an adult, he abandoned homosexuality and married a woman, yet he remained sexually adventurous. He "formed a lovers' quadrangle with his wife and two mistresses, Itō Noe, the editor of *Seitō* [a feminist magazine], and Kamichika Ichiko, a journalist."[81] However, this experiment ended in disaster, as Kamichika became overwhelmed with jealousy and stabbed Ōsugi in the throat in a teahouse in Hayama. Ōsugi spent several days in hospital and Kamichika was sentenced to two years in jail.

Ōsugi himself served several stints in prison for his political activities, including a three-month term just before he was approached by the Comintern in June 1920. As predicted, Ōsugi was bold enough to establish contact, not least because he was in financial difficulties and had been forced to suspend publication of his newspaper, *Rōdō Undō* (*The Labour Movement*). Arriving in Shanghai in October, Ōsugi met several Comintern representatives, including Voitinskii, and accepted 2,000 yen for the relaunch of his publication. In return, Ōsugi was required to add two Communists, Kondō Eizō and Takatsu Masamichi, to the staff of *Rōdō Undō*. Consequently, from the start of 1921, Ōsugi's anarchist newspaper began to include at least some Bolshevik material, giving Moscow a propaganda outlet within Japan.[82]

This relationship did not last. Ōsugi never accepted Marxism-Leninism, and, angered by the Bolsheviks' mistreatment of Russian anarchists, he began to distance himself from Moscow. In any case, Ōsugi's political activities were brought to a premature end on 16 September 1923, when, in the aftermath of the Great Kantō Earthquake, Ōsugi, Itō Noe, and his six-year-old nephew, Tachibana Munekazu, were murdered by *Kenpeitai* officer Amakasu Masahiko. Ōsugi and Itō were badly beaten before all three were strangled. The bodies were then stripped naked, wrapped in *tatami* mat coverings, and dumped in an abandoned well.[83] As if this were not awful enough, Ōsugi's ashes were stolen from the funeral home by the nationalist group, *Taika-kai*, and were never recovered.[84]

After Ōsugi Sakae, the next figure to play a prominent connecting role between the Comintern and Japan was Kondō Eizō, the communist who had been assigned to work for Ōsugi's *Rōdō Undō*. Kondō was a close associate of Yamakawa Hitoshi and Sakai Toshihiko, who, after their initial hesitance, had moved closer to the communist camp by the start of 1921. In April of that year, all three were involved in a meeting in a *soba* restaurant near Tokyo's Ōmori station, at which an initial Japanese Communist Committee was created. All participants agreed that this group should submit to the leadership of the Comintern, and Kondō was selected as the group's "secret messenger" to be sent to Shanghai without delay. On this journey, Kondō carried an English translation of the committee's prospectus, which was typed on thin paper and hidden within the binding of an English novel. Into his clothes was also sewn a small piece of silk on which the names of the committee's members were written.[85]

In Shanghai, Kondō met the Comintern representatives and submitted a proposed budget of 20,000 yen per month for the fledgling Japanese party's organisational expenses, as well as for issuing propaganda and covering some members' living costs. The officials of the Far Eastern Bureau agreed in principle but said they would need to confirm with Moscow. In the meantime, Kondō was given 6,500 yen, of which 5,000 yen was in US dollars. Kondō explains that the 5,000 yen was to support the activities of the new communist grouping, while 1,000 yen was for himself and 500 yen for Ōsugi, who, at that time, was still cooperating with the Comintern.[86]

This initial financing was essential for getting the new Japanese Communist Party off the ground, yet, as Kondō transported the funds back to Japan in May 1921, he revealed himself to be far from a master conspirator. Aboard ship, Kondō became acquainted with a Polish man who had lived in Moscow. When they landed at Shimonoseki and passed through customs, Kondō made himself useful by serving as the Polish man's interpreter. This, however, caused Kondō to miss the express train to Tokyo. It was then that Kondō committed what he described as a "once-in-a-lifetime failure."[87]

With time to kill until the night express and with the Comintern's money in his pocket, Kondō installed himself in a restaurant and set about drinking with a woman he describes as a "geisha." Enjoying the pleasures of being back in Japan, Kondō got drunk and belatedly realised that the train was soon to depart. He raced to the station in the company of his new friend but missed the train and ripped up his ticket in disgust. This scene was witnessed by a detective. Kondō was followed back to the restaurant, where he resumed drinking, before taking the "geisha" off to bed. He was woken in the night by four police officers, who discovered the money and bundled the half-cut communist off to jail. Kondō gave a fake name and claimed he had won the money at the horse races in Shanghai. However, the police placed a 16-year-old informer in his cell and Kondō foolishly asked the boy, who was soon to be released, to deliver a coded message to fellow communist Sakai Toshihiko in Tokyo. When this was discovered, Kondō came clean and admitted that the funds were from the Comintern to finance the establishment of a Communist Party within Japan. Remarkably, the money was then returned, and Kondō was permitted to continue to Tokyo. Kondō suspected that the police did this because following the money would enable them to track the group's underground activity.[88]

The farce was not quite over. Kondō sent fellow communist Shigeda Yōichi to Shanghai in November 1921 to update the Comintern on developments within Japan. However, documents sent with Shigeda were intercepted. As a result, the Japanese police were waiting when Shigeda returned to Japan in the company of B. Grey, an English Comintern agent, whose task was to deliver a further 7,000 yen to the Japanese communists. Grey claimed the funds were to purchase medical instruments, yet his notebook was found to contain the names of several communists, including Kondō.[89]

It was far from an auspicious beginning, but, with contacts with the Comintern firmly established, a Japanese Communist Party was now ready for launch. This officially occurred on 15 July 1922. This is the same Japanese Communist Party (JCP) whose representatives continue to sit in the Japanese parliament today. In its 100-year history, the JCP has undergone significant changes, including distancing itself from the Soviet Union from the early 1960s.[90] Yet, as Robert

Scalapino explains, "the evidence is overwhelming that the Japanese Communist Party, in its origins, was the creature of the Comintern and hence of the Soviet Union."[91] In addition to the provision of funds,

> the [JCP's] initial party program was drafted on the basis of detailed discussions with Soviet leaders in Moscow, and its main provisions most certainly had been "cleared" with them; all members of the party, moreover, recognized that they were a *branch* of an international movement having its headquarters in Moscow.[92]

In subsequent years, Moscow's grip remained firm, with the Comintern instructing JCP leaders to pursue a two-stage revolution—as had occurred in Russia—and to seek the toppling of the Japanese emperor. To begin with, the Japanese party was required to send a messenger to Shanghai every two weeks.[93] However, after diplomatic relations were established, management of Japan's communist movement could be secretly conducted from Soviet legations within Japan. From 1925, Soviet trade representative Yakov D. Yanson served as the main contact for Japanese communists. To give just one example, Kitaura Sentarō, a labour activist, admits that he met with Yanson every two weeks to receive guidance on how to proceed with union activism. Yanson also gave him 300 yen per month for organising a youth movement.[94]

Another source of control was education. In 1921, the Comintern created the Communist University of the Toilers of the East, which trained such notable alumni as Ho Chi Minh and Deng Xiaoping. In Japan's case, around 40 youths were dispatched annually to Moscow to attend the university. Their courses lasted a year or two and they received instruction in Marxist theory as well as in practical matters such as party management and propaganda techniques. It was also here that the students met prominent Japanese communists in exile, such as Katayama Sen and, later, Nosaka Sanzō, who himself deserves closer attention.[95]

Nosaka was born in 1892 as the son of a prosperous merchant. He grew up in comfortable circumstances and attended Keiō University. It was here that he became interested in left-wing politics. After university, Nosaka left Japan for England, where, in 1920, he became a founding member of the Communist Party of Great Britain. Chased out of the country by the police, Nosaka spent time in Russia, before returning to Japan in 1922.[96]

Nosaka quickly became one of the JCP's leading lights, but he was arrested in 1928 as part of the March 15 Incident. This was a mass crackdown on communists and socialists by the government of Prime Minister Tanaka Gi'ichi. Nosaka pleaded ill health and was released for medical treatment in 1931, whereupon he fled to the Soviet Union. According to some accounts, Nosaka evaded police surveillance by disguising himself as a woman and receiving assistance from make-up artists from the Takarazuka Revue, the famous Hyōgō theatre troupe that specialises in cross-dressing.[97] In Moscow, having presumably reverted to more conventional attire, Nosaka worked for the Comintern and became a member of its executive committee. After the Japanese Communist Party was legalised in 1945, Nosaka returned home. He became JCP leader in 1955 and served for decades as a member of the Japanese parliament. It was only in 1982 that he finally stepped down as JCP chairman, and he died, at the age of 101, in November 1993.[98]

The reason why this JCP stalwart concerns us here is because of post-Soviet revelations about Nosaka's role as a Comintern agent. Nosaka is said to have had "the air of a British gentleman," and, as party leader, he had promised to create "a lovable Communist Party."[99] However, evidence that came to light during the early 1990s exposed a very different figure.

The documents in question were discovered by Japanese journalists in the archives of the Communist Party of the Soviet Union. After reaching Moscow in 1931, Nosaka was deployed to the United States for a period of four years. Three coded letters that were sent by Nosaka from New York to Moscow in 1934 reveal the nature of his work there. Nosaka requested money and support staff to set up a large-scale communist network on the West Coast "by setting up 'sailors' clubs' in Los Angeles, Seattle and other cities." The letters also mention a plan to send Japanese and American recruits to Japan to establish a store in Yokohama to serve as a communist front.[100]

During the Second World War, Nosaka was active in communist-held Yan'an. There, under the name Okano Susumu, Nosaka conducted psychological warfare against Japanese troops fighting in

China. As well as propaganda, this included running camps for re-education of Japanese POWs. The aim was to turn the POWs away from militarism and have them embrace communism before sending them back to Japan at the end of the war. According to Koji Ariyoshi, a US Army sergeant who observed these communist re-education efforts in Yan'an, "The Japanese national who undoubtedly contributed most in the war against Japanese militarism is Sanzo Nosaka."[101]

It was, however, the post-Soviet revelations about Nosaka's time in Moscow during the 1930s that created the real scandal. Nosaka's role in the Soviet capital was as liaison between the Comintern and the JCP. In this capacity, he worked alongside Yamamoto Kenzō, another communist who had fled Japan shortly before Nosaka. Yamamoto was arrested by the Soviet authorities in 1939, and Nosaka reported that he had died of pneumonia in 1942. Nosaka claimed that he had tried to help his comrade, and, in 1973, he even proposed that a monument be built in Yamamoto's memory. It was therefore a shock when it was discovered that it was Nosaka who had falsely denounced Yamamoto.

The proof was a letter sent by Nosaka to the head of the Comintern Georgii M. Dimitrov on 23 February 1939. Nosaka informed Dimitrov that he suspected Yamamoto of being an anti-Soviet spy and he volunteered to provide evidence against him. Nosaka claimed that Yamamoto had suspiciously evaded arrest on several occasions during the 1920s in Japan. He also stated that a Japanese student, who was travelling to Moscow on an itinerary arranged by Yamamoto, had been detained in Shanghai. Due to these allegations, Yamamoto was arrested, charged as a Japanese spy, and executed in 1939.[102]

Nosaka's transgressions continued after the war. In 1952, Nosaka submitted a damning report to the Chinese Communist Party on Itō Ritsu, a fellow Japanese communist and Nosaka's rival for the JCP leadership. One of the suspicions raised against Itō was that he was a police informer and may have played a role in providing information that led to the arrest of Richard Sorge in Tokyo in October 1941. This is discussed in chapter 8. Following Nosaka's report, Itō was arrested. Although Nosaka is alleged to have requested his rival's execution, Itō was kept alive, serving 27 years in a Chinese prison before being released in 1979.[103]

After these revelations came to light in 1992, Nosaka was stripped of his honorary chairmanship of the JCP and expelled from the party. The new JCP leadership added allegations of its own, claiming Nosaka had maintained secret contacts with the Soviet Union after the JCP had broken with Moscow in 1962. JCP chairman Fuwa Tetsuzō "claimed that Nosaka undertook such dealings as a KGB agent serving Soviet interests while undermining the JCP."[104]

Returning to the Comintern's activities in Japan during the 1920s, aside from creating the JCP, another priority was spreading propaganda. To this end, Kondō Eizō used Moscow's money to establish a literary agency. This was in line with the Comintern's aim of creating a global network of pro-communist newspapers, film production companies, and publishing houses. These international efforts were coordinated by International Workers' Relief, a Comintern offshoot founded by German communist Willi Münzenberg in 1921. Within Japan, by 1925, several publications had been placed under communist control, including the *Rōdō Shinbun*, *Musansha Shinbun*, and a journal called *Marxshugi*.[105]

In August 1921, Kondō established a secret group called the Gyōmin Kyōsantō (Men of the Dawn Communist Party), whose core members were students of Waseda University. This group engaged in radical political activities of the sort that became increasingly common during the first half of the 1920s. Japan's Justice Ministry recorded 291 incidents related to "social thought" between 1922 and 1925, and claimed that all of them had been instigated by the Comintern.[106] One example was in November 1921, when large-scale Japanese army drills were conducted in the Tokyo area. In the hope of emulating Russian Bolsheviks' success in recruiting soldiers, the Gyōmin Kyōsantō delivered hundreds of political pamphlets to the troops' billets. These carried slogans such as, "the time for your self-consciousness has come. Don't kill your brothers. Arise and strike. Disobey your senior officers! Communist Party HQ."[107]

Another focus was the trade union movement. In 1928, the communist-linked Nihon Rōdō Kumiai Zenkoku Kyōgikai (Zenkyō) was launched. This radical trade union sought to cripple the Japanese economy by targeting key sectors. Their strategy was to create cells in important factories, then instigate strikes, demonstrations, and sabotage. Violence was encouraged.

> For example, power plant assault units and car destruction units were organized in connection with the Tōkyō Transport Workers' strike. At one point, an assassination squad was created, a band that was supposed to operate against spies and betrayers. An effort was also made to organize a self-defense force.[108]

Ahead of the elections in 1930, Zenkyō proclaimed that the goal was not to control the Japanese parliament but to destroy it.[109]

As well as soldiers and factory workers, Japanese fishermen were a target. Under the fishery agreement of 1928, Japanese boats were permitted access to waters along the Soviet Pacific coast and thus visited Soviet territory. During these sojourns, the Comintern attempted to radicalise the crews.

> The propaganda was disseminated by pistol-packing Japanese and Korean Communists, who came to the Japanese fishing sheds allegedly under the protection of the Soviet secret police, made speeches and distributed printed material. ... If anyone ... spoke up in protest, he was immediately arrested and after a beating at the G.P.U. [office] was deported to Japan.[110]

It is clear from this extract that the Comintern was active in its work against Japan and saw the country as promising ground for a revolution. However, while Moscow expended considerable effort and the Japanese authorities were alarmed by the threat of communism, one should not exaggerate the JCP's success during the 1920s and 1930s. For a start, the Japanese police and *Kenpeitai* were effective in suppressing and infiltrating the communist movement. The March 15 Incident of 1928 has already been mentioned, when over 1,200 socialists and communists were arrested and 500 prosecuted, including Nosaka Sanzō. Prior to this, in June 1923, following clashes at Waseda University, a wave of arrests had already removed most party members in Tokyo. These detentions were so devastating that remaining members decided to disband the JCP. However, when this was discovered by the Comintern, the Japanese communists were rebuked by Voitinskii in Shanghai and ordered to quickly reestablish the party. This was dutifully done, but further arrests came in summer 1932, followed by yet another relaunch in January 1933. A cycle therefore began. The JCP built itself up, only to be decimated by arrests. It was then reseeded by Japanese students sent home from Moscow, who were themselves detained by the police.[111]

The severity of this repression forced the JCP to resort to desperate measures, especially after revision of the Peace Preservation Law in 1928 to enable imposition of the death penalty. JCP leaders began carrying firearms and talked of committing suicide rather than allowing themselves to fall into the hands of the police. Secrecy was also emphasised, and "at one point the code used for communicating with the Shanghai Bureau was carried in the muzzle of a pistol."[112] However, weakened by arrests, the JCP was far from exemplary in its functioning as a secret organisation. For example, when a senior party member was detained on 18 March 1929, an organisational chart for the JCP's operations in Tokyo was discovered at his house. This led to the arrest of another party leader, who was found to be in possession of the roster for the entire party. Although this list of names was in code, it was soon cracked by the police.[113]

Another problem for the JCP was that Kondō's antics in Shimonoseki were far from the only case of the misuse of Comintern funds. There were rumours that leading figures within the JCP and Zenkyō lived in luxury and were engaged in "the squandering of funds at houses of prostitution."[114] In one case from 1923, Japanese communist Yoshihara Tarō was given diamonds and a large sum of money to transport from Moscow to Tokyo. He disappeared en route.[115] The same problem bedevilled Soviet efforts to undermine Japanese rule in Korea. Kim Rip, one of the leaders of the Soviet-supported Korean government in exile, was accused of using Moscow's money to buy himself a farm in China "and to establish himself in luxurious quarters in Shanghai with a Chinese concubine."[116] These allegations led to his assassination.

Restricted by police action and its own indiscipline, formal membership of the JCP never climbed above 1,000 in the pre-war era.[117] Indeed, as Japanese authoritarianism reached its apogee during the second half of the 1930s, the party became largely dormant. The final straw was when Hakamada Satomi, another student returnee from Moscow, was arrested in 1935. From that point until the end of the war, Japanese communism existed less as an organised party, and more as the "secret thoughts nurtured in the minds of a few 'true believers', most of whom were in prison."[118]

The Tanaka Memorial

One further case from the 1920s deserves our attention. This is the so-called Tanaka Memorial. In this context, a "memorial" (*jōsōbun*) is a formal report to the emperor. This one was supposedly written following the Eastern Conference, which was held in Tokyo between 27 June and 7 July 1927 to discuss the situation in China. The document is long—34,000 characters in Japanese—and has 21 sections that address a wide range of topics.[119] However, the reason why the document is notorious and was described by Leon Trotsky as "one of the most important political documents of modern history" is because it also sets out a grand design for the expansion of Japanese imperialism throughout Asia and beyond.[120] Its most famous line states: "To conquer China Japan must first conquer Manchuria-Mongolia. To conquer the world, Japan must first conquer China."[121] Consequently, when Japan imposed its control over Manchuria in 1931, launched the Second Sino-Japanese War in 1937, and attacked Pearl Harbor in 1941, it looked as if Japan was acting in accordance with this blueprint.

The memorial was purportedly written by Baron Tanaka Gi'ichi, who was then both prime minister and foreign minister. Interestingly, Tanaka had a strong connection with Russia. He had lived there as a young army officer between 1897 and 1902, was fluent in Russian, and was well-acquainted with Russia's military, politics, and culture. However, while describing himself as "a friend of Russia," Tanaka took a cold-eyed view of geopolitics and believed that Japan needed to confront Russia to secure its position in Korea and expand influence over Manchuria. For this reason, Tanaka had been a leading proponent of Japan's Siberian Intervention.[122]

There are various accounts of how the Tanaka Memorial, a supposedly confidential document, came to global attention. According to one version, a Chinese delegation visiting Japan to attend a conference in Kyoto in October 1929 purchased it from "a friend in Tokyo" for 50,000 yen.[123] However, Soviet intelligence also claimed credit for its discovery. According to the official history of the Russian foreign intelligence service, the acquisition of the Tanaka Memorial represented the "finest hour" of the Harbin *rezidentura*. Praise is given to an officer named Ivan T. Ivanov-Perekrest, who is said to have had "extensive connections among Japanese military personnel, employees of counterintelligence, and Chinese working at Japanese institutions."[124] Yet, at the same time, the official history says that the Tanaka Memorial was acquired by the Soviet *rezidentura* in Seoul. In this second case, credit is given to the OGPU's Ivan A. Chichaev, who recruited a Japanese police official by posing as an employee of the firm Churin & Co. Consequently, the official history presents the Tanaka Memorial as an unusual case in which an important secret document was obtained almost simultaneously by two separate *rezidenturas*.[125]

Leon Trotsky, who was People's Commissar for Military Affairs from 1918 to 1925, offered an entirely different account of how Soviet intelligence acquired the document. In an article he was still writing when he had his unfortunate encounter with an ice axe in August 1940, Trotsky states that the Tanaka Memorial was photographed by a Japanese agent of the OGPU in the Ministry of Naval Affairs in Tokyo, then brought to Moscow as an undeveloped film. This operation was overseen by spy chief Felix Dzerzhinskii himself, who, according to Trotsky, "stated ecstatically that this document in and of itself could provoke international upheavals, events of vast importance, war between Japan and the United States."[126]

Trotsky recounted that Dzerzhinskii, "speaking with a Polish accent which always became thicker as he grew excited," explained that the agent had been working for the OGPU for some time, had excellent access to government files, and was known for his "great precision and conscientiousness in fulfilling his obligations as a foreign spy."[127] It is possible that this was agent Krotov, who, as mentioned earlier, was the star recruit of the Tokyo *rezidentura* during the late 1920s.

It is difficult to verify either of these versions, but Trotsky's account includes some puzzling elements. He claims Dzerzhinskii told him about the Tanaka Memorial in the summer or early autumn of 1925—that is, two years before it was supposedly written. His explanation is that the document was composed long before it was signed, and that it was sent to Moscow prior to it being submitted to the emperor. Another surprising feature is that Trotsky says that an OGPU technician had to be sneaked onto the premises of the ministry to copy the document, as the Japanese agent was insufficiently skilled in photography.[128] This would have been quite a feat in the police state that Japan had become in the second half of the 1920s.

However, the most fundamental question about the Tanaka Memorial is not how it was acquired but whether it is genuine. Right from the start, the Japanese authorities insisted it was fake. The Soviets, by contrast, affirmed it was real. Indeed, modern-day Russian school history textbooks still teach that the Tanaka Memorial is an authentic Japanese government document.[129] Additionally, Trotsky, who was certainly not a friend of the Soviet state in 1940, was unequivocal in stating that "The Tanaka Memorial is not a forgery."[130]

Despite Russian insistence, the Tanaka Memorial is almost certainly a fake. For a start, the occasionally rough language does not accord with the formality expected in a memorial. The style also does not match samples of Tanaka Gi'ichi's writing.[131] Additionally, there are factual errors, such as when stating the volume of Japanese investment in Manchuria and when recounting the history of Tanaka's overseas visits. The biggest clanger is that the memorial refers to a meeting between Emperor Taishō and senior statesman Yamagata Aritomo after the signing of the Nine-Power Treaty on 6 February 1922. This is despite the fact that, by this date, Emperor Taishō had retired from active duties due to mental incapacity and Prince Yamagata was already dead.[132] It is also revealing that no Japanese original has ever been discovered. All the Japanese versions are translations from other languages.[133]

This still leaves the question of who was responsible. Stanislav Levchenko, who served as head of the active measures group in the Tokyo *rezidentura* prior to defecting to the United States in 1979, claims that the Tanaka Memorial was a Soviet forgery.[134] They certainly had the means. Within the international section of the OGPU was a special department, known as *Kaneva*, which specialised in forgeries. These were used for influence operations but also to raise funds, since many fabrications were sold abroad for foreign currency.[135] There are also other examples of the Soviets using forged documents against Japan, including in 1960, ahead of the revision of the US-Japan Security Treaty, when Moscow propagated a fake secret agreement between Japanese Prime Minister Kishi Nobusuke and the US secretary of state that supposedly permitted the use of Japanese troops anywhere in Asia.[136] Furthermore, the Soviet Union had a motive, because the Tanaka Memorial was a powerful instrument to incite tensions between Japan and the capitalist powers, especially the United States, which feared Japan's expansionism.

However, other evidence suggests it was the Chinese who created the document. The first published copy was in Chinese and was printed in December 1929 in a Nanking magazine with ties to the Kuomintang.[137] Two Chinese also claimed involvement in disseminating the document. These were Cai Zhikan, a Taiwanese businessman in Japan, and Wang Jiazhen, who was an official on the staff of Zhang Xueliang, who was then ruler of Manchuria. Japanese scholars propose that Cai may have procured information about the proposals discussed at Japan's Eastern Conference. These were then sent to Mukden, where Wang wrote them up in the format of an official Japanese memorial. According to this version, the original source was therefore genuine, but the document's embellishment and presentation as the Tanaka Memorial was fraudulent.[138] Another factor pointing away from Moscow is that the document contains criticism of Soviet imperialism.

Even if the Soviets were not the authors of the Tanaka Memorial, they certainly helped propagate it and ensure that it retained public attention for years to come. Trotsky claimed that he himself proposed that the Tanaka Memorial be translated into English and published in the United States. Since the Soviet Union did not have an embassy in Washington until official relations were established in 1933, this was done with the assistance of Amtorg, the Soviet trade office in New York.[139]

The Comintern, for its part, contributed by publishing the Tanaka Memorial in full in its official journal in December 1931 and by translating it into five languages. In March 1932, they used a front organisation in San Francisco to publish the document in the United States in the *Pan-Pacific Worker*, a Communist magazine.[140] In the same year, a copy was smuggled into Japan, where this "official Japanese document" was translated into Japanese by members of the JCP and distributed as a pamphlet entitled "Naked Japanese imperialism exposed in all its audacity."[141]

These Soviet efforts were effective, especially in the United States, where there was strong appetite for anti-Japanese fare. In April 1940,

Joseph Taussig, who was then a rear admiral in the US Navy, testified to Congress that the Tanaka Memorial was real. In November the next year, *Click*, a popular magazine, ran an article describing the document as "Japan's Mein Kampf" and predicting that "America is next on Japan's list of victims!"[142] The attack on Pearl Harbor followed the next month. After that, the US needed no encouragement to publicise the Tanaka Memorial, since it became part of US wartime propaganda. Congress approved a resolution to make the text available to the broader public. The version they selected had been produced by the World Peace Movement in New York, which was later identified as a Soviet front organisation. The Tanaka Memorial also featured in the well-known US propaganda film, *Know Your Enemy—Japan* (1944), which was directed by Frank Capra.[143]

The Tanaka Memorial therefore had a major impact on how Americans understood the war. It reinforced the view that the attack on Pearl Harbor was part of a premeditated plan, and not an act of desperation taken by Japan as it sought to break the ring of containment and retain territorial gains in China. It is not far-fetched to suggest that US belief in the Tanaka Memorial may have contributed to support for the decision to attack Japan with nuclear weapons.

* * *

In short, by the mid-1930s, the Soviet Union had accumulated valuable experience of intelligence-gathering and subversive operations against Japan. As we will see in the next chapter, this provided a platform from which Soviet intelligence was able to reach new heights as the outbreak of conflict between Russia and Japan once more approached.

7

SOVIET INTELLIGENCE AT NOMONHAN

Fears of Japanese aggression had existed since the October Revolution of 1917. These intensified in September 1931, when Japan's Kwantung Army staged an attack on the South Manchuria Railway to justify the occupation of Manchuria and pave the way for the creation of the puppet state of Manchukuo in March 1932. With Manchuria under Japan's control, the Soviet leadership was alarmed at the prospect of a Japanese attack against Soviet territory. Aleksandr A. Troyanovskii, who served as Soviet plenipotentiary in Tokyo from 1927 to 1933, reported that "the danger is now very great and became so when the Japanese 'line of defence' came right up to our frontiers."[1] Troyanovskii's assessment was that, after Manchuria and China itself, Japan planned to seize the Soviet Far East. Troyanovskii supported his claim with reference to the Tanaka Memorial, showing no indication that he suspected the document of being a fabrication.

Troyanovskii's emphasis on the Tanaka Memorial was misplaced, but he was not wrong in suggesting that Japan was contemplating war on the Soviet Union. Vice President of the Privy Council Baron Hiranuma said in January 1933 that "the army advocated war with Russia."[2] War Minister Araki Sadao, who was appointed in December 1931, also stated: "If the Soviet does not cease to annoy us, I shall have to purge Siberia as one cleans a room of flies."[3]

Moscow's sense of alarm was especially pronounced given Soviet weakness at the beginning of the 1930s. The first five-year plan had been declared complete in 1932, yet its successes were largely fictional. The forced collectivisation of agriculture from 1928 had left the Soviet Union in a state of famine and unrest. Moreover, the Soviet Union lacked military capabilities in the Far East, with no Pacific Fleet nor air force in the region prior to 1932. Not surprisingly, information about this situation inspired confidence within Japan. In swaggering tones, a Kwantung Army report predicted that, in the event of conflict with Japanese forces, "internal conditions in Russia would seem to be such that it could not do much more than engage in propaganda work."[4]

Desperate to buy time, the Soviet Union offered Japan a non-aggression pact in December 1931. However, the Japanese were confident that they held the upper hand and rejected the proposal. Moscow thus decided it had no option but to appease the Japanese and deny the hotheads of the Kwantung Army a convenient *casus belli*. The Soviets therefore provided *de facto* recognition to Manchukuo by accepting the puppet state's consuls in 1932. In May 1933, Moscow then offered to sell the Chinese Eastern Railway. In reality, this remaining outpost of Soviet influence had already largely fallen under Japanese control and, without Soviet approval, was being used by Japan to ferry troops to fight the Chinese. The transfer of the CER was finalised on 23 March 1935 and, with this, the Soviets left Manchuria entirely under Japan's control.

While engaging in appeasement, the Soviets simultaneously sought to undermine Japan's military development. In February 1932, the Comintern secretariat ordered member parties to sabotage the production of arms for shipment to Japan.[5] Moscow also rapidly built up their own forces in the Far East. An air force was swiftly created, with 160 planes flown in by February 1932. The first elements of a Soviet Pacific Fleet were launched in April, and a military intelligence group was established in Zabaikal'sk to improve the Soviets' understanding of Japanese capabilities and intentions.[6]

This crash programme was successful. By the end of 1934, Soviet forces east of Chita exceeded 200,000 men.[7] This gave Stalin sufficient confidence to declare at that year's 17th Party Congress that "those who try to attack our country will receive a crushing repulse to teach them in future not to poke their pig snouts into our Soviet garden."[8] However, the military build-up came at a dreadful cost. Vast quantities of resources were transferred to the Far East to support the new deployments, including 120,000 tonnes of grain from Black Sea ports to Vladivostok from June to December 1933. This exacerbated the brutal famine in Ukraine, which claimed millions of lives.[9]

By 1935, the Soviet position in the Far East was therefore stronger, but the threat of Japanese attack had not abated. In fact, in March, Japan's Otsu plan for operations against the Soviet Union was approved by the emperor.[10] The Japanese military was also eagerly eyeing Outer Mongolia. Chief of Kwantung Army headquarters Itagaki Seishirō stated:

> If Outer Mongolia be combined with Japan and Manchukuo, Soviet territory in the Far East will fall into a very dangerous condition, and it is possible that the influence of the Soviet Union in the Far East might be removed almost without fighting. Therefore, the Army aims to extend Japanese-Manchurian power into Outer Mongolia by all means at hand.[11]

These Japanese ambitions provided the backdrop for the confrontation at Nomonhan in 1939.[12] That conflict was ultimately a major Soviet success, yet it was preceded by one of the Soviet Union's most embarrassing intelligence failures.

Lyushkov's defection

Genrikh S. Lyushkov was the most senior intelligence officer to defect from the Soviet Union in all its history. Born in Odessa in 1900, he was the son of a Jewish tailor from whom he inherited a life-long passion for fine clothing. Lyushkov was not, however, a naturally elegant figure. Just 5 feet 3 inches in height and stout, he sported a Charlie Chaplin moustache and bouffant hair. In 1938, this small, unprepossessing man was the chief of the NKVD for the entire Far Eastern region. He was also "arrogant, arbitrary, and a sadistic bully."[13]

Lyushkov began his intelligence career in 1920 and was involved in the liquidation of regime opponents in Moscow, Ukraine, and the

North Caucasus.[14] While Lyushkov's focus was counterintelligence, he boasted of being sent in 1930 to Germany, where he used his fluent German to gather intelligence on Junkers aircraft factories.[15] Lyushkov also contributed to the Kirov case of 1934, when Stalin used the assassination of senior Bolshevik Sergei Kirov as the pretext for a purge of communist rivals, including former Comintern chief Grigorii Zinov'ev. Lyushkov's role was to handle the investigation into the assassin Leonid Nikolaev, as well as to assist with the subsequent show trial and executions.[16]

Lyushkov had proved himself a ruthlessly effective NKVD officer and was awarded the Order of Lenin for his services. It was thus to Lyushkov that Stalin turned in 1937, when he decided that a new broom was needed for a sweeping purge of party and military officials in the Far East. Stalin met Lyushkov to issue confidential instructions. He told him that the incumbent NKVD leadership in the region "are Japanese spies, and Japan has a large base for spying and insurrection work by means of Koreans and Chinese." Lyushkov's job was to "terrorize the district and the frontier so as to prevent any Japanese work."[17] This, Lyushkov did with enthusiasm. Not only did he supervise the elimination of his NKVD predecessors, he also oversaw the mass deportation of ethnic Koreans and Chinese from the Far East due to the supposed threat they posed to Soviet security. With Lyushkov's assistance, 172,597 Koreans were deported from the Russian Far East to Central Asia in 1937–8. The mortality rate is estimated at 16.3%.[18]

Lyushkov was therefore not one of those sympathetic figures who fled the Soviet Union in revulsion at its inhumanity. Instead, Lyushkov's defection was all about self-preservation. As described by the Japanese interpreter who was assigned to Lyushkov during his first months in Tokyo, he, who "had taken the lives of 5,000 people in one year in the name of the purge, was faced by an unsettling problem when it became his turn to be purged as No. 5,001."[19]

The warning came in spring 1938, when Lyushkov received notification that he was to be transferred back to Moscow. He knew this meant liquidation. Determined to survive, he kept secret the news of his recall and began to plan his escape across the nearest border, which meant fleeing to Japanese-controlled Manchukuo. He did so by announcing a personal inspection of the border zone around Pos'et

Bay, southwest of Vladivostok, on 12 June. Once in the area, he told subordinates: "Stay here. I'm going over the bridge. A top-secret Japanese plant is supposed to meet me here. No one can see him but me."[20] Out of sight of his men, Lyushkov crept across the border and hid in the mist until discovered by a two-man Manchukuoan police patrol at 5:30am on 13 June.

Utter confusion followed as the Soviets scrambled to find their man. Troops were rushed to the border and Soviet artillery fired two rounds into Manchukuo on 16 June. When it became clear that Lyushkov had defected, a rapid reshuffle of the local command was ordered as regional officials were blamed for lax border security. The scandal contributed to the downfall of Vasilii K. Blyukher, Marshal of the Soviet Union and commander of military forces in the Far East. Blyukher was arrested on 22 October and accused of being a Japanese spy. After refusing to confess, Blyukher was beaten to death.[21] One source includes the gruesome detail that one of his eyeballs was beaten out of its socket.[22] Alvin Coox argues that Lyushkov's flight also hastened the demise of head of the NKVD and chief architect of the Great Purge, Nikolai Ezhov.[23]

The Stalinist regime was perfectly capable of acting brutally without the slightest justification. However, in the case of Lyushkov, Moscow had genuine cause for worry. Although having previously been a loyal NKVD officer, Lyushkov, upon his decision to defect, committed himself to doing as much damage as possible. In his words, "Guilty as I am of collaborating in Stalin's foul terror, I shall risk everything, flee to the nearest country, seek asylum as others had done, and carry on the good fight against Stalin from the outside."[24] He therefore told the Japanese everything they wished to know about the Soviet security services. Much of this information was stored in his prodigious memory, but Lyushkov also carried with him classified military papers hidden in an empty typewriter case.[25]

Lyushkov's best information was about Soviet intelligence activities in the Far East. He informed the Japanese that the NKVD had 40,000 troops in total, including 16,000 frontier guards. He also outlined the organisation's structure, operations, and priorities. Of particular value to Tokyo were details of Soviet espionage in China. Lyushkov told his hosts of Moscow's decision to boost support for

Chinese partisans and thus to weaken Japan's position by tying down as many of its troops as possible in China. He explained that the Soviet Union operated bases for Chinese operatives at Manzovka and Bikin in the Russian Far East. These individuals were tasked with penetrating Japanese military missions within Manchukuo, as well as on Sakhalin. There was also a special centre in Khabarovsk for training in terrorist operations.[26]

Lyushkov was equally well-informed about Soviet SIGINT and handed over the military codes of the Red Army in the Far East. He also informed the Japanese that, for the purpose of radio intercepts, the Soviet Union operated: "at Komsomolsk—two stations (10 kW and 110 kW), at Svobodni—two (10 kW each), at Vladivostok—one (110 kW), on Kamchatka—one (10 kW), on Sakhalin—one (10 kW)."[27] The scale of this activity must have been alarming to the Japanese authorities, though Lyushkov did reassure them that the Soviets had not yet broken Japanese military codes.[28]

Lastly in terms of intelligence, Lyushkov confirmed details of the Stalinist purges to which he had contributed and almost fell victim. He explained that more than two million had been arrested and several hundreds of thousands executed. He had brought with him the piteous final appeal of General Albert Ya. Lapin, who had been Far Eastern Air Force Commander until his arrest in 1937. Writing in his own blood on a scrap of paper, Lapin explained that he had been tortured into making false confessions. He pleaded with the Central Committee to intervene, stating "I served the Soviet Government faithfully for 17 years. Do I deserve to be treated like this?" No assistance was forthcoming, and in September 1937 Lapin committed suicide in his prison cell.[29]

Lyushkov's willingness to speak about Stalinist atrocities made him useful as a public relations tool. Tokyo informed the press of Lyushkov's defection on 1 July 1938, prompting every major newspaper to publish a special edition. The Japanese military also arranged a press conference at the Sanno Hotel at which Lyushkov emphasised the threat the Soviet Union posed to Japan.[30] Incidentally, this is the same hotel at which another Soviet intelligence officer, Stanislav Levchenko, approached a US official and offered to defect on 24 October 1979.[31]

While Lyushkov's revelations about the NKVD were valuable, the Japanese really wanted military intelligence. This was not Lyushkov's area of expertise, but he was still able to offer "copious detail about deployment sites, organization, and equipment of each Red Army division in the East."[32] Of greatest importance was Lyushkov's information that, as of 1938, the Soviet Far Eastern Army comprised 20 rifle divisions and 270,000 men. If the Trans-Baikal Military District and other forces were included, the Soviet Union had 400,000 troops deployed east of Lake Baikal and nearly 2,000 military aircraft. These figures far exceeded Japan's estimates and demonstrated the success of the Soviet Union's crash military buildup.[33] Among the many details, Lyushkov informed the Japanese about Soviet supplies of chemical weapons, explaining that the NKVD had stocks of mustard gas and perhaps phosgene at Khabarovsk, as well as on Sakhalin and Kamchatka.[34]

Lyushkov's intelligence on Soviet forces deployed in the Far East was greatly beneficial to Japan. Yet he excessively talked down their quality. Lyushkov emphasised the debilitating effect of Stalinist repression and highlighted serious problems with logistics and training. These were real issues, but Lyushkov, having embraced the role of dissident, allowed himself to exaggerate problems and ignore continuing strengths. For instance, as tensions gathered across the frontier between Japanese-controlled Manchukuo and the Soviet satellite of Mongolia, Lyushkov wrote off the Red Army's willingness to fight, saying "one cannot reasonably expect Red fighters to die bravely in order to defend, not the soil of their beloved Russia, but those desert spaces in Mongolia about which they know little and care less."[35] This was music to the ears of the Japanese military, who prided themselves on the superiority of the Yamato fighting spirit. However, such information was to prove catastrophically misleading when Japanese and Soviet forces met at Nomonhan between May and September 1939.

After the initial panic, the Soviets concentrated on finding out all they could about what information Lyushkov had provided the Japanese. This task fell primarily to Richard Sorge, whom we shall meet properly in the next chapter. Sorge's remarkable spy ring initially struggled to uncover further information. Yet, fortunately for Moscow, after a few weeks, the Japanese decided to share Lyushkov's intelligence with their Nazi partners. Admiral Wilhelm Canaris, chief of the Abwehr (German military intelligence), sent a special agent to Tokyo to produce a report based on Lyushkov's information. Given Sorge's excellent contacts within the German embassy in Tokyo, it was straightforward to gain access to this report. Sorge radioed the key information, thereby quickly apprising Moscow of what Lyushkov had handed over. Most crucially, this meant the Soviets could change the military codes for the Far East. Another service provided by Sorge was to use his influence at the embassy to discredit Lyushkov's intelligence, characterising the defector as unimportant and unreliable.[36]

Ultimately, it was not the Soviets but the Japanese themselves who liquidated Lyushkov. After his arrival in Tokyo, Lyushkov had been treated with great honour. He was provided with a general's salary and fitted out with custom-made suits from the Matsuya department store. Even after pumping him dry of intelligence, the Japanese found a role for Lyushkov by transferring him to the Army's 8th Section (Psychological Warfare and Sabotage). Here, Lyushkov assisted with anti-Stalinist propaganda as well as with preparations for hostilities with the Soviet Union.[37]

The Japanese also looked after Lyushkov's personal needs. Lyushkov was deeply anxious about the wife and daughter he left behind in the Soviet Union. This was with good reason. According to one account, Lyushkov's wife was detained in the Lubyanka prison, where "They simply tore her apart. Then they liquidated [Lyushkov's] parents in Odessa. And all his relatives."[38] To take his mind off these sorrows, the Japanese authorities took Lyushkov to one of Tokyo's red-light districts and issued him with 300 yen. The experience raised Lyushkov's spirits, though he also contracted gonorrhoea. As a longer-term solution, the Japanese arranged a home for Lyushkov near Ushigome-Mitsuke and set him up with a "housekeeper." The woman was middle-aged and rather unattractive, but, although Lyushkov was initially unenthused, the two eventually married.[39]

Lyushkov thus passed the war years in relative comfort. However, in 1945, as the prospect of a Soviet attack loomed, the Japanese military decided to send Lyushkov to Manchuria, where his Soviet expertise could be better used. Lyushkov was not opposed, but his departure was repeatedly delayed. It was not until 20 July 1945 that

Lyushkov (travelling as "Malatov") finally reached Manchuria. The timing could hardly have been worse, for, by this time, there was little anyone could do to help the doomed Japanese forces. This was recognised by the Kwantung Army leadership, who soon decided to liquidate Lyushkov, since, were he to fall into Soviet hands, he could divulge details of his work for the Japanese. The decision was made by Yanagida Genzō, Lieutenant General of the Kwantung Leased Territory Defence Command, who concluded, "It's a pity … and I feel sorry for Lyushkov but, in order to prevent such revelations, it would be best to do away with him now."[40]

The task of shooting Lyushkov fell to Captain Takeoka Yutaka, the 27-year-old chief of the Dairen branch of the Harbin Special Agency (*Tokumu Kikan*). Despite being a graduate of the Nakano School, Japan's tough training centre for military intelligence officers, Takeoka struggled with the assignment. He had to convince himself, "I will not be committing murder for personal advantage or personal gain. I am following my superior's order as a loyal subordinate within the military system."[41] The burden was somewhat lightened by the disdain that Takeoka, and other Japanese officers, felt for a defector who had betrayed his homeland.[42]

It was on 20 August that Takeoka visited Lyushkov at the Yamato Hotel in Dairen. By the time of Takeoka's arrival, the Soviet Union's crushing of the Kwantung Army, which had begun on 9 August, was almost complete. With the fall of the city imminent, Takeoka invited Lyushkov to the office of the Harbin special agency and urged him to commit suicide. When the Russian categorically refused, Takeoka concluded he had no option but to kill him. Around 10.30 pm, he told Lyushkov they would go in search of a ship on which he could escape. Then, as they were walking towards the exit, Takeoka turned and shot Lyushkov in the chest with his Colt pistol. Stunned by the noise, Takeoka dropped the weapon. A civilian employee picked it up and fired a second round into Lyushkov's head. Despite this intended *coup de grâce*, Lyushkov seems still to have been alive, as groans were heard from his body several hours later. Nonetheless, a death certificate was issued and Lyushkov was cremated on 21 August, one day before the arrival of Soviet troops.[43]

Overall, given Lyushkov's depth of knowledge about the NKVD and military, his defection should have been a disaster for Soviet intelligence. However, Sorge's unrestricted access to the Abwehr's report helped minimise the damage. Moreover, while Lyushkov did reveal the size of Soviet forces in the Far East, his persistent talking down of their quality fanned overconfidence in the Japanese military. In one typical comment, a Japanese military analyst wrote in 1938 that "the Russian armed forces are uncontrolled, in a state of confusion, and corrupt in morale."[44] As the outbreak of conflict on the Mongolian plains approached, such misinformation could not have been more helpful to Moscow had Lyushkov been a Soviet plant.[45]

The Nomonhan Conflict

The conflict at Khalkhin Gol/Nomonhan between May and September 1939 is usually described as a "battle" or even, in Japanese, as just an "incident" (*jiken*). Yet the scale and ferocity of the clashes between Soviet and Japanese forces across the frontier between the Mongolian People's Republic (a Soviet satellite) and Japan's puppet state of Manchukuo were such that it could equally be described as a war, albeit an undeclared one.

The Nomonhan conflict involved 75,738 Japanese troops versus an even larger number on the Soviet/Mongolian side.[46] Hundreds of aircraft and tanks, including flamethrowing ones, were revved into action, while fierce artillery duels pounded the soil of the Mongolian plain. There was plenty of heroism, including "human bullet" (*nikuhaku kōgeki*) attacks, when Japanese soldiers would leap upon Soviet tanks and throw grenades into their hatches. There were also numerous suicides as Japanese officers felt obliged, or were compelled, to throw away their lives rather than retreat or surrender.

The end result was a resounding defeat for the Japanese. The Kwantung Army was repulsed from the Khalkha River and forced to acquiesce to the Soviet Union's claim that the rightful border lay several kilometres to the northeast. In addition, the human losses were appalling. The Japanese are estimated to have lost nearly 20,000 men, including the near annihilation of the 23rd Division.[47] Soviet dead are reported to have been 9,824, though the real number was likely higher.[48]

What accounts for the extent of Japan's drubbing? There are several military explanations, including the Kwantung Army's inferiority in tanks and artillery. There is also the interesting question, to which we return later, of the leadership of divisional commander Komatsubara Michitarō. However, intelligence factors were also prominent. As noted, the Kwantung Army's underestimation of the quality of Soviet forces had a major impact. Yet the Soviet Union also scored several espionage successes both in the years preceding the conflict and on the battlefield itself.

Soviet intelligence successes before Nomonhan

One profitable source of Soviet intelligence prior to 1939 was Japan's own military attachés in Moscow. These officers were employed to gather information for the Japanese military yet, on several occasions, they (inadvertently or otherwise) provided intelligence to the Soviets. The NKVD kept the attachés under close surveillance. Colonel Hayashi Saburō, chief of the Soviet section of the General Staff, complained that the army's attachés were forced to reside in a certain hotel in Moscow and their correspondence was monitored. "When they went out, they were tailed by the NKVD officers and sometimes followed into public lavatories."[49]

This intense surveillance disrupted Japanese intelligence collection but also revealed weaknesses in Japanese security protocols and personal vulnerabilities among the attachés. Armed with this information, the Soviets succeeded in stealing several classified documents from Japan's Moscow embassy in the years preceding Nomonhan. Some of these were used by Soviet prosecutors at the International Military Tribunal for the Far East as proof of Japan's aggressive intentions against the Soviet Union. Military attaché Kawabe Torashirō was stunned when these papers were presented. He explains, "In order to get these documents out of the safe [in the Moscow embassy], four different keys were needed … this means that the documents were accessed by someone, photographed, then returned."[50]

The honey trap was a favoured tactic to compromise the military attachés. It was just such an attempt that led to the death of Captain Koyanagi Kisaburō in 1929. Koyanagi was the top graduate of Japan's Naval University and was posted as naval attaché to Moscow from 1927. There are various accounts of what happened to Koyanagi but each suggests that, having left wife and children at home in Japan, he enjoyed a hedonistic existence in the Soviet capital. One source suggests Koyanagi regularly held orgies in his apartment at 44 Novinskii Boulevard.[51] This licentiousness gave Soviet intelligence the opening it needed. The OGPU assigned a female Russian-language teacher named Lida Alekseevna to Koyanagi and the two soon became intimate. Matters came to a head on 3 February 1929, when Koyanagi held a party at his apartment to which Lida Alekseevna and her "friend," another female agent, were invited. Koyanagi became intoxicated and fell asleep. When he awoke, he found Lida in the process of stealing the keys to his safe. Enraged, Koyanagi prevented the theft "thanks to his ju-jitsu" but slightly injured Lida's hand. Trying a new tack, the Soviet agents sought to blackmail Koyanagi by claiming he had tried to force himself on them. The attempt failed since, shortly after, Koyanagi committed suicide by *harakiri* in his office at the embassy.[52]

Another case relates to the death aboard the Trans-Siberian Railway of Lieutenant Colonel Kaneko Masao, who was acting chief of the 11th Section (communications) of the 3rd Department of the General Staff. Although this occurred after the Nomonhan conflict, it provides another example of how the unprofessionalism of certain officers aided Soviet intelligence. In May 1945, Kaneko, who was travelling under the codename "Kanazaki," and a fellow officer called Shibata (codename "Satō") were carrying secret documents from Manchukuo to Moscow by train. Seated in First Class, Kaneko and Shibata began drinking vodka with a "Soviet major." Much alcohol was consumed as the three debated whether Japan would win the Pacific War. At some point Shibata passed out, waking to find Kaneko's lifeless body next to him. When Japanese officials arrived to retrieve the corpse at Ekaterinburg, they found clear signs that the envelope in which Kaneko had been carrying the secret documents had been opened.[53]

Aside from targeting frisky and bibulous Japanese officers within the Soviet Union, Moscow scored intelligence successes against Japan within China. An overall goal of the Soviet Union was to ensure that Japan sank deeper into the quagmire of conflict in China, since, as Deputy Commissar Vladimir Potemkin put it in 1937, Japan's intensifying military commitment in China would "have the effect of reducing the pressure which it exercises on our Manchurian frontier."[54] Moscow had already been assisting the Chinese Communist Party (CCP) for several years. Moscow was also instrumental in pressuring the CCP to accept an anti-Japanese United Front with the nationalist Kuomintang (KMT) in 1936.[55] Yet Soviet assistance was only ratcheted up to its full extent after the Marco Polo Bridge Incident of July 1937, which marked the start of the Second Sino-Japanese War.

Between September 1937 and June 1941, the Soviet Union provided the Chiang Kai-shek-led Chinese government with:

> 904 planes (318 medium and heavy bombers, 542 fighters and 44 trainers), 82 tanks, 602 tractors, 1516 automobiles, 1140 heavy guns, 9720 light and heavy machine-guns, 50 000 rifles, about 180 milllion cartridges, 31.6 thousand bombs, about 2 million shells and other equipment.[56]

Many heavy items were secretly driven across the Sino-Soviet land border. Drivers at the wheels of trucks loaded with one-tonne bombs endured a white-knuckle ride as they manoeuvred up mountain slopes and across freezing saltmarshes in areas where proper roads were rare. Additionally, between autumn 1937 and February 1939, 3,665 Soviet military specialists served in China. These included Aleksandr Cherepanov, who was Chiang's chief military advisor. The Soviet Union also dispatched 450 pilots by the end of 1937.[57]

This Sino-Soviet cooperation extended to the intelligence realm. In 1938, a joint centre for anti-Japanese intelligence work was created. The Soviets provided significant assistance in organising sabotage operations against Japanese troops. "Subversive work was mainly carried out through Chinese partisan detachments, which were supplied with money, weapons, and ammunition." Additionally, the Soviets passed on information about Japanese troop deployments and warned of forthcoming air raids on Chinese cities. The names of suspected Japanese agents were also handed over. In return, the Chinese provided the Soviets with intelligence on Whites and Trotskyites residing in China, and supplied intercepts of Japanese communications that were then transferred to Moscow for decryption. When leading Chinese communist Zhou Enlai visited Moscow in 1939, he brought with him three Japanese cyphers that had been captured by the Eighth Route Army.[58]

Information received from the Chinese was periodically useful, but the Soviets did their most valuable work on their own via their multiple *rezidenturas* in China. In Chongqing, which was Chiang Kai-shek's provisional capital from 1937, Aleksandr S. Panyushkin, aged just 34, served as both ambassador and *rezident*. Panyushkin met daily with leading KMT members and used "every opportunity—legal and unofficial—to prevent the outbreak of a civil war and the breakdown of cooperation between Chiang Kai-shek and Mao Zedong."[59] A further priority was to prolong Japan's agony by ensuring that Chiang did not concede to a peace agreement with the Japanese. Panyushkin excelled in this work and was awarded the Order of Lenin. Later, in the mid-1950s, he was appointed head of the First Chief Directorate of the KGB.

Another key centre of activity was Harbin in Manchukuo. Here, Soviet intelligence went head to head with Japan's Harbin Special Agency, which was staffed with 1,000–2,000 intelligence officers. Many had been educated in Russian at elite military intelligence schools, such as the Nakano School, which collectively churned out around 100 Russian-speaking officers a year.[60]

Just as Soviet spies sought to infiltrate Japanese networks, so the Japanese sought to penetrate Soviet ones. They achieved a breakthrough in 1936, when intelligence officer Lieutenant Colonel Yamamoto Hayashi recruited a Russian named Mikhailov, who was a telegrapher in the Soviet consular office in Harbin. Mikhailov was paid 5,000 yen per month. In return he passed on large quantities of secret material, which the Japanese labelled "Harbin Special Intelligence."[61] However, as historian of intelligence Kotani Ken points out, the Soviets soon turned the tables. Realising that Mikhailov was selling information, the Soviets left him in place and used him to channel disinformation to the Japanese.[62]

Another Soviet success was recruitment of a spy named "Abe." The official history of Russian foreign intelligence only gives the name "Abe."[63] It was assumed this was a codename, but historian Tomita Takeshi claims the individual's real name was Abe Kōichi, although he also used the name Nakamura.[64] Abe was a Japanese officer who served in the Russian Far East during the Siberian Intervention. After the withdrawal of Japanese troops in 1922, Abe was transferred to Japan's Korean Army. His role was to train Korean, Chinese, and White Russian agents to conduct covert reconnaissance in the Primorskii and Amur regions. Another of Abe's responsibilities was to liaise with the Soviet consulate general in Seoul, and, in so doing, to collect intelligence on Soviet diplomats. However, while these contacts were supposed to help identify Soviet intelligence officers, they resulted in Abe's own recruitment.[65]

According to the official Russian account, Abe more or less recruited himself. "At meetings and in conversations with employees of the consulate general, he did not hide what he was doing, displayed willingness to render services, spoke openly about his financial difficulties, and A offered his service to the consulate as an intermediary."[66] Ivan A. Chichaev, who became consul general in Seoul in 1927 but was really an OGPU officer, took Abe up on his offer. As is customary, the new recruit was broken in with easy assignments. Abe was asked to purchase some publications with restricted circulation, and, in return, received a small payment. Later, as the relationship developed, Abe was asked to provide more sensitive information. This included documents from Japan's General Staff, plus files from the headquarters of the Korean Army and the Governor General of Korea.[67]

After several years of work for the Soviets in Seoul, Moscow sought Abe's transfer to Harbin. This was achieved in the early 1930s and resulted in a significant increase in his output. Indeed, Abe handed over such large quantities of information that, in February 1934, the Harbin *rezident* asked Moscow Centre for additional translators. The documents included information about Japanese troop deployments in Manchuria and described units' weapons, technical equipment, and state of combat readiness. Abe also handed over material on Japanese intelligence activities against the Soviet Union. This exposed several Japanese spies and provided forewarning of the arrest of Soviet agents, thus enabling their withdrawal from Manchukuo.[68]

Money was part of Abe's motivation. He is said to have been from an ancient but impoverished samurai family and dreamed of getting rich.[69] Ego was also important, since Abe "was notable for his excessive self-confidence." As is often the case with turncoats, Abe considered himself intellectually superior to his bosses and thought himself undervalued. He told his Soviet handler that Japanese senior officers were "idiots and idlers," and he regularly complained that he had to "receive and obey orders from people who are beneath him in terms of ability."[70] An added factor may have been affection for Russian culture, since, in a manner less than ideal for a Russian secret agent, he began to dress like a Russian, drink vodka, and play the guitar at home.[71]

Aside from stealing secrets, Abe was a useful recruiter. "On the instructions of the *rezidentura*, Abe recruited officers of the Korean Army 'Chon' and 'Tur', employees of the Main Gendarmerie Directorate 'Saya' and 'Li', employee of the Korean Governor General 'Maka', as well as his brother 'Kim', and the soldier 'Kan'."[72] Of these, Tur was the most valuable. Recruited in 1932, Tur supplied numerous original Japanese documents, including:

1) Secret reports and journals of the General Staff and other central organs;
2) reports and operational documents of Japanese organs in Manchuria—the headquarters of the Kwantung Army, the Harbin military mission and other military missions;
3) reports and other intelligence and operational-strategic materials from the headquarters of the Korean Army;
4) descriptions of manoeuvres, combat training manuals etc and materials from the War Ministry.[73]

There were also Soviet spies among the White Russians employed by the Japanese in Manchukuo. Some of these were employed by the Chinese Eastern Railway (CER). When the CER was purchased by Manchukuo/Japan in March 1935, all Soviet employees lost their jobs and were replaced by 1,500 White Russians. The Imperial Japanese Army later estimated that around 200 of these had actually been Soviet agents.[74] There were also White Russians who directly penetrated the Japanese security forces on behalf of the Soviets. One was "Osipov." Originally from Odessa, Osipov arrived in Manchuria in 1923 and was recruited by the Soviets in 1928. On Moscow's instructions, he first gained a job with the Japanese as a driver, then, with assistance from Abe, he was promoted to a position within the special department (political) of the Japanese gendarmerie. From here,

Osipov passed back information about White Russians working for the Japanese. He also seeded doubts about the reliability of Japan's own agents and succeeded in having some of them eliminated. Despite this work, Soviet suspicions fell on Osipov, as the officer who had recruited him was purged in 1938. The exact details of Osipov's demise are unclear, but the official history of Russian foreign intelligence records that he died during military action in China in 1945.[75]

Abe himself was more fortunate. Despite years of service to Soviet intelligence, he too came under suspicion of being a Japanese agent. As a result, when Soviet forces overran Manchukuo in August 1945, Abe received no special treatment and, along with hundreds of thousands of other Japanese personnel, he was dispatched to a Siberian labour camp, where he served as an interpreter for the camp authorities and may have informed on fellow prisoners. An investigation by Soviet intelligence found no substance to the allegations against him and he was permitted to return to Japan in December 1947. Although he was subsequently interrogated by Japan's Counter-Intelligence Corp, he appears to have been left at liberty.[76]

Soviet intelligence during the Nomonhan conflict

As with many wars, the conflict at Nomonhan was sparked by a seemingly innocuous incident. On the night of 10–11 May 1939, a 20-man group of Mongolian People's Republic (MPR) cavalry led their horses onto the flat grassland on the right bank of the Khalkha River into territory claimed by Japan as part of Manchukuo. After light skirmishing had failed to dislodge the Mongolians, General Komatsubara ordered a 2,000-strong force under Colonel Yamagata Takemitsu to attack. They were assisted by a 200-man reconnaissance unit under Lieutenant Colonel Azuma Yaozō, whose role was to get behind the enemy forces and cut off their retreat. However, due to inadequate intelligence, the Japanese had failed to realise that the MPR border troops holding the bridgehead had been reinforced by Soviet infantry. Unprepared for the enemy's strength, the Japanese attack was repulsed and Azuma's unit was destroyed, with only four men escaping. Seeking revenge, the Kwantung Army launched air and ground offensives (which had not been authorised by the General Staff in Tokyo) across the Khalkha into undisputed Mongolian territory. These efforts failed too, and Japanese troops had to scramble back across the river. Throughout the summer, intense fighting continued until August, when Soviet forces, under the command of Georgii Zhukov, launched a major counteroffensive, which crushed Komatsubara's 23rd Division and forced Tokyo to accept an armistice and, ultimately, an MPR-Manchukuo boundary that was far to the east of the Khalka.[77]

In prosecuting this conflict, the Soviets were eager to show their mettle and thus deter future Japanese aggression. Yet, at the same time, they did not want a full-scale war with Japan in 1939. This was because Soviet forces in eastern Siberia were not yet at full strength. Moscow was also determined to avoid fighting Germany and Japan at the same time. At the start of the Nomonhan conflict, the Nazi-Soviet Non-Aggression Pact of August 1939 had not yet been negotiated. Consequently, a leading Soviet intelligence priority during the Nomonhan conflict was to learn the degree to which the Japanese authorities were willing to escalate. This knowledge would enable the Soviets to calibrate their action so that it was sufficient to give the Kwantung Army a bloody nose yet not so forceful as to provoke a full-blown war. This task of ascertaining Japan's intentions fell to Sorge's spy ring.

Further to his unsurpassed access to the German embassy in Tokyo, Sorge's Japanese agents, especially Ozaki Hotsumi, were well-placed to harvest intelligence from the Japanese political leadership. However, despite these advantages, it was not straightforward for Sorge to ascertain Japan's intentions at Nomonhan. This was because the Japanese military enjoyed autonomy from the civilian government and was loath to share information with the political leadership. Indeed, Prime Minister Hiranuma Kiichirō subsequently claimed that he "knew nothing" of the fighting at Nomonhan.[78] Japan's Kwantung Army was even reluctant to cooperate with the military's high command in Tokyo, whose "armchair generals" were seen as interfering with the real business of warfare in the field. Tsuji Masanobu, a highly influential officer in the Kwantung Army's Operations section, went so far as to complain that the Kwantung Army was having to wage a two-front campaign, against Soviet-Mongolian forces on the one hand and against the Army General Staff on the other.[79]

Notwithstanding these obstacles, following several weeks of intense activity, Sorge's spy ring was able to amass a considerable amount of valuable intelligence. First, in a 10-page document submitted to Moscow on 4 June 1939, Sorge reported that the Japanese leadership believed it would be difficult to wage war against the Soviet Union without the support of Germany. Moreover, Sorge noted that Tokyo's priority remained the conflict in China and that it was to this theatre that most Japanese resources were being directed.[80] In a subsequent message, Sorge reassured that, despite the Japanese attacks against Soviet positions within the Mongolian People's Republic, "The Japanese armed forces, army, fleet and air force require fundamental reorganisation that would take 1.5 to 2 years more; i.e. Japan will be ready for a big war no earlier than 1941."[81] Sorge therefore urged the Soviet leadership to take tough action since, as he saw it, the Japanese could only be managed with whips and would become impudent unless treated roughly.[82]

Some of Sorge's intelligence came from his own meetings with Colonel Gerhard Matzky, military attaché at the German embassy, who shared details of his contacts with the Japanese General Staff. Ozaki Hotsumi, who had been appointed consultant to the cabinet of Prime Minister Konoe Fumimaro in summer 1938, chipped in with news that Japan's leadership was "adopting a policy of solving the problem locally and not expanding it. It does not have any intention of daring an overall war with Russia."[83] Another member of the spy ring, Miyagi Yotoku, used connections within the military and Japan's arms industry to learn that, although some tanks and aircraft were being sent to Nomonhan, there were no plans for a larger-scale deployment.[84]

One of Sorge's team even succeeded in visiting Nomonhan. This was Branko Vukelić, a Yugoslav communist whose cover job in Tokyo was as a journalist for Agence Havas (forerunner of Agence France-Presse). Vukelić was able to join a group of 10 foreign journalists who were invited by the Japanese army to travel to the vicinity of the battlefield in July 1939. Sorge ordered his man "to watch tanks and heavy guns carefully."[85] Vukelić witnessed some of the fighting and even interviewed Lieutenant General Komatsubara. Based on his observations, Vukelić reported that successes claimed by the Kwantung Army were exaggerated. It was also his strong impression that Japan would keep the conflict limited and not permit escalation into a full-scale war.[86]

Armed with this intelligence, the Soviet leadership concluded they were safe to give the Kwantung Army a thrashing so long as the fighting was contained to the area of disputed territory. Therefore, despite the success of Zhukov's August offensive, Soviet forces halted their advance at what they claimed to be the rightful border of the Mongolian People's Republic and did not extend attacks into undisputed areas of Manchukuo. Up-to-date intelligence was also an advantage for the Soviets during the ceasefire and border negotiations since Sorge learned that the High Command in Tokyo had ordered that the Nomonhan affair be conclusively settled. As Alvin Coox puts it, the Japanese negotiators "were operating in a near vacuum in terms of intelligence. Gut reactions were no substitute for Sorge's entrees in Japan and Manchuria."[87]

The Soviet side also had the upper hand in battlefield intelligence. In part, this was due to skilled and innovative work by Soviet intelligence officers, yet, in a reversal of the Russo-Japanese War, Soviet superiority was also a reflection of Japanese weakness. The chief intelligence officer of the 23rd Division, Major Suzuki Yoshiyasu, had no experience in intelligence before joining the division.[88] During the first stages of the conflict, despite Japan dominating the skies, the Kwantung Army failed to conduct adequate aerial reconnaissance.[89] Moreover, what was seen was often misinterpreted. At the end of June, Japanese scout planes spotted a massive number of trucks leaving the front in the direction of the Mongolian interior. This was interpreted as a Soviet withdrawal. In reality, these trucks were on their return journey from the front as they shuttled between the combat zone and the distant railway depot, bringing in vast quantities of matériel.[90]

Limited intelligence was also an impediment during the artillery duels that defined the combat during July. The Kwantung Army was already at a disadvantage due to the shorter range of their guns and more limited stocks of shells. Their task was made more difficult by a lack of information about Soviet positions. As one Major Ogata lamented, the Japanese forces only knew that the enemy was "'roughly in that direction' and that artillery was 'over there,' for the simple reason that shells were emanating from 'over there'."[91]

Overconfidence accounts for this failure to devote more attention to intelligence. Convinced of Japan's superiority of combat spirit and persuaded that the purges had decimated the Soviet military, the Kwantung Army initially assumed they could prevail at Nomonhan with little difficulty. Japanese troops were told that "the enemy was supposed to flee at the first appearance of Japanese regulars." Consequently, when setting off for the front, the divisional staff packed bags with necessities sufficient for little more than a week.[92]

The Japanese also assisted their enemy through the ill-advised practice of carrying large amounts of documentation into combat. Before their positions were overrun, Japanese forces were under orders to destroy or conceal classified material. Sometimes this was possible and Japanese soldiers did manage to bury several footlockers on the Nomonhan battlefield. This was one reason why the Kwantung Army was desperate to receive Soviet permission to return to the scene of the fighting after a ceasefire had been agreed.[93] However, on many occasions, Japanese troops had no time to destroy or hide their documentation. Alvin Coox records one bizarre instance when a Japanese commander ordered his men to burn their documents (*shorui yake*), yet, in the heat of battle, his troops misunderstood this as an order to burn their vehicles (*sharyō yake*). The soldiers therefore set fire to their own trucks and tractors.[94]

From the pockets of dead Japanese soldiers, the Soviets were able to collect numerous letters, memos, and operational orders. So voluminous was this material that Grigorii M. Shtern, chief of staff of the Far Eastern Military District, rejoiced that the Japanese army was authentically bureaucratic and loved writing a lot. He boasted that the Soviets had amassed so many documents that they could accurately predict Japan's next moves.[95] A particularly large number of confidential documents was lost when the Kwantung Army launched their ill-fated sally across the Khalkha River on 3 July, then quickly had to withdraw. Among the documents left behind were files specifying the composition of the 23rd Division and the 2nd Air Division.[96] Early in the conflict, the Soviets also found a map in the staff car of Lieutenant Colonel Azuma Yaozō, which is said to have confirmed the legitimacy of the Soviet-claimed MPR border.[97] Some of these captured documents were presented at the Tokyo Tribunal as proof of Japan's aggressive intentions against the Soviet Union.

The Soviets also benefitted from occasional windfalls when Japanese aircraft were shot down above their lines. On 2/3 July, anti-aircraft fire brought down a Japanese scout plane. When Soviet forces scoured the wreckage, they discovered a briefcase containing orders by Lieutenant General Giga Tetsuji, commander of the 2nd Air Division. The historian Hata Ikuhiko identifies the aircraft as having been that of Lieutenant Colonel Shimanuki Tadamasa, Giga's senior operations expert.[98] Shimanuki was a Russian-speaking regional expert and had been the first Japanese airman to be sent on an officer exchange to the Soviet Union. The shooting down of Shimanuki's aircraft therefore not only provided the Soviets with classified documents, it also deprived Japan of one of their leading Soviet experts.

Other factors that contributed to the Soviet Union's intelligence superiority at Nomonhan are more directly attributable to the quality of the Soviets' own work. One example is decryption. As part of the Sino-Soviet intelligence cooperation, the Soviet Union sent a task force of cryptographers to China in early 1938. During the subsequent year the Soviet experts broke 10 ciphers that were widely used by the Japanese military and were able to decrypt around 200 telegrams each month. After the fighting on the MPR-Manchukuoan border began in 1939, Soviet cryptographers were moved to the settlement of Tamsag Bulak, around 120 kilometres from the frontline. Even before arriving, they had begun work on Kwantung Army code 1357. This was then comprehensively broken after codebooks were captured during the early stages of the conflict. Since the code remained unchanged until late 1939, the Soviets were able to decipher "valuable information about the location of enemy units, the course of battles, losses, consumption of ammunition, and other data." The cryptographic team issued a daily summary of these intercepts to General Zhukov.[99]

Another area of Soviet strength is what Alvin Coox describes as "white magic" or what might otherwise be called "*maskirovka*" (military deception).[100] Some of this was basic. Before the serious fighting began, the air force commander of the MPR eastern military district ordered all Soviet aircraft to be repainted with Mongolian markings, thereby concealing the scale of Soviet involvement.[101] Other actions were more theatrical. One Soviet reconnaissance unit is said to have got close to Japanese positions by donning sheepskin coats and infiltrating a large flock of sheep.[102]

The most significant instance of *maskirovka* at Nomonhan was undoubtedly the Soviet effort to conceal preparations for the major offensive on 20 August 1939. Soviet commanders took the view that the best way to fool the enemy was to fool their own men. Soviet troops were thus told they would be digging in and adopting a defensive posture. The details of the real plan were shared with a minimum of senior officers. Notebooks with misleading information were also distributed to Soviet soldiers in the days before the offensive in the expectation that some of them would be captured by the Japanese.[103]

The efforts at deception did not stop there. A handbook entitled *What the Soviet Soldier Must Know in Defence* was issued to Zhukov's units and steps were taken to ensure it fell into Japanese hands. The construction of extensive defensive works was also commenced.[104] This was supplemented by extensive radio traffic about preparations for bedding down for autumn and winter, which the Soviets sent in a code they knew could be broken.[105] However, most innovative was the Soviet side's use of sound. Two weeks before the offensive, General Zhukov arranged for powerful speakers to emit sounds mimicking the noise of tanks, aircraft, and construction work. The Japanese soon realised that these were fake and learned to ignore them, but, as Zhukov explained, this "was exactly what we wanted because it was extremely important for us during the real regrouping and concentration of forces."[106] To add to the confusion, the Soviets generated real noise from their aircraft and trucks to drown out the sound of Soviet armour being manoeuvred into position at night. This had the added benefit of preventing the Japanese from sleeping. Tank noise was also minimised by removing the vehicles' metal treads and having them run on just wheels.[107]

These ruses worked so well that the Japanese refused to believe that a major Soviet attack was imminent. In the days before the offensive, heavy rain prevented the Kwantung Army from conducting aerial reconnaissance. When this resumed and a scout plane spotted "an enormous number" of enemy tanks readying to attack, the report was dismissed as outlandish.[108] Japanese forces were also at a disadvantage since they did not know where Soviet forces might cross the

Khalkha River. This is because the Soviets at Nomonhan pioneered the use of underwater bridges. These spans were installed approximately one foot below the surface of the river and were invisible from the air.[109] Ultimately, when the August offensive roared into action, the Japanese were caught unawares. As a post-Nomonhan Kwantung Army report admitted, "We had no prior clue from intelligence at any level, from the front to army headquarters, to lead us to expect there would be an offensive on such a scale at this time."[110]

Was Komatsubara a Soviet agent?

The Soviets undoubtedly had an intelligence advantage over Japan before and during the Nomonhan conflict. However, did Moscow have the ultimate advantage of having the main Japanese commander in their pocket? In other words, was Lieutenant General Komatsubara Michitarō, commander of the 23rd Division, a Soviet spy?

Born in Yokohama in 1886, Komatsubara graduated from the Imperial Japanese Army Academy in 1905. Having shown promise in the Russian language, he was selected in 1909 to spend a year in Russia. This was the first of three occasions in which Komatsubara lived in Russia. The second was from autumn 1919, when he served as assistant military attaché during the Russian Civil War. The third was for three years from early 1927, when Komatsubara was appointed military attaché in Moscow. Historian Kuromiya Hiroaki alleges that it was during Komatsubara's third stint in Russia that he was recruited as a Soviet agent. Drawing on research by Soviet historians Teodor Gladkov and N.G. Zaitsev, Kuromiya claims that Komatsubara and Miyamoto (presumably a colleague) were prone to "drinking, debauchery, and profiteering." Soviet intelligence took advantage of these vulnerabilities and ensnared Komatsubara in a honey trap, most likely in early 1927. In Kuromiya's telling, "on one occasion Komatsubara got so drunk with his mistress that he lost the keys to the safe in his room. Komatsubara (and 'Miyamoto') were said to have been 'ready to agree to anything' in order to prevent their misbehavior from being reported to Tokyo."[111]

Kuromiya suggests that, having been compromised in 1927, Komatsubara remained under Moscow's control for more than a decade. He asserts that Komatsubara began to pass secret documents to the Soviets, both during his time as military attaché in Moscow and while working as an intelligence officer in Harbin. Kuromiya claims that "Sufficient ground exists to suspect that Komatsubara betrayed his own men in Nomonhan."[112] The implication is that Komatsubara deliberately escalated a minor border skirmish into a large-scale conflict, thus giving the Soviets the opportunity for a short, victorious war that would puncture Japanese ambitions to attack the Soviet Union.[113] Moreover, Komatsubara made sure to lead his forces so incompetently that it guaranteed Soviet victory.

If true, this would be one of the most remarkable cases of infiltration of an enemy's military leadership in modern history. However, the evidence is insufficient to justify the claims. First, regarding Komatsubara's alleged sexual entrapment, aside from the claim by the Soviet historians, the only other piece of information presented by Kuromiya is the following:

> Around 1960, when a Japanese specialist of Hungarian and Uralic languages visited Estonia to attend an academic meeting, a Soviet lady came to his hotel to inquire about Komatsubara with whom she said she had been "intimate" when he was a Military Attaché "in Estonia" (obviously the Japanese linguist's mistake for "in Moscow").[114]

It is peculiar, to say the least, that this woman should suddenly approach an unknown foreigner in an Estonian hotel to confess to an affair she had some three decades earlier.

Even supposing that Komatsubara was compromised in 1927, it is far from certain that he continued to serve Moscow during the subsequent 12 years leading up to Nomonhan. In arguing that he did, Kuromiya points to a memorandum sent by Komatsubara to Tokyo in 1929 in which he played down the aggressiveness of Soviet foreign policy.[115] Kuromiya regards this as suspicious, yet, as Jonathan Haslam explains, Moscow's stance was not belligerent in the Far East at that time and, into the early 1930s, the Soviet Union maintained a policy of appeasement towards Japan.[116] Another piece of purported evidence is that several confidential telegrams were leaked to the Soviets from Harbin after 1932 when Komatsubara was head of the Harbin Special Agency.[117] This is also not conclusive, since we know that the

Soviets had other spies among the Japanese authorities in Harbin, including Abe.

What about Komatsubara's behaviour during the Nomonhan conflict? It is true that his leadership was poor. According to Owen Matthews: "The Nomonhan incident was, in effect, a freelance war begun 'single-handedly' (in the words of a subordinate) by the local Japanese commander, Lieutenant General Michitaro Komatsubara."[118] Major Ōgi Hiroshi added that Komatsubara's decision to launch an offensive in August, for which the 23rd Division was ill-prepared, was "the worst in history."[119] Another source of suspicion is Komatsubara's order to suspend night attacks against the Soviet bridgehead on the right bank of the Khalkha River on 12 July. This is despite the fact that, at 4 am that morning, lead elements of the 1st Battalion were within 500 yards of the river and seemed on the verge of taking the bridge.[120] A final point is the extraordinary loss ratio suffered by Komatsubara's men, with a full 76% of the 23rd Division reported killed, wounded, or missing.[121]

The scale of this disaster requires explanation, yet to move from these facts to the conclusion that Komatsubara was a Soviet spy is an unsupported leap. A closer look finds there are alternative explanations at every step. First, for the decision to escalate a minor border skirmish into a large-scale conflict, it makes more sense to blame Major Tsuji Masanobu. Despite his modest rank, Tsuji, by force of personality and length of service, dominated the Operations Section of the Kwantung Army. In this role, Tsuji drafted new principles for how Kwantung Army commanders should respond to border incidents. These guidelines, which were promulgated on 25 April 1939 as Operations Order 1488, included the following:

> if the enemy crosses the frontiers … annihilate him without delay. … To accomplish our mission, it is permissible to enter Soviet territory, or to trap or lure Soviet troops into Manchukuoan territory. … In the event of an armed clash, fight until victory is won regardless of relative strengths or of the location of the boundaries.[122]

Previously, Komatsubara had avoided escalation of border incidents, including in November 1938, when two Japanese personnel had been killed. This changed after Tsuji's new principles were issued. Indeed, it so happens that Komatsubara was discussing the new guidelines at the very moment on 13 May when the first reports of skirmishing reached him. "According to the officers who were present, the general, 'decided in a minute to destroy Outer Mongolian forces,' in conformity with Order 1488."[123]

Similarly, Komatsubara's misjudged decision to dash across the Khalkha River on 3 July and attack Soviet forces within the MPR was not his own initiative but was a plan devised by Major Tsuji, which had been approved by General Ueda Kenkichi, commander-in-chief of the Kwantung Army, without authorisation from the Army General Staff in Tokyo.[124] In later years, Tsuji begrudgingly acknowledged the responsibility of his Operations Section, stating "I have to admit that we at KwAHQ [Kwantung Army Headquarters] could have acted more wisely."[125]

Factors other than betrayal also explain the poor performance of the 23rd Division. Komatsubara had no prior combat experience. The division itself was brand new, having been formed in 1938, and was considered only good for defensive duties. Colonel Chikazawa Yoshimi, who was ordnance chief of the 23rd, was so depressed by the "awful equipment" with which the division was sent to fight that he shot himself on the day the main units were dispatched to the front lines at Nomonhan.[126] The only reason that the operation was assigned to the 23rd Division, rather than the better-prepared 7th Division, is because General Ueda feared that taking it away from Komatsubara would be a blow to his pride.[127]

As for combat losses, these were so high partly because of the Kwantung Army's institutional preference for death over retreat. Indeed, some officers who did make it back alive, such as Lieutenant Colonel Ioki Eiichi, were then pressured to kill themselves.[128] There is even a good reason for Komatsubara's seemingly strange decision to break off the attack when his troops were within striking distance of the river on 12 July. This followed a request by Major General Uchiyama Eitarō, who worried that persisting with the offensive would force the Soviets to draw back their artillery, putting it out of range of the less-capable Japanese guns.[129]

Lastly, Komatsubara's conduct on the battlefield is more suggestive of personal despair than calculated intrigue. On 29 August, when the scale of the 23rd Division's defeat became evident, Komatsubara prepared to commit suicide. However, he was interrupted by a call over the radio from General Ogisu Ryūhei, commander of the 6th Army, who ordered Komatsubara to break the enemy encirclement with as many of his men as possible. Komatsubara complied, leading 400 soldiers to safety. During this march, he was so distraught that he had to have his arms held by subordinates to prevent him from seizing his sword and taking his own life. After Nomonhan, Komatsubara was a broken man. His "previously black hair was now shockingly white." He died of stomach cancer one year later, aged 55.[130]

The argument that Komatsubara was a Soviet spy is tempting, especially for Japanese nationalists who prefer the notion that Japan was stabbed in the back to the reality that the defeat at Nomonhan was caused by the Kwantung Army's misjudged decision to escalate, as well as by its poor equipment, hubristic underestimation of Soviet forces, and inadequate military intelligence. Unless more convincing evidence comes to light, it is best to assume Komatsubara was not a Soviet agent.

* * *

The impact of the Soviet victory at Nomonhan can scarcely be exaggerated, not least because it dissuaded the Japanese leadership from joining Nazi Germany in attacking the Soviet Union in the latter half of 1941. This is a point stressed by Colonel Inada Masazumi, who stated that:

> the Nomonhan incident destroyed our guiding principle of preparing for global conflict by consolidating our position in the North, which would have been achieved by settling the China War and building up our strength against the Soviet Union. Instead, after the Nomonhan incident Japan unexpectedly drifted toward the decision to move south … The Nomonhan incident was a turning point which had a great influence on the history of Japan.[131]

Meanwhile, for the Soviets, Georgii Zhukov's impressive leadership, including his masterful use of disinformation, secured him the title of Hero of the Soviet Union and contributed to Stalin's decision to assign him command over the defence of Moscow of 1941. Zhukov was not the only veteran of Nomonhan present at the Battle of Moscow. He was joined by thousands of ordinary soldiers who had fought the Japanese on the plains of Mongolia. How they came to be transferred west just in time to rescue the capital is the most famous story in the history of Soviet espionage against Japan. It is addressed in the next chapter.

8

THE SORGE-OZAKI SPY RING

Even before picking up this book, most readers will have known something of Dr Richard Sorge, the high-living Soviet illegal whose reports from Tokyo are credited with turning the tide of the Second World War. His story has been told many times and, like many popular tales, aspects have become romanticised. Moscow contributed to this process by posthumously lionising their former spy, though, while he was still alive, they were far less solicitous.

When Sorge was first arrested by the Japanese authorities in October 1941, the Soviets denied all knowledge of him and made no effort to save him via the prisoner swap he expected. After he was hanged in November 1944, it was left to his long-term mistress, Ishii Hanako, to pay for his body to be exhumed from the graveyard near Sugamo prison and moved to a more dignified resting place at Tama cemetery. This neglect lasted until the 1960s, when Soviet leader Nikita Khrushchev, having ordered the construction of the Berlin Wall, decided that the East German people needed a pro-Soviet role model. The half-German Sorge was thus awarded the status of Hero of the Soviet Union in 1964. This veneration continued into the 1970s, when KGB director Yurii Andropov tried to glamorise his organisation by promoting Sorge as "a dashing Soviet version of James Bond."[1]

Even in recent times, Sorge has not been permitted to rest in peace. On regular occasions each year, the Russian ambassador leads a delegation to the graveside. When Ishii Hanako died in 2000, ownership of the grave was initially transferred to her niece. However, when the niece died in 2018, the Russian embassy gained the rights to the burial site.[2] Having done so, Foreign Minister Sergei Lavrov proposed exhuming Sorge's body, separating him from Ishii, whose remains are interred beside him, and reburying him on the Kuril Islands or southern Sakhalin, where the spy never once set foot.[3] By the start of 2025, no steps had been taken to implement this plan.

Yet, even if one strips away Moscow's glamorisation, the Sorge story remains remarkable. Since several book-length accounts already exist,[4] this chapter restricts itself to a comparably brief overview of the members of the Tokyo spy ring, an explanation of their achievements and techniques, and a description of their eventual downfall.

The Tokyo spy ring

Dr Richard Sorge (codenames: RAMSAY, FIX, INSON)

Introvert and extrovert, author of dull economics texts and brash seducer of women, undisciplined drunk and meticulous secret agent, these contradictions, as well as his contribution to Soviet victory in World War II, make Richard Sorge one of the most intriguing characters in the history of espionage. He was born in Baku in 1895, where his father, Wilhelm, a German drilling engineer, was profitably engaged in the Russian Empire's oil industry. While Wilhelm was a bourgeois nationalist, Sorge's uncle, Friedrich Adolf Sorge, had been a communist and had served as secretary general of the First International in New York. Another man drawn to Baku's business opportunities was the merchant Semyon Kobolev, who had moved to the city from Kyiv. Wilhelm married Kobolev's 18-year-old daughter, Nina, and Richard Sorge was one of their five children.[5]

The future communist spy was therefore a cosmopolitan from the start, with a German father, a Russian mother, and born in what became Azerbaijan. This contributed to Sorge's lifelong sense of being an outsider. However, the family moved to Berlin when Richard was just four years old, and he was brought up as a German. Even his mother seems to have spoken to him in German, since Sorge had to learn Russian as an adult. In the German capital, the Sorges enjoyed a comfortable lifestyle. Even when Sorge's father died in 1911, Richard and his siblings were left with generous private incomes. This bourgeois German upbringing was key to Sorge's later ability to win the confidence of German high society in Shanghai and Tokyo.

Another factor that contributed to Sorge's ability to bond with German peers was his experience as a soldier in World War I. Sorge signed up in August 1914 and served with distinction, receiving the Iron Cross (second class). He was wounded three times. On the third occasion, which occurred near Minsk, he was almost killed. "I was hit by a great deal of shrapnel, two pieces of which smashed bone."[6] After surgery, Sorge's left leg was left two centimetres shorter than the right, giving him a permanent limp. It is interesting to reflect that, had that Russian shell killed the young German soldier, he would not have been able to contribute the intelligence that helped save Moscow from German invaders some 25 years later.

As with another well-known soldier of the German army who was also injured during World War I, Sorge's wartime experience had a radicalising effect. However, while Adolf Hitler turned to the far right, Sorge looked left. He felt revulsion at the purposeless slaughter of warfare, began reading Marxist tomes during his recuperation in Königsberg, and became convinced that human progress could only be achieved through revolution. Following this hospital-bed conversion, Sorge remained a Marxist for the rest of his life. His last words before the trapdoor opened and the noose snapped tight around his neck were "Red Army! International Communist Party! Soviet Communist Party!"[7]

After being given a medical discharge from the army, Sorge joined the Independent Social Democratic Party in 1918 and committed himself to fostering a workers' revolution in Germany. He gave rousing speeches to sailors in Kiel and organised socialist cells among coalminers in Aachen. Amid this feverish activity, Sorge found time to study for a doctorate in Political Science in Hamburg, to steal the wife of his academic mentor, Dr Kurt Gerlach, and to join the German Communist Party.[8]

Sorge first came to the attention of Moscow in April 1924 when a communist convention was held in Frankfurt. The 28-year-old Sorge was tasked with looking after Soviet attendees and ensuring they avoided arrest since they were in Germany illegally. The delegation included the head of the Comintern's International Department, Osip A. Pyatnitskii. Impressed by his eager German guide, Pyatnitskii invited Sorge to Moscow to work for the Comintern. Sorge agreed and set off for the Soviet Union by train in October 1924.[9]

Christiane (the former Mrs. Gerlach), whom Sorge had been forced to marry in Germany, followed her husband to Moscow. However, she found she preferred socialism in theory than in practice and disliked the unrefined table manners of Sorge's communist friends. After several miserable months, Christiane returned to Germany in 1926. Sorge, by contrast, was in his element. He began taking Russian lessons from a young actress, Ekaterina A. Maksimova, and started a love affair with her. They moved in together in 1928.[10]

Professionally too, Sorge was hard at it. He was working for Pyatnitskii, who had been tasked with creating a secret organisation within the Comintern to conduct illegal activity abroad. This was the Department of International Communications (OMS). Sorge excelled in this sort of risk-taking, and, in April 1926, he was promoted to the secretariat of the Comintern's Executive Committee (IKKI). Sorge was sent abroad on several occasions, including to Germany, Scandinavia, and Britain. It is not entirely clear what Sorge did during these trips but, before his departure for Britain, he was warned by superiors to maintain an abstemious existence and avoid entanglements with "slim, long-legged English girls."[11] There is also the theory that, while in London, Sorge met an important Soviet agent. According to Peter Wright's *Spycatcher*, this may have been Charles "Dickie" Ellis, an SIS recruit, who is suspected of having been a Soviet double agent.[12]

Despite his ideological ardour, Sorge was ultimately pushed out of the Comintern. This was less because of Sorge's incessant drinking and womanising, and more because of the fratricidal nature of Soviet politics. While Sorge was on the up, he had cultivated ties with the head of the Comintern, Nikolai Bukharin. This proved a liability when Stalin grew suspicious of Bukharin, accusing him of rightist deviationism and removing him as Comintern chief in April 1929. Bukharin later faced a show trial and was executed in 1938. After

Bukharin's removal, Sorge was excluded from the IKKI and his career was put on ice. This could have been the end of Sorge's days serving the Soviet Union, yet his talents had been noted by General Yan K. Berzin, head of the Fourth Directorate of the Red Army's General Staff, better known by its later name, the GRU.

At the end of the 1920s, Soviet foreign intelligence was in a state of flux. Comintern intelligence networks were increasingly seen as insecure and unprofessional. The British police raid in 1927 on the Arcos organisation in London, which was responsible for Anglo-Soviet trade, had, in one fell swoop, largely destroyed Soviet intelligence networks in Britain. This encouraged the view in Moscow that institutions directly connected with the Soviet state, such as embassies and trade representative offices, needed to be supplemented by other channels. This drove the Soviets to rely more on "illegals," that is, "an officer of strategic intelligence performing the tasks of the Centre on the territory of a foreign state, who passes himself off as a foreigner but not as a Soviet citizen."[13] The subsequent years came to be known as "the time of the great illegals," and Sorge was certainly one of the greatest.[14]

After being recruited by Berzin, Sorge was quickly prepared for dispatch to China. This was a logical choice since, as noted, the Soviet Union's focus had shifted to the Far East after hopes of revolution in Europe had faded. Sorge arrived in Shanghai in January 1930 as part of a four-man team headed by Aleksandr P. Ulanovskii, who subsequently served as *rezident* for Soviet military intelligence in the United States (1931–2). Moscow decided that Sorge should use his real name and should present himself as a foreign correspondent. Sorge offered his services to German publications, including *Deutsche Getreide Zeitung* (*German Grain News*), who agreed to publish his articles and provided him with letters of introduction. It was at this time that Moscow assigned Sorge his famous codename, RAMSAY.[15]

In Shanghai, Sorge gathered intelligence on the nationalist Kuomintang government and its struggles with the Chinese Communist Party. Sorge also found himself caught up in the Noulens Affair. This was sparked by the arrest in June 1931 of Yakob Rudnik, a Comintern agent in Shanghai who was posing as a Belgian professor called Hilaire Noulens. Rudnik was a central player in Soviet subversion in East Asia. In the 10 months preceding his arrest, he had "dispensed a staggering £82,200 to communists in China, the Malay states, Japan, Burma, Indochina, Formosa and the Philippines."[16] Despite the risk to his cover, Sorge was ordered to do everything possible to overturn the arrest of "Noulens." This was part of a remarkably successful propaganda campaign by the Soviets which garnered the support of international figures, including Albert Einstein and H.G. Wells.[17] The memory of Moscow's efforts to free their spy in 1931 must have been galling to Sorge, as he spent three years from 1941 awaiting execution in Sugamo Prison as the Soviet leadership sat on their hands.

Aside from these activities, Sorge made crucial contacts among the cosmopolitan crowd that populated pre-war Shanghai. One was Agnes Smedley, a US communist who was working in China as correspondent for the left-leaning *Frankfurter Zeitung* and *Manchester Guardian*. Sorge had been told that Smedley was someone he could trust, and, soon after meeting, Sorge asked her to assist "in establishing an intelligence gathering group in Shanghai."[18] She readily agreed. Predictably, they became lovers, though, this time, Sorge seems to have been driven by professional considerations rather than lust. While Smedley was smitten with her "Sorgie," Sorge himself said that "As a wife [by which he meant a sexual partner] her value was nil. ... In short, she was like a man."[19]

What did make Smedley attractive was her network of contacts. She introduced Sorge to the left-wing crowd that frequented Shanghai's branch of Zeitgeist Buchhandlung, a chain of Comintern-funded bookstores. One such individual was Ursula Hamburger. Born Ursula Kuczynski in Berlin in 1907, she had moved to Shanghai with her architect husband in 1930. Sorge recruited the 23-year-old into the Fourth Directorate and she became Agent SONYA, who, while in Britain during the 1940s, was the handler of Klaus Fuchs, the nuclear scientist who passed atomic secrets to the Soviet Union. Sorge's love affair with Ursula Hamburger began when Agnes Smedley was away in the Philippines. His seduction technique was to get her astride his motorcycle and drive her at high speed through the countryside. She later recalled that, "After this ride, I no longer felt inhibited."[20]

Even more significant was the introduction provided by Smedley to the Shanghai-based Japanese journalist Ozaki Hotsumi, who is the subject of the next section. Sorge immediately recruited him too, leading Ozaki to believe he would be working for the Comintern (i.e. international communism), rather than the Fourth Directorate (i.e. the Soviet military). The timing was fortuitous, because, after the puppet state of Manchukuo had been established on the Soviet Union's eastern flank in 1932, Japan had become Moscow's leading intelligence priority in the Far East. It was therefore no surprise that, after Sorge departed Shanghai in December 1932, his next foreign assignment was Tokyo.

Before setting off for Japan, Sorge spent some time at the headquarters of the Fourth Directorate in Moscow, where he was informed of the objectives of his mission. He was tasked with answering seven questions:

> What was Japan's policy toward the Soviet Union, with particular attention to whether or not Japan planned to attack? Were there any signs of reorganisation and strengthening of such Japanese Army and air units that might be directed against Russia? Were Germany and Japan planning to form an alliance? Was Japan planning any further expansion in China? Was Japan likely to strike any deals with Britain and America to encircle the USSR? Was the influence of the Japanese Army on national policies growing? What was the status of Japan's breakneck industrialisation?[21]

The Fourth Directorate also taught Sorge the cipher codes he would need to contact "Wiesbaden," the radio receiver in Vladivostok through which Sorge would communicate with Moscow. These codes were based on the 1933 edition of the *German Statistical Yearbook*, a volume that would not look out of place on the bookshelf of a German journalist.

This was the entirety of Sorge's training. By contrast, former GRU officer Viktor Suvorov explains that, after World War II, there was a specialist training programme for illegals. Trainees were confined, for three to four years, to dachas in the Moscow suburbs, where they were immersed in a simulacrum of the lifestyle into which they were to be dropped. As Suvorov explains:

> he wears the clothes and shoes, and eats the food, even smokes the cigarettes and uses razor blades procured from overseas. In each room a tape recorder is installed which runs twenty-four hours a day while

> he is occupying the *dacha*. These tape recorders continuously broadcast news from the radio programmes of his target country.[22]

Sorge was subjected to none of this. In part, this was because his career preceded the professionalisation of the illegals programme. It was also because he was a very different type of illegal. Rather than trying to blend in with the local population, Sorge's approach was to make himself the centre of attention of the expatriate German community and thus attract those with information to voluntarily share it with him.

To prepare for Tokyo, Sorge also visited Berlin in May 1933. Hitler was now chancellor and Sorge found the atmosphere oppressive. He even gave up drinking during his stay for fear he might say something compromising when drunk. Rather than carousing in beer halls, Sorge set about acquiring letters of introduction to journalistic and diplomatic circles in Tokyo. The most important of these was that sent by Dr Eduard Zeller, the editor-in-chief of *Tägliche Rundschau* (*Daily Review*), to an old military friend residing in Japan. This told the friend to trust Richard Sorge "in everything; that is, politically, personally and otherwise."[23] That friend was Eugen Ott, and he was to become a central participant in Sorge's spy ring, albeit an unwitting one.

Letters of introduction in hand, Sorge set off for Japan, arriving in Yokohama in September 1933. After first staying at the Sanno Hotel, then the Meguro Hotel, Sorge took up residence at 30 Nagasaka-chō, in the small wooden house that was to be his home until he was ushered from it by Japan's *Tokkō* (Special Higher Police) some eight years later.

Even before Sorge had found himself permanent accommodation, he had got his feet under the table with Tokyo's German community. This numbered just 1,118 individuals in 1933. When Ambassador Herbert von Dirksen took over the embassy that year, its staff comprised just one counsellor, two attachés, two typists, and four secretaries.[24] While the German embassy is now in Minami-Azabu, prior to World War II it was next to the National Diet Building, where the National Diet Library now stands. It was to this location that Sorge strolled just three days after his arrival in Japan. In scarcely more time, he had established himself as a leading member of the German community. He became the most respected German journalist writing on Japanese affairs, a valued advisor at the embassy, and the community's roguish "social lion."[25]

Sorge also made strides into elite Japanese society. By 1938 he had become a member of the Tokyo Club, a British-style gentlemen's club that was founded in 1884 and whose members, then as now, included many senior bureaucrats and businessmen. In 1938 Sorge became one of only 110 foreign members of this exclusive club whose president was Prince Kan-in Kotohito, chief of the Army General Staff. This public prominence would have counted for little in terms of intelligence had Sorge not also enjoyed the confidence of Eugen Ott. In accounts of the Sorge story, Ott comes across as a pathetic figure, not only professionally exploited by the man he considered a friend but cuckolded by him. Yet Ott was a capable individual. He had been a prominent figure in Sondergruppe R, the secret group within the German armed forces that had been created by General Kurt von Schleicher in 1921 to manage the clandestine cooperation with the Bolsheviks that enabled Germany to rearm in violation of the Versailles Treaty. German pilots and tank commanders trained on Soviet territory, and the concept of *blitzkrieg* was developed during exercises in Soviet Belorussia with the assistance of Soviet advisors.[26]

Ott's career had been blown off course when his mentor, von Schleicher, who had become German chancellor in December 1932, was shouldered aside by Hitler just two months later. This accounted for Ott's presence in Japan and the lowly position he occupied. At the end of 1933, Ott was a mere liaison officer to the Japanese Third Artillery Regiment in Nagoya. He was therefore especially pleased when Sorge, of whom Dr Eduard Zeller had written so favourably, took the trouble to visit him there in October. The two found they had served in the same division on the Eastern Front during World War I, and Ott was immediately charmed by his more charismatic companion.

From Sorge's point of view, the effort expended cultivating Ott paid off many times over. This is because Ott's career progression soon resumed. In March 1934, Ott was made senior military attaché in Tokyo. By the next year, Ott was effectively running the embassy, as Ambassador Dirksen was incapacitated by asthma. Ott's appointment as Dirksen's replacement was then formalised in April 1938. Since this coincided with the transformation of Germany into Japan's closest ally, Ott soon found himself not only Germany's most senior official in Japan but the best-connected diplomat of any country. As US Ambassador Joseph Grew put it, "Of all his foreign colleagues, only Ott had real access to Japanese politics and the holders of power."[27] Furthermore, as a military officer, Ott found it easy to develop contacts with counterparts in the Japanese military, many of whom viewed Germany as a role model.

Throughout Ott's rise and service as ambassador, Sorge was there beside him. In September 1934, Sorge joined Ott on a visit to Manchukuo and was able to observe Japanese activities there. After the Marco Polo Bridge Incident in July 1937, Sorge was invited to join a three-man study team within the embassy to evaluate the expansion of Japan's conflict in China. Sorge was even trusted to make courier runs to Hong Kong and Shanghai, using the opportunity to smuggle microfilm for the Soviets within German diplomatic pouches. This close cooperation culminated in Ott's offer in 1939 for Sorge to formally accept a high position within the embassy. Sorge declined in order to retain the freedom he needed for spy work, yet he accepted a compromise that provided him with a desk at the embassy at which he worked most mornings. Sorge also breakfasted regularly with Ott. During these discussions over freshly baked German rolls, the ambassador shared details of confidential correspondence from Berlin.[28]

Ott was certainly enamoured with his raffish friend, yet this was a mutually beneficial relationship. Ott understood that the information he gave Sorge assisted his work as a journalist and boosted his reputation. In return, Sorge provided the embassy with first-class insight into the inner workings of Japanese politics. This information, which was given to Sorge by Ozaki Hotsumi, was highly valued in Berlin, thus simultaneously raising Ott's profile as ambassador. Sorge was therefore something of a double agent. Although Sorge may never have officially been a German intelligence officer, he was seen within the embassy as playing the role of a special officer, and Brigadeführer Walter Schellenberg, deputy head of the SS intelligence service, wrote with appreciation of the value of "Sorge's intelligence material."[29]

Despite being the most famous Soviet spy ever to have worked in Japan, Sorge did not actually spy on the Japanese, at least not directly. That task was the specialism of Ozaki Hotsumi.

Ozaki Hotsumi (codenames: OTTO, INVEST)

At the same time as the Soviet Union belatedly began eulogising Sorge, the Japanese left started doing the same with Ozaki. In 1962, a play called *Ottō to Yobareru Nihonjin* (*A Japanese Called Otto*) by playwright Kinoshita Junji began to be performed in Japan.[30] This sought to rehabilitate the executed spy and to present him not as a traitor who betrayed his country to a rival that was soon to attack Japan, but as a passionate idealist. Ozaki's new image as a sensitive humanist was assisted by publication in 1946 of the love poetry he had written to his wife when in prison.[31]

Ozaki also found international admirers, most notably Chalmers Johnson, whose *An Instance of Treason* is an essential source on the Sorge spy ring. Johnson makes the case that Ozaki was "a martyr rather than a traitor," and questions, "Is treason a meaningful concept when the leadership of a nation has fallen into the hands of men who are driving it toward its own destruction?"[32] This is a reasonable question, yet, while Ozaki may have been a martyr, he certainly was not a saint.

As we have seen, Ozaki was first introduced to Sorge by Agnes Smedley in Shanghai in late 1930. Initially, Ozaki did not know Sorge's real name, since the Soviet spy presented himself as an American journalist called Richard Johnson. Ozaki was working at the time as China correspondent for Japan's *Asahi Shimbun*. In Johnson/Sorge, Ozaki found someone who shared his intellectual commitment to communism. He also found a man as gregarious as himself, or, to put it less politely, a fellow boozer and skirt chaser. They hit it off immediately.

Ozaki Hotsumi was born into a former samurai family from West Shirakawa village in Gifu prefecture. While this accounts for his pen name—Shirakawa Jirō—Ozaki was actually born in the Shiba ward of Tokyo, now part of Minato ward. Appropriately for this future champion of proletarian revolution, his birthday was 1 May 1901. Ozaki's family moved to Taiwan when he was a baby and he remained there until he was 18 years old. The island had been acquired from China just six years earlier and Japan was beginning to colonise its new possession. Ozaki lived in a compound for Japanese residents and attended a school for the colonial elite. Despite his detachment from local society, Ozaki began to learn Chinese and to study Chinese history. These were foundations that helped him become one of Japan's leading Sinologists. Another legacy was Ozaki's abiding sense of guilt about his childhood, which included being carted around in rickshaws while other boys walked in the dust.[33] He reflected that, "This experience later aroused in me an extraordinary interest in the problem of national liberation."[34]

Ozaki's social conscience had been pricked, but he only turned to communism after returning to Japan. He enrolled at Tokyo Teikoku University, the forerunner of the University of Tokyo, and undertook his studies at a time of political unrest. In June 1923, there was a mass arrest of Communist Party members. Then, following the Great Kantō Earthquake of September 1923, thousands of Koreans were massacred, supposedly because they were conspiring with socialists to exploit the disaster.[35] These incidents had a radicalising effect on Ozaki, who later described 1923 as "the first major turning point of my life."[36]

Ozaki's future course was still not set. In 1924, he sat the Higher Civil Service Entrance Examination. Had he passed, there is every chance Ozaki would have put aside his youthful dalliance with socialism and devoted himself to a career as a bureaucrat and servant of empire. But he failed the exam. Apparently, this is because he was besotted with a young divorcée and preferred wooing her to committing to his studies.[37]

Having failed to become a bureaucrat, Ozaki opted for journalism, becoming an *Asahi Shimbun* reporter in 1926. Here too, things did not get off to a good start. His first supervisor lamented that, "as a city desk reporter, both his news sense and his writing style were completely hopeless."[38] Still, the paper stuck with him, directing him towards analysis, where he showed greater promise. In November 1928, they sent him to Shanghai as the *Asahi*'s special correspondent.

Ozaki's affection for China strengthened considerably while in Shanghai from 1928 to 1932. He even selected one of the characters from the Yangtze River for the name of his daughter, who was born in 1929.[39] Politically too, his time in China had an impact. He witnessed the exploitation of the Chinese people at the hands of his own countrymen and became convinced that only radical change could liberate them. It was, he said, "the observation of factual developments of the

'China problem' that matured my interests in the Marxist theory."[40] Therefore, when the heavily accented "Mr Johnson" asked Ozaki to work for the Comintern, it seemed natural he should accept.

In Shanghai, Ozaki helped Sorge compile information on Chinese politics and Japanese activity in Manchuria. He also began to recruit sub-agents. The most notable was Kawai Teikichi, a fellow Japanese journalist. Ozaki and Sorge dispatched Kawai to Manchuria, and he was told to "pay strict attention to the possibility of an invasion of Siberia by the Japanese Army."[41] Kawai proved himself a dogged agent, yet his involvement nearly brought the spy ring to a premature end. He was arrested on suspicion of espionage in January 1936 and shipped to Manchukuo, where he was interrogated and beaten with an iron bar. Even though Kawai was by then working for the Sorge-Ozaki ring in Tokyo, he revealed nothing. The thoroughness of the beating may have helped him, since "He could only gasp out a brief 'yes' or 'no' between blows, and through the blur of pain he could not think clearly enough to give detailed information." He was eventually released.[42]

Ozaki was useful to Sorge in Shanghai. Consequently, when Ozaki was recalled to Japan in early 1932, Sorge urged him to give up his job and stay. Ozaki ignored the suggestion and returned to the *Asahi*'s bureau in Osaka. From the Soviet perspective, this was just as well, since it was in Japan that the Sorge-Ozaki collaboration really began to flourish, going from helpful to truly historic.

Ozaki lived a quiet existence in Kansai for two years before "Mr Johnson" came calling again. Their rendezvous in May 1934 was in Nara Park, which is famous for its tame deer. Sorge asked Ozaki to resume cooperation, and Ozaki bowed to the request, recalling later, "I made up my mind to do spy activity with Sorge again."[43] Ozaki continued to insist that he thought he was working for the Comintern and not the Soviet state. This is questionable, since, by the early 1930s, it was apparent to everyone that Stalin had eliminated the distinction between the two.

When Sorge re-recruited Ozaki in 1934, he had no inkling that, in a little over four years, Ozaki would have a desk in the prime minister's office and access to Japan's highest policymaking circles. That Ozaki was initially a low priority is demonstrated by the fact that it was eight months after Sorge's arrival in Japan that he arranged to meet Ozaki in Nara. The metamorphosis in Ozaki's standing began with a transfer to the *Asahi*'s Tokyo office in 1934. This coincided with the paper's decision to create a think tank called the Tōa Mondai Chōsa Kai (Investigation Committee for East Asian Problems), which brought together *Asahi* journalists with government officials, commercial figures, and intellectuals. As one of the paper's China experts, Ozaki was invited to join.[44]

An equally important step was Ozaki's attendance at the conference of the Institute of Pacific Relations in August 1936 in California. As with most conferences, what occurred within the formal sessions was less important. What really mattered was the chance to forge contacts. In Ozaki's case, the long voyage to California gave him the opportunity to connect with other Japanese delegates, especially Saionji Kinkazu and Ushiba Tomohiko. Both became key to Ozaki's penetration of senior political circles.

Prince Saionji Kinkazu was the adopted grandson of Prince Saionji Kinmochi, who served as prime minister from 1911 to 1912. With his blue-blood connections, Saionji Kinkazu enjoyed close links with prominent politicians, including a future prime minister, Konoe Fumimaro, to whom Saionji became an advisor. As Ozaki later explained, after their long trip to California, "Saionji trusted me well, treated me as a bosom friend, and disclosed secret matters to me without any caution."[45] There are indications that Saionji's collaboration may not have been entirely unwitting. After Ozaki's arrest, Saionji was detained as an accomplice and given a three-year suspended sentence. Following the war, Saionji openly displayed his socialism and in 1958 moved to the People's Republic of China, where he became a friend of Zhou Enlai.[46]

While lacking Saionji's famous name, Ushiba Tomohiko was similarly important in providing Ozaki with access to the corridors of power. Ozaki and Ushiba had actually been acquainted since 1919, when they had studied together at Daiichi Kōtō Gakkō (First Higher School).[47] Ushiba later became private secretary to Prime Minister Konoe, giving Ozaki a second contact within the premier's office.

Ozaki's jovial personality made him a welcome companion during the dreary days aboard ship. Yet Ozaki's rise and growing list of contacts was due to much more than his conversation skills and readiness to share a drink. Ozaki might have been a second-rate news reporter, but he was a first-rate analyst of Chinese politics. His growing reputation in this field ensured that he was increasingly sought out by Japan's political elite, for whom the "China problem" was the dominant issue of the day.

Ozaki's breakthrough in becoming a renowned China expert was achieved with an article entitled "The Significance of Chang Hsueh-liang's Coup d'Etat." This was an analysis of the Xi'an Incident of December 1936, when Chang Hsueh-liang, the "Young Marshall" who had been warlord of Manchuria, took Premier of the Republic of China Chiang Kai-shek hostage for two weeks. At the time, Chiang had been focused on fighting the Chinese communists, whom he considered a "disease of the heart," rather than the Japanese, whom he saw as a mere "disease of the skin."[48] The Xi'an Incident changed this. Following his release, Chiang reversed course and made common cause with the communists against the Japanese. This paved the way for the Second United Front. In his article, Ozaki accurately predicted that the Xi'an Incident would be prejudicial to Japan's interests. This insight earned him membership of the Shōwa Kenkyū Kai (Shōwa Research Association), which functioned as an advisory group for Prince Konoe Fumimaro, who began his first stint as prime minister in June 1937.

Ozaki's espionage work for Moscow was, of course, a secret, but his left-wing sympathies were not. How is it that, in the rabidly nationalist environment of late 1930s Japan, a figure like Ozaki was granted a seat at such a top table? The explanation is that, while members of the Shōwa Kenkyū Kai were nationalist, they "relied heavily on Marxism for their analysis of society and rejected the principles of capitalism and liberalism in favor of the nationalization of industries, a single-party regime, and a state-regulated economy."[49] Ozaki's ideological views were therefore not out of place.

Further appointments soon followed. In July 1938, Ozaki received the title of *naikaku shokutaku*, or "cabinet consultant," and worked closely with Chief Cabinet Secretary Kazami Akira. In this capacity, Ozaki received an office in the prime minister's residence and gained access to government papers. Ozaki was also invited by Ushiba

Tomohiko, Konoe's private secretary, to the regular *Asameshi Kai* (Breakfast Club). This was an informal council at which advisors, experts, and government ministers would chew over key issues and formulate advice for the prime minister. As Ozaki himself put it, "It can be said that this meeting made me achieve a substantial result for my spy activity."[50] The spy ring therefore achieved the remarkable feat that, while one member was sipping miso soup at an inner council of the Japanese prime minister, another was breaking bread with the German ambassador.

Yet another appointment came in June 1939, when Ozaki was hired by the investigation department of the South Manchuria Railway (Mantetsu). This might seem a step down, but Mantetsu was much more than a railway company. It was the locomotive of Japanese imperialism in Manchuria. Established in 1906, Manetsu was a semi-governmental organisation modelled on Britain's East India Company that became involved in all key sectors of the Manchurian economy, including industry, energy, telecommunication, and logistics.[51] From Ozaki's perspective, what was important was that Mantetsu's investigation department was a hub for information about Japan's activities in Manchukuo. If Japan were preparing an attack against the Soviet Far East, it would be immediately apparent from the data flooding into the Mantetsu Building in Tokyo's Toranomon. "Every movement of troops, armour and war materials across Japan and China could be traced in precise detail through the Mantetsu's meticulous hour-by-hour timetables."[52]

Due to this access, Ozaki was Sorge's most valuable agent. However, how should history judge him? One controversial point is Ozaki's support for Japan's Greater East Asia Co-Prosperity Sphere. During his time with Konoe's Shōwa Kenkyū Kai, Ozaki, along with Rōyama Masamichi and Miki Kiyoshi, played a leading role in formulating this concept, which provided a fig leaf of intellectual decency to conceal the rapacity of Japanese imperialism. This was not about maintaining cover. Rather, Ozaki genuinely favoured a Greater East Asia Co-Prosperity Sphere, albeit in a different form from that pursued by the Japanese government from 1940. In Ozaki's vision, the Greater East Asia Co-Prosperity Sphere would begin as a Japanese government project but would take its true form after communist revolutions had swept both China and Japan. National tensions would then evaporate, and a new era of peace and prosperity would dawn. Ozaki hoped that Prime Minister Konoe's vision of a New Order could be harnessed in pursuit of this goal. In Ozaki's words, "By advancing him [Konoe], we can switch the so-called New Order in East Asia into socialism on the basis of close cooperation with the Communist Parties of the Soviet Union and China." Referring to the politician who led the Russian provisional government between the revolutions of February and October 1917, Ozaki claimed that "Konoye is a Kerensky; he is a bridge to the next political power."[53]

Another questionable feature of Ozaki's thinking was his support for the war in China. This was not so Japan could win. Rather, it was so Japan would experience a defeat that was as protracted and debilitating as possible. This was based on Lenin's concept of "revolutionary defeatism."[54] This idea, which was informed by Russia's experience of World War I, was that the hardship and instability caused by military failure can be exploited to ferment civil unrest and, ultimately, revolution. An added benefit was that the demands of a long war entailed shifting Japan further towards a Soviet-style state-managed economy. Ozaki therefore argued for yet more resources to be committed to the conflict in China. Indeed, the last article he wrote before his arrest in October 1941 was entitled "To Fight the Great War to the Very End."[55] This shows the cold consequentialism of Ozaki's thinking. He was willing to shove ever more of his compatriots into the meat grinder, and to accept the concomitant massacre of Chinese, so long as, in the end, it led to the promised land of communist revolution.

Ozaki's personal morals were also not to everyone's taste. His posthumous image is that of a devoted husband, yet, when alive, he was far from an exemplary family man. After marriage, Ozaki made no effort to be faithful. Contemporaries describe him as an "*enpukuka*" (a ladies' man) and a "hormone tank," who liked to boast to friends about his latest conquests. It is suspected that, when in Shanghai, he too may have slept with Agnes Smedley, as well as with the sister of Irene Wiedemeyer, the owner of the Zeitgeist Bookstore.[56] This was at a time when Ozaki's wife was at home nursing their baby daughter.

Additionally, Ozaki's commitment to equality was more intellectual than real. Chalmers Johnson concedes that Ozaki had "a 'feudal' attitude toward women and that he considered the idea of the emancipation of women bizarre." Moreover, while Ozaki was supposedly devoted to the interests of the working class, he avoided their company and had "a typically Japanese 'elitist' attitude toward the masses."[57] For some who got to know him, Ozaki's bonhomie seemed a mask. As one acquaintance put it, "Ozaki was always in smile; however, his eyes were not. Although his eyes were narrow and meek as those of an elephant, there was always something strikingly cold at the bottom."[58]

Max Clausen (codenames: HANS, FRITZ)

Sorge and Ozaki were the kingpins of the spy ring, yet their success was dependent on the support of lower-ranking figures. Above all, the intelligence gathered would have been worthless if it could not be communicated to Moscow. Courier runs to Shanghai and Hong Kong, where material could be handed off to Soviet contacts, were possible but were slow and laborious. They were primarily used for sending microfilm and collecting funds. Such trips became more difficult after 1939, when Germans became unwelcome among those cities' international residents. What was needed was a reliable "musician"—that is, a clandestine radio operator.

The Fourth Directorate initially selected Bruno Wendt (codename BERNHARDT). However, Sorge complained that he was so panic-stricken that he would only send short, infrequent messages. Sorge also criticised Wendt's excessive drinking, which must have been quite something to attract the opprobrium of Sorge.[59] Consequently, during a covert visit to Moscow in 1935, Sorge requested Wendt's replacement, ultimately selecting Clausen, whom he had met during his mission in China.

Max Clausen was born in 1899 on the windswept island of Nordstrand, in Schleswig-Holstein, close to Denmark. He was the only member of the spy ring's inner circle with working-class credentials, having toiled in his father's bicycle repair shop and having worked as an apprentice blacksmith.[60] However, it was Clausen who ultimately lost his faith in communism and became a devoted capitalist.

Clausen's path towards becoming a radio expert began when he was drafted into the Germany army's Signal Corps in 1917. He served on the Western Front and was injured in a friendly-fire gas attack "that left him coughing blood for a month."[61] Already embittered, his political radicalisation intensified after World War I due to the widespread unemployment he witnessed in Germany during the 1920s. Clausen entered the Merchant Navy, became an activist in the Seaman's Union, and joined the German Communist Party. He made a visit to the Soviet port of Murmansk in 1924 and was impressed by the fledgling workers' state. As with Sorge, Clausen's skills were noted by Moscow. He was invited in 1928 to the Soviet Union, where he underwent training at the Fourth Directorate's Technical School.[62] Talented radio operators were in short supply, so Clausen was soon activated and dispatched to China. Clausen was part of a different Fourth Directorate team in China from Sorge, but Sorge came to know Clausen and respected his technical work.

After Clausen returned to the Soviet Union in the autumn of 1933, he was punished by the security services. This was due to his relationship with Anna Wallenius. Anna Zhdankova was born in Novonikolaevsk (modern-day Novosibirsk) in 1899. At 18, she married Eduard Wallenius, the Finnish owner of a leather workshop. Wallenius took Anna to Semipalatinsk on the Kazakh steppes, where he purchased a flour mill. They looked set for a comfortable bourgeois existence, yet their timing could not have been worse. After the Bolsheviks seized power, Wallenius's property was expropriated and he and Anna, along with thousands of other White (i.e. anti-Bolshevik) Russians, fled to Shanghai. Eduard tried to restore the couple's fortunes, but the stress was too much and he died of a heart attack in 1927. This left Anna in financial distress and with an abiding hatred for communism. In her view, under communism, "there is no life, no freedom, and no peace."[63] It was an unusual background for a woman who was to become the wife of a Red Army intelligence officer.

Max Clausen met Anna in 1929 and the two quickly became lovers. However, Moscow denied them the right to marry for six years. Part of the reason was that Anna had been born in Russia and Fourth Directorate illegals were supposed to avoid all contact with Russians. A bigger factor was that, as a White Russian émigrée, Anna was a "former person," who was suspected of anti-Soviet attitudes, which, in Anna's case, she certainly did hold.

It is testimony to the strength of the couple's relationship that it survived Anna's discovery that Max was a Soviet spy. She did, however, draw the line at having a child in such circumstances, opting to have three abortions even though she wanted children.[64] Max too made sacrifices. He refused to abandon Anna even though, following the couple's return to the Soviet Union in 1933, it meant being sent to a collective farm in the Volga German Autonomous Republic for "reform through labour."[65]

The fact that Clausen was rehabilitated and ultimately permitted to marry Anna says much about his exceptional skills as a radio operator. This included building all the equipment himself since, for operational security, he was not permitted to travel to Japan with any technical kit. The transmitter that Clausen constructed was a creative marvel. According to a radio expert who examined the equipment after the breakup of the spy ring, it was "one of the strangest conglomerations of various stray parts I have ever seen—a terrific assortment of materials that included one or two beer bottles and other miscellaneous items."[66]

Clausen was terrifically hard-working, doing all the encoding and decoding himself. This required working in English, which had been selected by the Fourth Directorate as the language of communication. He was also brave. Clausen's ingenious transmitter was portable and could be set up in ten minutes. This had the advantage of allowing Clausen to operate from multiple sites, yet it meant he had to travel around Tokyo clutching a large case, which, if discovered, would lead to his immediate arrest. This almost happened when a taxi in which Clausen was travelling was stopped by a police officer. Fortunately, the officer did not demand to inspect the passenger's luggage. Despite the risks involved, this system of transmitting from several locations was wise, since, unbeknown to Clausen, the Japanese police had, since 1938, been intercepting all the spy ring's radio communications. These were filed away under the title "Dal X," yet, until the group's arrest and the revelation of the system of enciphering, the police were able neither to read the messages nor to identify their source.[67]

It seemed Sorge had selected the perfect radio man, yet the constant pressure began to take its toll. In May 1940, the heavy-set Clausen had a major heart attack. Even then, he rigged up a special table and continued to encode and decode from his sickbed. Unable to go out, he transmitted from his own home in Shinryūdo-chō, Azabu-ku, making use of an antenna he had built into the roof.[68]

More than declining health, what ultimately turned Clausen from an asset to a liability was his disillusionment with socialism. Repugnance at unemployment had been a major factor in enticing Clausen towards the far left. However, he now saw that this had largely been eliminated in Germany. This turned the Red Army officer into a man who held "a very favorable attitude toward Hitler's way of doing things."[69]

Clausen also inadvertently became a successful capitalist. For cover, Clausen had been instructed by the Fourth Directorate to set up a business in Japan. He experimented with various ideas before eventually focusing on producing and selling machines for copying blueprints. With the Japanese arms industry booming, the company, named M. Clausen Shōkai, became enormously successful. Clausen increasingly found that he preferred the world of commerce to that of clandestine operations, and he became the very image of a fat cat, with an ever-expanding waistline as he cruised around Tokyo in his Mercedes. Clausen also began to resent Sorge, who took his radio man for granted and used the profits from Clausen's firm to cover the spy ring's expenses.[70]

Eventually, Clausen's patience snapped, and, from November 1940, he began to sabotage communications, sending a fraction of the material Sorge handed him. Clausen made just 21 transmissions (13,103 word groups) in 1941 in contrast to 60 transmissions (29,179 word groups) in 1940.[71] However, fortunately for the Soviet Union, Clausen retained some residual loyalty or perhaps just feared being discovered. As such, he transmitted enough material during 1941 to permit the most crucial messages to get through.[72]

Miyagi Yotoku (codenames: JOE, INTERI)

Other than a radio operator, the spy ring needed a reliable Japanese fixer. Rather than an intelligence agent like Ozaki, this person's role was to handle the miscellaneous legwork that kept the group ticking. Finding such a figure was not simple. While there were still plenty of left-wing sympathisers in Japan, Moscow feared using them, since those with known socialist connections were kept under close surveillance by Japan's *Tokkō*. The recruit would also need fluent English, as Sorge spoke only broken Japanese. To find such an individual, Moscow looked to America.

Miyagi Yotoku was born in 1903 in Nago, Okinawa, close to where the controversial US Marine Corps Air Station is now being built at Henoko Bay. Miyagi's father was a poor farmer who left Okinawa in search of a better life when his son was just two years old, and finally settled in Baldwin Park, Los Angeles County. Miyagi was brought up by his maternal grandfather and might have stayed in Okinawa had it not been for the tuberculosis that showed itself at age 16. This encouraged him to follow in his father's footsteps and to soothe his lungs in the drier air of southern California.[73]

Miyagi was never a fervent Marxist. His passion was for art, and he graduated with a diploma from the San Diego Public Art School. Yet Miyagi did have an emotional commitment to the marginalised of society. This owed much to his own status as a double outsider. As a boy, Miyagi had been taught by his grandfather about how Okinawans were discriminated against and about how Japanese from the main islands had turned the formerly independent Ryūkyū Kingdom into a "palm-tree hell [*sotetsu jigoku*] of wanton exploitation by Kagoshima capital."[74] As an immigrant in California, Miyagi also felt resentment at the "inhuman discrimination practiced against the Asiatic races in the United States."[75]

In 1926, Miyagi and three Japanese friends began a social science study group, which they first called the Shakai Mondai Kenkyū-Kai (Association for the Research of Social Problems), then later, Reimei Kai (Society of the Dawn). He also joined the Proletarian Arts Society, a Comintern front. But he was not very committed to political activities, preferring to spend his time painting. Miyagi had married a fellow Japanese immigrant in 1927, though the relationship broke down in 1932. This left Miyagi living on his own in lodgings rented from a landlord named Kitabayashi Yoshisaburō, whose wife, Tomo, was also part of the Proletarian Arts Society and a member of the Communist Party of the United States.[76] This seemingly unimportant connection made in West Los Angeles in the early 1930s would prove the loose thread that led to the unravelling of the Sorge-Ozaki network in Tokyo almost a full decade later.

Miyagi's recruitment for Soviet intelligence was carried out by Japanese communist Yano Tsutomu (alias "Takeda") during visits at the end of 1932 and in spring 1933. Yano urged Miyagi to return to

Japan. Miyagi was unenthusiastic, but he was told he would be helping the Comintern promote world peace. He was also handed $200. Miyagi was assigned the codename JOE and reassured that he need only stay in Tokyo for a couple of months.[77] In fact, he was never to see the United States again.

Miyagi arrived in Japan in autumn 1933 and had his first meeting with Sorge at an art museum in Ueno. It did not take Miyagi long to discover the reality of his work for Moscow. He later admitted, "I participated in the ring, understanding completely that this activity was against the laws of Japan and that I would be executed in wartime for my espionage."[78] It may seem strange that Miyagi did not walk away when he realised he had been duped. As much as anything, this was due to the artist's indecisiveness. As he told fellow recruit Kawai Teikichi, "It is foolish for people like us to engage in this sort of thing. … I never intended to do this on a permanent basis. Now I can't seem to get away from it."[79]

Despite qualms about spying for Moscow against his own country, Miyagi proved an excellent assistant. He reliably did basic tasks, such as translations, but he was also effective at collecting intelligence himself. His profession as an artist was an asset, since it gave him freedom to travel. Moreover, a jobbing painter is someone who straddles the creative and the toiling classes, helping Miyagi feel at home in all company. When wishing to meet Ozaki, Miyagi used the cover story that he was giving painting lessons to the journalist's daughter. The clutter of an artist's studio also seemed a convenient place to conceal secret notes.[80]

Some of the intelligence gathered by Miyagi was open-source. Much valuable data was printed in Japanese military magazines and in pamphlets featuring articles by Japanese officers.[81] These were available in specialist bookshops but, written as they were in technical Japanese, for Sorge, they might as well have been in code. The appearance of a foreigner in one of those shops would also have aroused suspicions. Separately, Miyagi started hanging out in bars frequented by Japanese soldiers and gently probing for information on where they might be deployed. This sometimes generated useful intelligence but Miyagi, who lacked the hollow legs of Sorge and Ozaki, disliked the amount of alcohol he had to drink.[82]

Even more hazardous to the health of the spy ring was the decision to encourage Miyagi to recruit his own sub-agents. This he did with abandon. One, Akiyama Kōji, was an old acquaintance from California who had fallen on hard times. Miyagi employed him for 100 yen a month to assist with translations. There were also leftists who had spent time in jail, such as Yamana Masazano, whom Miyagi sent to Hokkaidō to survey Japanese troop movements. Miyagi even signed up his own doctor, Yasuda Tokutarō, in case he should pick up any gossip from his well-connected patients.

The intelligence provided by these individuals did not justify the risk involved, but Miyagi also had genuinely valuable informants. Most were connected to the military. Yabe Shu was a leftist sympathiser who was secretary to General Ugaki Kazushige, a former army minister.[83] Another was Koshiro Yoshinobu, who more commonly went by the surname "Kodai." Kodai was a former soldier who, after being conscripted in 1936, served in Manchuria as well as various parts of China. He retained friends in uniform and was urged by Miyagi to get a job with the War Ministry's mobilisation bureau. Under the codename MIKI, Kodai provided valuable information, including, in summer 1939, the reassurance that Japan would not send large numbers of reinforcements to Nomonhan.[84]

On most occasions, Miyagi told sub-agents they were serving international communism. Yet in some cases, Miyagi's informants were entirely unaware of his leftist leanings. Two right-wing journalists, Sano Masahiko and Kikuchi Hachirō, were fooled into believing that Miyagi was associated with ultra-nationalist groups.[85] Miyagi also became the principal handler of Shinotsuka Torao. An old acquaintance of Ozaki, Shinotsuka owned a factory that produced military equipment. Ozaki introduced Shinotsuka to Miyagi and told the factory owner that Miyagi was assisting him in his work with the Shōwa Kenkyū Kai. Happy to help this high-profile grouping, Shinotsuka provided Miyagi with data "about Japan's newest aircraft, the Kawasaki 88 and the Mitsubishi 92, as well as the exact numbers, armament and capabilities of the army's bomber fleet and details of the navy's complement of 'reconnaissance planes, scout planes, attack planes, fighters and torpedo planes'."[86]

Miyagi was therefore a key link in the spy ring and much more than a dogsbody. Yet, in the end, it was Miyagi's overly eager recruitment of sub-agents and his readiness to do a favour for an old friend that contributed to the downfall of the Sorge-Ozaki group.

Branko Vukelić (codename: GIGOLO) and Günther Stein (codename: GUSTAF)

The last two members to introduce before turning to the ring's achievements and downfall are Branko Vukelić and Günther Stein. Branko Vukelić was born in 1904 in what is now Croatia. He studied architecture at the University of Zagreb, where he became interested in communism. However, in 1926, his mother took him to Paris, where he studied in the law faculty of the Sorbonne. His political ardour had considerably cooled and Vukelić looked set for a conventional life. He found a job with the Compagnie Générale d'Electricité and married his Danish girlfriend, Edith Olsen, who had recently become pregnant. What changed all this was his trip to Yugoslavia in 1931 for his military service. Although absent for only four months, he returned to Paris to find his job had been abolished. It was at this moment of vulnerability that Vukelić happened upon two old friends from Zagreb, who were still involved in communist circles. Although Vukelić told them "I'm not a convinced Communist any longer," they insisted on putting him in contact with a female intelligence officer named "Olga," who is said to have had a Finnish or Baltic accent. It was she who recruited Vukelić.[87] It is almost certain that this "Olga" was Lydia Stahl, a Soviet military intelligence operative who was active in Paris during the early 1930s. She is known to have used the alias "Olga la Balte" and is said to have used sexual favours as a recruitment technique.[88]

Vukelić, along with Edith and their three-year-old son, Paul, was dispatched to Tokyo in December 1932, thus arriving months before Sorge. Their wait proved difficult, since Moscow had miscalculated their living expenses, leaving the young family with just 10 yen per day. Consequently, when the call finally came in November 1933 and arrangements were made for a meeting with "Johnson," Sorge found his new colleague in "a pitiful state ... ill, homesick and broke."[89]

Provided with financial resources, Vukelić set himself up, like Sorge, as a foreign correspondent in Tokyo. He worked for the French magazine *Vue* and the Belgrade daily *Politika*, and, later, for the Havas news agency. Although Vukelić and Sorge saw each other regularly at press events, they moved in different circles. Vukelić had closer relations with French and British journalists whose ties with German correspondents became distant as international tensions rose. He also had "many intimate talks with the British Military Attaché, Major General Francis S. Piggott," and was friendly with Eugene H. Dooman, Counselor at the US embassy.[90] Vukelić was therefore able to pass on political gossip that Sorge might not otherwise hear. He also served as courier for the spy ring during overseas trips and handled the group's photography.[91]

Yet Vukelić was the least valuable member of the spy ring. He lacked ideological commitment and preferred journalism to spying. As a result, Sorge always thought of him "as an outsider" and dismissed his intelligence as "neither secret nor important."[92] Vukelić's love life was also a risk. Vukelić had tired of Edith and began courting Yamasaki Yoshiko, a pretty translator he met at the theatre in 1934. Vukelić did not handle the situation tactfully. It became "'common knowledge' that Vukelić made love to his Japanese mistress downstairs while his wife wept upstairs."[93] The danger was that the spurned wife, who knew everything about Vukelić's work, would betray the group to the authorities. Sorge's solution was to pay Edith 400 yen a month plus expenses in exchange for maintaining her silence and allowing Clausen to use her home as a site for radio transmissions. After the divorce was finalised and Vukelić married Yoshiko, Edith and Paul left Japan for Australia on 25 September 1941, less than a month before Vukelić was arrested.[94]

Günther Stein was also a foreign correspondent in Tokyo, writing for several British publications, including the *Manchester Guardian* and *Daily Telegraph*. He also authored a book in 1935 analysing the causes of Japan's rapid industrialisation.[95] Stein was German by birth (in 1900), but, as a half-Jewish socialist, he had lost his job after Hitler took power and left for Britain, where he became a citizen. There remains confusion over whether Stein was really part of the Tokyo spy ring. This is because Moscow rejected Sorge's request to formally recruit him. Additionally, Stein was not arrested with the rest of the group in October 1941, since he was not in Japan at the time. And yet there is substantial evidence to support the claim of Major General

Charles A. Willoughby, General MacArthur's chief of intelligence during the occupation of Japan, that Stein was a "top level member of the ring."[96]

Sorge had known Stein "for a long time," presumably through socialist circles in Germany. He also trusted him, for he admitted to Stein that he was "working for the Moscow authorities."[97] Despite Moscow Centre's instructions not to recruit Stein, Sorge used him as another source on what was being discussed within European circles in Tokyo. Stein also spent time in China covering the war against the Japanese and was thus able to report back his observations.[98] Additionally, Stein made courier runs, and it was at his house that Clausen built his radio and first transmitter.[99] Indeed, rather than being only "a sympathizer," as Sorge told the Japanese police, Stein seems to have contributed more to the spy ring than Vukelić.[100] As Chalmers Johnson explains:

> Stein's sources of information—ncted and praised by Sorge—were the British Ambassador; the Commercial Counsellor of the British Embassy (1925–40), and the West's best-known historian of Japan, Sir George Sansom; various British and American journalists; and the Dōmei News Agency.[101]

In 1945, Stein moved to the United States but, when US occupation forces in Japan discovered information suggesting Stein's connection with the Sorge ring, Stein fled to Paris. He remained there until November 1950, when he was arrested by the French authorities, charged with being a Soviet spy, and deported to Great Britain. It is unclear if he was ever convicted, and several aspects of Stein's career remain opaque. This has led to speculation that Stein may have worked for British intelligence.[102]

The spy ring delivers

Predicting Barbarossa

Although based in Tokyo, Sorge's German contacts were so excellent that he was one of the best-placed operatives to report on Berlin's intentions after signing the Nazi-Soviet Non-Aggression Pact in August 1939. Some of the signs that Hitler would abandon the pact were oblique. Sorge noted that a German economic commission dispatched to Tokyo was interested in securing alternative supplies of resources such as rubber, soybeans, and whale oil that Germany was then importing from the Soviet Union. German officers visiting Japan at the end of 1940 also let slip that a new reserve army of 40 divisions had been created in eastern Germany, and that a force of 80 divisions had been deployed in Romania, close to the Soviet border.[103]

By spring 1941, there was greater clarity. On 2 May, Sorge cabled Moscow to report: "Ott informed me that Hitler is full of determination to destroy the USSR and seize the European part of the USSR as a grain and raw materials base in order to control all of Europe."[104] All that remained was the question of timing. The answer was provided by Major Erwin Scholl. Scholl had been assistant military attaché in Japan but had finished his tour and returned to Germany. He was now visiting Tokyo en route to a new posting in Thailand. Sorge took his old friend out for a night on the town. They dined at the Imperial Hotel and, as the alcohol flowed, Scholl revealed that the Nazi invasion of the Soviet Union would begin on 20 June.[105] He was out by just two days.

Sorge was, of course, not the only source to inform Moscow of the impending launch of Operation Barbarossa. One study argues that Moscow received 84 distinct warnings of the German invasion.[106] Notoriously, Stalin dismissed these as Anglo-American disinformation. This is because he did not wish to accept that his decision to make common cause with Hitler had been a colossal folly. However, it was also due to Stalin's distrust of his own security services. Stalin feared that the military had been infiltrated by German agents during the decade-long collaboration between Moscow and Berlin that had helped rebuild the German military after World War I. When Stalin visited the headquarters of the Fourth Directorate of the Red Army in May 1937, he muttered darkly that "the whole Directorate has fallen into German hands."[107] This was the justification for the widespread purge of Soviet military intelligence. The Comintern was similarly targeted, with 133 imprisoned or executed out of a total staff of 492.[108]

In this context, it is no surprise that Sorge's intelligence on Barbarossa was not trusted. From Stalin's perspective, Sorge ticked all the wrong boxes. He was German, a Red Army officer, had a background in the Comintern, and had spent many years overseas. Furthermore, Sorge defied an order in November 1936 to return to Moscow. This likely prolonged his life, since many of those who did return were locked up or liquidated. Yet Sorge's refusal left him with the image of being unreliable. On the report sent by Sorge predicting the date of the start of the German invasion, Stalin wrote: "Suspicious. To be listed with telegrams intended as provocations."[109] More broadly, Stalin dismissed Sorge as a lying "shit who has set himself up with some small factories and brothels in Japan."[110]

Sorge took no pleasure when proved correct. Instead, on the night of 22 June, as three million German and Axis troops poured across the Soviet frontier, Sorge retreated to the bar of the Imperial Hotel and drank himself into a stupor. The German embassy's radio attaché, Erwin Wickert, happened to be in the hotel that evening and overheard Sorge shouting in English to a group of foreigners that Hitler was "A fucking criminal." "Why does nobody kill him? For instance, some army officers?" This was reckless talk by a supposedly loyal Nazi. Yet, fortunately for Sorge, instead of reporting him, Wickert got him a room at the Imperial and helped him upstairs. The future Hero of the Soviet Union vomited in the sink then fell asleep in his clothes.[111]

Stalin's unforgivable disregard for the intelligence on Barbarossa might have caused Sorge to question the purpose of his work. However, he and his ring toiled on. This involved passing on information about German military strategy, including intelligence, which was transmitted by Clausen on 14 September, that the German advance would be directed towards the Caucasus, thus providing forewarning of the Battle of Stalingrad.[112] Even more crucially, Sorge's team investigated whether Japan would join its German ally in attacking the Soviet Union in 1941.

Ripe fruit?

The Nazi invasion was a catastrophe and would have proven fatal had Japan attacked the Soviet Far East, forcing Moscow to fight a two-front war. According to Major General A.K. Kazakovtsev, the Soviet operations chief in Khabarovsk, "If the Japanese enter the war on Hitler's side ... our cause is hopeless."[113] There were some in Tokyo who certainly did favour attacking north. One of the most prominent was Foreign Minister Matsuoka Yōsuke, who, despite having signed the Soviet-Japanese Neutrality Pact in April 1941, now advocated casting it aside. German officials were also lobbying hard. Minister of Foreign Affairs Joachim von Ribbentrop instructed his embassy in Tokyo to "Do everything … to rouse the Japanese to begin war against Russia … the quicker this happens the better. Our goal remains to shake hands with the Japanese on the Trans-Siberian railway before the beginning of the winter."[114]

On the other side were those who preferred *jukushi-shugi*, literally, the "ripe persimmon doctrine." Those in this camp did not oppose attacking the Soviet Union. They merely urged patience. Their argument was that Japan should wait until Nazi forces had softened up the Soviet Union. In this way, the fruit of victory would fall into Japan's lap and Japanese forces could occupy territory in Siberia and the Soviet Far East at minimal cost. In the meantime, Japan could concentrate on fighting the war in China, while preparing to strike south into Southeast Asia and readying for confrontation with Great Britain and the United States.

The Tokyo spy ring's crowning achievement was to accurately report that the latter group had prevailed and that Japan would not attack the Soviet Union until at least 1942. This was a collective effort. Ozaki used his position in the Mantetsu investigation department to discover that, while most Japanese army officers wanted to attack the Soviet Union, the Kwantung Army was more hesitant on account of its experience at Nomonhan. Specifically, the Kwantung Army leadership only favoured an attack on two conditions: "if it had a three-to-one superiority in troops over the Soviet Far East Army, and if the German invasion produced disunity and broken morale among the Siberian forces."[115] Reassuringly for Moscow, Japanese forces were far from achieving such superiority. In summer 1941, the Soviet Union had 700,000 men in the Far East versus the Kwantung Army's 300,000 to 350,000.[116] More concrete information followed. On 2 July, a *gozenkaigi* (Imperial Council) was held at which Emperor Hirohito approved the decision to prioritise a southward attack and to merely continue preparations for an eventual strike northward. Ozaki learned the details of this supposedly secret meeting from his aristocratic friend Saionji Kinkazu.[117]

German sources provided confirmation. Ott lamented to Sorge that he had failed to persuade the Japanese to attack the Soviet Union.[118] The ambassador added that the Japanese were unlikely to join the conflict before Nazi forces took Sverdlovsk (now Ekaterinburg), some 1,400 km east of Moscow. Miyagi also chipped in with the observation "that one of the battalions of 14th infantry division destined for North has been stopped in the barracks of the guards division in Tokyo."[119]

These details were transmitted to the Soviet Union in a series of increasingly confident radio communications. A cable of 12 July stated: "If the Red Army suffers defeat then there is no doubt that the Japanese will join the war, and if there is no defeat, then they will maintain neutrality."[120] More certainty was offered at the end of August: "They [the Japanese High Command] decided not to launch the war within this year, repeat, not to launch the war this year."[121] This was reiterated in a transmission of 14 September, which stated, "the possibility of Green [Japan] launching an attack, which existed until recently, has disappeared at least until the end of winter. There can be absolutely no doubt about this."[122]

This time, Sorge's intelligence was believed, and, by the end of September 1941, a massive transfer of military resources was underway, with 15 infantry divisions, 3 cavalry divisions, 1,700 tanks, and 1,500 aircraft withdrawn from Siberia and the Far East and sent west, with most deployed to defend Moscow. They arrived just in time, helping stop the Nazi advance just 30 km from the Kremlin. As Stalin admitted to British Foreign Minister Anthony Eden in December, "The bringing in of fresh reinforcements was the cause of the recent success."[123] Had the Soviet leadership not been forewarned of Japan's intentions, it is a real possibility that the capital would have fallen and the Soviet Union would have faced defeat in the winter of 1941–2.

The Sorge-Ozaki ring certainly reported on Japan's strategy in the second half of 1941, but did they also shape it? Some observers contend that Ozaki had amassed such influence within the government of Konoe Fumimaro, whose second administration lasted from July 1940 to October 1941, that he was able to shift Japanese policy away from conflict with the Soviet Union and promote a strike south.[124]

Ozaki did try to push Japanese policy in this direction. He used his position in the Breakfast Club to caution against an attack on the

Soviet Union, warning that, even after the Nazi invasion, Soviet forces remained strong, and expectations that Leningrad and Moscow would fall quickly were "oversimplified." He also argued that a Russo-Japanese war was precisely what Britain and the United States were seeking, and that, instead of falling into this trap, Japan should advance south.[125]

Ozaki got his wish, but his influence on this fateful decision was not decisive. He simply added his voice to an existing majority. In addition to the Kwantung Army's reluctance to renew conflict with the Soviet Union, the Japanese navy was eager to strike south. Moreover, within both Konoe's inner circle and the Foreign Ministry, there was a strong belief that the neutrality pact with Moscow, which was signed after the Tripartite Pact with Germany and Italy, should take priority, and that there was no obligation for Japan to join the Nazi invasion of the Soviet Union.[126] In short, without Ozaki's contribution, Japan's selection of the southern strategy would likely have remained the same, though Moscow may not have been tipped off about it until it was too late.

Impeccable spycraft?

The Sorge-Ozaki espionage network achieved historic results and evaded detection for eight years. Four factors were key to this success: charisma, expertise, professional spycraft, and luck.

Charisma

One factor that helped the spy ring secure its remarkable access was the charisma of its key members. Sorge had this in spades, as demonstrated by his skill in befriending Ott. Sorge also had the talent of being able to charm his adversaries yet never to warm to them on the inside. He spent years in the company of Nazis but never wavered in his personal commitment to communism. To him, a German official, no matter how close an acquaintance, always remained a quarry, who, when the time came, he would gut "like a fat Christmas goose."[127] This was in contrast to Clausen, for whom the role of capitalist and Nazi sympathiser increasingly became the reality.

Ozaki was similarly gifted in his ability to turn on the charm and cultivate close ties with nationalists without this affecting his ideological commitment. Indeed, Ozaki regarded his personality as one of his main strengths. When asked about his techniques as a spy, he replied:

> I have never given any thought to the so-called technical aspects of espionage. You might say that my non-technical attitude was a technique in itself. I am a sociable person and I like to mix with people from all walks of life; I find great sources of information just by being gregarious.[128]

Expertise

Sorge's swagger and Ozaki's ready smile ensured them a wide range of contacts, but they would not have been so prolific in receiving intelligence if they did not have information to share in return. For both, their reputation for expertise was a key reason why officials shared confidential material with them. Their expert knowledge meant that Sorge and Ozaki mostly did not need to risk quizzing contacts for information, since they offered it up voluntarily. The officials did so to compare their understanding of a subject with that of a well-known expert. As Sorge explained, the data he received from the embassy "were not obtained by means of plot, conspiracy, or violence ... I was shown them by Scholl and Ott, who asked for my cooperation."[129] Likewise, Ozaki reflected, "It is convenient to be a specialist of some kind. ... I was able to gather much data from men who came to ask me questions."[130]

Sorge's expertise owed much to the political intelligence he received from Ozaki, but he also impressed by the depth of his knowledge of Japanese history, economics, and culture. This was the product of intense study, and Sorge was immensely proud of his personal library of foreign-language books on Japan. Armed with this knowledge, Sorge was able to place new intelligence in context and to analyse its significance for Moscow.[131]

Ozaki's expertise on China was at least as impressive. He authored two well-received books: *Gendai Shina Ron* (*On Modern China*) (1939) and *Shina Shakai Keizai Ron* (*On China's Society and Economy*) (1940). At a time when the Japanese government was desperate for insight on how to successfully conclude the war in China, such publications helped Ozaki maintain elite access.

Professional spycraft

The spy ring was mostly professional in the spycraft it employed, though an account of their activities reads like an old-fashioned spy novel. When the team was first being assembled in 1933, Vukelić was instructed to place an advert in *The Japan Advertiser* seeking to purchase *ukiyo-e* (woodblock prints). This was an appropriate subject given that the person looking out for the message was Miyagi, an artist. Vukelić and Miyagi had also been issued with dollar bills with consecutive serial numbers so they could verify the other's identity.[132]

In his post-arrest testimony, Sorge detailed the techniques used for meeting unknown individuals, such as couriers in Shanghai. Arrangements included that the parties would wear pre-determined colours of tie or would be carrying parcels of certain colours. Another of Sorge's methods was to make contact "in restaurants by folding a newspaper I was reading in a special peculiar way when the other party entered." Alternatively, "I would be in a restaurant holding an odd-shaped pipe and the other man would be there with a large cigar. The cue was to light and begin smoking at the same time after each had become aware of the other's presence."[133]

Just as important was the spy ring's success in preventing the Japanese police from identifying the location of their radio transmissions and from reading the intercepted material. This was thanks to Clausen's diligence in moving between transmission sites and the simple but effective code that was used. As David Kahn puts it, the Sorge ring's communications, as well as those of other contemporary Soviet networks, were delivered to Moscow "through a pipeline that, despite the most strenuous bangings and poundings of counterintelligence, remained hermetically sealed against cryptanalysis."[134]

Luck

While there was much that was impressive about the operations of the Sorge-Ozaki ring, it was far from impeccable. This was primarily due to Sorge himself. One problem was his alcohol consumption. The prodigious drinking bouts served to loosen the tongues of contacts, but they also made Sorge dangerously indiscreet. The incident on 22 June 1941, when Sorge abused Hitler at the Imperial Hotel, was just one of several cases. Ott began to worry if he should continue to share information with his friend. As the German ambassador explained, "I had him watched for months … because I feared that while drunk he might talk about things from our conversations."[135]

Lack of mental clarity due to alcohol abuse also led to carelessness. Sorge travelled to the United States in 1935 on a false passport yet, when buying a ticket at a steamship office, he could not remember what was supposed to be his own name. As Sorge explains, during the same trip,

> When I was leaving New York, I had a suit tailored, giving the tailor my real name, and on my return trip I went to the same tailor and gave him the name in the forged passport. The tailor remembered me and noted that my name was different, but he was not interested in the change.

Sorge then forgot to pay the US exit tax and bribed the customs officer to look the other way. A more honest official could have had Sorge arrested on the spot.[136]

Sorge's worst drunken lapse was on 14 May 1938, when he crashed his 498cc Zündapp motorbike into a wall in Toranomon, near the US embassy. Sorge had already come off his motorbike in Shanghai in September 1931. That incident had left him with a broken leg, but the May 1938 crash was much worse. He suffered a fractured skull and a smashed jaw. In his pockets was a large quantity of US currency, plus several intelligence reports, which were written in English in preparation for encoding.[137] Fortunately for the Soviet Union, Clausen arrived at St Luke's Hospital in the nick of time to remove the incriminating material before it was discovered by either the Japanese police or German embassy officials. Sorge recovered well from his physical injuries, though a friend remarked that his face was left "somewhat like a mask, demonical."[138] Most of Sorge's teeth also fell out and he had to be fitted with dentures.

Another of Sorge's faults was his promiscuity. According to Major General Charles Willoughby, Sorge was intimate with around 30 women during his years in Tokyo.[139] These included waitresses from the city's German bars. This was how Sorge met Ishii Hanako, who became his mistress. Another waitress was so infatuated with Sorge that, when she saw him with another woman, she set off for Ōshima of the Izu archipelago to throw herself into the volcano. Fortunately, her German employer learned of her intended suicide and intervened to save her. Sorge also regularly visited brothels and amused himself by leaving their matchboxes around his home for his elderly maid to find.[140]

What made Sorge's sexual appetite a risk is that he seduced the partners of those connected with his spy work. Willoughby suggests Sorge may have had an affair with Yamasaki Yoshiko, Vukelić's beloved wife.[141] Yamasaki herself denied ever having laid eyes on Sorge.[142] He certainly did have a relationship with Helma Ott, the wife of the German ambassador. Given that Sorge's friendship with Eugen Ott was central to his espionage work, this was extremely reckless. Sorge also slept with Anita Mohr, a glamorous blonde with whom the ambassador was madly in love.[143]

These conquests were not for recruitment or soliciting information. Sorge was utterly dismissive of women's potential as spies. In his mind,

> They have no understanding of political and other affairs and I have never received satisfactory information from them. Since they were useless to me, I did not employ them in my group. Even upper class women have no comprehension of what has been said by their husbands and are, therefore, very poor sources of information. This does not apply merely to Japanese women; in my opinion, no woman in the world has the aptitude for espionage work.[144]

So why did Sorge jeopardise relations with co-conspirators and contacts for the sake of a fling? Part of it was the loneliness that is a common problem for those with secret lives. It was also because the art of seduction came so easily to him. The same charisma that made him a first-class spy also made him irresistible to many women, notwithstanding his false teeth and chauvinism.

Lastly, Sorge risked his group's operations by being a negligent personnel manager. Despite working closely with Ozaki for years, Sorge only learned that the journalist was married when he tried to get Ozaki to marry Hanako after he decided their relationship was over.[145] Ozaki did not seem to mind Sorge's lack of solicitude, but the more sensitive Clausen did. Clausen felt that Sorge looked down on him, never offered him a kind word, and forced him to continue working after his heart attack. In his post-arrest testimony, Clausen described his former boss as someone who "was not considerate of others" and who "would kill his best friend if it were necessary for communism."[146] Sorge's thoughtless behaviour thereby contributed to Clausen's decision to sabotage radio transmissions at just the time when the intelligence was of greatest importance.

That Sorge's personal shortcomings did not destroy the group was purely a matter of fortune. Rather than an impeccable spy, Sorge was a gifted intelligence officer on whom Lady Luck long smiled, until one day, quite suddenly, she stopped.

Arrest and execution

There are two competing accounts of the downfall of the Sorge-Ozaki group. One points the finger at Itō Ritsu, a member of the Japanese Communist Party. This version was popularised by Ozaki Hotsuki, the half-brother of Ozaki Hotsumi, who published a book in 1959 accusing Itō of betraying the spy ring.[147] The alternative account gives greater emphasis on Kitabayashi Tomo, the wife of the landlord from whom Miyagi had rented a room in the early 1930s in West Los Angeles.[148] In fact, both are correct.

Itō Ritsu had a long history of involvement with communism and was well-known to the *Tokkō*. He had spent two years in jail from 1933. Despite this, Itō received a job in the investigation department of the South Manchurian Railway in August 1939, just two months after Ozaki joined the organisation. Itō worked as Ozaki's deputy and the two became close. Itō was arrested again in November 1939 but released in August 1940 and immediately returned to his job. It appears that Itō bought his freedom by agreeing to become a police informer. This conclusion is supported by the post-war discovery of a *Tokkō* application for a meritorious service citation for Assistant Inspector Itō Taketora (no relation), who is credited with interrogating Itō Ritsu and uncovering "the first clue leading to the exposure of the Sorge-Ozaki case."[149]

Ozaki was not suspected of being a Soviet spy but his contacts among leftists did make him a person of moderate interest. The *Tokkō* therefore began gathering information about those who visited Ozaki at his Mantetsu office. Itō helped keep tabs on Ozaki, but it was not he who unmasked Ozaki, at least not directly. Instead, under pressure to identify communists, especially those who had returned to Japan from the United States, Itō gave the police the name of Kitabayashi Tomo, who happened to be the aunt of his housekeeper. Itō had no idea of her connection with the Sorge-Ozaki ring for he had no knowledge of the ring's existence. Instead, Itō simply tried to placate the police with a minnow. The fact that Kitabayashi had renounced communism and become a Christian may also have shaped his decision to throw her to the sharks.[150]

Itō appears to have given the police Kitabayashi's name in May 1940, yet they took their time to act. Kitabayashi had returned to Japan on her own and initially took up residence in Shibuya ward, where she worked at the Los Angeles Dressmaking School. The *Tokkō* set up surveillance, but this was disrupted when her husband arrived back in Japan and the couple moved to his native Wakayama. It was only in summer 1941 that the *Tokkō* raised the idea of detaining Mrs Kitabayashi and bringing her to Tokyo for questioning. However, the chivalrous Tamazawa Mitsusaburō of the Thought Section delayed her arrest until September to save the older lady from the capital's oppressive heat. In any case, she was not thought important. The request for Kitabayashi to be arrested was thus only approved on 28 September.

When finally questioned, Kitabayashi named Miyagi Yotoku as someone engaged in espionage who sometimes gave her money.[151] Why Miyagi had recruited Mrs Kitabayashi as a sub-agent is something of a mystery, since the sewing teacher and lapsed communist seemed to have no intelligence value. The best guess is that Miyagi felt a sense of duty towards the family of his former landlord and wanted to help her financially. In any case, it is ironic that Sorge, the hard-drinking atheist, was ultimately brought down by a Seventh-Day Adventist and member of the Women's Christian Temperance Union.

As soon as the police had Miyagi's name, the dawdling investigation accelerated. At 7 am on 10 October, a police team burst into Miyagi's home to find the artist asleep and his table strewn with compromising papers, including a study of Japan's oil stocks in Manchuria.

Miyagi was hauled off to Tsukiji police station. He initially refused to talk and, seizing a moment when his guards were distracted, threw himself, headfirst, out of the second-floor window. Thinking that Miyagi was trying to escape, chief interrogator Sakai Tamotsu also leapt from the window. The two men's fall was broken by shrubbery, though Sakai's spine was badly bruised. The failure of this suicide attempt had a transformative impact on Miyagi. As prosecutor Yoshikawa Mitsusada later put it: "Miyagi had experienced no less than a resurrection, and what life remained to him he must live with clean hands. He must make a general confession and start over with an unmarked slate."[152] Miyagi therefore began recounting the details of his espionage activity and gave up the names of all his associates, including Sorge and Ozaki.

Ozaki was picked up on 15 October. The arrests of Sorge, Clausen, and Vukelić followed four days later. In detention, some of the unmasked spies held out for a few days, but, ultimately, all spoke, and in considerable detail, about their work. This encourages speculation that they were tortured. It is a reasonable assumption, since the Japanese authorities were notorious for abuse of prisoners. However, this does not seem to have been the case here. This may have been because the abundance of physical evidence meant that the prosecution case was already strong. The police had discovered the group's radio and a well-thumbed codebook at Clausen's home, enabling them to finally decipher the thick file of "Dal X" communications that had been intercepted since 1938. Negatives of photos of confidential documents and Japanese military installations were also discovered in Vukelić's darkroom.[153] Rather than resorting to forced confessions, the *Tokkō* treated the spy ring's members kindly, such as by allowing Vukelić the privilege of wearing socks since he suffered badly from the cold.[154] The police also played on the spies' professional pride. This worked well with Sorge, who, when provided with his typewriter, eagerly tapped out a boastful testimony of the network's techniques and achievements.[155]

The willingness of the group to cooperate with the police may also have been animated by the assumption they would be spared the death penalty. Ozaki was stunned when he realised that the hangman's noose was to be his fate. Although the amended Peace Preservation Law did authorise the death penalty against those who threatened the *kokutai*, no one, until Ozaki, had ever been executed under its provisions. Ozaki may have assumed his elite connections would save him. This was the case with Saionji Kinkazu. Saionji was arrested but the courts ruled he had been an unconscious collaborator and handed him a suspended prison sentence of three years. If Ozaki's grandfather had been prime minister, perhaps he too would have been shown leniency.

For his part, Sorge assumed that, in recognition of his faithful service, Moscow would do all they could to secure his release. The Japanese authorities were open to a deal, especially as they were anxious that the Soviet Union stayed neutral. However, although the Japanese contacted the embassy in Tokyo on three occasions, the Soviets denied all knowledge of Sorge. Sorge inadvertently made it easier for them to do so by agreeing to be tried as a Comintern agent, instead of a Red Army officer. Since Moscow maintained the fiction that the Comintern was unconnected with the Soviet state, this enabled them to close their eyes on him and for the Japanese to hang him without fear of damaging relations with the Soviet Union.

The executions of Ozaki and Sorge were carried out on 7 November 1944, the 27th anniversary of the Bolshevik Revolution. As is still the practice in Japan, the two prisoners were not notified of the timing until immediately beforehand. They were then led in turn to the execution chamber. Sorge's last request was to be permitted a cigarette, which the prison governor denied. A hood was placed over his head, and his ankles, legs, and arms were bound. The executioners then sprang the trap and the rope snapped tight. He took 19 minutes to die.[156]

As for the others, Miyagi was spared the execution chamber but only because he succumbed to pneumonia on 2 August 1943.[157] Perhaps the most pitiable demise was that of Vukelić. He was transferred from Sugamo to Abashiri prison in the freezing northeast of Hokkaidō. In this lonely corner, Vukelić starved to death. He weighed just 32 kilograms when he breathed his last on 13 January 1945.[158]

Of the ring's main protagonists, only Clausen survived the war. He too was transferred north, finding himself in a prison in Akita, northern Honshū. Previously hefty, Clausen's weight dropped to less than 45 kilograms and he was so weak he struggled to walk. However, he held on until US troops took over the prison on 8 October 1945, whereupon he was transferred to a military hospital. Amnestied by the occupation authorities, Clausen was taken to Vladivostok by Soviet military aircraft, where, despite his efforts to sabotage the spy ring, he was lauded as a hero. Reunited with his wife, Clausen settled in East Germany under the name "Christiansen."[159]

One might have expected that, even while refusing to save Sorge, the Soviet Union would at least have ensured the wellbeing of his wife, Katya Maksimova, whom Sorge had married before travelling to Japan in 1933. Yet Sorge outlived her. After Sorge's arrest in Tokyo in October 1941, Katya was regarded with suspicion by the Soviet authorities and placed under surveillance. In November 1942, she was fired from her factory job and arrested, supposedly for "criminal activity." She was sentenced to five years of internal exile in central Siberia yet survived only a few months. Her final letters to her sister complained of being hungry and freezing. She died in the summer of 1943, aged 38.[160] This was how Moscow showed its gratitude to the man they later venerated as a Hero of the Soviet Union.

9

SORGE'S CONTEMPORARIES

The achievements of the Sorge-Ozaki spy ring are so eye-catching that they have obscured the role of other Soviet spies operating against Japan both prior to and during the Second World War. This has occurred to such an extent that one might almost imagine the Soviet Union conducted no other espionage operations against Japan during this time. Clearly this is not the case. Such was the threat posed by Japan that Moscow would never allow itself to be dependent upon a single spy ring.

This chapter turns the spotlight on Dr Sorge's contemporaries. Some names, including Harry Dexter White and Alger Hiss, are well-known, albeit that their activities with respect to Japan are often overlooked. Others, such Kōzō Izumi (codename NERO), are hardly known at all. None have quite the star appeal of Sorge, but several have a claim to having exerted an impact on the outcome of the war and the world order that emerged from it.

Other spies in Japan

Legals

While Richard Sorge, Max Clausen, and Branko Vukelić were Soviet "illegals," Moscow also operated "legals" in Tokyo during the 1930s and 1940s—that is, individuals who were openly associated with the

Soviet government, usually via diplomatic status, but whose employment as intelligence officers was concealed. Two of these were Helge L. Vutokevich, who was officially Soviet consul, and Viktor S. Zaitsev (Serge), who was second secretary. There was also a sidekick named Butkevich.[1] Soviet "legals" were supposed to avoid all contact with "illegals," but, in the case of Sorge's operation, this principle had to be abandoned. After the outbreak of war made courier runs to Shanghai and Hong Kong difficult, it became necessary for the Soviet "diplomats" to meet members of Sorge's group to deliver cash and collect microfilm. These clandestine encounters were conducted during performances at the Imperial Theatre and at the Tokyo theatre of the Takarazuka Revue, the famous all-female musical troupe.[2]

This is a reminder that, as well as the Fourth Directorate's activities in Japan, there was an NKVD *rezidentura* within the Soviet embassy. Between July 1937 and September 1939, the Soviet plenipotentiary in Tokyo was Mikhail M. Slavutskii. It is believed he doubled as *rezident*.[3] The official history of Russian foreign intelligence notes that, after Slavutskii's withdrawal, the *rezident* from January 1940 was a man identified only as "Artem."[4] Then, between 1942 and 1945, the NKVD *rezident* in Tokyo was Grigorii G. Dolbin, who went on to serve as *rezident* in Washington, DC, from 1946 to 1948.[5] Another notable name is Boris I. Gudz'. Gudz' worked as NKVD *rezident* in Tokyo between 1933 and 1936 under the official cover of third secretary. In 1937, he was transferred to the Fourth Directorate in Moscow, where he worked on the Japan desk that oversaw Sorge's spy ring. Gudz''s claim to fame, or rather infamy, is that it was he who denounced the famous writer Varlam Shalamov for anti-Soviet attitudes. Shalamov was the husband of Gudz''s sister. Gudz' was himself denounced after a colleague who had worked with him in Tokyo was arrested, confessed to being a Japanese spy, and claimed Gudz' as an accomplice. Gudz' lost his job but somehow avoided arrest. He outlived not only the Stalinist purges but also the Soviet Union, dying in 2006 at the age of 104.[6]

Overall, the Great Terror had a ruinous impact on Soviet intelligence. In 1938 alone, three successive leaders of NKVD foreign intelligence were eliminated. As a result, "for 127 consecutive days during 1938, it [NKVD foreign intelligence] sent not a single intelligence report to Stalin."[7] There was similar carnage at the Fourth Directorate. Yan K. Berzin, who had been the one to send Sorge to the Far East as a Red Army spy, was executed in July 1938. Semen P. Uritskii, who had succeeded Berzin as head of the Fourth Directorate, was liquidated one month later. According to figures compiled by the KGB in 1956, around 19 million people were arrested between 1935 and 1940. Of these, at least seven million were shot or died in the labour camps.[8]

So many officers were recalled from the Tokyo NKVD *rezidentura* that there were times when it barely functioned. Two who are reported to have been liquidated were an intelligence officer named Golkevich, who used the cover of first secretary, and Lieutenant-General Ivan A. Rink, who was military attaché.[9] Those sent to replace purged officers had Communist Party credentials but little knowledge of the outside world. According to the official history of Russian foreign intelligence, "On the eve of the war, there was a time in the Tokyo *rezidentura* when not a single employee of the 'legal' *rezidentura* knew either Japanese or any other foreign language."[10] Unsurprisingly, the embassy's officers missed important developments, such as Japan and Germany's secret preparations for the signing of the Anti-Comintern Pact in November 1936. This oversight prompted a reprimand from Moscow.[11]

Yet, despite personnel difficulties, the legal *rezidentura* did record some accomplishments. In July 1941, Mikhail Privalov, who was officially third secretary, managed to purchase military information from a nightclub owner in Yokohama. However, Privalov was soon detained and was withdrawn from Japan.[12] Greater success was achieved when NKVD officers recruited three foreigners who furnished intelligence on contemporary thinking within Japanese military and political circles. Based on such sources, in 1941 and 1942 the *rezidentura* sent more than 30 reports to Moscow that addressed the question of whether Japan would attack the Soviet Union. One of these reports, which was sent on 26 June 1941, included the following:

> In connection with the Soviet-German war, the foreign policy of Japan will be as follows: at present Japan does not have active intentions to declare war on the USSR and stand on the side of Germany. It is not known how this policy will change in future but, at least for the present, there are no such intentions. A firm policy towards the

> USSR will also not be adopted; that is, no demands will be made and no definite position will be declared. Japan wants to keep silent as it watches the development of the war and international relations. This current Japanese policy is explained by the fact that Japan is not ready to fight the USSR.[13]

The NKVD's *rezidentura* in Shanghai added their voice. Reflecting on the outcome of the *gozenkaigi* of 2 July, the Shanghai *rezidentura* reported:

> no final decision regarding the Soviet Union was taken by the Japanese government. However, at the government level it was decided:
>
> 1) To facilitate a solution to operations against the USSR without direct intervention in the war, at least in the near future.
> 2) To prevent … an increase in American influence in the Far East, which may occur as a result of the US decision to help the Soviet Union.
> 3) To put the armed forces on full alert and, if the Soviet Union shows a sign of general weakness, to use this weakness to take advantage, either through diplomatic pressure to obtain benefits in the Far East or through quick military action against certain regions of the Soviet Far East.[14]

These reports are striking because they show that the Sorge-Ozaki network was not the only source of Soviet intelligence indicating that Japan would not attack the Soviet Union in 1941. Indeed, the NKVD reports preceded those of Sorge since it was not until late August that Sorge's ring radioed with confidence that "They [the Japanese High Command] decided not to launch the war within this year."[15]

"Legals" under diplomatic cover were assisted by Soviet journalists. A core function of these correspondents when stationed overseas was to operate as intelligence officers. Indeed, in his testimony to the Japanese police, Richard Sorge lists the news agency TASS as one of the Soviet Union's five organs for gathering foreign intelligence.[16] Aino Kuusinen, whose role as a Soviet spy is outlined shortly, described how TASS operated. The Soviet Union's journalists sent back two types of report. "[T]he first, on grey paper, carried news which could be published in the press, while the second, on pink paper, were only to be read by a limited number of Comintern officials and members of the Central Committee of the Soviet CP [Communist Party]."[17]

TASS had set up a Tokyo office in March 1922, a full three years before diplomatic relations were formally established. Captain Malcolm D. Kennedy, who worked as Reuters correspondent in Japan (1925–34), recalls meeting three TASS journalists. The first was named Slapec, and is said to have been too busy with subversive activities to have done much journalism. Kennedy found him "a slimy, shifty little creature."[18] Too overt in his espionage activities, Slapec was called for questioning by the Japanese police, then withdrawn by Moscow.

Vladimir Romm, who replaced Slapec in 1927, was a notable improvement. Kennedy considered him "well-trained and highly intelligent," as well as "likeable."[19] Romm did real journalism, leaving much of the work of liaising with Japanese communists to his assistant, Okura Akira.[20] After his time in Tokyo, Romm was caught up in the show trial of Karl Radek. Radek had been Secretary of the Comintern and was involved in drafting the 1936 Soviet Constitution. However, Radek fell afoul of Stalin's suspicions and was accused of participating in a Trotskyite conspiracy. At the staged proceedings in 1937, Romm was forced to confess to serving as a go-between between Radek and Trotsky.[21] Romm was shot, while Radek was initially spared, dying later in a labour camp.

The third of the TASS correspondents was Aleksei L. Nagi. Nagi, who began work in Tokyo in July 1931, was an experienced journalist and quickly gained the respect of Western and Japanese colleagues. Indeed, he may have placed too much emphasis on journalism since, in 1935, Nagi was ordered to increase his intelligence output. He did so by exploiting contacts with foreign embassies and Western journalists. Those from whom Nagi solicited information included A.R. Catto, who was assistant to the Tokyo correspondent of the Exchange Telegraph Company, Havas journalist Georges Alsot, and Melville James Cox, who was Kennedy's successor as Reuters correspondent. "Any information he obtained was reported to the Soviet Embassy at secret meetings."[22] Incidentally, Melville James Cox was arrested by the Japanese police on 27 July 1940 and accused of being a British spy. Two days later, Cox fell to his death from a window in the headquarters of the *Kenpeitai*. While the Japanese authorities claimed suicide, many suspected murder.[23]

By the time of Cox's death, Nagi was no longer in Japan. In September 1937, he had collided with a Japanese cyclist while driving without a licence, then fled the scene. The cyclist was not seriously hurt but the police traced the car and Nagi was summoned before the Tokyo District court, where he acknowledged violating traffic regulations. Two months later, Nagi was recalled to the Soviet Union. Soon after, he was arrested and executed.[24]

Illegals

Adding to Moscow's intelligence apparatus in Japan in the run-up to the Second World War were several other illegals. The main spy ring that Moscow sought to establish, aside from Sorge's network, was led by John L. Sherman. The details of this operation were revealed by Whittaker Chambers, who worked as a Soviet spy in the United States during the 1930s before turning his back on communism. According to Chamber's testimony to the House Un-American Activities Committee (HUAC) in December 1949, John L. Sherman, who was a US citizen, worked with Maxim Lieber (codename POL/PAUL), a literary agent in New York, to establish the American Feature Writers' Syndicate, a firm whose ostensible business was to acquire material for publication in US newspapers but which was really a communist front. In the guise of a representative of this organisation, Sherman (codename DON) was dispatched to Tokyo in 1934, using a passport in the name of Charles Francis Chase.[25]

Sherman needed Japanese collaborators and he requested that Chambers find him "a Communist Party member, Japanese by race and American by citizenship, highly connected in Japan."[26] Despite these exacting requirements, Chambers delivered, putting Sherman in touch with a young Japanese-American named Noda Hideo (codename NED), who, just like Sorge's Miyagi Yotoku, was an artist. Noda was a serious talent who had studied with Mexican painter Diego Rivera. Chambers also claimed that Noda was related to Prince Konoe Fumimaro, within whose think tank Ozaki Hotsumi later worked.[27]

Noda was sent to Tokyo at the end of 1934 and the spy ring set to work. However, after just eight months, it ceased operations. This was due to a mistake. In 1935, Chambers, who was overseeing the operation from New York, was informed by his Soviet handler that there had been arrests in Tokyo and that he should shut down Sherman's mission. Chambers did so immediately. He told Maxim Lieber to liquidate the American Feature Writers' Syndicate. They "destroyed all the stationery, closed out the bank account, and took the name off Lieber's door."[28] Although Chambers's handler got in touch the next day to tell him it had all been a mistake and there had been no arrests, it was too late. With the front organisation having been dismantled, Moscow recalled Sherman and Noda from Japan. The Sherman operation therefore came to an end before it produced any meaningful intelligence. Sherman himself did, however, achieve one minor victory. In the name of "Charles Chase," he won the 1935 Japanese handball championship at the Tokyo YMCA.[29]

There were no further Soviet spy rings operating in Tokyo at the same time as Sorge, but there were individuals. One was William Maxwell Bickerton, a young New Zealander who was teaching at Ichikō (First Higher School), which, incidentally, was Ozaki Hotsumi's alma mater. Bickerton was also a notable translator of haiku. He was arrested in March 1934 and charged under the Peace Preservation Law with "dangerous thoughts" and "communistic activities." This made Bickerton the first foreigner to be detained under this law. The young man was brutally treated, including, according to his own account, by being beaten with a baseball bat and having his head repeatedly bashed against a cupboard.[30] Nonetheless, Bickerton refused to confess. Thanks to the intervention of the British embassy, Bickerton was eventually released and fled Japan. It was long assumed Bickerton was an innocent victim but, according to Robert Whymant, "Sixty years after the event, documents released by Moscow prove conclusively that there was substance to the charges, and that Bickerton had indeed played a liaison role between the Comintern and Japanese communists.[31]

Another intriguing figure was Gerold Eckelman. Born in 1899 in Oelsnitz, Germany, Eckelman was active in Shanghai in the early 1930s at the same time as Sorge. Charles Willoughby suggests his codename was either ALEX or JIM. Eckelman followed Sorge to Tokyo but was detained by the Japanese police and deported to China in 1936. He succeeded in returning to Japan in 1940 by using fake documents in the name of Dr Fred Sanders. "He then practiced medicine without a license and enjoyed a surreptitious popularity as a discreet abortionist. He also had numerous suspicious contacts with questionable German and Russian nationals."[32]

Eckelman/Sanders remained in Tokyo after the war and took Soviet citizenship in 1946. He came under suspicion of the US occupation authorities since "he had sought the friendship of American soldiers, particularly those on duty with the Signal Corps."[33] Eckelman/Sanders was therefore designated an "undesirable alien" in 1948 and ordered to be deported to Germany. The military police took him into custody but permitted Eckelman/Sanders to visit his home in the company of a police officer to collect clothing. What followed was unexpected.

> He [Eckelman/Sanders] took a dose of potassium cyanide instead. The panicky police officer summoned an ambulance and for some obscure reason, he stepped outside, into the garden to unload his pistol, inadvertently firing one round. American medical authorities took over and cremated the deceased. The prostitutes of the neighborhood, to whom Sanders had been able to render occasional assistance, started a rumor that he had been killed by the MP.[34]

Since the cremation was conducted with unusual haste, the Soviet embassy suggested "it was done to prevent inspection by Soviet representatives, which might have disclosed bullet wounds."[35]

The Bickerton and Eckelman/Sanders cases demonstrate the variety of colourful characters that Moscow used for espionage in Japan. However, neither had any prospect of penetrating the Japanese elite. In this respect, Aino Kuusinen displayed much greater promise.

Aino Kuusinen (née Turtiainen) was born in March 1886 in Savonranta in the Grand Duchy of Finland. She trained as a nurse and, in 1909, married Leo Sarola, a railway engineer. The couple took up residence in a small house in the Helsinki suburbs. Aino appeared set for a conventional life until disturbed by a knock on the door one evening in 1919. The caller was a friend who asked if the couple could shelter a communist for whom the police were searching. The stranger was Otto Kuusinen, who had been leader of the short-lived communist uprising in Finland in January 1918. After the failure of his hopes for revolution in Finland, Otto Kuusinen fled to the Soviet Union, where he became a senior communist official, holding several positions, including leader of the Comintern.[36]

Aino became Otto Kuusinen's second wife and joined him in Moscow, where, during the 1920s, they lived like royalty. Aino Kuusinen's memoirs contain several vignettes about this time. She recalls holidaying at a Black Sea resort with Soviet head of state Mikhail I. Kalinin, who played tricks on his security detail by hiding from them on the beach. Another prominent Bolshevik, Nikolai I. Bukharin, gifted her a monkey, though she gave it away to the zoo after it mauled one of her hats. Aino Kuusinen also tells the story of when Palmiro Togliatti, the famous Italian communist, came to stay in 1926 or 1927. Togliatti, along with his wife and son, went to bed in an upstairs room, waking in the morning to find that thieves had crept in during the night and stolen all their clothes. When her guests failed to appear for breakfast, Aino Kuusinen went up to see what was wrong. "When I entered the room I found all three of them lying in bed with sheets drawn up to their chins."[37]

Aino Kuusinen also had several encounters with Stalin. She and her husband spent a couple of days with the Soviet dictator while holidaying near Sochi on the Black Sea coast. On one occasion, they took a boat trip during which much wine was consumed and Stalin began to dance to Georgian folk songs. As Aino Kuusinen recounts:

> It was a gruesome sight, and the more he drank the more fearful he looked. ... He bellowed with laughter, staggering and stamping round the cabin completely out of time with the lovely music. The general impression was not only coarse and vulgar, but so bizarre that it seemed like a kind of sinister threat. The most frightening thing of all was that, despite his drunkenness, he still seemed sober enough to observe my reaction to his conduct.[38]

When not hobnobbing with the Soviet leadership, Aino Kuusinen worked for the Comintern. This included being sent to the United States in January 1931 in the guise of a Swedish citizen named Fru Elisabeth Petterson. During her year and a half in New York, Aino Kuusinen managed left-wing newspapers that targeted the Finnish diaspora. Then, after returning to Moscow, she followed the same career path as Sorge and was transferred to the Fourth Directorate. She was eager to work abroad again and General Yan K. Berzin decided to reinforce the Fourth Directorate's position in Japan by sending her to Tokyo.[39]

When leaving the Soviet Union and travelling across Europe, Aino Kuusinen used a Swedish passport in the name of Hildur Nordström. Then, for the journey to Tokyo, she switched to documents in the name of Mrs Elisabeth Hansson, who was said to be a journalist from Luleå in the north of Sweden. This was the identity Kuusinen used throughout her time in Japan. Her codename was INGRID.[40]

After a brief stay in Shanghai, where she received money from Soviet *rezident* "Dr Bosch" (Colonel Yakov G. Bronin), Aino Kuusinen arrived in Japan in November 1934. She took up residence in Tokyo's Imperial Hotel and waited to be contacted by "Dr Somebody." This turned out to be Richard Sorge, whom Kuusinen already knew from Moscow. Both Sorge and Kuusinen were working for Berzin, but they were not part of the same network. Other than functioning as Kuusinen's communication link with Moscow, Sorge was not involved in Kuusinen's work. This suited Kuusinen, since she felt little sympathy for her fellow Soviet spy, whose tastes were more proletarian than her own. When they held their first proper meeting in Tokyo, Kuusinen complained that "The rendezvous appointed by Sorge turned out to be a low-class German bar, and I asked him reproachfully how he could expect a lady who had been living at the Imperial Hotel to meet him in such a place."[41]

Aino Kuusinen's mission in Japan was distinct from Sorge's. While Sorge prioritised penetrating the German embassy, Kuusinen's objective was to ingratiate herself with the Japanese elite. According to Berzin's instructions, she "was to live in style and cultivate the most prominent Japanese politicians, but have nothing to do with the Germans."[42] She was given plenty of time to establish herself and spent the first year learning Japanese and developing contacts among Japanese journalists. These included "Baron Nakano" of the *Asahi* (presumably Nakano Gorō) and a journalist for the *Japan Times* named "Uehara." Although she felt Nakano was initially sent by the police to keep tabs on her, "Later he became a good friend, and opened many doors to me which were usually shut to foreigners."[43]

Kuusinen regarded her time in Tokyo as a long holiday, writing, "With the help of the Soviet military secret service I spent there the happiest and most carefree years of my life."[44] It therefore came as a shock when she was suddenly recalled. Kuusinen was not told the reason, but she speculated that it was a precaution following the arrest of Shanghai *rezident* Yakov G. Bronin in May 1935. She also suspected that her husband, Otto Kuusinen, from whom she was now estranged, may have been involved. Whatever the cause, Kuusinen arrived back in Moscow to discover that General Berzin had been dismissed. His replacement, Semen P. Uritskii, judged that Kuusinen's recall had been a mistake and instructed her to return to Tokyo. As she recalled, he told her "to go on studying and cultivating acquaintances. He advised me, however, to avoid contact with Dr Sorge, with whom he was dissatisfied." When she passed on Max Clausen's request for $20,000 to open a radio shop, Uritskii reacted angrily. "The rogues, they do nothing but drink and spend money. I shan't give them a single kopeck."[45]

Kuusinen's long trip was not wasted, since Uritskii proposed that, before returning to Japan, she write a book. The aim of this volume was to praise Japan in the highest terms and thereby enable Kuusinen, in the guise of Elisabeth Hansson, to further endear herself to the Japanese elite. Uritskii told her that "I was on no account to criticize Japanese policy, but I might speak a little harshly of the USSR if I chose. What was one piece of anti-Soviet literature more or less? Expense was to be no consideration."[46]

Not one to deny herself the finer things in life, Aino Kuusinen took up residence in Stockholm's Grand Hotel and started writing. The result was *Det leende Nippon* (*Smiling Japan*), which described in unctuous terms "the charms of that sunny land and its engaging and friendly people."[47] The spy chiefs in Moscow were delighted with the volume and helped ensure it received a wide audience by quickly arranging translation from Swedish to English.

While Sorge and Ozaki demonstrated how expertise can secure access, Kuusinen is a case study in the value of flattery. Having published the adulatory book, Kuusinen returned to Japan in September 1936 and received "compliments on every hand."[48] The volume was especially valued given that, at the time, there was growing international criticism of Japan's militarism. "Elisabeth Hansson" was subsequently invited to an imperial garden party and a reception hosted by Emperor Hirohito. Kuusinen also met Prince Chichibu, the emperor's younger brother, whom she describes as "a man of unusual character, with excellent manners, who spoke very good English and was often seen with foreigners." Kuusinen also cultivated an interest in Buddhism and Asian philosophy. This led to meetings with the emperor's cousin, Umewaka Kangfusu, a Buddhist priest. Kuusinen explains that "Our acquaintance began when I was invited to an ancient Buddhist ceremony which the Imperial Court arranged for the benefit of foreign diplomats on the premises of an exclusive club."[49]

What was the intelligence value of these contacts? Kuusinen gives the impression that she harvested no intelligence whatsoever and that her time in Japan was just one pleasant social occasion after another. However, Kuusinen defected to the West in 1965 and had an interest in downplaying her contribution to the Soviet regime. In reality, the Fourth Directorate must have demanded some return on their considerable investment. While contact with the imperial family itself was unlikely to have generated much of importance, Kuusinen was well-placed to pick up inside information from the many journalists, foreign diplomats, and Japanese officials she met at high-profile events.

Kuusinen was successful in penetrating the Japanese elite and could have become more productive had she remained in Tokyo. However, in another example of Soviet intelligence's tendency towards self-harm, Kuusinen was recalled again. She learned this when visiting Sorge's house in November 1937. She found him "lying on the sofa half-seas-over with the remains of a bottle of whisky beside him on the table; he had evidently dispensed with a glass." He imparted the news that they had all been ordered back to Moscow.[50]

Sorge defied the order and went on to become one of history's greatest spies. Kuusinen did as she was told and fell victim to Stalin's Great Terror. She was arrested for "counter-revolutionary activity" and spent eight years in a forced labour camp, including in the notorious Vorkuta Gulag in the Arctic. Kuusinen survived the ordeal, thanks, she claims, to "my robust health, and perhaps also to unseen protectors, as well as ingenuity and what Finns call *sisu* (pluck and perseverance)."[51] Many others were less fortunate, dying of starvation and overwork. She recounts that "Every morning the naked, emaciated corpses were stacked in a little room and, when they had frozen stiff, piled on to a sledge and taken away." They were dumped in the tundra since the ground was too hard for burial. "When the snow melted, the reindeer used to feed on the bodies decomposing in the sun and became diseased."[52]

Spying on Japan in third countries

Aside from the other spies inside Japan, the Soviet Union had several officers and agents who, although based in third countries, made their main contribution by targeting Japan. One example is Operation "Postman" ("*Pochtal'on*"), which began in Italy around 1933.[53] The impetus was the observation that the Japanese military attaché received large volumes of correspondence to his home address. Although this included official documents, it was sent via the ordinary Italian postal service. This was a matter of convenience, since diplomatic couriers from Tokyo only visited the Italian capital every six months. Much diplomatic mail was therefore sent to Japan's mission in Switzerland, whence it was forwarded to Japan's representatives in Italy as well as to legations in neighbouring countries. The most secret material was only delivered by courier, but there was still much to be gained if the Soviet Union could access the material delivered by post. For this, the *rezidentura* would need the assistance of the postman responsible for the relevant Rome neighbourhood. This turned out to be a man named Paolo.

Since it would raise suspicion if a Soviet official were to court Paolo, the *rezidentura* used Pietro Capuzzi, an Italian anti-fascist who was run by Soviet intelligence under the codename "D-36." The *rezidentura* instructed Capuzzi to rent an apartment on the same street as the Japanese military attaché. When a suitable property was at last secured, the *rezidentura* sent frequent letters to this address, giving Capuzzi the opportunity to engage daily with Paolo. "Capuzzi began to pay attention to him in every possible way: invited him for a cup of coffee, gave him presents for the holidays. They became friends."[54]

Once trust had been established, Capuzzi confided in Paolo that he feared his wife was having an affair with the Japanese military attaché, who is named only as "Mr N." To discover if his suspicions had foundation, Capuzzi asked Paolo to show him the letters sent to "Mr N." so he could ascertain if any had been written by his wife. After conducting this inspection, he would return the material to Paolo to be delivered as normal. After some hesitation, the postman agreed. Capuzzi also gave Paolo a small payment.

Access to the correspondence had been achieved, but there remained the problem of concealing the fact that the mail had been opened. To resolve this, it was necessary to recreate official Japanese seals. Copies were therefore made of the imprinted wax, and these were sent to Moscow in special impact-resistant packages. Using this material, Soviet forgers were able to provide Capuzzi with precise replicas of the seals, as well as supplies of the exact type of sealing wax. With these, Capuzzi was able to re-seal the official envelopes and return them to Paolo.

The operation provides an example of the time and resources the Soviet intelligence services were willing to commit to an operation. Such investment did not always pay off, but in this case it did. At some point Paolo must have realised that Capuzzi was not simply a jealous husband. Still, he continued to cooperate, no doubt encouraged by payments. In total, the operation lasted seven years. It only came to an end when Paolo was conscripted into the Italian army.

Overall, operation "Postman" delivered a large volume of intelligence. According to the official history of Russian foreign intelligence, "Most of the materials received from this source was of great value as they concerned Japanese military installations and preparations on the Soviet far eastern border." There were monthly bulletins from the Japanese General Staff containing data about the political and economic situations of various countries, reports on individual military issues, especially in relation to China, and orders regarding army personnel matters as well as copies of both encrypted and unencrypted telegrams. Moreover, the packages contained Japanese intelligence about the Soviet Union. From this, the Soviets were relieved to learn in 1939 that Japanese intelligence about Soviet aircraft production in the Far East was years out of date.[55]

Iran was another country where the Soviets had success against Japan during the 1930s. At the end of 1937, a local resident approached the Soviet embassy in Tehran requesting help in leaving

Iran and becoming a Soviet citizen. Local station chief Andrei M. Otroshchenko made clear that assistance would only be forthcoming if the applicant provided something in return. The man was thus recruited as an agent, codenamed SEMEN.

Otroshchenko discovered that one of SEMEN's acquaintances was an official at the Japanese embassy in Tehran. This diplomat, who was given the codename ZHUK (beetle), was responsible for the embassy's diplomatic correspondence. This made ZHUK an attractive target. Even more promising was that SEMEN revealed that ZHUK had a weakness for alcohol and gambling, as well as financial problems due to an expensive mistress.

Acting on behalf of the NKVD *rezidentura*, SEMEN told ZHUK that a businessman from Czechoslovakia wanted to meet him. SEMEN further explained that ZHUK would receive a "good reward" if willing to provide information about his embassy colleagues. ZHUK rejected this crude approach but the *rezidentura* persisted. The lurid details are not revealed but the official history of Russian foreign intelligence explains that, after this initial rejection, "SEMEN tried to exert the necessary influence on ZHUK's mistress, whose demands were constantly growing. In the end, ZHUK himself was compelled to cooperate." As well as providing intelligence on his colleagues, ZHUK agreed to hand over the Japanese embassy's diplomatic bag for a period of up to two hours. "In this way, Soviet intelligence gained access to secret documents of Japan's Ministry of Foreign Affairs."[56]

Operation "Postman" and the suborning of the Japanese diplomat in Tehran show that Soviet intelligence was on the lookout globally for opportunities during the 1930s to gather intelligence on the Japanese. This included continuing operations in China, where, as well as stealing secrets, the Soviets were channelling assistance to Chinese fighting Japanese imperialism. One of those who played a prominent role in these efforts was Ursula Hamburger (née Kuczynski), the young mother who had been recruited by Richard Sorge in Shanghai in the early 1930s and had joined the ranks of his many lovers.

When working under Sorge in Shanghai, Ursula Hamburger's role had been limited to providing a safehouse for clandestine meetings and concealing weapons. However, after Sorge's departure in December

1932, Ursula (codename SONYA) became a fully fledged officer of the Fourth Directorate of the Red Army's General Staff. After months of training in Moscow, Ursula was dispatched to Manchuria. For this mission, she was paired with Johann Patra, a Lithuanian communist, who became her lover and the father of her second child.

The two Soviet operatives, along with Michael, Ursula's toddler, set off for Mukden in May 1934. As Ben Macintyre explains,

> As the main Soviet intelligence outpost in Manchuria, they would be responsible for furnishing the rebels with money, weapons and explosives, sheltering fugitives, identifying partisans for training back in Moscow, recruiting and training local radio operators, and passing messages and intelligence back and forth between the Centre and the guerilla leadership.[57]

Ursula took a leaf out of Sorge's book by hiding in plain sight. She installed herself and Michael in a small house within the grounds of a larger property that was occupied by Hans von Schlewitz, a German arms dealer and member of the Nazi Party who worked closely with the Japanese military in Manchuria. Despite Ursula's Jewish background, she soon won over the older man with some playful flirtation. Von Schlewitz was thus converted into Ursula's protector, both from the suspicions of the Japanese police and from more zealous Nazis within the local German community. He was also an occasional source, since he "was exceptionally talkative, especially when plastered, which was often."[58]

Ursula spent over a year in Mukden, where, in addition to Johann Patra, she had the assistance of a young Chinese man named Wang and his wife, Shushin. These two helped with radio operations, enabling Ursula to communicate with Vladivostok at least twice a week. In these transmissions, she provided the Fourth Directorate with intelligence "on sabotage, partisan morale, Japanese counterinsurgency measures, and military and political intelligence gleaned from fellow expatriates."[59] Furthermore, Ursula helped Chinese fighters conduct attacks on Japanese-run infrastructure, especially the railway system. For instance, in response to a request from a fighter named "Chu," Ursula helped prepare a bomb for an attack on the South Manchurian Railway. She carried out these tasks with pride, noting in July 1934 that "Last month anti-Japanese groups carried out 650 attacks in the Mukden province alone."[60]

Discovery was a constant fear, not least because Ursula's cover story, which claimed she was an itinerant bookseller, was flimsy. As much as possible she used her status as an attractive young mother to divert attention. Notes from meetings with Chinese fighters were sewn into her petticoat in the hope that the police would not dare search the underwear of a foreign woman. Components for the radio were smuggled to Mukden within her son's teddy bear. She also took Michael with her when shopping for bomb-making materials, which Ursula and Johann Patra had been trained to build from household chemicals. Once the hazardous ingredients had been acquired, Ursula stashed them in the pram and returned home with Michael perched on top.[61]

Whether through luck or skill, Ursula was never discovered by the Japanese authorities. Her Chinese assistants were less fortunate. In April 1935, Ursula was tipped off that Shushin had been arrested. Fearing that the young woman would break under Japanese torture, Ursula radioed for instructions and was told to immediately leave Mukden. Despite the abrupt end to the mission, Moscow was well-pleased with Ursula's contribution to espionage and sabotage against the Japanese in Manchuria. After leaving China, she was awarded the Order of the Red Banner, the highest Soviet military medal. Ursula went on to conduct further espionage work for the Red Army in Poland and Switzerland before settling in Britain where she served as the handler of Klaus Fuchs, the scientist who helped pass key details of the Anglo-American nuclear programme to the Soviet Union. After Fuchs's arrest in 1950, Ursula fled to the German Democratic Republic, where she lived for decades under the name Ruth Werner and penned several children's books. Following her death in 2000, the Russian Federation awarded her the Order of Friendship, and President Vladimir Putin issued a decree that heralded her as a "super-agent of military intelligence."[62]

Spying on Japan in the United States

During the 1930s and 1940s, the Soviet Union operated an extensive espionage network in the United States. Moscow was interested in information about the US itself, but America was also valuable as a location from which to gather intelligence about third countries. As Allen Weinstein explains, during the 1930s, "the United States as an uncommitted world power with a strong diplomatic network in every major country made it a valuable listening post for foreign spies."[63] This was made easier by the woeful state of US counterintelligence. As one Soviet intelligence officer later joked, "If you had worn a sign saying 'I AM A SPY' in America at that time … you might still not get arrested."[64] This was partly a question of resources. The FBI had barely 300 agents in 1933 and still fewer than 900 by 1939.[65]

Within the United States, Soviet spies were especially focused on gathering intelligence about Japan (as well as Germany). This emphasis became more pronounced after the signing of the Anti-Comintern Pact in 1936. William Akets was a staff member of the US Commerce Department, as well as a lieutenant in the Army Intelligence Corps reserve. He had been on active service in Japan, China, and the Philippines after the First World War, and, according to a 1933 KGB memo, "Speaks, reads and writes Japanese fluently." The same document notes that Akets "is better posted on Japanese internal affairs than most reserve officers or regular officers for that matter, as he keeps in close touch with Far Eastern economic data through employment in the Bureau of Foreign and Domestic Commerce." Akets provided the Soviets with material extracted from US intelligence reports on the Japanese military, as well as details of US military aircraft provided to China.[66]

The Soviets also used several US journalists and authors, including John L. Spivak. Spivak first assisted the Soviet Union in 1930 during the Whalen Forgeries case, when he argued that documents purporting to show that the Comintern was behind riots in New York were fabrications.[67] It is not clear when Spivak became a Soviet agent (codename GRIN), but a file in the KGB archives from 1935 mentions information he supplied in 1932.[68] Spivak's relevance to Japan is that he wrote a book, *Honorable Spy*, in 1939, which provided an alarmist account of penetration of the Americas by Japanese agents, who disguised themselves as barbers and dentists.[69] Arguing that this infiltration was preparation for invasion, the book sought to foster tensions between the United States and Japan. Spivak continued working for Soviet intelligence during the 1950s but, by the time he wrote his autobiography in 1967, he had become disillusioned with communism.[70]

Journalists can be useful propagandists, but they do not generally have access to classified government files. Two individuals who did were Julius J. Joseph and his wife, Bella. This communist couple was recruited by the NKVD in 1941 and assigned the codenames CAUTIOUS and COLLEAGUE. Bella Joseph was the first to achieve a breakthrough by gaining employment in 1943 as a stenographer in the photography department of the recently formed Office of Strategic Services (OSS), the forerunner of the CIA. A report from the NKVD's New York *rezidentura* noted that Bella had gained access to "Photographs of localities, mil. installations, inventions, weaponry." Bella's handlers then urged her to find an OSS job for her husband. This took time but, by December 1943, Julius was given an assignment by the OSS working "on questions pertaining to Japan's manpower reserves and has promised to give us a copy of his report." This temporary position was made permanent, and Julius remained with the OSS throughout the war, becoming deputy head of his division, which dealt principally with Japanese intelligence. Julius also ran sub-agents within the OSS, including Helen Tenney (codename MUSE) and Donald Wheeler (codename IZRA). However, the Josephs' professional success threatened to be undone by personal factors. Bella began an affair, asked Julius for a divorce, and threatened to quit her job at the OSS and run off to California with her new lover. Their handler, Jacob Golos (codename SOUND), had to play marriage counsellor and persuaded Bella to stay with her husband.[71]

Akets, Spivak, and the Josephs were all valuable to Moscow, yet the two figures of greatest significance to US-based espionage against Japan were Harry Dexter White and Alger Hiss.

Harry Dexter White (codenames RICHARD, JURIST, LAWYER, REED)

Harry Dexter White was a senior official in the US Treasury Department, rising to the position of Assistant Secretary of the Treasury in January 1945. He was also a trusted advisor of Henry Morgenthau, who, as Secretary of the Treasury (1934–45), expanded his department's responsibilities into the fields of foreign affairs and post-war reconstruction. This meant that White became "among the most powerful and influential men in the government."[72] What is more, White, along with Britain's John Maynard Keynes, was the leading figure at the Bretton Woods Conference of July 1944, which created the post-war financial order. White went on to assume the post of US executive director of the International Monetary Fund in May 1946.

The accusation that White was a Soviet agent first became public in 1948, when Elizabeth Bentley (codenames MIRNA, UMNITSA) and Whittaker Chambers (codename KARL) testified before the House Un-American Activities Committee. They each named White amongst those they knew to be working for Soviet intelligence. Chambers claimed that White began "to pass weekly or fortnightly longhand memos summarizing documents that had come to his attention during the course of his work in the Treasury Department."[73] From early 1937 to April 1938, White provided documents to Boris Bykov, the illegal *rezident* for the Red Army's Fourth Directorate.[74] White may have taken a two-to-three-year break, but, during the war years, he was again assisting Soviet intelligence, although this was now the NKVD instead of military intelligence. White's codename of JURIST features regularly in the VENONA decrypts of Soviet intelligence transmissions during this period. One example is the report on a meeting between White and an NKVD officer named KOL'TSOV (probably Nikolai F. Chechulin) in July 1944. On this occasion, White declared both himself and his wife "ready for any self-sacrifice." KOL'TSOV and White also discussed security arrangements for future meetings. According to the intercepted message, "He [White] proposes infrequent conversations lasting up to half an hour while driving in his automobile." The same source also eliminates any doubt as to whether JURIST knew whom he was assisting. The decrypt reads: "'J' knows where his info. goes, which is precisely why he transmits it in the first place."[75] White seems not to have been paid for his services, although he was given a valuable Bokhara rug.[76] His handler in the United States also asked Moscow for permission to finance the college education of White's daughter.[77]

Whittaker Chambers accused White of using his influence to secure government jobs for known communists. This contributed to the success of the Silvermaster spy ring, which was centred on the

Treasury and of which White was a key member. Nathan Gregory Silvermaster (codenames PEL, PAL, PAUL, ROBERT) was born in the Russian Empire in 1898 and emigrated to the United States aged 15. Moving to California in 1920, Silvermaster became active in radical politics, serving as courier for the chairman of the Communist Party of the USA, Earl Browder, as well as for Japanese communist Nosaka Sanzō (aka Okano Susumu), who was then living on the US West Coast.[78] Silvermaster relocated to Washington in 1935 and became a close friend of Harry Dexter White. Silvermaster found employment in the government's Farm Security Administration and sought to be reassigned to the Board of Economic Warfare in 1942. This was opposed by the Civil Service Commission, which, due to suspicions of disloyalty, "recommended that the applicant be declared ineligible for the position of head economist, Board of Economic Warfare. It is further recommended that all of his eligibilities be cancelled and that he be debarred for 3 years or for the duration of the emergency [i.e. the war]."[79] However, both White House advisor Lauchlin Currie, who was also alleged to be a Soviet spy (codename PAGE), and Harry Dexter White spoke up in Silvermaster's defence, enabling his government career to progress. Overall, Silvermaster's contributions to the spy ring were so great as to secure him a place in the KGB's hall of fame.[80] Other "econ-umists"—that is, communist economists—who are alleged to have been helped by White to secure jobs or promotion include Solomon Adler (codename SACHS), Harold Glasser (codename RUBLE), and William Ludwig Ullmann (codenames PILOT, DONALD, POLO).[81]

What makes White especially intriguing is that he was sufficiently senior to shape US policy in ways favourable to Soviet interests. He allegedly did so on several occasions, including at the Bretton Woods Conference, where he is said to have informed the Soviets of the US negotiating position and argued in favour of providing Moscow with a $10 billion loan on concessionary terms.[82] Robert Skidelsky, the biographer of John Maynard Keynes, goes further, alleging that White's intention at Bretton Woods was "to cripple Britain in order to clear the ground for a post-war American-Soviet alliance."[83]

White is similarly alleged to have served Soviet interests at the San Francisco conference of April–June 1945, at which the Big Four—the

United States, Great Britain, the Soviet Union, and China—agreed on the establishment of the United Nations. Controversial decisions included the awarding of veto powers to the permanent members of the Security Council and the acceptance of the Ukrainian and Belorussian Soviet Socialist Republics as UN members as if they were independent countries. White was present in San Francisco as a senior advisor to the US delegation. During the conference, White met NKVD officer Vladimir S. Pravdin, telling him that "'Truman and [Secretary of State Edward] Stettinius want to achieve the success of the conference at any price', and advised that if Soviet diplomats held firmly to their demand that the USSR get a veto of UN actions, the Americans 'will agree'."[84]

The relevance of Harry Dexter White to Japan is that, for much of his career, he took a special interest in monetary policy in East Asia. Frequently working on issues related to Japan and China, he was well-placed to pass on information and to shape US policy towards the region. Indeed, one of the key pieces of evidence proving White's connection with Soviet intelligence is related to Japan. This is the so-called White Memorandum. Consisting of four sheets of notes in the hand of White, the memorandum provides a summary of his work at the Treasury in January 1938. The memo describes:

> a confidential conversation between Morgenthau and Roosevelt over economic policies toward Japan; a secret mission to England by an American naval captain to discuss a possible joint trading boycott of Japan by the two countries [...]; Treasury reactions to future aggressive moves by Japan in the Far East.[85]

Former Soviet spy Whittaker Chambers claimed he received these notes from White in early 1938, just before Chambers's break with communism. After having them photographed, Chambers kept the originals and was able to produce them a decade later as proof of White's espionage. According to Bruce R. Craig, "one can conclude that the White Memorandum is *prima facie* evidence tending to establish White's complicity with the Soviet underground." He also notes that the notes contain "exactly the type of information the Soviets would have been seeking from their information gatherers in the 1930s."[86] Separately, Whittaker Chambers recalled an occasion in

1935 when White provided documents to Frank Coe (codename PEAK), who was another member of the Silvermaster spy ring within the Treasury. These documents comprised the "names and addresses of Japanese and Chinese agents in the employ of the Japanese government" who were then active in China and Manchuria.[87]

Additionally, White was influential in advocating financial assistance to the Chinese nationalists. White was not a natural supporter of Chiang Kai-shek's government but, during the late 1930s, he recognised the expediency of doing so. White took the view that China was "fighting Russia's war" because, by keeping the Japanese bogged down in China, Chinese nationalist forces were forestalling a Japanese attack on the Soviet Union.[88] Furthermore, if the United States provided more assistance to Chiang Kai-shek's government, it reduced the requirement for the Soviet Union to do so. Providing aid to China was not straightforward due to Congress's Neutrality Act of 1935. However, Harry Dexter White, as well as presidential advisor Lauchlin Currie, devised creative means by which millions of dollars could be channelled to China "that would substantially strengthen her staying power against Japan and decrease her dependence upon Russian assistance."[89] To complement these efforts, White sought to squeeze Japan economically. This included his involvement in devising plans to curtail US oil supplies to aggressive countries including Japan.[90]

Later in the war, White reversed his position and strived to block financial flows to Chiang Kai-shek's government. With Chinese nationalist forces no longer needed to keep the Japanese at bay, the priority became to ensure that the communists prevailed in the struggle for control over post-war China. White thus turned himself into a "one man embargo" on the provision of further funds to Chiang Kai-shek's government.[91] White opposed providing the Chinese nationalists with $20 million in gold bullion in October 1944. He also boasted that he and his colleagues had "stalled as much as we have dared," thereby ensuring that gold shipments between January and June 1945 were "virtually nonexistent."[92] Other members of the Silvermaster ring within the Treasury simultaneously sought to soften US fears of the Chinese communists. Sol Adler claimed that "the Communist political program is moderate … [and] that their interests do not run counter to those of the United States."[93] It is difficult to assess exactly the extent to which these efforts contributed to the communists' victory in the Chinese civil war. However, in the judgement of Senator Charles E. Potter in 1954, "Evidence is highly convincing ... [that Harry Dexter White and his associates] bear a major share of the responsibility for the destruction of the Nationalist government in China."[94]

Aside from debate about White's role in first supporting then undermining Chiang Kai-shek's government, there is also the contention that White influenced the drafting of the Hull Note. This was the famous communication sent from the United States to Japan on 26 November 1941 that served as the US's final proposal to resolve the countries' tensions and avoid conflict. Tokyo regarded the terms as unacceptable, and, eleven days after the Hull Note was delivered, Japan launched its attack on Pearl Harbor. The speculation is that White helped ensure the inclusion of provisions, especially the requirement that all Japanese forces be withdrawn from China, that were known to be unacceptable to Japan. It is argued that, in this way, a Soviet spy succeeded in pushing Japan and the United States into conflict, thereby weakening two Soviet adversaries.[95]

This intriguing thesis owes its origin to a book entitled *Operatsiya "Sneg"* (*Operation Snow*) that was published in 1996.[96] The author, Vitalii G. Pavlov, was a retired NKVD officer who was active in North America during the early 1940s. Pavlov's key claim relates to a meeting he held with White in the summer of 1941 at the Old Ebbitt Grill in Washington, DC. Pavlov presented White with points that had been drafted by Iskhak A. Akhmerov (codename BILL), who was illegal *rezident* in the United States during World War II. These points related to countering the threat of Japanese expansionism in East Asia. White is said to have agreed with Akhmerov's argument and, according to Pavlov, stated that "he would be able to undertake the necessary efforts in the appropriate direction." Pavlov asserts that it is evident that White "developed Bill's brief thesis, passed through me, into convincing arguments that were accepted by the military leadership of the USA."[97] Specifically, the NKVD's points are said to have featured in two memoranda written by White on the topic of Japan. The first was dated 6 June 1941, the second, 17 November. It is the second of these that some historians consider to be the precursor of the Hull Note.[98]

There is nothing in the official history of Russian foreign intelligence about Operation Snow or Akhmerov's attempts to influence Harry Dexter White. This, however, tells us little. Even if there had been such an operation, it is unlikely that the Russian intelligence services would publicly boast about it. After all, it would not reflect well on Moscow if it were revealed that Soviet intrigue had provoked the Pacific War and all that followed from it.

There is also nothing about the Hull Note in the notes of Alexander Vassiliev, who had access to KGB files relating to intelligence activities against the United States during the 1930s and 1940s. There is also no mention of it in the VENONA decrypts. These sources do, however, confirm that Laurence Duggan was a Soviet agent (codename "19"), whose handler was Iskhak Akhmerov. Duggan served as a personal advisor to Cordell Hull. In 1948, 10 days after being questioned by the FBI about his contacts with Soviet intelligence, Duggan jumped or fell to his death from the sixteenth floor of the Institute of International Education in Manhattan.[99]

All this shows that Soviet intelligence had proximity to key US policymakers in 1941 via Harry Dexter White and other agents. Yet the fact that these agents had access to decision-makers does not necessarily mean they crafted particular decisions. What is needed is direct evidence that Soviet agents affected the contents of the Hull Note.

Hull's memoirs provide a detailed account of how the note was drafted. The Secretary of State explains that the initial version was drawn up by the State Department's Far Eastern experts on 11 November. Hull says that he went over this draft "word for word" and gave it his approval. However, he then adds an intriguing detail:

> Secretary Morgenthau sent me a further draft written in his Department. Although this was a further example of what seemed to me to be the Secretary of the Treasury's persistent inclination to try to function as a second Secretary of State, some of its points were good and were incorporated in our final draft.[100]

Given White's closeness to Morgenthau, there is a high probability that he was involved in writing this "further draft." As such, it does seem that White may have shaped the Hull Note. At the same time, these "good" points were only accepted because they accorded with

Hull's existing thinking. As such, even without Akhmerov's input and the lunch between Pavlov and White, the Hull Note is unlikely to have been radically different. In any case, the importance of the Hull Note should not be exaggerated. Despite Japanese attempts to pretend otherwise, it was not an ultimatum, and the United States threatened no use of force if its terms were rejected. Furthermore, the Japanese strike force that attacked Pearl Harbor had already set sail from Hitokappu Bay on Etorofu (Iturup) before the Hull Note had been received.[101]

Many remain hesitant to call Harry Dexter White a Soviet spy. Bruce R. Craig settles for "a species of espionage" to describe White's activities. However, whatever the terminology, the evidence against White is damning. He held meetings with Soviet intelligence officers and took precautions to prevent these from being discovered. As a senior Treasury official, he hired several Soviet agents. He also supplied summaries of sensitive government documents to Soviet couriers, including material about Japan's financial position and military strength. Moreover, he influenced US policy by first advocating financial support for Chiang Kai-shek's regime, then undermining it. As such, irrespective of White's role in the drafting of the Hull Note, it is clear that he made a significant contribution to Soviet intelligence, including in ways that assisted Moscow vis-à-vis Japan.

Despite the strength of the case against him, White never faced prosecution. On 13 August 1948, he appeared before the House Un-American Activities Committee. There, he denied the allegations and, despite having assisted Stalin's intelligence services for so many years, claimed a devotion to what he described as the sacred principles of freedom, "untrammeled by machine guns, secret police, or a police state."[102] Almost immediately after this brazen performance, White suffered a heart attack and died.

Alger Hiss (codenames ALES, LEONARD, JURIST)

The case against Alger Hiss is even more famous than that against Harry Dexter White. In 1949, Hiss was found guilty of perjury for having lied under oath about transferring government documents to Whittaker Chambers during the 1930s. He was spared prosecution for espionage because the statute of limitations for federal crimes was then three years. Yet, despite Hiss being sentenced to a five-year jail term, for decades many continued to believe in his innocence. Many within the US elite simply could not believe that one of their own was a Soviet spy.

Hiss insisted on his innocence until his death in 1996, yet the evidence against him is overwhelming. Again, much of this was provided by Whittaker Chambers. Although Chambers provided evidence about the contributions to Soviet espionage of both White and Hiss, the nature of his relationship with each man was very different. Chambers acknowledged that his relationship with White "was never especially close. I had the impression that he did not like me nor did I especially like him."[103] This was a common attitude towards the pugnacious Treasury official. US diplomat Paul Nitze described White as a "stinker. … a nasty, self-centered triple-barrel son-of-a-bitch."[104] By contrast, Alger Hiss was all charm, and he and Chambers developed a friendship.

They made for an odd couple. Hiss was the image of respectability. Born into a well-to-do Baltimore family in 1904, he attended Johns Hopkins University and Harvard Law School, before clerking for Supreme Court Justice Oliver Wendell Holmes. Jobs in government soon followed; first, in 1933 for the Nye Committee, which was set up to investigate the role of US arms manufacturers in World War I, then, from 1935, for the Agricultural Adjustment Administration (AAA), a New Deal institution established by the Roosevelt administration to stablise agricultural prices. After a short stint at the Justice Department, Hiss joined the State Department in September 1936, working as assistant to Assistant Secretary of State Francis B. Sayre before being transferred to the Far Eastern Division in 1939. He was subsequently a member of the US delegation at the Yalta Conference in February 1945, and, as the crowning glory of his career, served as acting secretary-general at the 1945 San Francisco Conference that established the United Nations. Hiss's last role before the allegations of espionage broke was, from February 1947, as president of the Carnegie Endowment for International Peace.

Superficially, Whittaker Chambers was everything that Hiss was not. While Hiss was tall, suave, and handsome, Chambers was "a small, pudgy man with effeminate manners and shifty, colorless eyes."[105] He was born Jay Vivian Chambers in Philadelphia in 1901. Whittaker was his mother's maiden name. His childhood was not a happy one. His father, also named Jay, abandoned the family to pursue a love affair with a male friend. His brother, Richard, suffered depression and proposed a suicide pact. When Whittaker refused, Richard killed himself on his own, leaving Whittaker with an enduring feeling of guilt. Needing something to live for, he joined the Communist Party of the United States in 1925. In the early 1930s, he was recruited by Soviet military intelligence. One of Chambers's first roles was in assisting Soviet counterespionage against Japan on the US East Coast. According to fellow communist Herbert Solow, Chambers told him in 1933 "that some Jap spies had been caught in an aircraft plant on L.I. [Long Island] by the American counter-espionage [presumably military intelligence agents], and I understood from what he said that his organization had been instrumental in helping the Americans catch those Japs."[106]

During the perjury trial, the defence made much of the men's contrasting reputations. Hiss's lawyer appealed to the jury, asking "Was there a flaw or blemish in that man? … Alger Hiss … everywhere he has gone and everything he has done and every trail he has left behind is pure, wholesome, sound, clean, decent, strong, fine."[107] High-profile character witnesses, including two Supreme Court justices, testified in support of Hiss. By contrast, Hiss labelled Chambers "somewhat queer" and condemned his life "in the sewers."[108] This was Hiss's way of drawing attention to the fact that Chambers had had several homosexual flings. Hiss's lawyer went further, castigating Chambers as "A man who is an enemy of the republic, a blasphemer of Christ, a disbeliever in God, with no respect for matrimony or for motherhood."[109]

Yet the two men had more in common than Hiss would like to admit. For a start, Hiss's early years were far from idyllic. His father, Charles Alger Hiss, committed suicide in the family home in 1907 by slitting his throat with a razor. Alger's older brother, Bosley, died of degenerative kidney disease in 1926. Three years later, his sister committed suicide by drinking Lysol, a cleaning product. Additionally, while Chambers could not match Hiss for academic qualifications, he was certainly his intellectual equal. Chambers was a gifted linguist and supplemented his income with translation work. Incongruously for a Soviet spy, Chambers produced the first English translation of the children's classic *Bambi*. Furthermore, as a talented journalist, Chambers became a leading contributor and editor at *Time* magazine. During the 1930s, Hiss and Chambers could also bond over left-wing views. In the case of Hiss, these had strengthened following his marriage to Priscilla Hobson in 1929. Priscilla, known as "Prossy," was strongly committed to social justice and was a member of the Socialist Party from 1930 to 1932. Donald Hiss, Alger's brother, who is also alleged to have had connections with Soviet intelligence (codename JUNIOR), described her as a "red-hot Communist."[110] Alger Hiss himself became an admirer of Stalin and remained so in later life, telling an interviewer in 1986 that the Soviet dictator "was very impressive ... decisive, soft-spoken, very clear-headed."[111]

At the start of the hearings, Hiss claimed, "I do not know Mr. Chambers and, so far as I am aware, I have never laid eyes on him."[112] In reality, they had been close companions. For several years during the 1930s, Hiss and Chambers met regularly and their wives became friends. Hiss permitted Chambers, whom he knew as "George Crosley," to stay at one of his houses for around two months. They also made car trips together, including, according to Chambers, one to visit Harry Dexter White in August 1937.

Many books have been written about Hiss's contributions to Soviet intelligence. We will stick here to the basics and to those aspects with most relevance to Japan. Hiss began to provide Chambers with government documents when still at the Nye Committee. This was useful because the committee had access to State Department files. Hiss's theft of confidential documents then became more systematic after his move to State in 1936. In early 1937, Hiss met Fourth Directorate *rezident* Boris Bykov at a Brooklyn cinema. Chambers joined them as interpreter since Bykov spoke German but not English. Bykov asked Hiss to provide him with State Department files, and, seemingly without hesitation, Hiss agreed. Bykov was explicit about what the Soviets wanted. As Chambers later recalled, "Bykov indicated that he was generally interested in anything concerning Germany and the Far East."[113]

Between this meeting and Chambers's break with communism in April 1938, Hiss regularly handed over US government documents.

Hiss's method was to establish the custom of bringing files home to consult during the evening. Then, on an agreed night at intervals of one week to 10 days, Chambers collected these documents from Hiss and arranged for them to be photographed. The documents were returned to Hiss the same night, ready to be carried to work the next morning. This only served for files that happened to cross Hiss's desk on the day of the pick-up. On other days, Hiss took documents of interest home and typed up summaries on the family typewriter. The typing was most likely done by Priscilla, since she was the more accomplished typist. Lastly, for documents that could not be taken out of the State Department, Hiss made handwritten notes. These notes, as well as the typed summaries, were handed to Chambers at the next pick-up.[114]

At some point in late 1937, Chambers decided to turn his back on Moscow. Before making the final break, he decided to collect documentary evidence about Soviet espionage in the United States. He described these files as his "life preservers," since the threat of their release would deter Soviet retaliation. This was a genuine risk, since Soviet agents had already murdered several defectors during the 1930s. The stash of documents contained four notes in the handwriting of Alger Hiss, 65 typewritten documents that provided summaries or complete transcripts of 70 State Department cables and one War Department report, as well as two strips of developed film plus three cans of undeveloped film. Also included were the four handwritten notes by Harry Dexter White. Chambers hid these documents in the shaft of an unused dumb waiter in the Brooklyn home of his nephew, Nathan Levine. Chambers told Levine that the documents should be handed over to the authorities in the event of his death. The documents remained in Levine's home for a decade until extracted by Chambers during the Hiss trials in 1948. Since Chambers subsequently hid the cans of film in a hollowed-out pumpkin on his farm, the documents came to be known as the "pumpkin papers."[115]

The papers only cover the period from 5 January to 1 April 1938. One can only speculate as to the contents of the documents handed over by Hiss to Chambers during the preceding months. However, if the sample is at all representative, much of the other material also likely related to the Far East and especially to Japan.

To begin with the handwritten notes, these were Hiss's summaries of State Department cables from March 1938. Two are of particular interest. The first is a cable sent from the US embassy in Paris to Secretary of State Cordell Hull. Dated 2 March, the message provides details of the financial and military assistance given by the Soviet Union to bolster China's resistance to the Japanese invasion. This was useful to Moscow in clarifying the extent of US intelligence about Soviet activities in the Far East. The same cable included the views of the French ambassador to Japan, who had reported to his capital that "the Japanese may be preparing for a move against the Russian maritime provinces." This opinion was based on the boasts of unnamed Japanese army chiefs who claimed that "they will be able to wage a successful war against Russia while holding the Chinese in check on their flank with little difficulty." The second cable was dated 11 March and contained details of Japanese troop deployments to China.[116]

Hiss was forced to accept that these notes were in his own handwriting. He suggested that he had made them for legitimate work purposes, though his boss, Francis B. Sayre, said he had never asked Hiss to prepare such memos.[117]

The original documents, whose photographs appeared on the rolls of film, also included material about Japan. Three State Department cables from January 1938 all dealt with aspects of the Sino-Japanese War. An 11 January report summarised the latest fighting, while a 13 January missive assessed the Japanese military's supplies and tactics. Another cable from 13 January was marked "Strictly confidential for the secretary." This provided details of a conversation between recently recalled Chinese ambassador to Moscow Ting-fu Tsiang and Soviet Foreign Minister Maksim Litvinov. Litvinov is reported to have told the Chinese diplomat that the Soviet Union "had no intention whatsoever of going to war with Japan under any circumstances." All these files were marked with Hiss's initials. He suggested that the files could have been stolen from his office. The secretaries disputed this, asserting that confidential documents were kept in a locked box when not in the possession of Sayre or Hiss.[118]

Lastly, there were the typed summaries of the 70 State Department cables plus one War Department report. Again, material about Japan was prominent. Multiple documents addressed military and diplomatic aspects of the Sino-Japanese War. Specific topics included the Japanese occupation of Shanghai, as well as British and US attitudes to a possible war with Japan. The one War Department file, which was dated 7 January, addressed the "Sino-Japanese Situation" and detailed US military intelligence's assessment of "supply matters, troop movements, and other military developments in the Far Eastern war."[119] A separate batch comprised State Department cables on Japan's plans for the economic development of its puppet state of Manchukuo. One of these was a translation of a Japanese report entitled "New Economic Organization of 'Manchukuo'," which had been acquired by the US consul in Yokohama. Since Manchukuo bordered the Soviet Union, this information was of particular importance to Moscow. Separately, the documents contained material that had been sent in coded form. This was valuable because a comparison of the transcribed cables with the original coded transmissions could assist Soviet codebreakers.[120]

These typed documents played a key role in demonstrating that Hiss had lied about passing government files to Chambers. Expert witnesses certified that the documents held by Chambers had undoubtedly been produced on the Hiss family's typewriter. There was also a clear match with sample documents typed on the same machine by Priscilla Hiss. These comparisons were possible because typewriters of that era produced print with minute discrepancies, thus giving each machine its own "fingerprint." Typists also left their own mark due to their distinctive style of striking the keys. These facts left Hiss's defence team floundering. Hiss was laughed at by jurors when he stated with professed bemusement, "Until the day I die, I shall wonder how Whittaker Chambers got into my house to use my typewriter."[121]

The documents passed by Hiss to Chambers had genuine intelligence value and provide an interesting example of indirect espionage; that is, spying on a country to access their intelligence on a third country. However, as with Harry Dexter White, Hiss was also an agent of influence. This was how Chambers thought of him, describing Hiss's main function as being for "infiltrating the government and influencing government policy." On another occasion, Chambers added that Hiss's role within the US government "was to mess up policy."[122] This capacity to cause trouble rose significantly as Hiss's career progressed and reached its apogee during the final months of World War II.

The debate about Hiss's manipulation of US policy centres on his role at the Yalta Conference of February 1945. Hiss was included in the US delegation at the request of Secretary of State Edward Stettinius, with whom Hiss had close relations. It is not certain to what extent the Soviets had direct contact with their agent during the conference. Mikhail Milshtein, a retired Soviet military intelligence officer, recalled that he did meet one of his assets at the Yalta conference. It is possible that this was Hiss, but it has not been verified.[123]

As Hiss explained, at Yalta, "I was primarily responsible for the United Nations topics which were rather numerous and of considerable importance."[124] They were also controversial. The main point of contention was the Soviet Union's demand that the Ukrainian Soviet Socialist Republic and the Byelorussian Soviet Socialist Republic be permitted to join the UN as founder members. Since the Soviet Union would also have membership, this would give Moscow three votes in the UN General Assembly. Roosevelt initially opposed the Soviet claim but, during the Yalta Conference, he was persuaded to accept Moscow's demand for "just" three votes.

Writing in *American Affairs* in July 1945, Isaac Don Levine alleged that Hiss was instrumental in persuading Roosevelt to make this concession:

> Premier Stalin found an occasion, at the termination of a session, to chat with President Roosevelt when all the other American delegates, with the exception of one had left the room. The one was Alger Hiss, … With the aid of the Soviet interpreter, and in the absence of the official American interpreter, Stalin pressed President Roosevelt for consent to the Soviets having three votes at the world organization, one each for the Soviet Union, for the Ukraine and the White Russian Republic. The President, in the presence of Mr. Hiss, yielded.[125]

Hiss's defenders counter that, far from supporting the Soviet claim, he drafted a memo entitled "Arguments against Inclusion of Any of the Soviet Republics among the Initial Members." Hiss did indeed write such a memo at Yalta but its existence is not inconsistent with the claim that Hiss was working to further Soviet interests. For a start, no halfway competent spy would openly advocate a measure that so clearly favoured a foreign government. Instead, a talented agent would find more subtle means of furthering their employer's agenda. This is what Hiss may have been doing with the memo. Based on a careful examination of the document, Henry D. Fetter argues "that the Hiss Memorandum is not a flat-out rejection of the Soviet proposal." Also, "arguments put forth in the memorandum diverged from the position of the State Department and thereby raise the possibility that Hiss took advantage of the opportunity he enjoyed as a trusted and expert adviser to promote a case that was at odds with US interests."[126] Specifically, Hiss's memo dropped insistence on the principle that each member state should have only one vote. This had hitherto been central to the US's argument. Hiss also argued that, if the Soviet republics were not to be admitted, India's membership would also be in question, since "It, too, is not independent." Fetter suggests this was intended to provoke tensions between Roosevelt and Churchill, since the two had previously clashed over India's status.[127]

Of more direct relevance to Japan is the possibility that Hiss had a hand in depriving it of the Southern Kuril Islands, which, to this day, remain disputed between Japan and Russia. At the Yalta Conference, Roosevelt, Stalin, and Churchill signed a secret protocol in which the Soviet Union pledged to enter the war against Japan no later than three months after the end of the war in Europe in return for several promises. These included that "The southern part of Sakhalin as well as the islands adjacent to it shall be returned to the Soviet Union;" and that "The Kurile Islands shall be handed over to the Soviet Union."[128] This deal remains controversial because, while southern Sakhalin had been taken from Russia following Japanese victory in the Russo-Japanese War, the southernmost Kuril Islands had never belonged to any country aside from Japan and had a settled Japanese population. Additionally, the decision to give the islands to the Soviet Union went against the Atlantic Charter, which was signed by Roosevelt and Churchill in August 1941. This document, which is referenced in the Yalta Declaration, affirms:

> First, their countries seek no aggrandizement, territorial or other;

> Second, they desire to see no territorial changes that do not accord with the freely expressed wishes of the peoples concerned.[129]

In his memoirs, Charles E. Bohlen, who was part of the US delegation at Yalta, puts Roosevelt's decision down to a briefing failure. In his words:

> The President evidently thought that both Southern Sakhalin and the Kuriles had been seized by Japan in the 1904 war, and that Russia therefore was only getting back territories that had been taken from her. If the President had done his homework, or if any of us had been more familiar with Far Eastern history, the United States might not have given the Kuriles to Stalin so easily.[130]

Bohlen assumes that this was an oversight, yet it could have been conspiracy rather than cock-up.

Hiss was well-placed to control the flow of information to Roosevelt since he was responsible for compiling the memoranda to be included in the president's Yalta Briefing Book. As Hiss explained, "Stettinius put me in charge of assembling all the background papers and documentation of the State Department group before we left Washington." Moreover, Hiss had a leading role in matters related to Japan, since "I was also to be responsible for any general matters that might come up relating to the Far East or the Near East."[131] There is no possibility that Hiss was simply unfamiliar with the territory in question. In advance of Yalta, Hiss had served on the State Department's Inter-Divisional Area Committee on the Far East. This committee discussed the ownership of the Kuril Islands, explicitly recommending that, "if there was any doubt about the disposition of the southern islands, they should be retained by Japan."[132]

Did Hiss manipulate the decision-making process regarding the Kuril Islands at Yalta to ensure an outcome favourable to the Soviet Union? While we do not know for certain, it seems likely that Hiss did, at least, pass on information about the US negotiating position. This concern was held by Erle R. Dickover, a colleague of Hiss at State, who contacted security officer Frederick B. Lyons in 1948 to warn:

> If the recommendations of this [Inter-Divisional Area] Committee ... were conveyed to the Russians, it would explain some later occurrences. For example, the Committee recommended that South

> Sakhalin and the southern group of the Kuriles be retained by Japan. ... If the Russians knew our thinking on these subjects ... they were in a very advantageous position at Yalta and other conferences. They knew what we hoped to do and could make their plans accordingly. Hence, perhaps, their insistence upon their claims as their price upon entry into the war against Japan (return of South Sakhalin to the Soviets, handing over of all the Kuriles, restoration of most of the Czarist rights in Manchuria, etc). They perhaps would not have made these claims had they not known the disposition which we hoped to make of these territories.[133]

There is evidence that the Soviets did indeed have access to US files relating to the Kurils in advance of Yalta. Tsuyoshi Hasegawa reports that Stalin had a copy of a memorandum of the Division of Territorial Studies that had been prepared for Roosevelt by the State Department's George H. Blakeslee prior to the conference.[134] This document again clearly recommended that the Southern Kurils be retained by Japan, but it did not make it into the president's Yalta Briefing Book.[135] It is entirely conceivable that it was Hiss who was responsible both for providing this document to Stalin and for ensuring that it was never seen by Roosevelt.

Despite others' suspicions, Edward Stettinius's faith in Alger Hiss remained unshaken. However, after the war, he did acknowledge that both the issues considered here had been damaging to US interests. In comments made in 1948, the former Secretary of State conceded that "the extra votes and the Kuriles business with the Soviet Union gradually caused Yalta to become a symbol of appeasement."[136]

A few months after the Yalta Conference, Hiss was assigned an even more prominent role as temporary secretary-general of the San Francisco conference, which, between April and June 1945, finalised arrangements for the establishment of the United Nations. The Soviets therefore achieved the remarkable feat of having their agents present at the creation of both the UN and the IMF. Eager for Hiss to remain in an influential position, Soviet ambassador to the United Nations Andrei Gromyko told Stettinius on 7 September 1945 that Moscow would be very happy for Hiss to continue as acting secretary general until an election for the post could be held. The Soviet diplomat even praised Hiss for his fairness and impartiality.[137] However, as with White at the IMF, Hiss ultimately missed out on the top job, with the role of UN acting secretary-general assigned to British diplomat Gladwyn Jebb.

All Hiss's efforts to overturn his conviction failed. However, to this day, some still doubt whether Hiss was truly a Soviet spy. This owes much to Richard Nixon's involvement in the case. Nixon was a member of the House Committee on Un-American Activities that originally heard Chambers's allegations. The resulting publicity helped Nixon win a Senate seat in 1950, then the vice-presidential nomination in 1952. The assumption of some is that, given Nixon's crooked behaviour as president, he must also have engaged in trickery in the Hiss case, which made his political career.

Moscow also helped promote the view that the allegations against Hiss were a witch hunt. Similar to its propaganda efforts in the 1930s during the Noulens Affair, in the post-war era "the Soviets were conducting a massive public campaign protesting that Hiss was innocent."[138] This had a dual benefit. As well as helping defend their man, stoking support for Hiss gave longevity to a divisive debate that continued to rile US politics for decades. Moscow did not, however, accept all proposals for assisting Hiss. Researchers with access to the KGB archives discovered a cable sent by Soviet ambassador (and NKVD *rezident*) Aleksandr Panyushkin from Washington, DC to Moscow in December 1948. Panyushkin proposed that the Soviet Union discredit Chambers by fabricating evidence to show that he had been a Nazi rather than a Soviet agent. Using Chambers's codename, Panyushkin suggested that

> As "Karl" … is of German origin, lived and studied for some time in Berlin [it should be possible] …, "to find" in German archives "Karl's" file from which it would become clear that he is a German agent who by Gestapo instructions was carrying out espionage work in the US and penetrated into the American Communist Party. If we claim it in our press and publish some "documents" which could be produced at home, the effect of this will be very big. … and, as a result, positions of the Committee on Un-American Activities, the Grand Jury … and other organs will be strongly undermined.[139]

Moscow did not accept Panyushkin's proposal since they worried that, if Chambers's former collaborators were persuaded that he had really been a Nazi agent, it would encourage more of them to testify to the US authorities about their work with him during the 1930s. The scheme would also have converted Hiss from a Soviet spy into a Nazi one.[140]

Whatever the source of the doubt about Hiss's guilt, its dogged persistence makes necessary a review of the material that corroborates the testimony and documentary evidence provided by Chambers. Much of this comes from other defectors. First, as early as 1939, French Prime Minister Edouard Daladier warned US Ambassador William C. Bullitt about "two brothers named Hiss" who were both "Soviet agents" and worked in the State Department.[141] The French most likely heard this information from Walter G. Krivitsky, the head of Soviet military intelligence in Western Europe who defected to the West in 1937.[142] In September 1945, Igor S. Guzenko, a cipher clerk in the Soviet embassy in Ottawa, also defected, taking with him his wife, infant son, and 109 intelligence documents. Guzenko was not able to give Hiss's name, but he did reveal that Soviet military intelligence operated an "agent of influence" who was, at the time of the San Francisco conference, "an assistant secretary to the Secretary of State."[143] Furthermore, Elizabeth Bentley and Noel Field both named Hiss as part of the Soviet espionage network in the United States to which they had previously contributed.[144] Lastly, Oleg A. Gordievsky, a former KGB colonel who fled to Britain in 1985, revealed that Alger Hiss's codename had been ALES.[145]

Even more conclusive evidence surfaced in the 1990s. Shortly after the collapse of the Soviet Union in 1991, Crown Publishers and the KGB's Association of Retired Intelligence Officers signed an agreement to publish five books based on top-secret KGB archives. This deal reflected the spirit of cooperation that characterised the first years after the end of the Cold War. It also showed that the Russian intelligence services were desperate for cash. The man selected to research the volume on Soviet espionage in the United States during the 1930s and 1940s was Alexander Vassiliev, a Russian journalist who had previously worked for the KGB. Vassiliev was permitted access to Soviet foreign intelligence files and spent months taking detailed notes. The KGB-approved books were never published since Crown Publishers encountered financial difficulties and the political atmosphere in Russia became less permissive. Nonetheless, Vassiliev kept his extensive notes and smuggled them out of the country after he emigrated to Britain in 1996. These became the basis for two books co-written with US academics.[146] These volumes include many revelations about Soviet agents but the most eye-catching are about Hiss. As the authors explain,

> Alexander Vassiliev's notebooks quote KGB reports and cables from the mid-1930s to 1950 that document KGB knowledge of and contacts with Alger Hiss and unequivocally identify Hiss as a long-term espionage source of the KGB's sister agency, GRU, Soviet military intelligence. Hiss is identified by his real name as well as by cover names, "Jurist," "Ales," and "Leonard."[147]

Material from the VENONA project also began to be declassified during the 1990s. VENONA was an operation begun in 1943 by the US Army's Signal Intelligence Service to intercept and decrypt communications between Soviet spies in the United States and their bosses in Moscow. Beginning in 1995, the US government declassified almost 3,000 intercepted Soviet cables.[148] Within this archive is one telegram of particular importance to the Hiss case. Cable no. 1822 was sent by Soviet *rezident* in Washington Anatolii B. Gromov (codename VADIM) to Moscow on 30 March 1945. It reports the details of a "chat" between ALES and an NKVD officer identified as "A" (probably Iskhak Akhmerov). The key section is as follows:

> 1. ALES has been working with the NEIGHBORS [SOSEDI] [the standard NKVD designation for Soviet Military Intelligence] continuously since 1935.
> 2. For some years past he has been the leader of a small group of the NEIGHBORS' probationers [STAZhERY] [agents], for the most part consisting of his relations.

Additionally, the cable provides further evidence that ALES is almost certainly Hiss. It states:

> 5. Recently ALES and his whole group were awarded Soviet decorations.
> 6. After the YaLTA Conference, when he had gone to MOSCOW, a Soviet personage in a very responsible position (ALES gave to

> understand that it was Comrade VYSHINSKIJ [then Deputy Commissar of Foreign Affairs]) allegedly got in touch with ALES and at the behest of the Military NEIGHBORS passed on to him their gratitude and so on.[149]

It is a matter of public record that Hiss, along with Stettinius and six other US officials, did visit Moscow on the way back from Yalta. Of those who travelled to Moscow, it is only Hiss who is suspected of ties to Soviet intelligence. Furthermore, on 13 February 1945, Deputy Commissar Andrei Vyshinskii invited his American guests to a reception at the commissariat's guesthouse in Moscow. Several of the group, including Hiss, also attended a performance of *Swan Lake* at the Bolshoi Theatre. Vyshinskii, as well as director of Red Army intelligence Fedor Kuznetsov and military intelligence officer Mikhail Milshtein, sat in the same box. Vyshinskii therefore had several opportunities to express his gratitude.[150]

A second VENONA decrypt mentions Hiss by name, though regrettably not all of it was successfully deciphered. Sent on 28 September 1943 by Pavel P. Mikhailov (codename MOLIERE), who was Soviet vice consul in New York, this telegram (no. 1579) includes the line: "2. The NEIGHBOR [SOSED] has reported that (1 group unrecovered) from the State Department by the name of HISS (121 groups unrecoverable)."[151]

Until his death in 1996 at the age of 92, Alger Hiss continued to insist on his innocence. This indefatigability gained him supporters, with many assuming that no one could live a lie for half a century. Yet, while Hiss's tenacity convinced some that he had been framed, the mutually reinforcing evidence shows clearly that he really was an agent of Soviet military intelligence.

SIGINT

Lastly, when considering Sorge's contemporaries, is the topic of signals intelligence (SIGINT). This often receives less attention than human intelligence (HUMINT), since the technical work of decoding intercepts is less glamorous than undercover agents risking their lives to steal secrets from beneath their enemies' noses. Governments may also distract attention from SIGINT successes since, even years after the events, they may wish to conceal the code-breaking techniques used and the extent to which they had penetrated another country's communications. One leader who certainly did value SIGINT was Stalin. Indeed, he preferred it, since, as Robert Whymant explains, "Human spies were prone to the weaknesses of the flesh and might turn into traitors. Sigint did not lie, nor could the most alert and nimble agent match it for speed."[152]

Walter G. Krivitsky

In early spring 1936, Eugen Ott, who was then still German military attaché in Tokyo, rushed to tell his friend Richard Sorge of an intriguing rumour he had just heard. The news was that secret talks were underway between Japanese Major General Ōshima Hiroshi and German Foreign Minister Joachim von Ribbentrop. Sorge, who was keenly aware of Moscow's fears about a tie-up between Germany and Japan, pressed Ott for details. However, for once, neither Ott nor Sorge's other diplomatic sources could deliver. This was because the highly sensitive talks were being conducted without the involvement of the German diplomatic service. As Ott told Sorge: "It's so hush-hush that neither Ambassador Dirksen nor myself were told anything about this."[153] Only after the talks culminated in the Anti-Comintern Pact of November 1936 was Sorge able to discover the key facts. By then, Moscow already knew all about the agreement. This owed much to Walter G. Krivitsky and his success in accessing the communications between Major General Ōshima and Tokyo.

Walter Krivitsky was born Samuel Ginzberg in 1899 in Galicia, then part of the Austro-Hungarian Empire. As a young man, he "looked very frail and thin, obviously marked by the wartime famine years."[154] However, what Krivitsky lacked in physical stature, he made up for in ideological zeal. He was 18 when the October Revolution struck, and, as he explains, "I joined the Bolshevik Party with my whole soul."[155] He became a member of the Bolshevik security services and adopted the *nom de guerre* of "Krivitsky," which is derived from the Russian word "*krivoi*," meaning "crooked."

After years of dedicated service, Krivitsky was promoted in September 1935 to the position of illegal *rezident* in the Netherlands, where he presented himself as an Austrian antiquarian by the name of

Dr Martin Lessner. Shortly after taking on his new role, Krivitsky learned from one of his agents in Germany about the secret Japanese-German talks. He returned to Moscow for consultations and was given "all the necessary authority and means to pursue to the bitter end the quest for information on the Ōshima-Ribbentrop conversations."[156] Krivitsky's team did so by targeting Japanese communications, albeit indirectly.

Soviet military intelligence had learned that the Nazis were intercepting all coded messages between Ōshima and Tokyo. Consequently, rather than intercepting the Japanese cables themselves, they could simply piggyback on the work of the Germans. Soviet agents set to work in Berlin, and, as Krivitsky recounts, "Late in July, 1936, I received word that the complete file of this confidential correspondence had at last been secured in photostatic form."[157] The source was a German officer who was desperate for money to fund a love affair with a young actress.[158] Krivitsky explains that, as soon as he had the documents, "I went straight to Haarlem, where we had a secret photographic developing room. … I also had, awaiting us in Haarlem, a first-class Japanese-language expert, whom we had scoured Moscow to find."[159] The cables were encoded, but the Soviets already had the relevant codebook. Historian Miyake Masaki suggests that this had been stolen from the Japanese embassy in Moscow.[160]

The intelligence operation was a great success. As Krivitsky notes, several months before the Anti-Comintern Pact was signed, "all correspondence between General Oshima and Tokyo flowed regularly through our hands." This revealed that:

> the purpose of the negotiations was the conclusion of a secret pact to coordinate all the moves made by Berlin and Tokyo in Western Europe as well as in the Pacific. Under the terms of the secret agreement, Japan and Germany undertook to regulate between themselves all matters relating to the Soviet Union and to China, and to take no action either in Europe or in the Pacific without consulting each other. Berlin also agreed to place its improvements in weapons of war at the disposal of Tokyo and to exchange military missions with Japan.[161]

Equipped with this intelligence, Moscow tried to scupper the agreement by leaking parts of it to the international press.[162] When this failed, the Soviet leadership changed tack and attempted a rapprochement with Germany. As Krivitsky recounts, "The terms of that secret agreement, which came into Stalin's possession in the main through my efforts and those of my staff, incited him to a desperate attempt to drive a bargain with Hitler. Early in 1937 such a deal was actually pending between them."[163]

As well as revealing the details of the Anti-Comintern Pact, continued access to Ōshima's communications offered first-class insight into the thinking of the German leadership. This is because Ōshima spoke excellent German and had close relations with many senior Nazis. "He was variously called the Germans' 'pet' and 'Hitler's confidant'. Top-level people trusted and confided in him, giving his reports a 'from-the-horse's-mouth' quality."[164] Ōshima's telegrams to Tokyo included a prediction of a German invasion of the Soviet Union in 1941, providing yet another warning that was ignored by Stalin.[165]

For his work in securing Soviet access to Ōshima's communications, Krivitsky was recommended for the Order of Lenin. He never received it. Instead, in October 1937, he broke with the Soviet Union. This was prompted by the murder one month earlier of Krivitsky's friend and fellow Soviet spy Ignace Poretskii (Ignace Reiss) by a Soviet assassination squad in Switzerland. After Krivitsky's defection, he met Whittaker Chambers in New York. By that time Chambers had already broken with communism but was uncertain whether he should tell the US authorities what he knew about other Soviet agents. During an all-night discussion, Krivitsky persuaded Chambers that he must speak up, telling him, "In our time, informing is a duty."[166]

Krivitsky made his own efforts to warn the West of the threat posed by communist spies. In 1939, he published a book entitled *In Stalin's Secret Service*, in which he recounted his experiences in Soviet intelligence. In February 1941, he was found dead in a hotel room in Washington, DC with a gunshot wound to the head. Although the official verdict was suicide, many assumed the Soviet intelligence services had taken their revenge.

Izumi Kōzō (codenames NERO, GREEN)

The second SIGINT case is that of Izumi Kōzō. This individual remains little known within the history of intelligence, including within Japan. This is a considerable oversight given that Izumi's contribution to Soviet espionage during World War II is claimed by some to match, or even exceed, that of Richard Sorge. Unlike the drama of the downfall of Sorge and Ozaki, there was no climactic end to Izumi Kōzō's career as a Soviet agent. Indeed, Japanese counterintelligence never appears to have had this Japanese diplomat on their radar. His unmasking only occurred during the mid-1950s, following another Soviet defection.

Yurii A. Rastvorov was a lieutenant colonel in the MVD (another of the forerunners of the KGB). He was deployed to Japan in 1950 but became disillusioned with the Soviet system. This was as much for personal as political reasons. Rastvorov was married to ballerina Galina A. Godova but the relationship had soured. Rastvorov was therefore living on his own in Tokyo and craving female company. He gained a taste for Western lifestyle as a consequence of his membership of the Tokyo Lawn Tennis Club. The intention was for Rastvorov to cultivate contacts among this exclusive club's members, which included many diplomats. However, Rastvorov found that, having experienced the high life in Tokyo, he never wanted to return to Moscow.[167]

The push came in January 1954, when, having fallen out with the embassy's chargé d'affaires and his wife, Rastvorov was recalled to Moscow. This prompted Rastvorov to defect to the United States. Over the course of a debriefing that lasted several months, Rastvorov provided full details of his espionage work in Japan, naming dozens of agents. One of the most interesting was Izumi Kōzō.[168]

Izumi Kōzō was born near Tokyo in 1890. He attended the elite Ichikō high school but dropped out without graduating. Ozaki Hotsumi was a pupil at the same school but, since Izumi was more than 10 years older, it is unlikely these future Soviet spies met in the playground. Having failed to distinguish himself academically, Izumi began work as a provincial clerk. However, in 1914, he secured a job with the security department of the Ministry of Internal Affairs in Tokyo. After the October Revolution in 1917, Izumi, along with several other government officials, was ordered to study Russian so that Japan might better understand the Bolshevik threat. He was transferred to the Ministry of Foreign Affairs in 1918 and spent time in Vladivostok before returning to Tokyo in 1922 to continue working as a Soviet expert.[169]

Izumi emerged unscathed from his early experiences of the Soviet Union. This changed when, following the formal establishment of diplomatic relations in 1925, he was sent to Moscow as a member of staff in the newly reopened Japanese embassy. On arrival, Izumi immediately became a target for Soviet intelligence.

The Soviet security services exercised tight control over where foreign diplomats were permitted to live. In the case of Izumi, they arranged for him to rent a room in the house of Elizaveta V. Perskaya at 15 Merzlyakovskii Pereulok.[170] Perskaya was a woman of noble birth for whom the October Revolution had been a catastrophe. Her husband, a Tsarist army general, had died, either during World War I or following the Bolshevik seizure of power. Her only son was executed in 1925 on suspicion of counter-revolutionary activity. Vulnerable and fearful for the lives of her two daughters, Elizaveta Perskaya was compelled to work for the Soviet security services.[171]

As no doubt intended by the Soviet secret police, Izumi began a relationship with one of the daughters, Elena, and the two married in 1927. Soon after, Izumi and his new bride, accompanied by Elizaveta, left for Harbin, China, where Izumi served as vice consul. The younger daughter, Vera, remained behind. From this point, the Soviet security services' chief tool for exerting influence over Izumi changed from Elizaveta to Elena. She was assigned the unimaginative codename DAUGHTER.[172]

Izumi's next posting, from 1930, was in Blagoveshchensk, on the banks of the Amur River, which separates Russian and Chinese territory. Elena had become pregnant and returned to Moscow to have the child. Taking this opportunity, the Soviet authorities detained her and pressured her into helping steal documents from her husband's safe. The plan was for Elena to provide the files to a local intelligence officer, whose wife had gained employment in the Japanese consulate as a cleaning lady. This initial attempt failed, as Elena ultimately refused to give access to the safe. However, the Soviet security services did not give up.

In the following years, Izumi, accompanied by wife and child, was sent to work in Japanese legations in Petropavlovsk, Manchuli, and

Tehran. Then, in late 1936, Izumi was transferred to Prague. During this period, the Soviet authorities tightened their grip on Elena's family. Elena's sister, Vera, and her husband were arrested and executed, and her mother, Elizaveta, was sentenced to 10 years in the gulag. Elena knew nothing of this, but, having heard nothing from her family, she assumed they had been arrested. Moscow's leverage over Elena was heightened by the fact that her child, a boy named Tōyō, had serious medical problems. Fearing for her relatives and needing support for her son, Elena walked into the Soviet embassy in Prague in September 1937 and requested the restoration of her Soviet citizenship, which she had renounced when marrying a foreign diplomat. She asked for the release of her family members and wrote a statement of repentance for her failure to follow through with the operation in Blagoveshchensk. This marked the real start of Elena's intelligence career.[173]

In subsequent months, Elena began to inform on her husband. She revealed that Izumi was engaged in cipher work at the Japanese embassy and had contacts with Russian émigrés. This suggests he may have conducted intelligence as well as diplomatic work for the Japanese. Most significantly, "In March 1938 Elena gave to her handler nine notebooks of her husband, a card catalogue of Russian émigrés in Iran (Persia), replicas of keys to Izumi's safe, and his briefcase."[174] In return, Elena made the pitiable request that she be allowed to send her mother a letter, parcels, and £10 sterling.

It is unclear how much Izumi already suspected of his wife's collaboration with Soviet intelligence, but, during a trip to Italy in spring 1938, Elena openly proposed that he work for Moscow. Izumi agreed. His motivations are not entirely clear. It is said that he disliked the military clique then dominating Japanese politics, but Izumi does not appear to have betrayed his country for ideological reasons. Rather, one suspects he felt a duty to assist his wife and her family. Elena herself told the Soviet authorities of Izumi's deep attachment to her. Whatever the explanation, Izumi began to consciously assist Soviet intelligence. "On 3 May 1938 Elena brought to her Prague handler, Mikhail M. Adamovich (1898–1979), seven codebooks and their keys."[175] A meeting was then arranged between Izumi and Adamovich at which the Japanese diplomat requested that, in return for his cooperation, he receive £5,000 sterling plus £100 every month. The couple's cooperation was also rewarded through the transfer of Elena's mother from a gulag to a clinic within Butyrka prison in Moscow. In March 1941, she was fully released.

By providing codebooks and sample coded messages, Izumi enabled the Soviets to break Japan's diplomatic codes. He also undermined Japan's intelligence work by revealing the names of Japanese agents due to be sent to Soviet territory.[176] What is more, Izumi's assistance was recurring. When Japan changed its codes for European diplomatic communications in 1940, Izumi, who was then acting head of the Japanese legation in Sofia, Bulgaria, simply gave Moscow the new codebooks. The same occurred in June 1941 when, the day after the start of the Nazi invasion of the Soviet Union, Tokyo changed the diplomatic codes again. Thanks to Izumi's updates, "Moscow thus was able to read the war-time correspondence that took place between Tokyo and Japan's European legations and among these legations."[177]

The value of Izumi's espionage during World War II was enormous. Just as Sorge warned of Nazi Germany's plans to attack the Soviet Union in 1941, access to Japanese diplomatic correspondence provided insight into Berlin's intentions. On 30 May 1941, Deputy People's Commissar of State Security Bogdan Z. Kobulov sent a note to Stalin entitled "A message received by agents about the intention of Germany to start war with the USSR in the second half of June 1941." This top-secret message stated:

> The Japanese consul general in Vienna on 9 May 1941 reported the following to Japan's Ministry of Foreign Affairs: The German leadership now understands that to provide Germany with raw materials and products for a long war it is necessary to seize Ukraine and the Caucasus. They are accelerating their preparations in order to provoke conflict, probably in the second half of June, before the gathering of the harvest, and they hope to finish the whole campaign in 6–8 weeks. In connection with this, the Germans are postponing the invasion of England.[178]

As with all the other warnings of Barbarossa, this message was dismissed by Stalin.

Decryption of Japanese diplomatic correspondence also confirmed that Japan would not join Nazi Germany in attacking the Soviet Union in 1941. According to a report sent to Moscow on 17 July 1941, Soviet agents in London had intercepted a Japanese cable that revealed that the *gozenkaigi* of 2 July had prioritised a southward advance instead of an attack on the Soviet Union.[179] Furthermore, the Soviets were able to decrypt a telegram sent from Tokyo to the Japanese embassy in Berlin on 27 November 1941. This instructed the Japanese ambassador to "Explain to Hitler that the main Japanese efforts will be concentrated in the south and that we propose to refrain from deliberate operations in the north."[180] This provided further reassurance to the Soviet leadership that it was safe to transfer forces from the Far East to the defence of Moscow.

Izumi is also credited with informing Moscow of a 1939 Japanese plot to assassinate Stalin. Details of the scheme were recorded in German government files because Ambassador Ōshima discussed them with SS Reichsführer Heinrich Himmler on 31 January 1939 as part of broader talks on Japanese-German "long-range" espionage projects "aimed at the disintegration of Russia." The German records reveal that Ōshima told Himmler that he had "succeeded up to now to send ten Russians armed with bombs across the Caucasian frontier ... These Russians had the mission to kill Stalin."[181] Tipped off with the assistance of Izumi, the Soviet security forces intercepted and liquidated the Russian émigrés. Additionally, the Soviets used information from Izumi at the Nuremberg and Tokyo war crimes tribunals to demonstrate Japan's long-standing aggressive intentions and thus to justify Moscow's attack on Japan in 1945 in violation of the Soviet-Japanese neutrality pact.[182]

In making an overall assessment of Izumi Kōzō's intelligence work, Hiroaki Kuromiya and Andrzj Pepłoński conclude that it is "not an overstatement to say that Izumi was the equal of Richard Sorge." Indeed, these scholars suggest "that Izumi's contribution to Moscow was greater than that of Sorge's: Izumi enabled Moscow to acquire 'raw data', which Stalin wanted, whereas Stalin treated Sorge's dispatches from Tokyo with scepticism."[183] Historian of intelligence Christopher Andrew concurs, arguing that the intelligence that did the most to persuade Stalin that the Japanese would not attack came, not from Sorge, but from SIGINT. He also notes that the cracking of Japan's diplomatic cipher, which was facilitated by Izumi, made Sergei Tolstoi, the NKVD's chief Japanese specialist, "the most decorated Soviet cryptanalyst of the war."[184]

Why then does Izumi Kōzō remain so little known? Partly this is on account of his low-key end. In March 1946, Izumi returned to Japan. He was on his own since Elena and Tōyō had returned to the Soviet Union at the start of May 1941. Moscow had judged that, during the war, separating Izumi from his foreign wife would strengthen his position within the ministry. Soon after arriving back in Tokyo, Izumi reported to the Soviet embassy to ask about his family. After several weeks, he was informed that his son was living with his grandmother, Elizaveta, and that Elena was receiving treatment in a psychiatric hospital. It is unclear if any of this was true.[185]

After the war, Izumi stopped working for the Ministry of Foreign Affairs and began a small trading company. He no longer had access to state secrets but continued assisting Soviet intelligence, meeting his handler around 40 times between 1949 and 1952. He passed on information about US activities in Japan and titbits he picked up from former colleagues. He received money in return.[186]

In spring 1947, Izumi was interviewed by the US occupation authorities, but this was common practice with Japanese officials who had returned from overseas. The interviewers seem to have had no suspicion that Izumi was working for Moscow. This only changed following Rastvorov's revelations. After Rastvorov's defection in 1954, Izumi was questioned again. This time, he confessed to being a Soviet agent.[187] He avoided prosecution but died two years later of hypertension, aged 66.

While Izumi's spy work and ultimate demise are less cinematic than Sorge's, his contributions to Soviet victory in the Second World War might still have been honoured by Moscow. However, Izumi's case is harder to use for propaganda purposes. Richard Sorge was a dedicated communist who had a deep attachment to his Russian motherland. With skill and bravado, he penetrated the German embassy in Tokyo and built a broader spy network within Japan. By contrast, Izumi had little affection for either communism or Russia. Instead of volunteering to serve Soviet intelligence, he was entrapped through the ruthless exploitation of his wife's family. Rather than inspiring respect for the Soviet intelligence services, it is a story that reinforces their reputation for cruelty. It is therefore unsurprising that Moscow has remained silent about him.

* * *

Richard Sorge remains undiminished as one of the most memorable characters in the history of intelligence. Yet, as has been shown, the Soviets had several other irons in the fire when it came to spying on the Japanese during the late 1930s and early 1940s. Through these multiple sources, the Soviet Union amassed a clear picture of Japan's military resources and economic capabilities, and they learned crucial details about Japan's military strategy towards the Soviet Union. Moscow also gained insight into the status of Japan's ruinous war in China and the deteriorating strength of Japanese forces across the Soviet frontier in Manchuria. This intelligence served as vital preparation for August 1945, when the Soviet Union finally cast aside its neutrality pact with Japan and launched what has come to be known as Operation August Storm.

CONCLUSION

HOW TO SPY ON JAPAN

What can be learned from this history of Russian/Soviet espionage operations against Japan? The examples covered in this volume only extend to 1945, but there is much that remains relevant. What follows is a textbook account of how to spy on the Japanese that is based on these historical cases. By highlighting long-standing vulnerabilities and the means to exploit them, this conclusion shows areas where vigilance is needed. This is instructive as Japan confronts persistent activity from Russian operatives, as well as a heightened threat of Chinese espionage.

There is a widespread impression that Japan is a "spy paradise" (*supai tengoku*). This term gained prominence after it was used by Prime Minister Nakasone Yasuhiro in April 1983.[1] There are good reasons for this characterisation, yet, as this book has shown, over the centuries Japan has often been a hard target for espionage. During the *sakoku* era, the Japanese authorities went to extraordinary lengths to shield the country from foreign eyes. Adam Laxman was treated courteously when he arrived in 1792, yet his accommodation was surrounded by guards and curtains were installed to prevent him from glimpsing the country beyond. Nikolai Rezanov was subject to even tighter restrictions and felt that he and his officers were detained like zoo animals after arriving in Nagasaki in 1804. Neither man saw himself as leading a spy mission, yet, since the Bakufu regarded all information about Japan as secret, every attempt to penetrate Japan's seclusion was seen as spying.

While all foreigners were viewed warily, particular suspicion was directed against Russia. This owed something to ancient prophecies that "The time will be, when a people will come from the north, and conquer Japan."[2] However, enemies and rivals of Russia also fanned Japanese fears. This included Hungarian adventurer Maurice Benyovszky (Hanbengoro), who falsely told the Japanese in 1771 that he was a Russian spy and that the Russians were preparing to attack. The Dutch also sought to defend their privileged position in Nagasaki by inflaming Japanese fears of the supposedly cruel and untrustworthy Russians.

These outsized fears outlasted the end of national isolation in the 1850s. Ahead of the Russo-Japanese War of 1904–5, Japan was gripped by spy mania that caused several Japanese, including Diet member Akiyama Teisuke, to be accused of being "*rotan*," that is, "Russian agents." The irony is that these were the years when Russian espionage against Japan was at its most complacent and under-resourced. Suspicions were also intense during the 1930s, an era when the Japanese government operated anti-spy weeks and all manner of innocuous data, including bicycle production figures, were categorised as state secrets. Once again, Russian officials were subject to especially close surveillance, this time because of Bolshevik efforts to propagate communism within Japan.

Aside from the difficulties presented by Japanese government policies, those seeking intelligence on Japan have had to overcome other barriers, including language. From the earliest days of interaction, Russia has struggled to have sufficient personnel with the ability to converse in Japanese as well as to read and write Chinese characters. Efforts to compel castaways—most of whom were uneducated fishermen—to serve as language teachers had limited effectiveness. Language remained a problem before and during the Russo-Japanese War, with military attaché Nikolai Yanzhul writing in despair that the "gibberish" of *kanji* made it impossible for him to understand confidential papers.[3]

An added challenge has been Japan's relative homogeneity and the obvious physical differences between most Russians and Japanese. In the multi-ethnic United States, Soviet *rezidenty* during the 1930s simply called themselves "Bill" or "Peter" and presented themselves as naturalised citizens. This has not generally been an option for Russian spies operating against Japan. When Russian soldier Vasilii Ryabov dressed himself up as an East Asian to gather intelligence behind Japanese lines during the Russo-Japanese War, this "Russian samurai" was quickly captured and executed. Furthermore, even for someone who is Japanese, it is difficult to penetrate Japan's insular elite, whose interlocking bonds are forged through family ties and attendance at prestigious schools and universities.

Despite these factors making Japan a hard target, Russia has achieved considerable success in penetrating Japan for intelligence purposes. What accounts for this inconsistency? Richard Sorge offers a compelling explanation. In his words: "Japan is like a crab. Its outside has a hard, durable surface, but once you get on the inside, it is soft. And if you arrive at that point, it is easy to get information."[4]

One source of this softness is that same insular elite that seems to protect Japan from external infiltration. This is because, while the elite shows mistrust towards outsiders, it features high levels of internal trust. This means that access is permitted to those whom a more objective analysis would flag as a security risk. An example is Saionji Kinkazu, who, despite his socialist views, was granted privileged positions at the heart of government because he was the adopted grandson of a former prime minister, Prince Saionji Kinmochi. Within this narrow elite, information is exchanged freely. This is exacerbated by Japan's rigid age hierarchy, since *kōhai* (juniors) find it difficult to decline requests from their *senpai* (seniors). The Japanese practice of *nemawashi*—that is, the laborious process of consensus building before any decision is taken—also entails the widespread sharing of confidential information. Many of those who do not strictly need to know are nonetheless kept informed as a mark of respect. These factors mean that the top level of Japanese society is remarkably gossipy. In Sorge's assessment, "Although leakages of information may, strictly speaking, be punishable by law, in practice the Japanese social system is not amenable to the keeping of secrets."[5]

Adding to the softness is the fact that many Japanese, at least historically, have behaved with abandon when outside Japan. Freed of the conformity imposed by the presence of other Japanese, several officers have given way to licentiousness. This left them vulnerable to compromise, especially when alcohol has been mixed with "honey." During the 1920s and 1930s, a common tactic was for the Russian intelligence services to provide Japanese officers stationed in Russia with attractive female language teachers. A powerful sense of duty and shame also meant that some of those compromised would rather agree to work for a foreign power than face public humiliation.

Compounding these factors has been the historical weakness of Japanese counterintelligence. Japanese police have displayed plenty of activity in chasing spies but little of the skill or strategy needed to run them to ground. The impression has often been of effort over efficiency, hours amassed over output achieved. The Sorge-Ozaki spy ring was eventually broken up, but this was a matter of luck. When the Japanese authorities finally arrested Miyagi Yotoku, they had no idea of the scale of their catch. As for Izumi Kōzō (NERO), he was never caught at all.

In modern Japan, politicians often debate the need for a proper anti-spy law. The Japanese government proposed such legislation in the 1980s but backed off due to public opposition. This was not the issue before 1945. In addition to the Peace Preservation Law (1925), which was principally targeted at agents of the Comintern, Japan had the Military Secrets Protection Law (1899), the Military Resources Protection Act (1939), and the National Defence Security Law (1941). The last of these specified that state secrets included not only military information but also diplomatic, economic, and political matters. Yet, as Chalmers Johnson explains, these laws, while strict, "were intended more to strengthen totalitarian rule than to support counterespionage."[6]

As Richard Sorge reflected from prison, the problem with Japanese counterintelligence was not the legal structures but the police tactics. "In summation I would say that the Japanese police were interested too much in little things and not enough in big ones."[7] Fellow Soviet spy Max Clausen argued that, despite their fearsome reputation, "the Japanese police were too polite to aliens and, therefore, not as efficient at spy control as European police."[8] A further problem was the failure to learn lessons. Even after the momentous Sorge-Ozaki case, the priority of officials in the final report was not to learn lessons but to play down the scale of the espionage to conceal embarrassing failures of oversight.[9]

Cracking the crab

Given these strengths and weaknesses, what is the best way to spy on Japan? Firstly, this history of Russian espionage demonstrates that the ideal agent will be Japanese. This has been the case with Russia's most valuable agents, from Tachibana Kōsai in the 1850s right through to Ozaki Hotsumi and Izumi Kōzō in the 1930s and 1940s. Richard Sorge left his mark but, as has been shown, he really spied on the Germans and was dependent on Ozaki for his best intelligence about Japan.

The ideal agent also needs excellent access. This can be due to formal position, as was the case with KROTOV's role within the Japanese intelligence services during the 1920s, or Izumi Kōzō's position within the Ministry of Foreign Affairs during the 1930s. However, due to the weakness of information security within the Japanese elite, it is even better to have an agent who, while perhaps lacking formal title, is on intimate terms with individuals at the heart of the Japanese establishment. It is this quality, more than any official position he held, that made Ozaki Hotsumi the most impressive Japanese spy that Moscow ever operated.

To recruit Japanese agents, the usual four inducements of money, ideology, compromise, and ego (MICE) have proved effective. However, even when other motivations are involved, money tends to play a supporting role. This is because handlers want their agents to accept payment. It formalises the relationship and creates for the agent a feeling that they need to be productive to justify the cash they have received. Furthermore, if the agent signs a receipt, this evidence can be used to deter him/her from breaking with Moscow.

Some element of ego is also often there in the background. This was most evident in agent ABE's decision to supply secrets to the Soviets from Seoul and Harbin from the 1920s. He felt undervalued by his bosses and wanted to demonstrate, at least to himself, that he was superior to them. In other cases, agents get a thrill as the sparkle of the secret world brightens their otherwise dull lives. There is also the ego boost of being able to tell yourself that you are having an impact on the course of history.

Ideology has been a more irregular factor in the recruitment of Japanese agents. Few were motivated by an affection for Russia itself.

Unsurprisingly, Russian imperialism or nationalism did not stir the hearts of Japanese subjects. Left-wing ideology, however, was a different matter. There was a profound interest in socialist and anarchist ideas within Japan from the late 19th century, and many looked to Russian revolutionary movements for inspiration. This was evident in the High Treason Incident of 1910. Later, after the Bolshevik Revolution, several Japanese were persuaded to serve the Comintern. This continued to be an effective lure long after it was obvious that the Comintern served the interests of the Soviet state rather than international communism.

Additionally, the Soviet intelligence services, unburdened by any moral compass, made productive use of Japanese officials' strong sense of duty and shame. Izumi Kōzō was paid for the codebooks he handed over, yet a stronger motivation was his sense of duty to his wife and family. However, those blackmailing Japanese officials must be cautious not to pressure their targets too hard. This was demonstrated in the case of Japanese naval attaché Koyanagi Kisaburō in 1929. After Captain Koyanagi was successfully caught in a "honey trap," he chose suicide over becoming a tool of Soviet intelligence. It remains a matter of debate whether Moscow had greater success in compromising Lieutenant General Komatsubara Michitarō, who commanded Japanese forces at Nomonhan.

While recruiting agents within the political, military, and social elite has been the obvious priority, a broader range of Japanese recruits is also needed. They help Russian officers overcome the language barrier. They are also valuable because they are inconspicuous when visiting locations such as specialist bookshops or the vicinity of naval bases. This was a role performed by Takahashi Monsaku for Russian military attachés at the start of the 20th century. When recruiting such translators/fixers, it is profitable to look to outsiders and to those disaffected with Japanese society. Miyagi Yotoku proved a perfect fit because, as an Okinawan, he felt hostility towards the Japanese central government. This was complemented by fluent English on account of his education in the United States. Moreover, Miyagi demonstrated that the profession of artist can be good cover since it features flexible hours and creates opportunities for interactions with both bohemians and the bourgeois.

A further goal when building an espionage network should be volume and diversity. This is something of which Moscow has long been cognizant. As Whittaker Chambers learned when working as a courier for Soviet military intelligence during the 1930s, the Soviets believed in

> "the principle of parallel apparatuses." This is a swollen way of saying that a variety of self-contained underground apparatuses, ignorant of one another's existence, operate side by side for more or less the same purpose. For the Russians are great believers in bulk. They are not highly selective, and they mass their apparatuses in about the same way that they mass their artillery.[10]

One example is Moscow's attempt in 1934 to supplement Sorge's apparatus with a second spy ring in Tokyo involving John L. Sherman and Noda Hideo.

Alongside Japanese agents and their legal handlers within the embassy, Moscow has had success with illegals. There is no recorded case prior to 1945 of Russian spies posing as Japanese within Japan. However, there are several cases of Russia sending operatives to impersonate third-country nationals. This is especially useful given the historical suspicion with which Russia has been regarded in Japan. The logical choice has been other European countries. Lieutenant Subbotich was sent to Japan in 1905 in the guise of a Serbian journalist. Aino Kuusinen passed herself off as a Swedish journalist, and Richard Sorge as a correspondent from Germany. This is a reminder that journalism remains excellent cover for espionage, since journalists have a legitimate interest in political and military matters, and everyone expects them to cultivate a wide network of contacts.

Once an *illegal* is in place, various techniques can be used to promote their access. One of the best is to develop a reputation for expertise. This worked for Sorge, as he succeeded in presenting himself as a *Japankenner*. If a person has valuable knowledge about a subject of contemporary importance, highly placed officials will seek them out. As these individuals ask their questions, they will inevitably reveal pieces of information about what they know. An added benefit is that you are unlikely to suspect a person of spying on you if you have initiated the contact yourself. This technique is likely to work as well in the 2020s as it did in the 1930s. If Moscow had an operative in Tokyo who was posing as a citizen of a friendly country and was a recognised expert on a hot topic, such as the Chinese military or cybersecurity, there is no doubt that Japanese officials, as well as diplomats from foreign embassies, would make contact with them.

Flattery is also not to be underestimated. In the first half of the 20th century, Japan, as a late developer, still suffered from an inferiority complex. This made the Japanese elite desirous of praise, especially from established European countries. This accounts for the ease with which Aino Kuusinen was able to use an ingratiating book she had written to open the doors to Tokyo's high society. This tactic likewise has a good chance of success in the 21st century. Japan's economic stagnation, demographic collapse, and calcified politics are often criticised by international observers. In this context, any foreign commentator who offers up a rosy picture of the country's prospects is likely to be courted by the Japanese elite.

Aino Kuusinen's effectiveness was also enhanced by her being a northern European woman, a category that seems to appeal to many Japanese men. Then, as now, Japan was a male-dominated society, and there were plenty of men who were only too willing to take this "vulnerable" foreign woman under their wing and introduce her to Japanese culture. Similarly, Ursula Hamburger (agent SONYA) used her gender to advantage. She hid secret notes in her underwear and bomb-making materials in her son's pram, trusting that the Japanese police would not be so bold as to conduct an intrusive search of a foreign woman. The Japanese authorities belatedly recognised the threat posed by Moscow's use of women as sexual bait, but they still failed to appreciate the risk posed by women functioning as spies in their own right.

Another option for diversifying espionage activities is to use intermediaries. During the 19th century, Russia employed Ainu to collect intelligence about the Japanese on Sakhalin. In the early 20th century, Korean partisans were encouraged to foment rebellion against Japanese rule, whilst, during the Russo-Japanese War, efforts were made to use Chinese agents to gather intelligence on Japanese military deployments in Manchuria.

Separately, this book has shown that it has been productive for Russia to piggyback on the intelligence work of third countries. At times, this has been done collaboratively. After the signing of the Franco-Russian Alliance in 1894, Paris and St Petersburg shared much intelligence. For instance, Lieutenant Colonel Vladimir K. Samoilov, who was Russian military attaché in Tokyo from 1903, received valuable information about the Japanese military from his French counterpart, Baron Charles Corvisaire. On other occasions, Russia simply stole material about Japan from third countries. This was done in the 18th century, when Russian representatives purloined maps from the Beijing Palace Library. Two centuries later, Harry Dexter White and Alger Hiss not only shared US intelligence about Japan with their handlers but influenced US policy in a direction favourable to Soviet interests. Additionally, Moscow has demonstrated the value of taking advantage of intrigue carried out by others. The Tanaka Memorandum was most likely a Chinese forgery. However, it was the Soviets who benefited most by exploiting the opportunity to present Japan as a threat and to foment anti-Japanese sentiment within the United States.

In the 21st century, Russia has one close partner with sophisticated external intelligence capabilities and a shared interest in spying on Japan. This is, of course, China. Russia and China already cooperate in conducting military activities directed against Japan. One example is the joint patrols that have regularly been conducted by Russian and Chinese strategic bombers over the Sea of Japan since 2019. In theory, the potential for Sino-Russian cooperation in the field of intelligence is significant. The large Chinese diaspora in Japan offers major HUMINT possibilities, while Russia has unique skills in the area of "active measures." However, while this is a concern for Japan, such intelligence cooperation between Russia and China remains unlikely, since they lack mutual trust. Indeed, the countries regularly spy on each other. Even if a degree of cooperation is developed, the absence of shared history and cultural commonalities means that intelligence sharing between Moscow and Beijing is never likely to reach the level of the Five Eyes.

Lastly when considering how to spy on Japan, there is SIGINT, an area in which Japan has regularly shown vulnerability. This was exploited at the start of the 20th century, when Russia was able to read dozens of secret Japanese telegrams, including from Minister of Foreign Affairs Komura Jutarō. This was thanks to the codebreaking wizardry of St Petersburg's *cabinet noir*. However, SIGINT is often dependent on the work of spies in the field. This was true in the case of Soviet access to Major General Ōshima Hiroshi's correspondence from Berlin to Tokyo during the 1930s, which was facilitated by Walter Krivitsky's recruitment of a German officer who supplied his country's intercepts of Japanese communications. Most significant, however, was the Soviet Union's success in accessing Japan's broader diplomatic correspondence during the 1930s and 1940s by using Izumi Kōzō to supply Japanese codebooks. This intelligence was likely even more important than that provided by Sorge in persuading the Soviet leadership that Japan would not attack in 1941 since Stalin placed more faith in SIGINT than he did in his own intelligence officers.

* * *

Over the centuries, Russia did regularly "crack the crab" and achieve espionage success against Japan. Notable achievements include easing the path to the opening of official relations in 1855 and gaining the upper hand in the battle of intrigue in Korea and Manchuria at the end of the 19th century. Later, intelligence superiority made a sizeable contribution to Soviet victory at Nomonhan in 1939. Additionally, intelligence from several sources (and not just Richard Sorge) reassured the Soviet leadership that military units could be redeployed from the Far East to assist the defence of Moscow in the winter of 1941.

All these espionage coups impacted the history of Russia-Japan relations. However, those related to the Second World War stand out. The Soviet Union's intelligence-driven victory at Nomonhan played a significant role in deterring Japan from seizing the opportunity offered by Barbarossa to launch an attack against the Soviet Far East in 1941. Had Japan joined the invasion of the Soviet Union, Moscow may well have fallen. Moreover, having thrown its forces north, Japan would have been unlikely to have struck against the British and United States in December 1941, thus avoiding the Pacific War.

For all the successes, Russia did not get everything right in terms of espionage against Japan. For a start, good intelligence must be believed, even when it conflicts with established beliefs. This did not happen when Captain Martin Spanberg's expedition reported the location of Japan in 1739. Infamously, Stalin also disregarded Sorge's reports from Tokyo about German preparations for Barbarossa. According to Sir Richard Dearlove, the former head of MI6, this has been an enduring problem: "If you look at the history of Soviet intelligence ... they're massively successful at collecting intelligence. But relating intelligence production to making policy was a real weakness of the Soviet system."[11] A separate problem has been the tendency—most notable ahead of the Russo-Japanese War—to underestimate Japanese capabilities. Lastly, there was the self-destructive character of Soviet intelligence under Stalin, when effective spy chiefs, such as General Yan K. Berzin, and promising officers, including Aino Kuusinen, were destroyed or sent to the gulag. This hollowed out the Soviet intelligence services and encouraged defections, most prominently that by Genrikh S. Lyushkov, who fled to the Japanese in 1938.

Up until 1945, the strengths of Moscow's intelligence activities against Japan outweighed the weaknesses, often giving Russia an advantage in the relationship. Did this continue in the post-war period? The decades after 1945 certainly remained an active period for Soviet intelligence against Japan, featuring the recruitment of Siberian internees, the KGB's attempts to manipulate protest movements within Japan, and Moscow's efforts to steal science and technology as Japan became an economic powerhouse from the 1960s. There was even a Japanese cabinet minister in the 1970s who is alleged to have been a Soviet spy. However, the story of how Japan became a spy paradise for Moscow's intelligence services between 1945 and the present is the topic for another volume.

NOTES

INTRODUCTION

1. Richard Sorge quoted in Gordon W. Prange, 1985, *Target Tokyo: The Story of the Sorge Spy Ring* (New York: McGraw Hill), p. 469.

1. THE FIRST "RUSSIAN SPY" IN JAPAN (1771)

1. Quoted in Andrew Drummond, 2017, *The Intriguing Life and Ignominious Death of Maurice Benyovszky* (Oxford.: Taylor & Francis), pp. 171–2.
2. Donald Keene, 1954, *The Japanese Discovery of Europe. Honda Toshiaki and other Discoverers 1720–1798* (New York: Grove Press), p. 22.
3. Quoted in Drummond, *The Intriguing*, p. 163.
4. Memoirs of Maurice Benyovszky in David Wells, 2019, *The Russian Discovery of Japan* (London: Routledge), p. 108.
5. George A. Lensen, 1971, *The Russian Push Toward Japan: Russo-Japanese Relations, 1697–1875* (Tallahassee: University Presses of Florida), p. 80.
6. Drummond, *The Intriguing*, pp. 185, 196.
7. Quoted in Lensen, *The Russian Push*, pp. 81–2.
8. Tabohashi Kiyoshi quoted in Lensen, *The Russian Push*, p. 84.
9. For instance, both Flashman and Benyovszky found themselves at the centre of political intrigue on Madagascar, though, while the notorious British cad narrowly escaped with his life, Benyovszky was not so fortunate. See George MacDonald Fraser, 1988, *Flashman's Lady* (New York: Plume).
10. Quoted in Drummond, *The Intriguing*, p. 99.
11. Drummond, *The Intriguing*.
12. Drummond, *The Intriguing*, p. 10.
13. Drummond, *The Intriguing*, pp. 11–12.
14. Quoted in Drummond, *The Intriguing*, p. 18.
15. Lensen, *The Russian Push*, pp. 73–4.
16. Drummond, *The Intriguing*, p. 66.

17. Drummond, *The Intriguing*, p. 66.
18. Lensen, *The Russian Push*, p. 74.
19. Benyovszky quoted in Drummond, *The Intriguing*, p. 158.
20. Benyovszky quoted in Drummond, *The Intriguing*, p. 67.
21. Benyovszky quoted in Drummond, *The Intriguing*, pp. 4–6.
22. Wells, *The Russian Discovery of Japan*, p. 30.
23. Keene, *The Japanese Discovery of Europe*, p. 44.
24. Quoted in Drummond, *The Intriguing*, p. 18.
25. John A. Harrison, 1953, *Japan's Northern Frontier: A Preliminary Study in Colonization and Expansion with Special Reference to the Relations of Japan and Russia* (Gainesville: University of Florida Press), p. 18.
26. Lensen, *The Russian Push*, p. 83.
27. Quoted in Lensen, *The Russian Push*, p. 79.
28. Lensen, *The Russian Push*, p. 84.
29. Harrison, *Japan's Northern Frontier*, p. 14.
30. Lensen, *The Russian Push*, p. 252.
31. Watabe Kyōji, 2010, *Kurofune Zenya: Roshia, Ainu, Nihon no Sangokushi* [*Eve of the Black Ships: Annals of the Three Kingdoms of Russia, the Ainu, and Japan*] (Tōkyō: Yōsensha), pp. 9–28.
32. Tabohashi Kiyoshi quoted in Lensen, *The Russian Push*, p. 83.
33. Keene, *The Japanese Discovery of Europe*, pp. 45–52
34. Keene, *The Japanese Discovery of Europe*, p. 52; Harrison, *Japan's Northern Frontier*, p. 17.
35. Lensen, *The Russian Push*, p. 82.
36. Harrison, *Japan's Northern Frontier*, p. 14.
37. Keene, *The Japanese Discovery of Europe*, p. 46.
38. Keene, *The Japanese Discovery of Europe*, p. 59.
39. Quoted in Harrison, *Japan's Northern Frontier*, p. 21.
40. Keene, *The Japanese Discovery of Europe*, p. 54.
41. Watabe, *Kurofune Zenya*, pp. 145–50.
42. Keene, *The Japanese Discovery of Europe*, p. 47.
43. Harrison, *Japan's Northern Frontier*, p. 19.
44. Harrison, *Japan's Northern Frontier*, p. 63.
45. Harrison, *Japan's Northern Frontier*, p. 140.
46. Honda Toshiaki quoted in Keene, *The Japanese Discovery of Europe*, p. 222.
47. Keene, *The Japanese Discovery of Europe*, pp. 68–9.

2. EXPLORERS AND CASTAWAYS OF THE 18TH CENTURY

1. Evgenii Maksimovich Primakov, 1996, *Ocherki Istorii Rossiiskoi Vneshnei Razvedki* [*Essays on the History of Russian Foreign Intelligence*] (Moscow: Mezhdunarodnye Otnosheniya).
2. Gregory Afinogenov, 2020, *Spies and Scholars: Chinese Secrets and Imperial Russia's Quest for World Power* (Cambridge: Harvard University Press).
3. Primakov, *Ocherki*, vol. 1, essay 8.

4. Lensen, *The Russian Push*, p. 9.
5. Arlette Kouvenhoven and Matthi Forrer, 2000, *Siebold and Japan: His Life and Work* (Leiden: Hotei), p. 18.
6. Quoted in Kouvenhoven and Forrer, *Siebold and Japan*, p. 18.
7. Harrison, *Japan's Northern Frontier*, p. 145.
8. Report of Vladimir Atlasov quoted in Wells, *The Russian Discovery of Japan*, p. 60.
9. Report of Vladimir Atlasov quoted in Wells, *The Russian Discovery of Japan*, p. 67.
10. Lensen, *The Russian Push*, p. 28.
11. Lensen, *The Russian Push*, p. 30.
12. Report by Dembei in Wells, *The Russian Discovery of Japan*, p. 72.
13. Report by Dembei in Wells, *The Russian Discovery of Japan*, p. 71.
14. Afinogenov, *Spies and Scholars*, p. 20, p. 69.
15. Wells, *The Russian Discovery of Japan*, p. 4.
16. Lensen, *The Russian Push*, p. 29, p. 41.
17. Keene, *The Japanese Discovery of Europe*, p. 61.
18. Lensen, *The Russian Push*, p. 42.
19. Afinogenov, *Spies and Scholars*, p. 75.
20. Lensen, *The Russian Push*, pp. 40–1. David Wells attributes the same information not to Ivan-Lorents Lange but to Nikolai Pavel Krisnits, an Italian in Russian service who visited Beijing from 1719 to 1722. Wells, *The Russian Discovery of Japan*, pp. 75–7.
21. Afinogenov, *Spies and Scholars*, p. 112.
22. Wells, *The Russian Discovery of Japan*, pp. 4–5, p. 24. Kimura Hiroshi, 2005, *Nichiro Kokkyō Kōshō-shi* [*History of Border Negotiations between Japan and Russia*] (Tokyo: Kakugawa Sensho), pp. 51–2.
23. Harrison, *Japan's Northern Frontier*, p. 12. Harrison's account differs from that of David Wells in that he states that Kozyrevskii actually reached Kunashiri (now known as Kunashir in Russian), just 20km from Hokkaidō and one of the islands now disputed between Japan and Russia.
24. Tsuyoshi Hasegawa, 1998, *The Northern Territories Dispute and Russo-Japanese Relations: Between War and Peace, 1697–1985* (Berkeley: University of California Press), p. 16.
25. Quoted in Wells, *The Russian Discovery of Japan*, p. 25.
26. Lensen, *The Russian Push*, p. 36.
27. Lensen, *The Russian Push*, p. 38.
28. Lensen, *The Russian Push*, pp. 46–9.
29. Lensen, *The Russian Push*, p. 47.
30. There is some disagreement about the exact date of Spanberg's arrival. While George Lensen gives the date as 27 June 1739, David Wells records it as 16 June. Lensen, *The Russian Push*, p. 50; Wells, *The Russian Discovery of Japan*, p. 95.
31. Report by Martin Spanberg quoted in Wells, *The Russian Discovery of Japan*, p. 83.
32. Report by Martin Spanberg quoted in Wells, *The Russian Discovery of Japan*, p. 84.
33. Wells, *The Russian Discovery of Japan*, p. 6.
34. Lensen, *The Russian Push*, p. 50, p. 55.
35. Hiraoka Matsuhide, 1982, *Nichiro kōshō shiwa—Ishin zengo no Nihon to Roshia* [*The*

History of Negotiations between Japan and Russia: Japan & Russia around the Time of the Restoration] (Tōkyō: Harashobō), p. 35.

36. Lensen, *The Russian Push*, p. 56.
37. Harrison, *Japan's Northern Frontier*, p. 150.
38. Lensen, *The Russian Push*, p. 57.
39. Wells, *The Russian Discovery of Japan*, p. 7.
40. Lensen, *The Russian Push*, p. 66.
41. Anton Chekhov, 2019, *Sakhalin Island* (Surrey: Alma Classics), p. 207.
42. Lensen, *The Russian Push*, p. 68.
43. Lensen, *The Russian Push*, p. 68.
44. Lensen, *The Russian Push*, p. 85.
45. Lensen, *The Russian Push*, p. 84.
46. Lensen, *The Russian Push*, p. 88.
47. Lensen, *The Russian Push*, p. 88.
48. Lensen, *The Russian Push*, p. 88.
49. Lensen, *The Russian Push*, p. 87.
50. Afinogenov, *Spies and Scholars*, p. 12.
51. Lensen, *The Russian Push*, p. 87.
52. Lensen, *The Russian Push*, pp. 88–9.
53. Lensen, *The Russian Push*, pp. 89–91.
54. Quoted in Lensen, *The Russian Push*, pp. 92–3.
55. Wells, *The Russian Discovery of Japan*, p. 30.
56. Wells, *The Russian Discovery of Japan*, p. 31.
57. Quoted in Wells, *The Russian Discovery of Japan*, p. 31.
58. Quoted in Wells, *The Russian Discovery of Japan*, p. 30.
59. Wells, *The Russian Discovery of Japan*, p. 14.
60. Although Daikokuya is the surname, he has come to be known to history as Kōdayū.
61. Lensen, *The Russian Push*, pp. 96–7.
62. Keene, *The Japanese Discovery of Europe*, p. 61.
63. De Lesseps in Wells, *The Russian Discovery of Japan*, pp. 133–4.
64. Lensen, *The Russian Push*, p. 183.
65. Quoted in Lensen, *The Russian Push*, p. 119.
66. Quoted in Lensen, *The Russian Push*, p. 101.
67. Afinogenov, *Spies and Scholars*, pp. 197–200.
68. Quoted in Lensen, *The Russian Push*, p. 105.
69. Wells, *The Russian Discovery of Japan*, p. 149.
70. Wells, *The Russian Discovery of Japan*, p. 147.
71. Wells, *The Russian Discovery of Japan*, p. 149.
72. Watabe, *Kurofune Zenya*, pp. 191–204.
73. Kouwenhoven and Forrer, *Siebold and Japan*, pp. 44–7.
74. Wells, *The Russian Discovery of Japan*, p. 143.
75. Laxman in David Wells, 2004, *Russian Views of Japan, 1792–1913: An Anthology of Travel Writing* (London: Routledge), pp. 41–4.

76. Laxman in Wells, *Russian Views*, p. 53, p. 56.
77. Wells, *Russian Views*, p. 32
78. Wells, *The Russian*, p. 33.
79. Laxman in Wells, *Russian Views*, p. 39.
80. Lensen, *The Russian Push*, p. 106.
81. Honda Toshiaki in Keene, *The Japanese Discovery of Europe*, p. 177. Elsewhere, his name is given as Semion Ishiozov. Herbert Plutschow, 2007, *Philipp Franz von Siebold and the Opening of Japan* (Folkestone: Global Oriental), p. 82.
82. Honda Toshiaki in Keene, *The Japanese Discovery of Europe*, p. 177.
83. Honda Toshiaki in Keene, *The Japanese Discovery of Europe*, p. 227.
84. Wells, *The Russian Discovery of Japan*, p. 138.
85. Keene, *The Japanese Discovery of Europe*, p. 67.
86. Keene, *The Japanese Discovery of Europe*, p. 67.
87. Lensen, *The Russian Push*, p. 184.
88. Lensen, *The Russian Push*, p. 112.
89. Laxman in Wells, *Russian Views*, p. 41.
90. Wells, *The Russian Discovery of Japan*, p. 138.
91. Wells, *The Russian Discovery of Japan*, p. 143.
92. Laxman in Wells, *Russian Views*, p. 58.
93. Lensen, *The Russian Push*, p. 110.
94. Wells, *The Russian Discovery of Japan*, p. 143.
95. "Denied area" is a modern intelligence term meaning "An area under enemy or unfriendly control in which friendly forces cannot expect to operate successfully within existing operational constraints and force capabilities." Joint Chiefs of Staff, 2021, *DOD Dictionary of Military and Associated Terms*, https://www.jcs.mil/Portals/36/Documents/Doctrine/pubs/dictionary.pdf
96. Laxman in Wells, *Russian Views*, pp. 43–50.
97. Quoted in Lensen, *The Russian Push*, p. 120.
98. Harrison, *Japan's Northern Frontier*, p. 155.
99. A translation of this condensed account is provided in Wells, *The Russian Discovery of Japan*, pp. 136–50.

3. CAPTIVES AND THE OPENING OF JAPAN

1. Grigorii Shelikhov is a controversial figure. During two years on Kodiak Island (in what is now Alaska), Shelikhov is alleged to have participated in the killing of 150–200 Koniag islanders in 1784 in what is known as the massacre of Refuge Rock. Matthews, *Glorious Misadventures: Nikolai Rezanov and the Dream of a Russian America* (New York: Bloomsbury), pp. 64–5, pp. 100–1.
2. There are several alternative renderings of Krusenstern's name, including Ivan Fedorovich Krusenstern. Relations between Krusenstern and Rezanov became extremely strained during the long voyage. This was, in part, because each considered himself the true commander of the expedition. Ultimately, Krusenstern became so infuriated with Rezanov, whom he described as "thoughtless, mean, partial and

roaring," that he arranged for a panelled partition to be built within the Great Cabin of the *Nadezhda* so that he and his officers did not have to share the same space with Rezanov. Matthews, *Glorious Misadventures*, p. 150, p. 156.

3. Lensen, *The Russian Push*, p. 128. Owen Matthews suggests that five castaways, rather than four, were repatriated aboard the *Nadezhda*. Matthews, *Glorious Misadventures*, p. 141.
4. Fourth Lieutenant Hermann Ludwig von Löwenstern quoted in Matthews, *Glorious Misadventures*, p. 141.
5. Quoted in Lensen, *The Russian Push*, p. 128.
6. Lensen, *The Russian Push*, p. 132.
7. Adam Krusenstern in Wells, *Russian Views*, p. 60.
8. Adam Krusenstern in Wells, *Russian Views*, p. 60.
9. Adam Krusenstern in Wells, *Russian Views*, p. 61. Hirado was the trading post in Nagasaki that was used by the Dutch before they were forced to relocate to the confines of Dejima.
10. Lensen, *The Russian Push*, p. 155.
11. Quoted in Matthews, *Glorious Misadventures*, pp. 296–7.
12. Lensen, *The Russian Push*, p. 163.
13. Lensen, *The Russian Push*, p. 164.
14. Quoted in Matthews, *Glorious Misadventures*, p. 297.
15. Lensen, *The Russian Push*, p. 166.
16. Quoted in Matthews, *Glorious Misadventures*, pp. 297–9.
17. Lensen, *The Russian Push*, p. 167.
18. Lensen, *The Russian Push*, pp. 168–9.
19. Lensen, *The Russian Push*, pp. 167–70.
20. Lensen, *The Russian Push*, pp. 170–2.
21. Lensen, *The Russian Push*, p. 174.
22. Lensen, *The Russian Push*, pp. 174–5.
23. Matthews, *Glorious Misadventures*, p. 316.
24. Matthews, *Glorious Misadventures*, pp. 302–3.
25. Kimura, *Nichiro Kokkyō*, p. 63.
26. Keene, *The Japanese Discovery of Europe*, pp. 65–6.
27. Matthews, *Glorious Misadventures*, p. 194.
28. Iwashita Tetsunori and Anna L. Carlander, 2021, *Mu-ru no kunō* [*Moor's agony*] (Tōkyō: Yūbunshoin), p. 41.
29. Plutschow, *Siebold and the Opening*, p. 83.
30. Lensen, *The Russian Push*, p. 160.
31. Rumyantsev quoted in Lensen, *The Russian Push*, pp. 132–3.
32. Lensen, *The Russian Push*, p. 131.
33. Vasilii Golovnin quoted in Harrison, *Japan's Northern Frontier*, p. 24.
34. Golovnin, Vasilii, 2020, *Captive in Japan*, edited by William de Lange (Toyo Press), p. 156.
35. Adam Krusenstern quoted in Wells, *Russian Views*, p. 77.
36. Watabe, *Kurofune Zenya*, p. 218.

37. Adam Krusenstern quoted in Wells, *Russian Views*, pp. 73–4.
38. Adam Krusenstern quoted in Wells, *Russian Views*, p. 75.
39. Adam Krusenstern quoted in Wells, *Russian Views*, p. 75.
40. Harrison, *Japan's Northern Frontier*, p. 154.
41. Adam Krusenstern in Wells, *Russian Views*, p. 61.
42. Matthews, *Glorious Misadventures*, p. 185.
43. Adam Krusenstern in Wells, *Russian Views*, p. 62, p. 69.
44. Lensen, *The Russian Push*, p. 151. "Deshima" is an alternate spelling of "Dejima."
45. Lensen, *The Russian Push*, p. 153.
46. Adam Krusenstern in Wells, *Russian Views*, p. 66.
47. Adam Krusenstern in Wells, *Russian Views*, pp. 67–8.
48. Adam Krusenstern in Wells, *Russian Views*, p. 73.
49. Harrison, *Japan's Northern Frontier*, p. 23. "Yezo" is an alternate spelling of "Ezo."
50. Golovnin, *Captive*, pp. 2–3.
51. Golovnin, *Captive*, p. 11.
52. Wells, *Russian Views*, p. 14.
53. Golovnin, *Captive*, p. 278.
54. Golovnin, *Captive*, p. 47.
55. Despite being captured by the Russians and held for a time on Kamchatka, Takadaya Kahei became an advocate for closer Japan-Russia relations and declared himself to have become "half-Russian." This enthusiasm led to suspicions of him being a Russian spy. Takadaya's younger brother was also later suspected of conducting secret trade with Russia and his property was confiscated by the Japanese authorities. Lensen, George A., 1954, *Report from Hokkaido: The Remains of Russian Culture in Northern Japan* (Hakodate: The Municipal Library of Hakodate), p. 51, p. 62.
56. Lensen, *The Russian Push*, p. 247.
57. Plutschow, *Siebold and the Opening*, p. 83.
58. Golovnin, *Captive*, p. 103.
59. Golovnin, *Captive*, p. 162.
60. Golovnin, *Captive*, p. 61.
61. Golovnin, *Captive*, p. 18, p. 22.
62. Golovnin, *Captive*, p. 18, p. 218.
63. Golovnin, *Captive*, p. 83.
64. Golovnin, *Captive*, p. 214.
65. Golovnin, *Captive*, pp. 28–9.
66. Golovnin, *Captive*, p. 76, p. 102.
67. Golovnin, *Captive*, pp. 13–14.
68. Golovnin, *Captive*, p. 270.
69. Golovnin, *Captive*, p. 155.
70. Matthews, *Glorious Misadventures*, p. 87.
71. Lensen, *The Russian Push*, p. 250.
72. Lensen, *The Russian Push*, pp. 257–8.
73. Golovnin, *Captive*, p. 111.
74. Golovnin, *Captive*, p. 63.

75. Lensen, *The Russian Push*, p. 251.
76. Golovnin, *Captive*, pp. 114–15.
77. Golovnin, *Captive*, p. 37.
78. Lensen, *Report from Hokkaido*, p. 42.
79. Golovnin, *Captive*, pp. 91–3.
80. Golovnin, *Captive*, p. 208.
81. Iwashita and Carlander, *Mu-ru no kunō*, pp. 7–8.
82. Golovnin, *Captive in Japan*, p. 194.
83. Golovnin, *Captive in Japan*, p. 239.
84. Golovnin, *Captive in Japan*, p. 238, p. 283. Mur was aged 30 when he killed himself.
85. Chekhov, *Sakhalin Island*, p. 47.
86. John J. Stephan, 1969, "The Crimean War in the Far East," *Modern Asian Studies*, 3:3, pp. 257–77, pp. 268–74. The strait had, in fact, already been discovered by Japanese explorer Mamiya Rinzō in 1809. Kimura, *Nichiro Kokkyō*, p. 66.
87. Lensen, *The Russian Push*, pp. 289–90.
88. Lensen, *The Russian Push*, p. 292. It was surely a fertility shrine, of which there are several in Japan.
89. Lensen, *The Russian Push*, p. 295.
90. Nikolai Busse quoted in Lensen, *The Russian Push*, p. 294.
91. Lensen, *The Russian Push*, p. 294.
92. Nikolai Busse quoted in Lensen, *The Russian Push*, p. 294.
93. Lensen, *The Russian Push*, p. 296.
94. Nikolai Busse quoted in Lensen, *The Russian Push*, p. 294.
95. Nikolai Busse quoted in Lensen, *The Russian Push*, p. 297.
96. Edyta M. Bojanowska, 2018, *A World of Empires: The Russian Voyage of the Frigate* Pallada (Cambridge, MA: Belknap Press), p. 1.
97. Ivan Aleksandrovich Goncharov, 2018, *Fregat 'Pallada'* [*Frigate 'Pallada'*] (St Petersburg: Azbuka).
98. Edgar Franz, 2005, *Philipp Franz von Siebold and Russian Policy and Action on Opening Japan to the West* (Munich: Iudicium), p. 122.
99. Ivan Goncharov in Wells, *Russian Views*, p. 104.
100. Bojanowska, *World of Empires*, p. 123.
101. George A. Lensen, 1955, *Russia's Japan Expedition of 1852 to 1855* (Westport, CT: Greenwood Press), p. 113.
102. Ivan Goncharov quoted in Bojanowska, *World of Empires*, p. 123.
103. Ivan Goncharov in Wells, *Russian Views*, p. 108.
104. Quoted in Lensen, *Russia's Japan Expedition*, pp. 19–20.
105. Ivan Goncharov in Wells, *Russian Views*, p. 116.
106. Ivan Goncharov quoted in Bojanowska, *World of Empires*, p. 129.
107. Ivan Goncharov quoted in Bojanowska, *World of Empires*, p. 121, p. 148.
108. Ivan Goncharov quoted in Bojanowska, *World of Empires*, p. 223.
109. Bojanowska, *World of Empires*, p. 243.

110. Bojanowska, *World of Empires*, p. 265, p. 275. "greedily read…" is a quotation from contemporary critic Apollon Grigorev.
111. Lensen, *The Russian Push*, p. 344.
112. With the border placed between Etorofu and Urup, the four most southerly islands of the Kuril chain—Etorofu, Kunashiri, Shikotan, and the Habomais—were assigned to Japanese sovereignty. A century later, in 1945, these were occupied by Soviet forces, yet they continue to this day to be claimed by Japan as its Northern Territories. To highlight its assertion that the border established in the Shimoda Treaty is the legitimate dividing line between the countries, each year the Japanese government marks Northern Territories Day on 7 February, the date on which the treaty was signed. The status of Sakhalin remained unsettled until the Treaty of St Petersburg (1875), in which Japan ceded its rights to the island in exchange for possession of all the Kuril archipelago, leading right up to Kamchatka.
113. The Treaty of Edo reproduced in Lensen, *The Russian Push*, pp. 484–94.
114. Lensen, *The Russian Push*, p. 318.
115. Mizuno Hironori, 1931, "The Japanese Navy" in Inazo Nitobe and others, *Western Influences in Modern Japan* (Chicago: University of Chicago Press), p. 417.
116. Harrison, *Japan's Northern Frontier*, p. 43.
117. Matthew Perry quoted in Lensen, *Russia's Japan Expedition*, p. 128.
118. Bojanowska, *World of Empires*, pp. 75–6.
119. Bojanowska, *World of Empires*, pp. 112–13.
120. Bojanowska, *World of Empires*, p. 111.
121. Plutschow, *Siebold and the Opening*, p. 17.
122. Franz, *Siebold and the Opening*, p. 42.
123. Plutschow, *Siebold and the Opening*, p. 86.
124. Plutschow, *Siebold and the Opening*, pp. 90–100, p. 150. Kimura, *Nichiro Kokkyō*, pp. 71–3.
125. Franz, *Siebold and the Opening*, p. 93.
126. Plutschow, *Siebold and the Opening*, pp. 17–18.
127. Plutschow, *Siebold and the Opening*, p. 149.
128. Plutschow, *Siebold and the Opening*, pp. 136–7.
129. Philipp Franz von Siebold quoted in Plutschow, *Siebold and the Opening*, p. 132.
130. Lensen, *Russia's Japan Expedition*, p. 128.
131. Philipp Franz von Siebold quoted in Plutschow, *Siebold and the Opening*, p. 151.
132. Lensen, *Russia's Japan Expedition*, p. 119.
133. Francis Hawks quoted in Bojanowska, *World of Empires*, p. 116.
134. Lensen, *The Russian Push*, pp. 266–71, p. 332; John J. Stephan, 1969, "The Crimean War in the Far East," *Modern Asian Studies*, 3:3, pp. 257–77, p. 259.
135. Nakamura Yoshikazu, 1970, "Tachibana Kōsai-den" ["The life of Tachibana Kōsai"], *Hitotsubashi Ronsō*, 63:4, pp. 138–64, p. 144.
136. This requirement was specified in the Treaty of Nagasaki, a supplementary treaty signed between Japan and Russia in 1857. This treaty is reproduced in Lensen, *The Russian Push*, pp. 478–83.

137. Lensen, *Report on Hokkaido*, pp. 65–6.
138. Nakamura, "Tachibana Kōsai-den," p. 147.
139. Lensen, *The Russian Push*, p. 342.
140. Nakamura, "Tachibana Kōsai-den," p. 149.
141. Bojanowska, *World of Empires*, p. 11.
142. Stephan, "The Crimean War in the Far East," p. 259.
143. Admiral Bruce quoted in Stephan, "The Crimean War in the Far East," p. 267. The British decided to burn part of the town anyway.
144. Harrison, *Japan's Northern Frontier*, p. 53.
145. Bojanowska, *World of Empires*, p. 11, p. 115.

4. INFLUENCE IN JAPAN, INTRIGUE IN MANCHURIA AND KOREA

1. Sergei Maksimov, 2004, "In the East (Hakodate, late 1850s)," ch.6 in Wells, *Russian Views*, p. 126. The building described is not the same as the former Russian consulate that still stands in Hakodate and in 2021 was in the process of being converted into a boutique hotel. The consulate building that remains was constructed in 1908. Goshkevich's first consulate was damaged by fire in 1865 and nothing is left of the original.
2. Victor de Mars quoted in Lensen, *The Russian Push*, pp. 453–4.
3. Victor de Mars quoted in Lensen, *The Russian Push*, p. 454.
4. Lensen, *The Russian Push*, p. 391.
5. Victor de Mars quoted in Lensen, *The Russian Push*, pp. 453–4.
6. Harrison, *Japan's Northern*, p. 49.
7. Shmagin, Viktor, 2017, "They fear us, yet cling to us: Russian negotiations with Tsushima domain officials during the 1861 Tsushima incident," *The International History Review*, 39:3, pp. 521–45, p. 523.
8. Lensen, *The Russian Push*, p. 450.
9. Afinogenov, *Spies and Scholars*.
10. Father Nikolai quoted in Lensen, *The Russian Push*, pp. 401–2.
11. Sawabe Takuma quoted in Lensen, *The Russian Push*, p. 402.
12. Lensen, *The Russian Push*, p. 413.
13. Naganawa Mitsuo, 1989, *Nikoraidō no hitobito* [*The people of the Nikolai Cathedral*] (Tokyo: Gendaikikakushitsu), p. 181.
14. Betsy C. Perabo, 2017, *Russian Orthodoxy and the Russo-Japanese War* (London: Bloomsbury), p. 56.
15. John Takahashi, 2010, "The beginning of the Orthodox Church in Japan: The long-lasting legacy of Saint Nicholai," *Studies in World Christianity*, 16:3, pp. 268–85.
16. Father Nikolai quoted in Lensen, *The Russian Push*, p. 416.
17. Aleksandr Kulanov, 2011, "Vasilii Oshchepkov: Put' ot niotkuda v nikuda" ["Vasilii Oshchepkov: The path from nowhere to nowhere"], *Yaponiya Nashikh Dnei*, 1:7, pp. 85–101, pp. 86–7.
18. Kulanov, "Vasilii Oshchepkov."
19. Kulanov, "Vasilii Oshchepkov," p. 89.

20. Kulanov, "Vasilii Oshchepkov," pp. 89–90.
21. NKVD Order No. 00593 quoted in Kulanov, "Vasilii Oshchepkov," p. 97. The NKVD (Narodnyi Komissariat Vnutrennikh Del, People's Commissariat for State Security) was a forerunner of the KGB.
22. Kulanov, "Vasilii Oshchepkov," p. 99.
23. Aleksandr Kulanov, 2012, "Agent 'R'", *Rodina* 8, pp. 93–5.
24. *RIA Novosti*, "V Yaponii otkrylsya chempionat po sambo na kubok prezidenta Rossii" ["Sambo championship, the Russian President's Cup, begins in Japan"], 12 February 2018, https://ria.ru/20180212/1514432131.html, accessed 21 July 2021.
25. Lensen, *The Russian Push*, pp. 444–5.
26. Mutsu Munemitsu in June 1894 quoted in George A. Lensen, 1982, *Balance of Intrigue: International Rivalry in Korea & Manchuria 1884–1899* (Tallahassee: University Presses of Florida), p. 138.
27. Komura Jutarō quoted in Lensen, *Balance of Intrigue*, p. 137.
28. Lensen, *Balance of Intrigue*, p. 85.
29. Lensen, *Balance of Intrigue*, p. 78.
30. "Convention between Russia and China for lease to Russia of Port Arthur, Talienwan, and the adjacent waters," 1910, *The American Journal of International Law*, 4:4, October 1910, pp. 289–91.
31. Rotem Kowner, 2006, *Historical Dictionary of the Russo-Japanese War* (Lanham: Scarecrow Press), p. 375.
32. S.C.M. Paine, 2007, "The triple intervention and the termination of the First Sino-Japanese War," ch.7 in Elleman, B.A. and Paine, S.C.M. (eds), *Naval Coalition Warfare* (London: Routledge), p. 78.
33. Li Hung-chang's name is also romanised as Li Hongzhang.
34. Quoted in Lensen, *Balance of Intrigue*, p. 778.
35. Lensen, *Balance of Intrigue*, p. 787.
36. The bribed official, Viktor Grot, was in fact a Russian subject who had been appointed to represent the Chinese side in the negotiations. Lensen, *Balance of Intrigue*, p. 498.
37. George A. Lensen, 1966, *Korea and Manchuria Between Russia and Japan 1895–1904: The Observations of Sir Ernest Satow* (Tallahassee: The Diplomatic Press), p. 108.
38. Lensen, *Balance of Intrigue*, pp. 243–7.
39. Lensen, *Balance of Intrigue*, p. 510.
40. Ian Nish, 1985, *The Origins of the Russo-Japanese War* (London: Longman), p. 29.
41. Lensen, *Observations of Sir Ernest Satow*, p. 206.
42. Lensen, *Observations of Sir Ernest Satow*, p. 114.
43. Hamada Kenji, 1936, *Prince Ito* (Tokyo: Sanseido), p. 118.
44. Lensen, *Observations of Sir Ernest Satow*, p. 28.
45. Yoji Koda, 2005, "The Russo-Japanese War: Primary causes of Japanese success," *Naval War College Review*, 58:2, pp. 10–44, p. 16.
46. Gustave Montebello quoted in Lensen, *Balance of Intrigue*, p. 298.
47. Lensen, *Balance of Intrigue*, p. 323.

48. Lensen, *Balance of Intrigue*, p. 203.
49. Itō Hirobumi quoted in Lensen, *Observations of Sir Ernest Satow*, p. 24. "Hitrovo" is an alternate spelling of "Khitrovo."
50. Lensen, *Balance of Intrigue*, p. 287.
51. Lensen, *Balance of Intrigue*, p. 218.
52. Lensen, *Balance of Intrigue*, p. 259.
53. Lensen, *Balance of Intrigue*, p. 258.
54. James B. Palais, 2014, "Political leadership in the Yi dynasty," ch.1 in Suh Dae-Sook and Lee Chae-Jin (eds) *Political Leadership in Korea* (Seattle: University of Washington Press), p. 13.
55. Lensen, *Balance of Intrigue*, p. 531.
56. Danny Orbach, 2018, *Curse on this Country: The Rebellious Army of Imperial Japan* (Ithaca: Cornell University Press), p. 118.
57. Lensen, *Observations of Sir Ernest Satow*, p. 48, p. 79, p. 92. Satow mentions Secretary of Legation Sugiyama and another Japanese named Okamoto Ryūnosuke as the queen's probable assassins.
58. Orbach, *Curse on this Country*, p. 101.
59. Lensen, *Balance of Intrigue*, p. 563.
60. Lensen, *Balance of Intrigue*, pp. 583–4.
61. Lensen, *Balance of Intrigue*, p. 589.
62. Lensen, *Balance of Intrigue*, p. 607.
63. David Fedman, 2020, *Seeds of Control: Japan's Empire of Forestry in Colonial Korea* (Seattle: University of Washington Press), pp. 59–60.
64. Aleksei Shpeier quoted in Lensen, *Balance of Intrigue*, p. 587.
65. Lensen, *Balance of Intrigue*, p. 588.
66. Sergei Witte quoted in Lensen, *Balance of Intrigue*, p. 755.

5. ESPIONAGE AND THE RUSSO-JAPANESE WAR

1. Oku Takenori, *Rotan: Nichiro sensō-ki no media to kokumin ishiki* [*Rotan: Media and Public Consciousness at the Time of the Russo-Japanese War*] (Tōkyō: Chūo Kōron Shinsha).
2. Edvard Radzinsky, 1993, *The Last Tsar: The Life and Death of Nicholas II* (New York: Anchor), p. 29.
3. Patrick Parr, 2019, "Russia's Nicholas II is scarred for life in 1891 Japan," *Japan Today*, 24 May, https://japantoday.com/category/features/lifestyle/russia%E2%80%99s-nicholas-ii-is-scarred-for-life-in-1891-japan
4. Oku, *Rotan*, pp. 64–5.
5. Oku, *Rotan*, p. 63.
6. Nicholas II quoted in Radzinsky, *The Last Tsar*, p. 29.
7. Parr, "Russia's Nicholas II."
8. Oku, *Rotan*, pp. 67–8.
9. Ishimitsu Makiyo quoted in Oku, *Rotan*, p. 79.
10. Oku, *Rotan*, pp. 78–9.

11. Oku, *Rotan*, p. 37.
12. Unger, Frederic William, 1905, *Russia and Japan and a Complete History of the War in the Far East* (Philadelphia), p. 78.
13. Oku, *Rotan*, p. 91.
14. "*Ro*" means "Russia," but the character read as "*tan*" more commonly means "search for," and features in words such as "*tankyū*" ("investigation"). In this case, "*rotan*" means "agent of the Russian enemy." Oku, *Rotan*, p. 8, p. 14. In modern Japanese, more usual words for "spy" are "*kōsaku-in*," "*chōhō-in*," or simply the loanword "*supai*."
15. Oku, *Rotan*, p. 15.
16. Oku, *Rotan*, p. 28, p. 43, p. 52.
17. Oku, *Rotan*, p. 97, p. 107.
18. Oku, *Rotan*, pp. 111–18.
19. Yamaguchi Kōji, 2000, "Popurizumu toshite no shinbun (2): Akiyama Teisuke to 'Niroku Shinpō'" ["A newspaper as populism (2): Akiyama Teisuke and 'Niroku Shinpō"], *Hyōron Shakaikagaku*, 62, pp. 125–53, p. 140.
20. Miles Fletcher, 1979, "Intellectuals and fascism in early Showa Japan," *The Journal of Asian Studies*, 39:1, pp. 39–63.
21. Oku, *Rotan*, pp. 204–12.
22. Oku, *Rotan*, pp. 47–52.
23. Oku, *Rotan*, pp. 108–29.
24. Oku, *Rotan*, pp. 212–14.
25. Oku, *Rotan*, pp. 210–25.
26. Konstantin Zvonarev quoted in Evgeny Sergeev, 2007, *Russian Military Intelligence in the War with Japan, 1904–05* (London: Routledge), p. 7.
27. Nikolai Shebuev quoted in Lensen, *The Russian Push*, pp. 464–5.
28. Sergeev, *Russian Military Intelligence*, p. 21.
29. Sergeev, *Russian Military Intelligence*, p. 15.
30. Sergeev, *Russian Military Intelligence*, p. 44.
31. Sergeev, *Russian Military Intelligence*, p. 18.
32. Il'ya Derevyanko, 2018, *Nauchnye i Nauchno-Populyarnye Proizvedeniya. Tom 2. Russkaya Razvedka i Kontrrazvedka v Voine 1904–1905 gg.* [*Scientific and Popular Scientific Works. Vol. 2. Russian Intelligence and Counterintelligence in the War of 1904–05*] (Moscow: Yauza), p. 16.
33. Sergeev, *Russian Military Intelligence*, p. 18.
34. Nikolai Yanzhul quoted in Derevyanko, *Russkaya Razvedka*, p. 256.
35. Nikolai Yanzhul quoted in Sergeev, *Russian Military Intelligence*, p. 42.
36. Primakov, *Ocherki*, vol. 1, essay 27, p. 109.
37. Primakov, *Ocherki*, vol. 1, essay 27, p. 109.
38. Sergeev, *Russian Military Intelligence*, p. 37.
39. Gleb Vannovskii quoted in Sergeev, *Russian Military Intelligence*, pp. 37–8.
40. Primakov, *Ocherki*, vol. 1, essay 27, p. 110.
41. Primakov, *Ocherki*, vol. 1, essay 27, p. 110; Sergeev, *Russian Military Intelligence*, pp. 38–42.

42. Vladimir Samoilov quoted in Primakov, *Ocherki*, vol. 1, essay 27, p. 110.
43. Vladimir Samoilov quoted in Primakov, *Ocherki*, vol. 1, essay 27, p. 112.
44. Sergeev, *Russian Military Intelligence*, p. 42.
45. Sergeev, *Russian Military Intelligence*, p. 21.
46. Sergeev, *Russian Military Intelligence*, p. 40.
47. Bruce W. Menning, 2006, "Miscalculating one's enemies: Russian military intelligence before the Russo-Japanese War," *War in History*, 13:2, pp. 141–70, p. 147.
48. Sergeev, *Russian Military Intelligence*, p. 40.
49. Sergeev, *Russian Military Intelligence*, p. 41.
50. Sergeev, *Russian Military Intelligence*, p. 42.
51. Oku, *Rotan*, p. 142.
52. Oku, *Rotan*, p. 142.
53. Oku, *Rotan*, pp. 137–42.
54. Igor' L. Bunich, 2000, *Dolgaya Doroga na Golgofa* [*The long road to Golgotha*] (St Petersburg: Energii), p. 363.
55. Aleksei Rusin quoted in Sergeev, *Russian Military Intelligence*, p. 41.
56. Menning, "Miscalculating," p. 154.
57. Yakov Zhilinskii quoted in Sergeev, *Russian Military Intelligence*, p. 75.
58. Report from Colonel Aleksandr Nechvolodov to Quartermaster-General of Field Headquarters of Manchurian Army, 28 April 1904, reproduced in Derevyanko, *Russkaya Razvedka*, pp. 146–8.
59. Report from Colonel Aleksandr Nechvolodov in Derevyanko, *Russkaya Razvedka*.
60. Dmitrii B. Pavlov, 2007, "Russia and Korea in 1904–1905: 'Chamberlain' A.I. Pavlov and his 'Shanghai Service,'" ch.11 in J.W.M. Chapman and C. Inaba (eds), *Rethinking the Russo-Japanese War, vol. 2: The Nichinan Papers* (Leiden: Brill), p. 165.
61. Primakov, *Ocherki*, vol. 1, essay 27, p. 114.
62. Sergeev, *Russian Military Intelligence*, p. 76.
63. Kimitaka Matsuzato, 2016, *Russia and Its Northeast Asian Neighbors: China, Japan, and Korea 1858–1945* (Lanham: Lexington Books), pp. 102–3.
64. There is some disagreement as to the correct rendering of his name. While Dmitrii Pavlov gives it as "Balais," Matsuzato Kimita gives it as "Balet" and Alex Marshall as "Bale." Pavlov, "Russia and Korea," p. 169; Matsuzato, *Russia and Its Northeast Asian Neighbors*, p. 103; Alex Marshall, 2006, *The Russian General Staff and Asia, 1860–1917* (Abingdon: Routledge), p. 89.
65. Pavlov, "Russia and Korea," p. 169.
66. *Japan Times*, 2004, "French Reporter Conducted Espionage for Russia in Russo-Japanese War," 24 October, https://www.japantimes.co.jp/news/2004/10/24/national/french-reporter-conducted-espionage-for-russia-in-russo-japanese-war/
67. Pavlov, "Russia and Korea," p. 169.
68. Sergeev, *Russian Military Intelligence*, p. 137.
69. Aleksandr Vineken quoted in Derevyanko, *Russkaya Razvedka*, p. 162. After Balais's withdrawal in March 1905, two other French citizens, named Echare and Plare,

were also sent to Japan. Their primary goal was to report on Japanese reinforcements being prepared for deployment. They were also tasked with looking out for any sign that Japan was readying its forces for an attack on Vladivostok or Sakhalin. Sergeev, *Russian Military Intelligence*, pp. 117–18.

70. Derevyanko, *Russkaya Razvedka*, p. 162.
71. Derevyanko, *Russkaya Razvedka*, p. 162.
72. Sergeev, *Russian Military Intelligence*, p. 83.
73. Oku, *Rotan*, pp. 146–50; *Cardiff Times*, 1905, "Trial of a spy," Press Association Special War Telegram, 21 January, https://newspapers.library.wales/view/3432542/3432549
74. Derevyanko, *Russkaya Razvedka*, p. 191, pp. 201–2.
75. Sergeev, *Russian Military Intelligence*, p. 118.
76. José Maria Guedes quoted in Derevyanko, *Russkaya Razvedka*, pp. 216–17, p. 232.
77. Oku, *Rotan*, pp. 152–3.
78. République Française, Archive Nationale, "Bougouin, Alexandre Etienne," no. de notice: LO312006, https://www.leonore.archives-nationales.culture.gouv.fr/ui/notice/47219
79. Oku, *Rotan*, pp. 151–8.
80. Sergeev, *Russian Military Intelligence*, p. 66.
81. Quoted in Sergeev, *Russian Military Intelligence*, p. 115.
82. Sergeev, *Russian Military Intelligence*, p. 155.
83. Quoted in Sergeev, *Russian Military Intelligence*, p. 68.
84. Alex Marshall, 2007, "Russian intelligence during the Russo-Japanese War, 1904–05," *Intelligence and National Security*, 22:5, pp. 682–98, p. 684.
85. Sergeev, *Russian Military Intelligence*, p. 13, p. 16.
86. V.G. Datsyshen, 2021, "Military Japanese studies in the Russian Far East in the early 20th century," *Russian Japanology Review*, 1, pp. 117–43, p. 121.
87. Sergeev, *Russian Military Intelligence*, p. 115.
88. Sergeev, *Russian Military Intelligence*, p. 87.
89. Vladimir Kosagovskii quoted in Sergeev, *Russian Military Intelligence*, p. 83.
90. Sergeev, *Russian Military Intelligence*, p. 56.
91. Julian Corbett, 2015, *Maritime Operations in the Russo-Japanese War, 1904–1905: Vol. 1* (Annapolis: Naval Institute Press), p. 88, p. 114.
92. Sergeev, *Russian Military Intelligence*, p. 60.
93. Bennett Burleigh, 1905, *Empire of the East; or, Japan and Russia at War, 1904–5* (London: Chapman & Hall), p. 97.
94. Sergeev, *Russian Military Intelligence*, p. 60.
95. Quoted in Alistair Horne, 2015, *Hubris: The Tragedy of War in the Twentieth Century* (London: Weidenfeld & Nicolson), p. 30.
96. Vladimir Kosagovskii quoted in Sergeev, *Russian Military Intelligence*, p. 103.
97. Sergeev, *Russian Military Intelligence*, p. 84.
98. Sergeev, *Russian Military Intelligence*, p. 138.
99. Sergeev, *Russian Military Intelligence*, pp. 102–3.

100. Quartermaster General of the Manchurian Army quoted in Primakov, *Ocherki*, essay 27, p. 115.
101. Sergeev, *Russian Military Intelligence*, p. 126.
102. Derevyanko, *Russkaya Razvedka*, pp. 138–40.
103. Sergeev, *Russian Military Intelligence*, p. 122, p. 127, p. 140.
104. Lieutenant General Nadarov quoted in Sergeev, *Russian Military Intelligence*, p. 130.
105. Colonel Mikhail Kvetsinskii quoted in Sergeev, *Russian Military Intelligence*, p. 127.
106. Sergeev, *Russian Military Intelligence*, p. 99.
107. Fedor Barmin, 2013, "Russkii Samurai Ryabov," *Spetsnaz Rossii*, 31 May, http://www.specnaz.ru/articles/200/8/1838.htm
108. Datsyshen, "Military Japanese studies," p. 126.
109. Primakov, *Ocherki*, vol. 1, essay 27, pp. 115–16.
110. Richard M. Connaughton, 2003, *Rising Sun and Tumbling Bear: Russia's War with Japan* (London: Cassell), pp. 132–3.
111. Russian General Staff quoted in Sergeev, 2007, p. 82.
112. Connaughton, *Rising Sun*, p. 302.
113. Connaughton, *Rising Sun*, p. 301.
114. Horne, *Hubris*, p. 52; Corbett, *Maritime Operations*, p. 35. This is the same *Aurora* that famously fired the shot that signalled the start of the assault on the Winter Palace during the October Revolution of 1917. She is now a museum ship in St Petersburg.
115. Admiral Zinovii Rozhestvenskii quoted in Corbett, *Maritime Operations*, p. 29.
116. Quoted in Sergeev, *Russian Military Intelligence*, p. 148.
117. Corbett, *Maritime Operations*, p. 30, p. 32.
118. Sergeev, *Russian Military Intelligence*, p. 145.
119. Connaughton, *Rising Sun*, p. 300.
120. For further discussion of the Siege of Port Arthur, see Connaughton, *Rising Sun*; Reginald Hargreaves, 1962, *Red Sun Rising: The Siege of Port Arthur* (Philadelphia: Lippincott).
121. Menning, "Miscalculating," p. 164.
122. Sergeev, *Russian Military Intelligence*, p. 97.
123. Colonel Sergei Rashevskii quoted in Sergeev, *Russian Military Intelligence*, p. 98.
124. Colonel Sergei Rashevskii quoted in Sergeev, *Russian Military Intelligence*, p. 97.
125. Tat'yana Soboleva, 2002, *Istoriya Shifroval'nogo Dela v Rossii* [*The History of Encryption in Russia*] (Moscow: Olma Press), p. 130.
126. Sergeev, *Russian Military Intelligence*, p. 57.
127. Connaughton, *Rising Sun*, p. 264.
128. Sergeev, *Russian Military Intelligence*, p. 136.
129. Connaughton, *Rising Sun*, p. 265.
130. Pavlov, "Russia and Korea," p. 70.
131. Connaughton, *Rising Sun*, p. 161.
132. Quoted in Primakov, *Ocherki*, vol. 1, p. 115.
133. Primakov, *Ocherki*, vol. 1, pp. 117–18.
134. Sergeev, *Russian Military Intelligence*, p. 74.

135. Andrew, Christopher, 2018, *The Secret World: A History of Intelligence* (New Haven: Yale University Press), p. 455, p. 467.
136. Sergeev, *Russian Military Intelligence*, p. 100.
137. Sergeev, *Russian Military Intelligence*, p. 100.
138. Sergeev, *Russian Military Intelligence*, pp. 92–3.
139. Sergeev, *Russian Military Intelligence*, p. 20.
140. Sergeev, *Russian Military Intelligence*, p. 20.
141. Primakov, *Ocherki*, vol. 1, p. 103.
142. Primakov, *Ocherki*, vol. 1, p. 114.
143. King Gojong quoted in Pavlov, "Russia and Korea," p. 161, p. 162.
144. Pavlov, "Russia and Korea," pp. 166–9.
145. Pavlov, "Russia and Korea," p. 167.
146. Pavlov, "Russia and Korea," pp. 159–60.
147. Pavlov, "Russia and Korea," p. 163.
148. Sergeev, *Russian Military Intelligence*, p. 94.
149. Encyclopædia Britannica, "Stepan Osipovich Makarov." Britannica Academic.
150. Sergeev, *Russian Military Intelligence*, p. 89, p. 93.
151. Pertti Luntinen and Bruce W. Menning, 2005, "The Russian navy at war, 1904–05," ch.11 in John W. Steinberg et al. (eds), *Russo-Japanese War in Global Perspective: World War Zero* (Leiden: Brill), p. 235.
152. Luntinen and Menning, "The Russian navy," pp. 236–7.
153. Ben B. Fischer, 1997, *Okhrana: The Paris Operations of the Russian Imperial Police* (Washington, DC: Center for the Study of Intelligence), p. 1, pp. 7–8, p. 105.
154. Fischer, *Okhrana*, p. 15.
155. Fischer, *Okhrana*, p. 30.
156. Andrew, *The Secret World*, pp. 467–8.
157. Andrew, *The Secret World*, p. 470.
158. Chiharu Inaba, 1998, "Franco-Russian intelligence cooperation against Japan during the Russo-Japanese war, 1904–05," *Japanese Slavic and East European Studies*, 19, pp. 1–23, p. 11.
159. Inaba, "Franco-Russian intelligence," pp. 10–13.
160. Inaba, "Franco-Russian intelligence," p. 5.
161. Samuels, Richard J., 2019, *Special Duty: A History of the Japanese Intelligence Community* (Ithaca: Cornell University Press), p. 39.
162. Andrew, *The Secret World*, p. 469.
163. Jacob, Frank, 2018, *The Russo-Japanese War and its Shaping of the Twentieth Century* (London: Routledge), p. 102.
164. Connaughton, *Rising Sun*, p. 343.
165. Sergei Witte quoted in Jacob, *Russo-Japanese War*, p. 100.
166. Horne, *Hubris*, p. 96.
167. Theodore Roosevelt quoted in *Jacob, Russo-Japanese War*, p. 13.
168. Jacob, *Russo-Japanese War*, p. 5.
169. Horne, *Hubris*, p. 22.
170. Quoted in Lensen, *Observations of Sir Ernest Satow*, p. 36.

171. T. Bogdanovich quoted in Lensen, *The Russian Push*, p. 465.
172. Sergeev, *Russian Military Intelligence*, p. 52.
173. Derevyanko, *Russkaya Razvedka*, p. 25.

6. BOLSHEVIK SPIES

1. Marshall, "Russian intelligence," p. 682.
2. Sergeev, *Russian Military Intelligence*, p. 179.
3. Sergeev, *Russian Military Intelligence*, pp. 167–70.
4. Sergeev, *Russian Military Intelligence*, pp. 172–3.
5. Primakov, *Ocherki*, vol. 1, essay 27, p. 118.
6. Sergeev, *Russian Military Intelligence*, p. 176.
7. Quoted in Sergeev, *Russian Military Intelligence*, p. 185.
8. Igor Saveliev, 2004, "Militant diaspora: Korean immigrants and guerillas in early twentieth century Russia," *Forum of International Development Studies*, 26, March, p. 156.
9. Dunscomb, Paul E., 2011, *Japan's Siberian Intervention, 1918–1922: "A great disobedience against the people"* (Lanham: Lexington), p. 68.
10. Dunscomb, *Japan's Siberian Intervention*, p. 46.
11. Connaughton, Richard M., 2017, *The Republic of the Ushakovka* (London: Routledge), p. 83.
12. Dunscomb, *Japan's Siberian Intervention*, p. 1.
13. Connaughton, *Ushakovska*, p. 170.
14. Dunscomb, *Japan's Siberian Intervention*, p. 163.
15. Dunscomb, *Japan's Siberian Intervention*, p. 192.
16. Article from the *Contemporary Review* (April 1922) quoted in Lensen, George A., 1970, *Japanese Recognition of the U.S.S.R.: Soviet-Japanese Relations, 1921–1930* (Tokyo: Sophia University Press), p. 9.
17. Lensen, *Japanese Recognition*, pp. 99–100.
18. Vladimir I. Lenin quoted in Tatiana Linkhoeva, 2020, *Revolution Goes East: Imperial Japan and Soviet Communism* (Ithaca: Cornell University Press), p. 2.
19. Vladimir Lenin quoted in Andrew, Christopher and Gordievsky, Oleg, 1990, *KGB: The Inside Story of Its Foreign Operations from Lenin to Gorbachev* (New York: Harper Collins), p. 65.
20. Joseph Stalin quoted in Lensen, *Japanese Recognition*, p. 367.
21. Linkhoeva, *Revolution Goes East*, p. 31.
22. Linkhoeva, *Revolution Goes East*, pp. 30–1.
23. Shimane Kiyoshi, 1983, *Nihon Kyōsan-tō Supai-shi* [*History of Japanese Communist Party Spies*] (Tokyo: Shinjinbutsuōraisha), pp. 31–54.
24. Linkhoeva, *Revolution Goes East*, p. 33, p. 129.
25. Richard H. Mitchell, 1973, "Japan's Peace Preservation Law of 1925: Its origins and significance," *Monumenta Nipponica*, 28(3), pp. 317–45, p. 334.
26. Ōsugi Sakae quoted in Linkhoeva, *Revolution Goes East*, p. 136.

27. Linkhoeva, *Revolution Goes East*, p. 135.
28. Kevin McDermott and Jeremy Agnew, 1996, *The Comintern: A History of International Communism from Lenin to Stalin* (London: Macmillan), p. 10.
29. Quoted in Primakov, *Ocherki*, vol. 2, essay 5, p. 23.
30. Primakov, *Ocherki*, vol. 2, essay 5, pp. 23–4.
31. Primakov, *Ocherki*, vol. 2, essay 5, p. 28.
32. Primakov, *Ocherki*, vol. 2, essay 5, pp. 28–9.
33. Linkhoeva, *Revolution Goes East*, pp. 105–6.
34. Dunscomb, *Japan's Siberian Intervention*, p. 102.
35. Shimane, *Nihon Kyōsan-tō*, p. 79.
36. Linkhoeva, *Revolution Goes East*, p. 62.
37. Robert A. Scalapino and Lee Chong-Sik, 1960, "The origins of the Korean communist movement (I)," *The Journal of Asian Studies*, 20:1, pp. 9–31, p. 20.
38. Erich von Salzmann quoted in Lensen, *Japanese Recognition*, pp. 13–14.
39. Scalapino and Lee, p. 21.
40. Scalapino and Lee, p. 16.
41. Vladimir Tikhonov, 2017, "'Korean nationalism' seen through the Comintern prism, 1920s–30s," *REGION, Regional Studies of Russia, Eastern Europe, and Central Asia*, 6:2, pp. 201–24, pp. 206–7.
42. Lensen, *Japanese Recognition*, p. 138.
43. Lensen, *Japanese Recognition*, p. 139.
44. Commissar of Foreign Affairs Georgii V. Chicherin quoted in Lensen, *Japanese Recognition*, p. 7.
45. Viktor L. Kopp quoted in Lensen, *Japanese Recognition*, p. 345.
46. Lensen, *Japanese Recognition*, pp. 210–13.
47. Georgii S. Agabekov quoted in Andrew and Gordievsky, *KGB*, p. 80. OGPU (*Ob"edinennoe Gosudarstvennoe Politicheskoe Upravlenie*—Joint State Political Directorate) was the name used by the KGB between 1923 and 1934. After his defection, Agabekov wrote several condemnatory books about the Soviet intelligence services. He was assassinated in 1937.
48. Primakov, *Ocherki*, vol. 2, essay 33, p. 158.
49. Primakov, *Ocherki*, vol. 2, essay 33, p. 159.
50. Primakov, *Ocherki*, vol. 2, essay 33, p. 159.
51. Primakov, *Ocherki*, vol. 2, essay 33, p. 160.
52. Primakov, *Ocherki*, vol. 2, essay 33, p. 160.
53. Primakov, *Ocherki*, vol. 2, essay 33, p. 161.
54. Shimane, *Nihon Kyōsan-tō*, p. 94.
55. Quoted in Andrew and Gordievsky, *KGB*, pp. 87–8.
56. Filip Kovacevic, 2022, "Ian Fleming's Soviet rival: Roman Kim and Soviet spy fiction during the early Cold War," *Intelligence and National Security*, 37:4, pp. 593–606, p. 595.
57. Kovacevic, "Ian Fleming's Soviet," p. 595.
58. Kovacevic, "Ian Fleming's Soviet," p. 595.

59. Kovacevic, "Ian Fleming's Soviet," p. 597, p. 604.
60. Kovacevic, "Ian Fleming's Soviet," p. 598.
61. Gotō Shinpei quoted in Linkhoeva, *Revolution Goes East*, p. 85.
62. Linkhoeva, *Revolution Goes East*, pp. 92–3.
63. Wakatsuki Reijirō quoted in Linkhoeva, *Revolution Goes East*, p. 120.
64. Quoted in Mitchell, "Japan's Peace Preservation Law," p. 339.
65. Linkhoeva, *Revolution Goes East*, p. 121.
66. McDermott and Agnew, *The Comintern*, p.xix.
67. Linkhoeva, *Revolution Goes East*, p. 90.
68. Quoted in Lensen, *Japanese Recognition*, p. 199.
69. Andrew and Gordievsky, *KGB*, p. 66.
70. Owen Matthews, 2019, *An Impeccable Spy: Richard Sorge, Stalin's Master Agent* (London: Bloomsbury), p. 29.
71. McDermott and Agnew, *The Comintern*, p. 43.
72. McDermott and Agnew, *The Comintern*, p. 68.
73. Joseph Stalin quoted in McDermott and Agnew, *The Comintern*, p. 67.
74. Veteran German Communist Clara Zetkin quoted in McDermott and Agnew, *The Comintern*, p. 86.
75. "Theses on the conditions for admission to the Communist International," reproduced in McDermott and Agnew, *The Comintern*, pp. 226–8.
76. McDermott and Agnew, *The Comintern*, p. 22.
77. Andrew and Gordievsky, *KGB*, p. 93.
78. Linkhoeva, *Revolution Goes East*, p. 147.
79. Linkhoeva, *Revolution Goes East*, p. 138.
80. Ōsugi Sakae, 1992, *The Autobiography of Ōsugi Sakae*, translated by Byron K. Marshall (Berkeley: University of California Press), p. 44.
81. Miles Fletcher, 1983, "Review of *Ōsugi Sakae, Anarchist in Taishō Japan* by Thomas A. Stanley," *The Journal of Japanese Studies*, 9:2, pp. 399–404, p. 401.
82. Kondō Eizō, 1949, *Cominterun-no-missshi-Nihon Kyōsantō Sōsei Hiwa* [*The Secret Messenger of the Comintern—Secret History of the Founding of the JCP*] (Tokyo: Bunkahyōronsha), pp. 105–6; Linkhoeva, *Revolution Goes East*, p. 138; Robert A. Scalapino, 1967, *The Japanese Communist Movement, 1920–1966* (Berkeley: University of California Press), p. 12.
83. Thomas A. Stanley, 1982, *Ōsugi Sakae, Anarchist in Taishō Japan: The Creativity of the Ego* (Cambridge, MA: Harvard University Press), pp. 159–60.
84. Linkhoeva, *Revolution Goes East*, p. 153.
85. Kondō, *Cominterun-no-missshi*, pp. 113–14; Scalapino, *Japanese Communist Movement*, pp. 15–17.
86. Kondō, *Cominterun-no-missshi*, p. 132.
87. Kondō, *Cominterun-no-missshi*, p. 133.
88. Kondō, *Cominterun-no-missshi*, pp. 133–53; Scalapino, *Japanese Communist Movement*, pp. 16–17.
89. Scalapino, *Japanese Communist Movement*, p. 17.

90. Scalapino, *Japanese Communist Movement*, pp. 171–2.
91. Scalapino, *Japanese Communist Movement*, p. 19.
92. Scalapino, *Japanese Communist Movement*, p. 19.
93. Yamanouchi Akito, 2006, "Katayama Sen, zai Ro nihonjin Kyōsan shugi-sha to shoki kominterun" [Katayama Sen, Japanese communists in Russia and the Comintern's early days], *Journal of Ōhara Institute for Social Research*, 566, pp. 29–53, p. 45.
94. Shimane, "*Nihon Kyōsan-tō*," p. 94.
95. Scalapino, *Japanese Communist Movement*, p. 35.
96. Scalapino, *Japanese Communist Movement*, pp. 4–5; Tu Xiaofeng, 2020, "Between the Comintern, the Japanese Communist Party, and the Chinese Communist Party: Nosaka Sanzo's Betrayal Games," ch.7 in Drachewych, O. and McKay, I. (eds), *Left Transnationalism* (Montreal: McGill-Queen's University Press), p. 206.
97. Tu, "Between the Comintern," p. 209.
98. Tu, "Between the Comintern," pp. 204–5.
99. Tu, "Between the Comintern," p. 205.
100. *The Japan Times*, 2000, "Spy against Japan: Letters shed new light on Nosaka's acts," 22 October, https://www.japantimes.co.jp/news/2000/10/22/national/letters-shed-new-light-on-nosakas-espionage-acts/
101. Koji Ariyoshi, 2000, *From Kona to Yenan: The Political Memoirs of Koji Ariyoshi*, edited by Beechert, A.M. and Beechert, E.D. (Honolulu: University of Hawai'i Press), pp. 122–3.
102. Tu, "Between the Comintern," pp. 209–12.
103. Tu, "Between the Comintern," pp. 212–15.
104. Tu, "Between the Comintern," p. 212.
105. Andrew and Gordievsky, *KGB*, p. 82; Kondō, *Cominterun-no-missshi*, p. 154; Scalapino, *The Japanese Communist Movement*, p. 25.
106. Linkhoeva, *Revolution Goes East*, p. 117.
107. Kondō, *Cominterun-no-missshi*, pp. 155–7.
108. Scalapino, *The Japanese Communist Movement*, p. 38.
109. Scalapino, *The Japanese Communist Movement*, p. 41.
110. Lensen, *Japanese Recognition*, pp. 349–50.
111. Scalapino, *The Japanese Communist Movement*, pp. 19–43.
112. Scalapino, *The Japanese Communist Movement*, pp. 40–1.
113. Scalapino, *The Japanese Communist Movement*, p. 40.
114. Scalapino, *The Japanese Communist Movement*, p. 41.
115. Linkhoeva, *Revolution Goes East*, p. 175.
116. Scalapino and Lee, p. 18.
117. Scalapino, *The Japanese Communist Movement*, p. 45.
118. Scalapino, *The Japanese Communist Movement*, p. 44.
119. Hattori Ryūji, 2012, "Controversies over the Tanaka Memorial," ch.4 in Yang, D., Liu, J., Mitani, H., and Gordon, A. (eds) *Toward a History Beyond Borders* (Cambridge, Mass.: Harvard University Asia Center), p. 147.

120. Leon Trotsky, 1941, "The Tanaka Memorial," *Fourth International*, 4:5, June, pp. 131–5, p. 135.
121. Tanaka Memorial quoted in Hattori, "Controversies," p. 122.
122. Linkhoeva, *Revolution Goes East*, pp. 22–3, p. 84.
123. John J. Stephan, 1973, "The Tanaka Memorial (1927): Authentic or spurious?," *Modern Asian Studies*, 7:4, pp. 733–45, p. 736.
124. Primakov, *Ocherki*, vol. 2, essay 32, p. 156.
125. Primakov, *Ocherki*, vol. 2, essay 32, p. 158.
126. Trotsky, "The Tanaka Memorial," p. 133.
127. Trotsky, "The Tanaka Memorial," p. 134.
128. Trotsky, "The Tanaka Memorial," p. 134.
129. V.R. Medinskii and A.O. Chubar'yan, 2023, *Vseobshchaya Istoriya, 10 Klass* [*General History, 10th Class*] (Moscow: Ministry of Education), p. 131.
130. Trotsky, "The Tanaka Memorial," p. 131.
131. Stephan, "The Tanaka Memorial," p. 740.
132. Stephan, "The Tanaka Memorial," p. 741.
133. Thomas Rid, 2020, *Active Measures: The Secret History of Disinformation and Political Warfare* (New York: Farrar, Straus and Giroux), p. 40.
134. Herbert Romerstein and Stanislav Levchenko, 1989, *The KGB Against the 'Main Enemy': How the Soviet Intelligence Service Operates Against the United States* (Lexington: Lexington Books), p. 267.
135. Deacon, Richard, 1975, *A History of the Russian Secret Service* (London: New English Library), p. 172.
136. Romerstein and Levchenko, *The KGB*, p. 268.
137. Stephan, "The Tanaka Memorial," p. 737.
138. Hattori, "Controversies," p. 136.
139. Trotsky, "The Tanaka Memorial," pp. 134–5.
140. Rid, *Active Measures*, p. 38.
141. Hattori Ryūji, 2010, *Nitchū rekishi ninshiki: "Tanaka jōsōbun" o meguru sōkoku 1927–2010* [*Understanding Sino-Japanese History—Conflict over the Tanaka Memorial 1927–2010*] (Tokyo: Tokyo Daigaku Shuppankai), p. 138.
142. Rid, *Active Measures*, p. 40.
143. Rid, *Active Measures*, p. 42.

7. SOVIET INTELLIGENCE AT NOMONHAN

1. Haslam, Jonathan, 1992, *The Soviet Union and the Threat from the East, 1933–41* (Pittsburgh: University of Pittsburgh Press), p. 7.
2. Haslam, *The Soviet Union*, p. 9.
3. War Minister Araki Sadao quoted in Alvin D. Coox, 1985, *Nomonhan: Japan Against Russia, 1939* (Stanford: Stanford University Press), p. 77.
4. Kwantung Army report quoted in in Haslam, *The Soviet Union*, p. 27.
5. Christopher Andrew and Oleg Gordievsky, 1990, *KGB* (New York: HarperCollins), p. 179.

6. Haslam, *The Soviet Union*, pp. 27–8.
7. Stuart D. Goldman, 2012, *Nomonhan 1939: The Red Army's Victory that Shaped World War II* (Annapolis: Naval Institute Press), p. 19.
8. Joseph Stalin quoted in Haslam, *The Soviet Union*, p. 37, p. 43.
9. Haslam, *The Soviet Union*, p. 29.
10. Haslam, *The Soviet Union*, p. 46.
11. Chief of Kwantung Army headquarters Itagaki Seishirō quoted in Haslam, *The Soviet Union*, p. 48.
12. The confrontation is known as Khalkhin Gol in Russian and Nomonhan in Japanese. This book will follow Alvin D. Coox's masterful work in calling it Nomonhan. Coox, *Nomonhan*.
13. Alvin D. Coox, 1998, "The lesser of two hells: NKVD general G.S. Lyushkov's defection to Japan, 1938–1945, part 1," *The Journal of Slavic Military Studies*, 11:3, pp. 145–86, pp. 145–50.
14. Coox, "The lesser: part 1," p. 145.
15. Riehle, *Soviet Defectors*, p. 65.
16. Coox, "The lesser: part 1," pp. 146–9.
17. Stalin's instructions recounted by Lyushkov quoted in Coox, "The lesser: part 1," pp. 151–2.
18. Jon K. Chang, 2016, *Burnt by the Sun: The Koreans of the Russian Far East* (Honolulu: University of Hawai'i Press), pp. 156–60.
19. Lyushkov's Japanese interpreter quoted in Coox, "The lesser: part 1," p. 168.
20. Lyushkov quoted in Coox, "The lesser: part 1," p. 161.
21. Arch J. Getty and Oleg V. Naumov, 1999, *The Road to Terror: Stalin and the Self-Destruction of the Bolsheviks, 1932–1939* (New Haven: Yale University Press), p. 521.
22. Hiroaki Kuromiya, 2016, "The Battle of Lake Khasan Reconsidered," *The Journal of Slavic Military Studies*, 29:1, pp. 99–109, p. 108.
23. Coox, "The lesser: part 1," p. 166.
24. Riehle, *Soviet Defectors*, p. 49.
25. Coox, "The lesser: part 1," p. 146.
26. Alvin D. Coox, 1998, "The lesser of two hells: NKVD general G.S. Lyushkov's defection to Japan, 1938–1945, part 2," *The Journal of Slavic Military Studies*, 11:4, pp. 72–110, pp. 78–89.
27. Coox, "The lesser: part 2," p. 75.
28. Coox, "The lesser: part 2," p. 75, p. 89.
29. Coox, "The lesser: part 1," p. 176.
30. Coox, "The lesser: part 1," pp. 171–3.
31. Stanislav Levchenko, 1988, *On the Wrong Side: My Life in the KGB* (Virginia: Pergamon Brassey's), pp. 157–8.
32. Coox, "The lesser: part 2," p. 74.
33. Coox, "The lesser: part 1," p. 172.
34. Coox, "The lesser: part 2," pp. 77–9.
35. Coox, "The lesser: part 2," p. 92.

36. Coox, "The lesser: part 2," pp. 73–5.
37. Coox, "The lesser: part 1," pp. 177–9.
38. Quoted in Coox, "The lesser: part 1," p. 177.
39. Coox, "The lesser: part 1," p. 177.
40. Lieutenant General Yanagida Genzō quoted in Coox, "The lesser: part 2," p. 99.
41. Captain Takeoka Yutaka quoted in Coox, "The lesser: part 2," p. 100.
42. Coox, "The lesser: part 2," p. 100.
43. Coox, "The lesser: part 2," pp. 100–1.
44. Coox, *Nomonhan*, p. 86.
45. Coox, "The lesser: part 2," p. 108.
46. Coox, *Nomonhan*, p. 915.
47. Coox, *Nomonhan*, p. 915.
48. Haslam, *The Soviet Union*, p. 132.
49. Colonel Hayashi Saburō quoted in Kotani Ken, 2008, "Japanese intelligence and the Soviet-Japanese border conflicts in the 1930s," 33rd Conference of International Military History, National Institute of Defence Studies (NIDS), http://www.nids.mod.go.jp/publication/senshi/pdf/200803/09.pdf, pp. 132–3.
50. Military attaché Kawabe Torashirō quoted in Iwaki, *Nomonhan-jiken*, p. 167.
51. Kuromiya, Hiroaki, 2011, "The mystery of Nomonhan, 1939," *Journal of Slavic Military Studies*, 24:4, pp. 659–77, p. 662
52. Iwaki, *Nomonhan-jiken*, pp. 171–2; Kuromiya, "The mystery," pp. 662–3.
53. Iwaki, *Nomonhan-jiken*, pp. 184–5
54. Deputy Commissar Vladimir Potemkin quoted in Haslam, *The Soviet Union*, p. 92.
55. Haslam, *The Soviet Union*, pp. 55–6.
56. Haslam, *The Soviet Union*, pp. 93–4.
57. Haslam, *The Soviet Union*, p. 94, p. 124.
58. Primakov, vol. 3, essay 20, pp. 137–8, vol. 4, essay 27, p. 202.
59. Primakov, *Ocherki*, vol. 3, essay 20, p. 133.
60. Kotani, "Japanese intelligence," p. 133.
61. Hata Ikuhiko, 2014, *Mei-to-An-no Nomonhan Senshi* [*Light and Dark in the History of the Battle of Nomonhan*] (Tōkyō: PHP Kenkyūjo), p. 331.
62. Kotani, "Japanese intelligence," pp. 133–4.
63. Primakov, *Ocherki*, vol. 3, essay 21, pp. 139–42.
64. Tomita Takeshi, 2011, "Soren jōhō kikan 'Abe' no nazo" ["The mystery of the Soviet intelligence agent 'Abe'"], *Rekishi Dokuhon*, September 2011, pp. 222–30.
65. Primakov, *Ocherki*, vol. 3, essay 21, p. 139.
66. Primakov, *Ocherki*, vol. 3, essay 21, p. 139.
67. Primakov, *Ocherki*, vol. 3, essay 21, p. 140.
68. Primakov, *Ocherki*, vol. 3, essay 21, p. 142.
69. Primakov, *Ocherki*, vol. 3, essay 21, p. 138.
70. E.M. Kaluzhskii quoted in Primakov, *Ocherki*, vol. 3, essay 21, p. 141.
71. Primakov, *Ocherki*, vol. 3, essay 21, p. 141; Tomita, "Soren jōhō," pp. 225–6.
72. Primakov, *Ocherki*, vol. 3, essay 21, p. 140.

73. Primakov, *Ocherki*, vol. 3, essay 21, p. 141.
74. Coox, *Nomonhan*, p. 81.
75. Primakov, *Ocherki*, vol. 3, essay 21, pp. 142–4.
76. Tomita, "Soren jōhō," pp. 220–30.
77. Goldman, *Nomonhan 1939*, pp. 1–5.
78. Prime Minister Hiranuma Kiichirō quoted in Coox, *Nomonhan*, p. 886.
79. Coox, *Nomonhan*, p. 682.
80. Iwaki, *Nomonhan-jiken*, pp. 219–20.
81. Richard Sorge quoted in Haslam, *The Soviet Union*, p. 131.
82. Iwaki, *Nomonhan-jiken*, p. 220.
83. Quoted in Matthews, *An Impeccable*, p. 211.
84. Matthews, *An Impeccable*, p. 212.
85. Gordon W. Prange, 1984, *Target Tokyo: The Story of the Sorge Spy Ring* (New York: McGraw-Hill), p. 245.
86. Hata, *Mei-to-An*, p. 337; Iwaki, *Nomonhan-jiken*, pp. 221–7.
87. Coox, *Nomonhan*, p. 910.
88. Goldman, *Nomonhan 1939*, p. 91.
89. Coox, *Nomonhan*, p. 317.
90. Goldman, *Nomonhan 1939*, p. 112.
91. Major Ogata Kyūichirō quoted in Coox, *Nomonhan*, p. 383.
92. Coox, *Nomonhan*, p. 345.
93. Coox, *Nomonhan*, p. 922.
94. Coox, *Nomonhan*, p. 768.
95. Iwaki, *Nomonhan-jiken*, p. 187.
96. Coox, *Nomonhan*, p. 574.
97. Coox, *Nomonhan*, p. 247.
98. Hata, *Mei-to-An*, p. 340.
99. Soboleva, *Istoriya Sifroval'nogo Dela*, p. 209.
100. Coox, *Nomonhan*, p. 582.
101. Coox, *Nomonhan*, p. 253.
102. Coox, *Nomonhan*, p. 547.
103. Coox, *Nomonhan*, pp. 579–84.
104. Horne, *Hubris*, p. 146.
105. Coox, *Nomonhan*, p. 573.
106. General Georgii Zhukov quoted in Coox, *Nomonhan*, p. 582.
107. Coox, *Nomonhan*, pp. 582–3.
108. Coox, *Nomonhan*, p. 586, p. 683.
109. Coox, *Nomonhan*, p. 286.
110. Kwantung Army report quoted in Coox, *Nomonhan*, p. 578.
111. Kuromiya, "The mystery," pp. 661–2.
112. Kuromiya, "The mystery," pp. 675.
113. Matthews, *An Impeccable*, p. 214.
114. Kuromiya, "The mystery," pp. 664–5.

115. Kuromiya, "The mystery," p. 665.
116. Haslam, *The Soviet Union*, pp. 1–22.
117. Kuromiya, "The mystery," p. 665.
118. Matthews, *An Impeccable*, p. 211.
119. Major Ōgi Hiroshi quoted in Matthews, *An Impeccable*, p. 212.
120. Goldman, *Nomonhan, 1939*, p. 126.
121. Horne, *Hubris*, p. 153.
122. Kwantung Army Operations Order 1488 quoted in Goldman, *Nomonhan, 1939*, p. 1.
123. Goldman, *Nomonhan, 1939*, p. 89.
124. Goldman, *Nomonhan, 1939*, pp. 104–5.
125. Major Tsuji Masanobu quoted in Goldman, *Nomonhan, 1939*, p. 181.
126. Coox, *Nomonhan*, p. 264.
127. Goldman, *Nomonhan, 1939*, p. 105.
128. Coox, *Nomonhan*, p. 961.
129. Goldman, *Nomonhan, 1939*, p. 127.
130. Goldman, *Nomonhan, 1939*, pp. 148–52.
131. Colonel Inada Masazumi quoted in Goldman, *Nomonhan, 1939*, p. 173.

8. THE SORGE-OZAKI SPY RING

1. Owen Matthews, 2019, *An Impeccable Spy: Richard Sorge, Stalin's Master Agent* (London: Bloomsbury), pp. 340–50.
2. *TASS*, 2020, "Posol'stvo Rossii v Tokio poluchilo prava na mogilu razvedchika Zorge" ["Russian embassy in Tokyo receives rights to the grave of intelligence officer Sorge"], 20 October, https://tass.ru/obschestvo/9844691
3. *RIA Novosti*, 2022, "Trutnev podderzhal pozitsiyu MID o perezakhoronenii prakha Zorge na Kurilakh" ["Trutnev supports the position of the Foreign Ministry on the reburial of Sorge's remains on the Kurils"], 27 January, https://ria.ru/20220127/zorge-1769779204.html
4. Chalmers Johnson, 1964, *An Instance of Treason: Ozaki Hotsumi and the Sorge Spy Ring* (Stanford: Stanford University Press); Matthews, *An Impeccable*; Gordon W. Prange, 1985, *Target Tokyo: The Story of the Sorge Spy Ring* (New York: McGraw Hill); Robert Whymant, 1996, *Stalin's Spy: Richard Sorge and the Tokyo Espionage Ring* (New York: St Martin's Press); Charles A. Willoughby, 1952, *Shanghai Conspiracy: The Sorge Spy Ring* (New York: E.P. Dutton).
5. Matthews, *An Impeccable*, pp. 9–11.
6. Richard Sorge quoted in Whymant, *Stalin's Spy*, p. 16.
7. Matthews, *An Impeccable*, p. 347. Other versions report that Sorge merely thanked the prison officials "for all your kindnesses." Willoughby, *Shanghai Conspiracy*, p. 127.
8. Prange, *Target Tokyo*, pp. 11–13.
9. Prange, *Target Tokyo*, p. 14.
10. Matthews, *An Impeccable*, pp. 33–41.

11. Richard Sorge quoted in Matthews, *An Impeccable*, p. 43.
12. Peter Wright, 1987, *Spycatcher: The Candid Autobiography of a Senior Intelligence Officer* (New York: Viking), pp. 328–9.
13. Viktor Suvorov, 1984, *Soviet Military Intelligence* (London: Hamish Hamilton), p. 75.
14. Wright, *Spycatcher*, p. 226.
15. Matthews, *An Impeccable*, p. 55. The Fourth Directorate later used the codename of INSON for Sorge.
16. Ben Macintyre, 2021, *Agent Sonya* (London: Penguin), p. 60.
17. Matthews, *An Impeccable*, pp. 84–5.
18. Richard Sorge quoted in Matthews, *An Impeccable*, pp. 63–4.
19. Macintyre, *Agent Sonya*, p. 39. Smedley's alias is given in Willoughby, *Shanghai Conspiracy*, p. 282.
20. Macintyre, *Agent Sonya*, p. 51.
21. Matthews, *An Impeccable*, pp. 143–4.
22. Suvorov, *Soviet Military Intelligence*, p. 77.
23. Dr Eduard Zeller quoted in Prange, *Target Tokyo*, p. 35.
24. Prange, *Target Tokyo*, p. 38.
25. Matthews, *An Impeccable*, p. 103, p. 120, p. 135.
26. Matthews, *An Impeccable*, p. 173.
27. US Ambassador Joseph Grew quoted in Prange, *Target Tokyo*, p. 317.
28. Johnson, *An Instance*, p. 16; Prange, *Target Tokyo*, pp. 260–1.
29. Brigadeführer Walter Schellenberg quoted in Whymant, *Stalin's Spy*, p. 154.
30. Kinoshita Junji, 1973, *Ottō to Yobareru Nihonjin* [*A Japanese Called Otto*] (Tōkyō: Kōdansha).
31. Ozaki Hotsumi, 2003, *Aijō ha Furuboshi no Gotoku* [*Love is Like a Falling Star*] (Tōkyō: Iwanami Gendai Bunko).
32. Johnson, *An Instance*, p. 8, p. 19.
33. Johnson, *An Instance*, pp. 21–4; Prange, *Target Tokyo*, p. 23.
34. Ozaki Hotsumi quoted in Johnson, *An Instance*, p. 23.
35. Ezaki Michio, 2017, *Kominterun no bōryaku to Nihon no haisen* [*The Comintern conspiracy and Japan's defeat*] (Tōkyō: PHP Shinsho), p. 396.
36. Ozaki Hotsumi quoted in Johnson, *An Instance*, p. 28.
37. Prange, *Target Tokyo*, p. 24.
38. Suzuki Bunshirō quoted in Johnson, *An Instance*, p. 34.
39. Johnson, *An Instance*, p. 10.
40. Ozaki Hotsumi quoted in Prange, *Target Tokyo*, p. 26.
41. Johnson, *An Instance*, p. 80.
42. Prange, *Target Tokyo*, pp. 109–11.
43. Ozaki Hotsumi quoted in Matthews, *An Impeccable*, p. 129.
44. Matthews, *An Impeccable*, pp. 129–30.
45. Ozaki Hotsumi quoted in Prange, *Target Tokyo*, p. 152.
46. *The New York Times*, 1993, "Kinkazu Saionji; Japanese statesman, 86," 23 April 1993, https://www.nytimes.com/1993/04/23/obituaries/kinkazu-saionji-japanese-statesman-86.html

47. Johnson, *An Instance*, p. 26.
48. Matthews, *An Impeccable*, p. 183.
49. Linkhoeva, *Revolution Goes East*, p. 209.
50. Ozaki Hotsumi quoted in Prange, *Target Tokyo*, p. 185.
51. Kato Kiyofumi, 2006, *Mantetsu Zenshi* [*The Comprehensive History of Mantetsu*] (Tōkyō: Kōdansha).
52. Matthews, *An Impeccable*, p. 300.
53. Ozaki Hotsumi quoted in Johnson, *An Instance*, pp. 6–7.
54. Kevin McDermott and Jeremy Agnew, 1996, *The Comintern: A History of International Communism from Lenin to Stalin* (London: Macmillan), p. 5.
55. Ezaki, *Kominterun*, p. 357.
56. Johnson, *An Instance*, p. 36; Matthews, *An Impeccable*, p. 81, p. 85.
57. Johnson, *An Instance*, p. 13, p. 36.
58. Quoted in Prange, *Target Tokyo*, p. 23.
59. Johnson, *An Instance*, p. 101; Matthews, *An Impeccable*, p. 127.
60. Prange, *Target Tokyo*, p. 18.
61. Matthews, *An Impeccable*, p. 66.
62. Matthews, *An Impeccable*, p. 67.
63. Johnson, *An Instance*, pp. 103–4; Matthews, *An Impeccable*, p. 67; Prange, *Target Tokyo*, p. 133.
64. Prange, *Target Tokyo*, p. 21.
65. Matthews, *An Impeccable*, pp. 145–6.
66. Quoted in Prange, *Target Tokyo*, p. 102.
67. Matthews, *An Impeccable*, p. 332.
68. Matthews, *An Impeccable*, p. 227; Clausen later moved to Hiroo, part of Shibuya ward.
69. Quoted in Prange, *Target Tokyo*, p. 271.
70. Matthews, *An Impeccable*, p. 166, p. 225.
71. Willoughby, *Shanghai Conspiracy*, p. 100.
72. Matthews, *An Impeccable*, p. 239.
73. Johnson, *An Instance*, p. 92; Prange, *Target Tokyo*, p. 55.
74. Miyagi Yotoku quoted in Johnson, *An Instance*, p. 93.
75. Miyagi Yotoku quoted in Matthews, *An Impeccable*, p. 116.
76. Johnson, *An Instance*, p. 94; Matthews, *An Impeccable*, pp. 116–17; Prange, *Target Tokyo*, p. 56.
77. Prange, *Target Tokyo*, p. 56.
78. Miyagi Yotoku quoted in Prange, *Target Tokyo*, p. 61.
79. Miyagi Yotoku quoted in Whymant, *Stalin's Spy*, p. 190.
80. Willoughby, *Shanghai Conspiracy*, p. 79.
81. Matthews, *An Impeccable*, p. 151.
82. Willoughby, *Shanghai Conspiracy*, p. 212.
83. Edan Corkill and Chalmers Johnson, 2010, "Sorge's spy is brought in from the cold: A Soviet-Okinawan connection," *The Asia-Pacific Journal: Japan Focus*, 8:6, no. 1.

84. Corkill and Johnson, "Sorge's spy," p. 8; Johnson, *An Instance*, p. 151; Willoughby, *Shanghai Conspiracy*, pp. 85–7.
85. Matthews, *An Impeccable*, p. 182.
86. Matthews, *An Impeccable*, p. 152.
87. Prange, *Target Tokyo*, p. 49.
88. William T. Murphy, 2019, "Lydia Stahl: A secret life, 1885–?," *Journal of Intelligence History*, 18:1, pp. 38–62, p. 41.
89. Richard Sorge quoted in Prange, *Target Tokyo*, p. 59.
90. Prange, *Target Tokyo*, p. 393; *Willoughby*, *Shanghai Conspiracy*, p. 58.
91. Prange, *Target Tokyo*, p. 60.
92. Prange, *Target Tokyo*, p. 59; Willoughby, *Shanghai Conspiracy*, p. 122.
93. Matthews, *An Impeccable*, p. 224.
94. Matthews, *An Impeccable*, p. 224; Matt Wilce, n.d., "Journalist, gymnast, schoolboy, spy," *ASIJ Stories*, https://www.asij.ac.jp/asij-stories/journalist-gymnast-schoolboy-spy
95. Guenther Stein, 2011, *Made in Japan* (Oxford: Routledge).
96. Willoughby states that Stein did have a codename (though he does not give it) and that he was listed in the personnel records of Soviet military intelligence. Willoughby, *Shanghai Conspiracy*, p. 77, p. 276.
97. Richard Sorge quoted in Prange, *Target Tokyo*, p. 104.
98. Erwin D. Canham, 1958, *Commitment to Freedom: The Story of The Christian Science Monitor* (Boston: Houghton Mifflin), p. 341.
99. Johnson, *An Instance*, pp. 163–5.
100. Richard Sorge quoted in Johnson, *An Instance*, p. 108.
101. Johnson, *An Instance*, p. 107.
102. Canham, *Commitment*, pp. 342–3; Johnson, *An Instance*, pp. 107–8.
103. Whymant, *Stalin's Spy*, p. 123.
104. Quoted in Matthews, *An Impeccable*, p. 257.
105. Prange, *Target Tokyo*, pp. 339–40.
106. Christopher Andrew and Oleg Gordievsky, 1990, *KGB* (New York: HarperCollins), p. 260.
107. Joseph Stalin quoted in Matthews, *An Impeccable*, p. 173.
108. Matthews, *An Impeccable*, p. 171.
109. Joseph Stalin quoted in Matthews, *An Impeccable*, p. 280.
110. Joseph Stalin quoted in Christopher Andrew, 2018, *The Secret World: A History of Intelligence* (New Haven: Yale University Press), p. 626.
111. Whymant, *Stalin's Spy*, p. 182.
112. Matthews, *An Impeccable*, p. 316.
113. Major General A.K. Kazakovtsev quoted in Alvin D. Coox, 1985, *Nomonhan: Japan Against Russia, 1939* (Stanford: Stanford University Press), p. 1,079.
114. Minister of Foreign Affairs Joachim von Ribbentrop quoted in Andrew, *The Secret*, p. 627.
115. Johnson, *An Instance*, p. 157.

116. Coox, *Nomonhan*, p. 1,036.
117. Whymant, *Stalin's Spy*, p. 196.
118. Stuart D. Goldman, 2012, *Nomonhan, 1939: The Red Army's Victory that Shaped World War II* (Annapolis: Naval Institute Press), p. 176.
119. Matthews, *An Impeccable*, p. 296, p. 315.
120. Sorge ring radio transmission of 12 July 1941 quoted in Matthews, *An Impeccable*, p. 296.
121. Sorge ring radio transmission of 25/6 August 1941 quoted in Whymant, *Stalin's Spy*, p. 234.
122. Sorge ring radio transmission of 14 September 1941 quoted in Whymant, *Stalin's Spy*, p. 244.
123. Joseph Stalin quoted in Goldman, *Nomonhan, 1939*, p. 177.
124. Ezaki, *Kominterun*, p. 358.
125. Ozaki Hotsumi quoted in Johnson, *An Instance*, pp. 160–1.
126. Johnson, *An Instance*, p. 155.
127. Max Clausen quoted in Matthews, *An Impeccable*, p. 60.
128. Ozaki Hotsumi quoted in Johnson, *An Instance*, p. 127.
129. Richard Sorge quoted in Matthews, *An Impeccable*, p. 231.
130. Ozaki Hotsumi quoted in Willoughby, *Shanghai Conspiracy*, p. 63.
131. Willoughby, *Shanghai Conspiracy*, p. 64.
132. Prange, *Target Tokyo*, p. 37. *The Japan Advertiser* later merged with *The Japan Times*, which continues to publish to this day.
133. Richard Sorge quoted in Willoughby, *Shanghai Conspiracy*, p. 72. This "pipe of extraordinary design" appears to have been sourced for Sorge by Günther Stein in Shanghai. Willoughby, *Shanghai Conspiracy*, p. 277.
134. Kahn, David, 1996, *The Code-Breakers: The Comprehensive History of Secret Communication from Ancient Times to the Internet* (New York: Scribner), p. 650.
135. Eugen Ott quoted in Prange, *Target Tokyo*, pp. 42–3.
136. Richard Sorge quoted in Willoughby, *Shanghai Conspiracy*, p. 73.
137. Prange, *Target Tokyo*, p. 200.
138. Quoted in Whymant, *Stalin's Spy*, p. 103.
139. Willoughby, *Shanghai Conspiracy*, p. 27.
140. Prange, *Target Tokyo*, pp. 92–6, p. 101.
141. Willoughby, *Shanghai Conspiracy*, p. 60.
142. Whymant, *Stalin's Spy*, p. 134.
143. Matthews, *An Impeccable*, p. 133, p. 272.
144. Willoughby, *Shanghai Conspiracy*, pp. 64–5.
145. Prange, *Target Tokyo*, p. 347.
146. Testimony of Max Clausen in Willoughby, *Shanghai Conspiracy*, p. 241.
147. Ozaki Hotsuki, 1959, *Ikiteiru Yuda* [*The Living Judas*] (Tōkyō: Hachi-un Shoten).
148. Matthews, *An Impeccable*, pp. 319–21.
149. Johnson, *An Instance*, p. 176.
150. Willoughby, *Shanghai Conspiracy*, p. 117.

151. Matthews, *An Impeccable*, p. 321.
152. Prosecutor Yoshikawa Mitsusada quoted in Matthews, *An Impeccable*, p. 323.
153. Matthews, *An Impeccable*, p. 329.
154. Prange, *Target Tokyo*, p. 452.
155. It is claimed that much of Sorge's testimony was lost during the firebombing of Tokyo towards the end of World War II. What remains is reprinted in Willoughby, *Shanghai Conspiracy*, pp. 133–230.
156. Prange, *Target Tokyo*, p. 511.
157. Johnson, *An Instance*, p. 97.
158. Matthews, *An Impeccable*, p. 347.
159. Prange, *Target Tokyo*, p. 502.
160. Matthews, *An Impeccable*, pp. 344–5.

9. SORGE'S CONTEMPORARIES

1. Gordon W. Prange, 1985, *Target Tokyo: The Story of the Sorge Spy Ring* (New York: McGraw Hill), p. 312; Owen Matthews, 2019, *An Impeccable Spy: Richard Sorge, Stalin's Master Agent* (London: Bloomsbury), p. 341.
2. Charles A. Willoughby, 1952, *Shanghai Conspiracy: The Sorge Spy Ring* (New York: E.P. Dutton), p. 102.
3. Haslam, *The Soviet Union*, p. 95.
4. Evgenii Maksimovich Primakov, 1996, *Ocherki Istorii Rossiiskoi Vneshnei Razvedki* [*Essays on the History of Russian Foreign Intelligence*] (Moscow: Mezhdunarodnye Otnosheniya), vol. 4, essay 43, pp. 326–7.
5. Andrew, Christopher and Gordievsky, Oleg, 1990, *KGB: The Inside Story of Its Foreign Operations from Lenin to Gorbachev* (New York: Harper Collins), pp. 657–63.
6. Matthews, *An Impeccable Spy*, pp. 175–6.
7. Christopher Andrew, 2018, *The Secret World: A History of Intelligence* (New Haven: Yale University Press), p. 620.
8. Andrew and Gordievsky, *KGB*, p. 140.
9. Malcolm D. Kennedy, n.d., *Captain Malcolm Kennedy & Japan, 1917–1945*, the University of Sheffield, Kennedy Papers, MS 117, 236, https://www.sheffield.ac.uk/library/special/polopoly_fs/1.694153!/file/KennedyBiography.pdf, p. 119, p. 125.
10. Primakov, *Ocherki*, vol. 3, p. 11.
11. Quoted in Haslam, *The Soviet Union*, p. 80.
12. George A. Lensen, 1972, *The Strange Neutrality* (Tallahassee: The Diplomatic Press), pp. 251–2.
13. Quoted in Primakov, *Ocherki*, vol. 4, p. 333.
14. Quoted in Primakov, *Ocherki*, vol. 4, p. 334.
15. Sorge ring radio transmission of 25/6 August 1941 quoted in Goldman, *Nomonhan 1939: The Red Army's Victory that Shaped World War II* (Annapolis: Naval Institute Press), p. 176.

16. Richard Sorge quoted in Charles A. Willoughby, 1952, *Shanghai Conspiracy: The Sorge Spy Ring* (New York: EP Dutton), p. 170.
17. Aino Kuusinen, 1974, *The Rings of Destiny: Inside Soviet Russia from Lenin to Brezhnev* (New York: William Morrow), p. 48.
18. Malcolm D. Kennedy, 1969, *The Estrangement of Great Britain and Japan, 1917–35* (Manchester: Manchester University Press), p. 114.
19. Kennedy, *The Estrangement*, p. 114.
20. Kennedy, *Captain Malcolm Kennedy*, p. 123.
21. *The Daily News*, 1937, "Radek's concession in Soviet trial amazes packed court," 25 January.
22. Kennedy, *Captain Malcolm Kennedy*, p. 125.
23. Hugh Cortazzi, "The Death of Melville James Cox (1885–1940) in Tokyo on 29 July 1940," ch.39 in H. Cortazzi, 2013, *Britain and Japan: Biographical Portraits, Vol. III* (Leiden: Brill).
24. Kennedy, *Captain Malcolm Kennedy*, p. 125.
25. Charles A. Willoughby, 1952, *Shanghai Conspiracy: The Sorge Spy Ring* (New York: EP Dutton), pp. 253–4; US House of Representatives Committee on Un-American Activities, 1951, *Hearings Regarding Communist Espionage, First and Second Sessions* (Washington: Government Printing Office), p. 3,577.
26. Prange, *Target Tokyo*, p. 73.
27. Prange, *Target Tokyo*, p. 73.
28. Allen Weinstein, 2013, *Perjury: The Hiss-Chambers Case* (Stanford: Hoover Institution Press), p. 140.
29. Prange, *Target Tokyo*, p. 73.
30. William Maxwell Bickerton, 1934, "Third degree in Japan," *The Living Age*, 1 September 1934, pp. 30–4.
31. Robert Whymant, 1996, *Stalin's Spy: Richard Sorge and the Tokyo Espionage Ring* (New York: St Martin's Press), p. 69.
32. Willoughby, *Shanghai Conspiracy*, pp. 18–19.
33. Willoughby, *Shanghai Conspiracy*, p. 18.
34. Willoughby, *Shanghai Conspiracy*, p. 19.
35. Willoughby, *Shanghai Conspiracy*, p. 19.
36. Kuusinen, *The Rings*, pp. 18–19.
37. Kuusinen, *The Rings*, p. 70, p. 77, p. 229.
38. Kuusinen, *The Rings*, p. 30.
39. Kuusinen, *The Rings*, p. 88, pp. 103–5.
40. Kuusinen, *The Rings*, pp. 103–7.
41. Kuusinen, *The Rings*, pp. 112–13.
42. Kuusinen, *The Rings*, p. 107.
43. Kuusinen, *The Rings*, p. 111.
44. Kuusinen, *The Rings*, p. 16.
45. General Semen P. Uritskii quoted in Kuusinen, *The Rings*, p. 119.
46. Kuusinen, *The Rings*, p. 119.

47. Kuusinen, *The Rings*, p. 121.
48. Kuusinen, *The Rings*, p. 122.
49. Kuusinen, *The Rings*, pp. 122–3.
50. Kuusinen, *The Rings*, p. 124.
51. Kuusinen, *The Rings*, p. 16.
52. Kuusinen, *The Rings*, p. 170.
53. Primakov, *Ocherki*, vol. 3, essay 14, p. 106.
54. Primakov, *Ocherki*, vol. 3, essay 14, p. 106.
55. Primakov, *Ocherki*, vol. 3, essay 14, pp. 106–7.
56. Primakov, *Ocherki*, vol. 3, essay 18, pp. 128–9.
57. Ben Macintyre, 2021, *Agent Sonya* (London: Penguin), p. 101.
58. Macintyre, *Agent Sonya*, p. 111.
59. Macintyre, *Agent Sonya*, p. 115.
60. Ursula Hamburger quoted in Macintyre, *Agent Sonya*, p. 113.
61. Macintyre, *Agent Sonya*, p. 106, p. 113, p. 118.
62. Macintyre, *Agent Sonya*, p. 327.
63. Weinstein, *Perjury*, p. 210.
64. Nadezhda Ulanovskaya quoted in Weinstein, *Perjury*, p. 619. Nadezhda Ulanovskaya was the wife of Alaksandr Ulanovskii, who was Richard Sorge's senior officer when Sorge was first sent to Shanghai in 1930.
65. John Earl Haynes and Harvey Klehr, 1999, *Venona: Decoding Soviet Espionage in America* (New Haven: Yale University Press), p. 87
66. Haynes, John Earl, Harvey Klehr, and Alexander Vassiliev, 2009, *Spies: The Rise and Fall of the KGB in America* (New Haven: Yale University Press), pp. 214–15.
67. Thomas Rid, 2020, *Active Measures: The Secret History of Disinformation and Political Warfare* (New York: Farrar, Straus and Giroux), p. 52.
68. Haynes et al., *Spies*, p. 162.
69. John L. Spivak, 1939, *Honorable Spy: Exposing Japanese Military Intrigue in the United States* (New York: Modern Age Books).
70. Haynes et al., *Spies*, p. 164.
71. Haynes et al., *Spies*, pp. 322–3.
72. Bruce R. Craig, 2004, *Treasonable Doubt: The Harry Dexter White Spy Case* (Lawrence: University Press of Kansas), p. 196.
73. Craig, *Treasonable Doubt*, p. 42.
74. Andrew and Gordievsky, *KGB*, p. 230.
75. Venona decrypt quoted in Haynes et al., *Spies*, p. 260.
76. Craig, *Treasonable Doubt*, p. 46.
77. Haynes and Klehr, *Venona*, p. 141.
78. Haynes et al., *Spies*, p. 258.
79. Civil Service Commission file quoted in US House of Representatives, 1948, *Hearings Regarding Communist Espionage in the United States Government*, Public Law 601 (Washington: Government Printing Office), p. 615.
80. Craig, *Treasonable Doubt*, p. 107.

81. Haynes and Klehr, *Venona*, pp. 136–45.
82. Craig, *Treasonable Doubt*, pp. 149–51.
83. Robert Skidelsky, 2000, *John Maynard Keynes: Fighting for Britain, 1937–1946* (London: Macmillan), p. 253.
84. Haynes et al., *Spies*, p. 260.
85. Weinstein, *Perjury*, p. 257.
86. Craig, *Treasonable Doubt*, p. 52, p. 54.
87. Craig, *Treasonable Doubt*, p. 44.
88. Craig, *Treasonable Doubt*, p. 181.
89. Craig, *Treasonable Doubt*, p. 182.
90. Saitō Michio, 2022, *Nichi-Bei Kaisen to Futari no Soren Spai* [*Two Soviet Spies and the Outbreak of the Japan-US War*] (Tōkyō: PHP Kenkyūjo).
91. David Rees, 1973, *Harry Dexter White: A Study in Paradox* (New York: Coward, McCann & Geoghegan), p. 341.
92. Craig, *Treasonable Doubt*, p. 193.
93. Craig, *Treasonable Doubt*, p. 192.
94. Senator Charles E. Potter quoted in Craig, *Treasonable Doubt*, p. 178.
95. John Koster, 2012, *Operation Snow: How a Soviet Mole in FDR's White House Triggered Pearl Harbor* (Washington, DC: Regnery History); Saitō, *Nichi-Bei Kaisen*.
96. Vitalii G. Pavlov, 1996, *Operatsiya 'Sneg'* [*Operation Snow*] (Moskva: Geya).
97. Quoted in Craig, *Treasonable Doubt*, p. 250.
98. Craig, *Treasonable Doubt*, pp. 250–1.
99. Haynes et al., *Spies*, p. 220, p. 238.
100. Cordell Hull, 1948, *Memoirs of Cordell Hull* (New York: Macmillan), p. 1,073.
101. Norman Hill, 1948, "Was there an ultimatum before Pearl Harbor?," *The American Journal of International Law*, 42:2, pp. 355–67, p. 364.
102. Harry Dexter White quoted in Benn Steil, 2013, "Red White: Why a founding father of postwar capitalism spied for the Soviets," *Foreign Affairs*, March/April, p. 125.
103. Whittaker Chambers quoted in Weinstein, *Perjury*, p. 256.
104. Paul Nitze quoted in Craig, *Treasonable Doubt*, p. 292.
105. *The Daily Worker* quoted in Weinstein, *Perjury*, p. 301.
106. Herbert Solow quoted in Weinstein, *Perjury*, p. 137.
107. Lloyd Stryker quoted in Weinstein, *Perjury*, p. 485.
108. Alger Hiss quoted in Weinstein, *Perjury*, p. 79.
109. Lloyd Stryker quoted in Weinstein, *Perjury*, p. 485.
110. Weinstein, *Perjury*, p. 35.
111. Alger Hiss quoted in Susan Jacoby, 2009, *Alger Hiss and the Battle for History* (New Haven: Yale University Press), p. 173.
112. Weinstein, *Perjury*, p. 18.
113. Weinstein, *Perjury*, pp. 155–6, p. 188, p. 249.
114. Weinstein, *Perjury*, pp. 251–2, pp. 260–1.
115. Weinstein, *Perjury*, p. 185, p. 338.

116. Quoted in Weinstein, *Perjury*, p. 262.
117. Weinstein, *Perjury*, p. 266.
118. Weinstein, *Perjury*, pp. 270–1.
119. Weinstein, *Perjury*, p. 275.
120. Weinstein, *Perjury*, pp. 277–80.
121. Alger Hiss quoted in Weinstein, *Perjury*, p. 318.
122. Whittaker Chambers quoted in Weinstein, *Perjury*, p. 69, p. 389.
123. Serhii Plokhy, 2011, *Yalta: The Price of Peace* (New York: Penguin), p. 357.
124. Alger Hiss quoted in Fetter, Henry D., 2020, "Alger Hiss at Yalta: A Reassessment of Hiss's Arguments against Including Any of the Soviet Republics as Initial UN Members," *Journal of Cold War Studies*, 22:1, pp. 46–88, p. 47.
125. Isaac Don Levine quoted in Fetter, "Alger Hiss," p. 48.
126. Fetter, "Alger Hiss," p. 48, p. 70.
127. Fetter, "Alger Hiss," p. 79.
128. Wilson Center Digital Archive, "Yalta Conference Agreement," 11 February 1945.
129. Avalon Project, "Atlantic Charter," 14 August 1941.
130. Charles E. Bohlen, 1973, *Witness to History, 1929–1969* (New York: W.W. Norton & Co.), p. 196.
131. Alger Hiss quoted in Weinstein, *Perjury*, p. 373.
132. State Department Inter-Divisional Area Committee on the Far East quoted in Seokwoo Lee, 2001, "Towards a Framework for the Resolution of the Territorial Dispute over the Kurile Islands," *Boundary and Territory Briefing*, 3:6, pp. 1–55, p. 1.
133. State Department official Erle R. Dickover quoted in Weinstein, *Perjury*, pp. 380–1.
134. Hasegawa, Tsuyoshi, 2005, *Racing the Enemy: Stalin, Truman, and the Surrender of Japan* (Cambridge, MA: The Belknap Press), p. 34
135. US State Department, Office of the Historian, "261, 'Memorandum of the division of territorial studies,' CAC-302, December 28, 1944," https://history.state.gov/historicaldocuments/frus1945Malta/d261
136. Edward Stettinius quoted in Fetter, "Alger Hiss," p. 85.
137. Weinstein, *Perjury*, p. 381.
138. Maria Schmidt quoted in Weinstein, *Perjury*, p. 598.
139. Aleksandr Panyushkin quoted in Weinstein, *Perjury*, pp. 301–2.
140. Eduard Mark, 2009, "In *Re* Alger Hiss: A final verdict from the archives of the KGB," *Journal of Cold War Studies*, 11:3, pp. 26–67, p. 36.
141. Weinstein, *Perjury*, p. 370.
142. W.G. Krivitsky, 1939, *In Stalin's Secret Service* (New York: Harper & Brothers).
143. Bruce Craig, 2008, "A matter of espionage: Alger Hiss, Harry Dexter White, and Igor Gouzenko—The Canadian Connection Reassessed," *Intelligence and National Security*, 15:2, pp. 211–24, pp. 214–18.
144. Weinstein, *Perjury*, p. 376.
145. Andrew and Gordievsky, *KGB*, p. 285.

146. Haynes et al., *Spies*; Allen Weinstein and Alexander Vassiliev, 1999, *The Haunted Wood: Soviet Espionage in America—The Stalin Era* (New York: Random House).
147. Haynes et al., *Spies*, p. 1.
148. Haynes and Klehr, *Venona*.
149. VENONA, 1945, "KGB interviews GRU agent and net controller name ALES 30 March (Release 3)," https://media.defense.gov/2021/Aug/01/2002818545/-1/-1/0/30MAR_KGB_INTERVIEWS_GRU_AGENT.PDF
150. Mark, "In *Re*," p. 62; Plokhy, *Yalta*, p. 353. Others report that only four US officials visited Moscow after the Yalta conference. Two were Stettinius and Hiss. The others were Director of the Office of European Affairs H. Freeman Matthews and Stettinius's press aide Wilder Foote. Haynes and Klehr, *Venona*, p. 172
151. VENONA, 1943, "Five GRU sources are named. Milton Schwartz needs a loan to pay off debts. KGB (or perhaps Naval GRU) has mentioned a person from State Department named Hiss, 28 September 1943" (Release 4), https://media.defense.gov/2021/Jul/29/2002815608/-1/-1/0/28SEP_GRU_SOURCES.PDF
152. Whymant, *Stalin's Spy*, p. 89.
153. Quoted in Whymant, *Stalin's Spy*, p. 87.
154. Poretsky, *Our Own*, p. 22.
155. Walter Krivitsky quoted in Gary Kern, 2004, *A Death in Washington: Walter G. Krivitsky and the Stalin Terror* (New York: Enigma Books), p. 6.
156. Krivitsky, *In Stalin's*, p. 16.
157. Krivitsky, *In Stalin's*, p. 17.
158. Miyake Masaki, 2010, *Stalin-no-tainichi jōhō kōsaku* [*Stalin's intelligence manoeuvres against Japan*] (Tōkyō: Heibonsha), p. 33.
159. Krivitsky, *In Stalin's*, p. 17.
160. Miyake, *Stalin-no-tainichi*, p. 33.
161. Krivitsky, *In Stalin's*, p. 18.
162. Miyake, *Stalin-no-tainichi*, p. 50.
163. Krivitsky, *In Stalin's*, p. 4.
164. Ben Fisher, 1999, "An unwitting spy: The ambassador who knew too much," *American Intelligence Journal*, 19:1/2, pp. 67–9, p. 67.
165. Andrew and Gordievsky, *KGB*, p. 267.
166. Whittaker Chambers, 1952, *Witness* (New York: Random House), p. 30.
167. Gordon Brook-Shepherd, 1989, *The Storm Birds* (New York: Weidenfeld & Nicolson), pp. 69–76.
168. Brook-Shepherd, *The Storm Birds*, pp. 80–4.
169. Hiroaki Kuromiya and Andrzj Pepłoński, 2013, "Kōzō Izumi and the Soviet breach of Imperial Japanese diplomatic codes," *Intelligence and National Security*, 28:6, pp. 769–84, pp. 770–1.
170. Kuromiya and Pepłoński, "Kōzō Izumi," p. 771.
171. Kuromiya and Pepłoński, "Kōzō Izumi," p. 771.
172. Kuromiya and Pepłoński, "Kōzō Izumi," p. 772.

173. Kuromiya and Pepłoński, "Kōzō Izumi," pp. 772–3.
174. Kuromiya and Pepłoński, "Kōzō Izumi," p. 774.
175. Kuromiya and Pepłoński, "Kōzō Izumi," p. 774.
176. Kuromiya and Pepłoński, "Kōzō Izumi," p. 775.
177. Kuromiya and Pepłoński, "Kōzō Izumi," p. 777.
178. Primakov, *Ocherki*, vol. 3, p. 316.
179. Primakov, *Ocherki*, vol. 4, pp. 326–7.
180. Primakov, *Ocherki*, vol. 4, p. 328.
181. Shalett, Sidney, 1946, "Axis plot to kill Stalin confirmed," *The New York Times*, 22 September.
182. Hiyama Yoshiaki, 1982, *Sokoku wo Soren ni utta 36 nin no nihonjin* [*36 Japanese who sold out their fatherland to the Soviet Union*] (Sankei), pp. 30–1.
183. Kuromiya and Pepłoński, "Kōzō Izumi," p. 783.
184. Andrew, *The Secret*, p. 627.
185. Kuromiya and Pepłoński, "Kōzō Izumi," p. 777, p. 782.
186. *Shokun!*, 1994, "Futari no nihonjin supai—gokuhi shiryō ga terashi dashita gendai-shi no anbu" ["Two Japanese spies: The dark side of modern history illuminated by top-secret materials"], 26:6, June, pp. 128–42.
187. Kuromiya and Pepłoński, "Kōzō Izumi," p. 782.

CONCLUSION: HOW TO SPY ON JAPAN

1. *Nihon Keizai Shimbun*, 1983, "Supai Tengoku," 14 April.
2. Lensen, *The Russian*, p. 252.
3. Nikolai Yanzhul quoted in Derevyanko, *Russkaya Razvedka*, p. 256.
4. Richard Sorge quoted in Prange, *Target Tokyo*, p. 469.
5. Richard Sorge quoted in Prange, *Target Tokyo*, p. 498.
6. Johnson, *An Instance*, p. 170.
7. Richard Sorge quoted in Willoughby, *Shanghai Conspiracy*, p. 72.
8. Max Clausen quoted in Willoughby, *Shanghai Conspiracy*, p. 238.
9. Nagai Yasuji, 2019, "Final report to Hirohito about Sorge spy ring hid lax oversight," *Asahi Shimbun*, 5 November, https://www.asahi.com/ajw/articles/13057472
10. Whittaker Chambers, 2014, *Witness* (Washington, DC: Regnery History), pp. 6–7.
11. Sir Richard Dearlove quoted in Simon Kuper, 2021, *The Happy Traitor* (London: Profile Books), p. 118.

BIBLIOGRAPHY

Abrikossov, Dmitrii I., 1964, *Revelations of a Russian Diplomat: The Memoirs of Dmitrii I. Abrikossov* (Seattle: University of Washington Press).

Afinogenov, Gregory, 2020, *Spies and Scholars: Chinese Secrets and Imperial Russia's Quest for World Power* (Cambridge: Harvard University Press).

Ambrose, Stephen, 1984, *Eisenhower, vol. 2: The President* (New York: Simon & Schuster).

Andrew, Christopher, 2018, *The Secret World: A History of Intelligence* (New Haven: Yale University Press).

Andrew, Christopher and Gordievsky, Oleg, 1990, *KGB: The Inside Story of Its Foreign Operations from Lenin to Gorbachev* (New York: Harper Collins).

Andrew, Christopher and Mitrokhin, Vasili, 1999, *The Sword and the Shield: The Mitrokhin Archive and the Secret History of the KGB* (New York: Basic Books).

Andrew, Christopher and Mitrokhin, Vasili, 2005, *The World Was Going Our Way: The KGB and the Battle for the Third World* (New York: Basic Books).

Ariyoshi, Koji, 2000, *From Kona to Yenan: The Political Memoirs of Koji Ariyoshi*, edited by Beechert, A.M. and Beechert, E.D. (Honolulu: University of Hawai'i Press)

Auslin, Michael, 2004, *Negotiating with Imperialism: The Unequal Treaties and the Culture of Japanese Diplomacy* (Cambridge, MA: Harvard University Press).

Avalon Project, "Atlantic Charter," 14 August 1941, https://avalon.law.yale.edu/wwii/atlantic.asp.

Barmin, Fedor, 2013, "Russkii Samurai Ryabov" ["Russian samurai Ryabov"], *Spetsnaz Rossii*, 31 May, http://www.specnaz.ru/articles/200/8/1838.htm

Bickerton, William Maxwell, 1934, "Third degree in Japan," *The Living Age*, 1 September 1934, pp. 30–4.

Bird, Isabella, 2009, *Korea and Her Neighbours* (Oxford: Routledge).

Bojanowska, Edyta M., 2018, *A World of Empires: The Russian Voyage of the Frigate* Pallada (Cambridge, MA: Belknap Press).

Brook-Shepherd, Gordon, 1989, *The Storm Birds* (New York: Weidenfeld & Nicolson).

Budiansky, Stephen, 2000, *Battle of Wits: The Complete Story of Codebreaking in World War II* (New York: Free Press).

Bunich, Igor' L., 2000, *Dolgaya Doroga na Golgofa* [*The long road to Golgotha*] (St. Petersburg: Energii).

Burleigh, Bennett, 1905, *Empire of the East; or, Japan and Russia at War, 1904–5* (London: Chapman & Hall).

Canham, Erwin D., 1958, *Commitment to Freedom: The Story of The Christian Science Monitor* (Boston: Houghton Mifflin).

Cardiff Times, 1905, "Trial of a spy," Press Association Special War Telegram, 21 January, https://newspapers.library.wales/view/3432542/3432549

Chambers, Whittaker, 2014, *Witness* (Washington, DC: Regnery History).

Chang, Jon K., 2016, *Burnt by the Sun: The Koreans of the Russian Far East* (Honolulu: University of Hawai'i Press).

Chekhov, Anton, 2019, *Sakhalin Island* (Surrey: Alma Classics).

Chiba Isao, 2014, "From cooperation to conflict: Japanese-Russian relations from the formation of the Russo-Japanese entente to the Siberian Intervention," in Tosh Minohara, Tze-ki Hon, Evan Dawley (eds), *The Decade of the Great War: Japan and the Wider World in the 1910s* (Leiden: Brill),

Chuev, Feliks, 1993, *Molotov Remembers: Inside Kremlin Politics* (Chicago: Ivan R. Dee).

Clark, Grover, 1935, "The sale of the Chinese Eastern," *Current History*, 42:2, May 1935, pp. 221–4.

Clements, Jonathan, 2012, *Mannerheim: President, Soldier, Spy* (London: Haus).

Connaughton, Richard M., 2003, *Rising Sun and Tumbling Bear: Russia's War with Japan* (London: Cassell).

Connaughton, Richard M., 2017, *The Republic of the Ushakovka* (London: Routledge).

"Convention between Russia and China for lease to Russia of Port Arthur, Talienwan, and the adjacent waters," 1910, *The American Journal of International Law*, 4:4, Oct. 1910, pp. 289–91.

Coox, Alvin D., 1985, *Nomonhan: Japan Against Russia, 1939* (Stanford: Stanford University Press).

Coox, Alvin D., 1998, "The lesser of two hells: NKVD general G.S. Lyushkov's defection to Japan, 1938–1945, part 1," *The Journal of Slavic Military Studies*, 11:3, pp. 145–86.

Coox, Alvin D., 1998, "The lesser of two hells: NKVD general G.S. Lyushkov's defection to Japan, 1938–1945, part 2," *The Journal of Slavic Military Studies*, 11:4, pp. 72–110.

Corbett, Julian, 2015, *Maritime Operations in the Russo-Japanese War, 1904–1905: Vol. 1* (Annapolis: Naval Institute Press).

Corkill, Edan and Johnson, Chalmers, 2010, "Sorge's spy is brought in from the cold: A Soviet-Okinawan connection," *The Asia-Pacific Journal: Japan Focus*, 8:6, no. 1.

Cortazzi, Hugh, "The Death of Melville James Cox (1885–1940) in Tokyo on 29 July 1940," ch.39 in H. Cortazzi, 2013, *Britain and Japan: Biographical Portraits, Vol. III* (Leiden: Brill).

Cotterell, Arthur, 2009, *Western Power in Asia: Its Slow Rise and Swift Fall—1415–1999* (Singapore: John Wiley).

Craig, Bruce, 2008, "A matter of espionage: Alger Hiss, Harry Dexter White, and Igor Gouzenko—The Canadian Connection Reassessed," *Intelligence and National Security*, 15:2, pp. 211–24.

Craig, Bruce R., 2004, *Treasonable Doubt: The Harry Dexter White Spy Case* (Lawrence: University Press of Kansas).

Daily News, 1937, "Radek's concession in Soviet trial amazes packed court," 25 January.

Datsyshen, V.G., 2021, "Military Japanese studies in the Russian Far East in the early 20th century," *Russian Japanology Review*, 1, pp. 117–43.

Deacon, Richard, 1975, *A History of the Russian Secret Service* (London: New English Library).

Derevyanko, Il'ya, 2018, *Nauchnye i Nauchno-Populyarnye Proizvedeniya. Tom 2. Russkaya Razvedka i Kontrrazvedka v Voine 1904–1905 gg.* [*Scientific and Popular Scientific Works. Vol. 2. Russian Intelligence and Counterintelligence in the War of 1904–05*] (Moscow: Yauza).

Drummond, Andrew, 2017, *The Intriguing Life and Ignominious Death of Maurice Benyovszky* (Oxon: Taylor & Francis).

Dunscomb, Paul E., 2011, *Japan's Siberian Intervention, 1918–1922: "A great disobedience against the people"* (Lanham: Lexington).

Embassy of the Russian Federation to Japan, "History of the Russian Diplomatic Missions in Japan," https://tokyo.mid.ru/web/tokyo-en/hakodate, accessed 15 July 2021.

Encyclopædia Britannica, "Stepan Osipovich Makarov." Britannica Academic.

Fedman, David, 2020, *Seeds of Control: Japan's Empire of Forestry in Colonial Korea* (Seattle: University of Washington Press).

Fetter, Henry D., 2020, "Alger Hiss at Yalta: A Reassessment of Hiss's Arguments against Including Any of the Soviet Republics as Initial UN Members," *Journal of Cold War Studies*, 22:1, pp. 46–88

Fischer, Ben B., 1997, *Okhrana: The Paris Operations of the Russian Imperial Police* (Washington, DC: Center for the Study of Intelligence).

Fisher, Ben, 1999, "An unwitting spy: The ambassador who knew too much," *American Intelligence Journal*, 19:1/2, pp. 67–9.

Fletcher, Miles, 1979, "Intellectuals and fascism in early Showa Japan," *The Journal of Asian Studies*, 39:1, pp. 39–63.

Fletcher, Miles, 1983, "Review of *Ōsugi Sakae, Anarchist in Taishō Japan* by Thomas A. Stanley," *The Journal of Japanese Studies*, 9:2, pp. 399–404.

Flory, Harriette, 1977, "The Arcos raid and the rupture of Anglo-Soviet relations, 1927," *Journal of Contemporary History*, 12:4, pp. 707–23.

Foreign, Commonwealth & Development Office, "UK exposes series of Russian cyber attacks against Olympics and Paralympic Games," 19 October 2020, www.gov.uk/government/news/uk-exposes-series-of-russian-cyber-attacks-against-olympic-and-paralympic-games

Fowler, Josephine, 2004, "From East to West and West to East: Ties of Solidarity in the Pan-Pacific Revolutionary Trade Union Movement, 1923–1934," *International Labor and Working-Class History*, 66 (Fall 2004), pp. 99–117.

Franz, Edgar, 2005, *Philipp Franz von Siebold and Russian Policy and Action on Opening Japan to the West* (Munich: Iudicium).

Garver, John W., 1991, "The Soviet Union and the Xi'an Incident," *The Australian Journal of Chinese Affairs*, 26, pp. 145–75.

Getty, Arch J. and Oleg V. Naumov, 1999, *The Road to Terror: Stalin and the Self-Destruction of the Bolsheviks, 1932–1939* (New Haven: Yale University Press).

Gevorkyan, Nataliya, Natalya Timakova, Andrei Kolesnikov, 2000, *First Person: An Astonishingly Frank Self-Portrait by Russia's President Vladimir Putin* (New York: Public Affairs)

Goldman, Stuart D., 2012, *Nomonhan 1939: The Red Army's Victory that Shaped World War II* (Annapolis: Naval Institute Press).

Golovnin, Vasilii, 2020, *Captive in Japan*, edited by William de Lange (Toyo Press)

Goncharov, Ivan Aleksandrovich, 2018, *Fregat "Pallada"* [*Frigate "Pallada"*] (St Petersburg: Azbuka).

Gurinov, Sergey Leonidovich, 2021, "Activities of Russian naval intelligence during the Russo-Japanese War of 1904–1905," *Bulletin Social-Economic and Humanitarian Research*, 10:12, pp. 50–7.

Hamada Kenji, 1936, *Prince Ito* (Tokyo: Sanseido).

Harrison, John A., 1953, *Japan's Northern Frontier: A Preliminary Study in Colonization and Expansion with Special Reference to the Relations of Japan and Russia* (Gainesville: University of Florida Press).

Hargreaves, Reginald, 1962, *Red Sun Rising: The Siege of Port Arthur* (Philadelphia: Lippincott).

Haruna Mikio, 2000, *Himitsu no Fairu: CIA no tainichi kōsaku* [*Secret files: The CIA's work against Japan*] (Tōkyō: Shinchōsha).

Hasegawa, Tsuyoshi, 1998, *The Northern Territories Dispute and Russo-Japanese Relations: Between War and Peace, 1697–1985* (Berkeley: University of California Press).

Hasegawa, Tsuyoshi, 2005, *Racing the Enemy: Stalin, Truman, and the Surrender of Japan* (Cambridge, MA: The Belknap Press).

Haslam, Jonathan, 1992, *The Soviet Union and the Threat from the East, 1933–41* (Pittsburgh: University of Pittsburgh Press).

Haslam, Jonathan, 2016, *Near and Distant Neighbours: A New History of Soviet Intelligence* (Oxford: Oxford University Press).

Hata Ikuhiko, 2014, *Mei-to-An-no Nomonhan Senshi* [*Light and Dark in the History of the Battle of Nomonhan*] (Tōkyō: PHP Kenkyūjo).

Hattori Ryūji, 2010, *Nitchū rekishi ninshiki: "Tanaka jōsōbun" o meguru sōkoku 1927–2010* [*Understanding Sino-Japanese History—Conflict over the Tanaka Memorial 1927–2010*] (Tokyo: Tokyo Daigaku Shuppankai).

Hattori Ryūji, 2012, "Controversies over the Tanaka Memorial," ch.4 in Yang, D., Liu, J., Mitani, H., and Gordon, A. (eds), *Toward a History Beyond Borders* (Cambridge, MA: Harvard University Asia Center).

Haynes, John Earl and Harvey Klehr, 1999, *Venona: Decoding Soviet Espionage in America* (New Haven: Yale University Press).

Haynes, John Earl, Harvey Klehr, and Alexander Vassiliev, 2009, *Spies: The Rise and Fall of the KGB in America* (New Haven: Yale University Press).

Heller, Jeffrey, 2016, "Palestinian leader Abbas was KGB spy in 1980s—Israeli researchers," *Reuters*, 8 September, www.reuters.com/article/israel-palestinians-abbas-idINKCN11E29W

Hill, Alexander, 2016, *The Red Army and the Second World War* (Cambridge: Cambridge University Press).

Hill, Norman, 1948, "Was there an ultimatum before Pearl Harbor?" *The American Journal of International Law*, 42:2, pp. 355–67.

Hiraoka Matsuhide, 1982, *Nichiro kōshō shiwa—Ishin zengo no Nihon to Roshia* [*The History of Negotiations between Japan and Russia: Japan & Russia around the Time of the Restoration*] (Tōkyō: Harashobō).

Hiyama Yoshiaki, 1982, *Sokoku wo Soren ni utta 36 nin no nihonjin* [*36 Japanese who sold out their fatherland to the Soviet Union*] (Sankei).

Horne, Alistair, 2015, *Hubris: The Tragedy of War in the Twentieth Century* (London: Weidenfeld & Nicolson).

Hull, Cordell, 1948, *Memoirs of Cordell Hull* (New York: Macmillan).

Hunter, Janet, 1984, *Concise Dictionary of Modern Japanese History* (Berkeley: University of California Press).

Husel, Borjigin, 2001, "Manshūkoku-gun shōshō Guo Uen Ton ni tsuite—Jichi shugisha, Soren-gun chōhōin toshite no shōgai" ["A study of Guo Wen-tong, Major General of the Manchukuo Army—His life as an autonomist and USSR Army's secret agent"], *Bulletin of Japanese Association for Mongolian Studies*, 31, pp. 107–27.

Iklé, Frank W., 1967, "The Triple Intervention: Japan's lesson in the diplomacy of imperialism," *Monumenta Nipponica*, 22:1/2, pp. 122–30.

Inaba, Chiharu, 1998, "Franco-Russian intelligence cooperation against Japan during the Russo-Japanese war, 1904–05," *Japanese Slavic and East European Studies*, 19, pp. 1–23.

Iwaki Shigeyuki, 2013, *Nomonhan-jiken no kyozō to jitsuzō—Nichiro-no bunken de yomitoku sono shinsō* [*Falsehoods and realities of the Nomonhan Incident: Its depths deciphered from Japanese and Russian documents*] (Tōkyō: Sairyūsha).

Iwashita Tetsunori and Carlander, Anna L., 2021, *Mu-ru no kunō* [*Moor's agony*] (Tōkyō: Yūbunshoin).

Jacob, Frank, 2018, *The Russo-Japanese War and its Shaping of the Twentieth Century* (London: Routledge).

Japan Times, 2000, "Spy against Japan: Letters shed new light on Nosaka's acts," 22 October, https://www.japantimes.co.jp/news/2000/10/22/national/letters-shed-new-light-on-nosakas-espionage-acts/

Japan Times, 2004, "French Reporter Conducted Espionage for Russia in Russo-Japanese War," 24 October, https://www.japantimes.co.jp/news/2004/10/24/national/french-reporter-conducted-espionage-for-russia-in-russo-japanese-war/

Johnson, Chalmers, 1964, *An Instance of Treason: Ozaki Hotsumi and the Sorge Spy Ring* (Stanford: Stanford University Press).

Joint Chiefs of Staff, 2021, *DOD Dictionary of Military and Associated Terms*, https://www.jcs.mil/Portals/36/Documents/Doctrine/pubs/dictionary.pdf

Jones, Colin P.A., 2019, "How the last czar shaped Japan's courts," *The Japan Times*, 2 January, https://www.japantimes.co.jp/community/2019/01/02/issues/last-czar-shaped-japans-courts/

Kahn, David, 1996, *The Code-Breakers: The Comprehensive History of Secret Communication from Ancient Times to the Internet* (New York: Scribner).

Kaplan, Zackary, 2012, "Anti-Americanism in Zengakuren 1957–1960," *Studies on Asia*, series IV, 2:1, March.

Kapur, Nick, 2018, *Japan at the Crossroads: Conflict and Compromise after Ampo* (Cambridge, MA: Harvard University Press).

Kato Kiyofumi, 2006, *Mantetsu Zenshi* [*The Comprehensive History of Mantetsu*] (Tōkyō: Kōdansha).

Kennedy, Charles Stuart, 1986, "Interview with Douglas MacArthur II," The Association for Diplomatic Studies and Training Foreign Affairs Oral History Project, Library of Congress, https://tile.loc.gov/storage-services/service/mss/mfdip/2004/2004mac03/2004mac03.pdf

Kennedy, Malcolm D., n.d., *Captain Malcolm Kennedy & Japan, 1917–1945*, The University of Sheffield, Kennedy Papers, MS 117, 236, https://

www.sheffield.ac.uk/library/special/polopoly_fs/1.694153!/file/KennedyBiography.pdf

Kennedy, Malcolm D., 1969, *The Estrangement of Great Britain and Japan, 1917–35* (Manchester: Manchester University Press).

Kern, Gary, 2004, *A Death in Washington: Walter G. Krivitsky and the Stalin Terror* (New York: Enigma Books).

Kimura Hiroshi, 2005, *Nichiro Kokkyō Kōshō-shi* [*History of Border Negotiations between Japan and Russia*] (Tokyo: Kakugawa Sensho).

Kinoshita Junji, 1973, *Ottō to Yobareru Nihonjin* [*A Japanese Called Otto*] (Tōkyō: Kōdansha).

Kobayashi, Kai, 2021, *Resurrected* (Independently published).

Koda, Yoji, 2005, "The Russo-Japanese War: Primary causes of Japanese success," *Naval War College Review*, 58:2, pp. 10–44.

Kondō Eizō, 1949, *Cominterun-no-missshi-Nihon Kyōsantō Sōsei Hiwa* [*The Secret Messenger of the Comintern—Secret History of the Founding of the JCP*] (Tokyo: Bunkahyōronsha).

Kornilov, A., 2004, "News from Japan (Edo, 1859)," ch.5 in Wells, D. (ed.), *Russian Views of Japan, 1792–1913: An Anthology of Travel Writing* (London: Routledge).

Koster, John, 2012, *Operation Snow: How a Soviet Mole in FDR's White House Triggered Pearl Harbor* (Washington, DC: Regnery History).

Kotani Ken, 2008, "Japanese intelligence and the Soviet-Japanese border conflicts in the 1930s," 33rd Conference of International Military History, National Institute of Defence Studies (NIDS), http://www.nids.mod.go.jp/publication/senshi/pdf/200803/09.pdf

Kouvenhoven, Arlette, and Forrer, Matthi, 2000, *Siebold and Japan: His Life and Work* (Leiden: Hotei).

Kovacevic, Filip, 2022, "Ian Fleming's Soviet rival: Roman Kim and Soviet spy fiction during the early Cold War," *Intelligence and National Security*, 37:4, pp. 593–606.

Krivitsky, W.G., 1939, *In Stalin's Secret Service* (New York: Harper & Brothers).

Kulanov, Aleksandr, 2011, "Vasilii Oshchepkov: Put' ot niotkuda v nikuda" ["Vasilii Oshchepkov: The path from nowhere to nowhere"], *Yaponiya Nashikh Dnei*, 1:7, pp. 85–101.

Kulanov, Aleksandr, 2012, "Agent 'R'," *Rodina*, 8, pp. 93–5.

Kuromiya, Hiroaki, 2011, "The mystery of Nomonhan, 1939," *Journal of Slavic Military Studies*, 24:4, pp. 659–77.

Kuromiya, Hiroaki, 2016, "The Battle of Lake Khasan Reconsidered," *The Journal of Slavic Military Studies*, 29:1, 99–109.

Kuromiya, Hiroaki and Andrzj Pepłoński, 2013, "Kōzō Izumi and the Soviet breach of Imperial Japanese diplomatic codes," *Intelligence and National Security*, 28:6, pp. 769–84.

Kuper, Simon, 2021, *The Happy Traitor* (London: Profile Books).

Kuusinen, Aino, 1974, *The Rings of Destiny: Inside Soviet Russia from Lenin to Brezhnev* (New York: William Morrow).

Lee, Seokwoo, 2001, "Towards a Framework for the Resolution of the Territorial Dispute over the Kurile Islands," *Boundary and Territory Briefing*, 3:6, pp. 1–55.

Lensen, George A., 1954, *Report from Hokkaido: The Remains of Russian Culture in Northern Japan* (Hakodate: The Municipal Library of Hakodate).

Lensen, George A., 1955, *Russia's Japan Expedition of 1852 to 1855* (Westport, CT: Greenwood Press).

Lensen, George A.,1966, *Korea and Manchuria Between Russia and Japan 1895–1904: The Observations of Sir Ernest Satow* (Tallahassee: The Diplomatic Press).

Lensen, George A., 1970, *Japanese Recognition of the U.S.S.R.: Soviet-Japanese Relations, 1921–1930* (Tokyo: Sophia University Press).

Lensen, George A., 1971, *The Russian Push Toward Japan: Russo-Japanese Relations, 1697–1875* (Tallahassee: University Presses of Florida)

Lensen, George A., 1972, *The Strange Neutrality* (Tallahassee: The Diplomatic Press).

Lensen, George A., 1982, *Balance of Intrigue: International Rivalry in Korea & Manchuria 1884–1899* (Tallahassee: University Presses of Florida).

Levchenko, Stanislav, 1988, *On the Wrong Side: My Life in the KGB* (Virginia: Pergamon Brassey's).

Lewin, Ronald, 1982, *The American Magic: Codes, Ciphers and the Defeat of Japan* (New York: Farrar Straus and Giroux).

Linkhoeva, Tatiana, 2020, *Revolution Goes East: Imperial Japan and Soviet Communism* (Ithaca: Cornell University Press).

Luntinen, Pertti and Bruce W. Menning, 2005, "The Russian navy at war, 1904–05," ch.11 in John W. Steinberg et al. (eds), *Russo-Japanese War in Global Perspective: World War Zero* (Leiden: Brill).

MacDonald Fraser, George, 1988, *Flashman's Lady* (New York: Plume).

McDermott, Kevin and Jeremy Agnew, 1996, *The Comintern: A History of International Communism from Lenin to Stalin* (London: Macmillan).

Macintyre, Ben, 2021, *Agent Sonya* (London: Penguin).

Maksimov, Sergei, 2004, "In the East (Hakodate, late 1850s)," ch.6 in Wells, David N. (ed.), *Russian Views of Japan, 1792–1913: An Anthology of Travel Writing* (London: Routledge).

Male, Andrew, 2018, "Russia's answer to James Bond: Did he trigger Putin's rise to power?" *The Guardian*, 11 September, https://www.theguardian.com/tv-and-radio/2018/sep/11/russias-answer-to-james-bond-did-he-trigger-putins-rise-to-power-seventeen-moments-spring

Mark, Eduard, 2009, "In *Re* Alger Hiss: A final verdict from the archives of the KGB," *Journal of Cold War Studies*, 11:3, pp. 26–67

Marshall, Alex, 2006, *The Russian General Staff and Asia, 1860–1917* (Abingdon: Routledge).

Marshall, Alex, 2007, "Russian intelligence during the Russo-Japanese War, 1904–05," *Intelligence and National Security*, 22:5, pp. 682–98.

Massie, Robert K., 1991, *Dreadnought: Britain, Germany, and the Coming of the Great War* (New York: Ballantine Books).

Matsuzato, Kimitaka, 2016, *Russia and Its Northeast Asian Neighbors: China, Japan, and Korea 1858–1945* (Lanham: Lexington Books).

Matthews, Owen, 2013, *Glorious Misadventures: Nikolai Rezanov and the Dream of a Russian America* (New York: Bloomsbury).

Matthews, Owen, 2019, *An Impeccable Spy: Stalin's Master Agent* (London: Bloomsbury).

Medinskii, V.R. and A.O. Chubar'yan, 2023, *Vseobshchaya Istoriya, 10 Klass* [*General History, 10th Class*] (Moscow: Ministry of Education).

Menning, Bruce W., 2006, "Miscalculating one's enemies: Russian military intelligence before the Russo-Japanese War," *War in History*, 13:2, pp. 141–70.

Mitchell, Richard H., 1973, "Japan's Peace Preservation Law of 1925: Its origins and significance," *Monumenta Nipponica*, 28:3, pp. 317–45.

Miyake Masaki, 2010, *Stalin-no-tainichi jōhō kōsaku* [*Stalin's intelligence manoeuvres against Japan*] (Tōkyō: Heibonsha).

Mizuno Hironori, 1931, "The Japanese Navy" in Inazo Nitobe et al., *Western Influences in Modern Japan* (Chicago: University of Chicago Press).

Murphy, William T., 2019, "Lydia Stahl: A secret life, 1885–?," *Journal of Intelligence History*, 18:1, pp. 38–62.

Nagai Yasuji, 2019, "Final report to Hirohito about Sorge spy ring hid lax oversight," *Asahi Shimbun*, 5 November.

Nagai Yasuji, 2023, "Nazo toki tsudzuku '20 seiki saidai no supai'" ["Continuing to solve mysteries, 'The 20th Century's Greatest Spy'"], *Asahi Shimbun*, 7 January.

Naganawa Mitsuo, 1989, *Nikoraidō no hitobito* [*The people of the Nikolai Cathedral*] (Tokyo: Gendaikikakushitsu).

Nakamura Yoshikazu, 1970, "Tachibana Kōsai-den" ["The life of Tachibana Kōsai"], *Hitotsubashi Ronsō*, 63:4, pp. 138–64.

New York Times, 1993, "Kinkazu Saionji; Japanese statesman, 86," 23 April 1993, https://www.nytimes.com/1993/04/23/obituaries/kinkazu-saionji-japanese-statesman-86.html

Nihon Keizai Shimbun, 1983, "Supai Tengoku," 14 April.

Nihon Keizai Shimbun, "Roshia-gawa, 5G nirami sekkin ka, Sofutobanku jōhō rōei" ["Softbank information leak—Russia looking for access to 5G?"], 27 January 2020, www.nikkei.com/article/DGXMZO54911630X20C20A1CC1000/

Nish, Ian, 1985, *The Origins of the Russo-Japanese War* (London: Longman).

Oku Takenori, *Rotan: Nichiro sensō-ki no media to kokumin ishiki* [*Rotan: Media and Public Consciousness at the Time of the Russo-Japanese War*] (Tōkyō: Chūo Kōron Shinsha).

Orbach, Danny, 2017, *Curse on this Country: The Rebellious Army of Imperial Japan* (Ithaca, NY: Cornell University Press).

Ōsugi Sakae, 1992, *The Autobiography of Osugi Sakae*, translated by Byron K. Marshall (Berkeley: University of California Press).

Ozaki Hotsuki, 1959, *Ikiteiru Yuda* [*The Living Judas*] (Tōkyō: Hachi-un Shoten).

Ozaki Hotsumi, 2003, *Aijō ha Furuboshi no Gotoku* [*Love is Like a Falling Star*] (Tōkyō: Iwanami Gendai Bunko).

Packard, George R., 1966, *Protest in Tokyo: The Security Treaty Crisis of 1960* (Princeton, NJ: Princeton University Press).

Paine, S.C.M., 2007, "The triple intervention and the termination of the First Sino-Japanese War," ch.7 in Elleman, B.A. and Paine, S.C.M. (eds), *Naval Coalition Warfare* (London: Routledge).

Palais, James B., 2014, "Political leadership in the Yi dynasty," ch.1 in Suh Dae-Sook and Lee Chae-Jin (eds), *Political Leadership in Korea* (Seattle: University of Washington Press).

Parr, Patrick, 2019, "Russia's Nicholas II is scarred for life in 1891 Japan," *Japan Today*, 24 May, https://japantoday.com/category/features/life-style/russia%E2%80%99s-nicholas-ii-is-scarred-for-life-in-1891-japan

Pavlov, Dmitrii B., 2007, "Russia and Korea in 1904–1905: 'Chamberlain' A.I. Pavlov and his 'Shanghai Service,'" ch.11 in J.W.M Chapman and C. Inaba (eds), *Rethinking the Russo-Japanese War, vol. 2: The Nichinan Papers* (Leiden: Brill).

Pavlov, Vitalii G., 1996, *Operatsiya "Sneg"* [*Operation Snow*] (Moskva: Geya).

Perabo, Betsy C., 2017, *Russian Orthodoxy and the Russo-Japanese War* (London: Bloomsbury).

Plokhy, Serhii, 2011, *Yalta: The Price of Peace* (New York: Penguin).

Plutschow, Herbert, 2007, *Philipp Franz von Siebold and the Opening of Japan* (Folkestone: Global Oriental).

Poretsky, Elisabeth K., 1970, *Our Own People: A Memoir of "Ignace Reiss" and His Friends* (Ann Arbor: The University of Michigan Press).

Prange, Gordon W., 1985, *Target Tokyo: The Story of the Sorge Spy Ring* (New York: McGraw Hill).

Presidential Library, 1925, "The USSR and Japan signed the Basic Convention," Boris Yeltsin Presidential Library, https://www.prlib.ru/en/history/618963

Primakov, Evgenii Maksimovich, 1996, *Ocherki Istorii Rossiiskoi Vneshnei Razvedki* [*Essays on the History of Russian Foreign Intelligence*] (Moscow: Mezhdunarodnye Otnosheniya).

Prima Media, 2015, "Pamyatnik ubiytse yaponskogo prem'er-ministra privezli v Ussuriysk iz primorskoy stolitsy" ["Monument for the killer of the Japanese prime minister moved to Ussuriysk from the capital of Primor'e"], 28 February, https://primamedia.ru/news/423730/

Radzinsky, Edvard, 1993, *The Last Tsar: The Life and Death of Nicholas II* (New York: Anchor).

Records of the Security Service, 1927–1948, Soviet intelligence agents and suspected agents, "Eugene Pik or Pick, aliases Yevgeniy Kozhevnikov," The National Archives, KV 2/1895.

Rees, David, 1973, *Harry Dexter White: A Study in Paradox* (New York: Coward, McCann & Geoghegan).

RIA Novosti, "V Yaponii otkrylsya chempionat po sambo na kubok prezidenta Rossii" ["Sambo championship, the Russian President's Cup, begins in Japan"], 12 February 2018, https://ria.ru/20180212/1514432131.html, accessed 21 July 2021.

Rid, Thomas, 2020, *Active Measures: The Secret History of Disinformation and Political Warfare* (New York: Farrar, Straus and Giroux).

Riehle, Kevin, 2020, *Soviet Defectors: Revelations of Renegade Intelligence Officers, 1924–1954* (Edinburgh: Edinburgh University Press).

Romerstein, Herbert and Stanislav Levchenko, 1989, *The KGB Against the "Main Enemy": How the Soviet Intelligence Service Operates Against the United States* (Lexington: Lexington Books).

Russo-Japanese peace treaty (Treaty of Portsmouth), 5 September 1905, The World and Japan Database, GRIPS, https://worldjpn.grips.ac.jp/documents/texts/pw/19050905.T1E.html

Sablin, Ivan and Alexander Kuchinsky, 2017, "Making the Korean nation in the Russian Far East, 1863–1926," *Nationalities Papers*, 45:5, pp. 798–814.

Saitō Michio, 2022, *Nichi-Bei Kaisen to Futari no Soren Spai* [*Two Soviet Spies and the Outbreak of the Japan-US War*] (Tōkyō: PHP Kenkyūjo).

Samuels, Richard J., 2019, *Special Duty: A History of the Japanese Intelligence Community* (Ithaca: Cornell University Press).

Sankei Shimbun, "An'yaku suru Soren KGB, Seiyaku hikiagesha o tsūjite hanbei kōsaku, Kishi naikaku o 'kaku' de dōkatsu" ["Secret manoeuvres of the Soviet KGB, Anti-US manoeuvres via compromised returnees, Threatening the Kishi cabinet with 'nukes'"], 19 September 2015, https://www.sankei.com/premium/news/150506/prm1505060032-n1.html

Saveliev, Igor, 2004, "Militant diaspora: Korean immigrants and guerillas in early twentieth century Russia," *Forum of International Development Studies*, 26, March.

Saveliev, Igor R. and Yuri S. Pestushko, 2001, "Dangerous rapprochement: Russia and Japan in the First World War, 1914–1916," *Acta Slavica Iaponica*, 18, pp. 19–41.

Scalapino, Robert A. and Lee Chong-Sik, 1960, "The origins of the Korean communist movement (I)," *The Journal of Asian Studies*, 20:1, pp. 9–31.

Scalapino, Robert A., 1967, *The Japanese Communist Movement, 1920–1966* (Berkeley: University of California Press).

Sergeev, Evgeny, 2007, *Russian Military Intelligence in the War with Japan, 1904–05* (London: Routledge).

Shalett, Sidney, 1946, "Axis plot to kill Stalin confirmed," *The New York Times*, 22 September.

Shimane Kiyoshi, 1983, *Nihon Kyōsan-tō Supai-shi* [*History of Japanese Communist Party Spies*] (Tokyo: Shinjinbutsuōraisha).

Shmagin, Viktor, 2017, "They fear us, yet cling to us: Russian negotiations with Tsushima domain officials during the 1861 Tsushima incident," *The International History Review*, 39:3, pp. 521–45.

Shokun!, 1994, "Futari no nihonjin supai—gokuhi shiryō ga terashi dashita gendai-shi no anbu" ["Two Japanese spies: The dark side of modern history illuminated by top-secret materials"], 26:6, June, pp. 128–42.

Skidelsky, Robert, 2000, *John Maynard Keynes: Fighting for Britain, 1937–1946* (London: Macmillan).

Soboleva, Tat'yana, 2002, *Istoriya Shifroval'nogo Dela v Rossii* [*The History of Encryption in Russia*] (Moscow: Olma Press).

Spivak, John L., 1939, *Honorable Spy: Exposing Japanese Military Intrigue in the United States* (New York: Modern Age Books).

Stanley, Thomas A., 1982, *Ōsugi Sakae, Anarchist in Taishō Japan: The Creativity of the Ego* (Cambridge, MA: Harvard University Press).

Steil, Benn, 2013, "Red White: Why a founding father of postwar capitalism spied for the Soviets," *Foreign Affairs*, March/April.

Stein, Guenther, 2011, *Made in Japan* (Oxford: Routledge).

Stephan, John J, 1969, "The Crimean War in the Far East," *Modern Asian Studies*, 3:3, pp. 257–77.

Stephan, John J., 1973, "The Tanaka Memorial (1927): Authentic or spurious?," *Modern Asian Studies*, 7:4, pp. 733–45.

Suvorov, Viktor, 1984, *Soviet Military Intelligence* (London: Hamish Hamilton).

Takahashi, John, 2010, "The beginning of the Orthodox Church in Japan: The long-lasting legacy of Saint Nicholai," *Studies in World Christianity*, 16:3, pp. 268–85.

TASS, 2020, "Posol'stvo Rossii v Tokio poluchilo prava na mogilu razvedchika Zorge" ["Russian embassy in Tokyo receives rights to the grave of intelligence officer Sorge"], 20 October, https://tass.ru/obschestvo/9844691

Tikhonov, Vladimir, 2017, "'Korean nationalism' seen through the Comintern prism, 1920s–30s," *REGION, Regional Studies of Russia, Eastern Europe, and Central Asia*, 6:2, pp. 201–24.

Tilley, Henry Arthur, 1861, *Japan, the Amoor and the Pacific; with Notices of other Places Comprised in a Voyage of Circumnavigation in the Imperial Russian Corvette "Rynda," in 1858–60* (London: Smith, Elder & Co.).

Tomita Takeshi, 2011, "Soren jōhō kikan 'Abe' no nazo" ["The mystery of the Soviet intelligence agent 'Abe'"], *Rekishi Dokuhon*, September 2011, pp. 222–30.

Trotsky, Leon, 1941, "The Tanaka Memorial," *Fourth International*, 4:5, June, pp. 131–5.

Tu Xiaofeng, 2020, "Between the Comintern, the Japanese Communist Party, and the Chinese Communist Party: Nosaka Sanzo's Betrayal Games," ch.7 in Drachewych, O. and McKay, I. (eds), *Left Transnationalism* (Montreal: McGill-Queen's University Press)

United Nations Oral History Project," 1990, "Interview with Alger Hiss by James S. Sutterlin," 13 February and 11 October 1990, https://digitallibrary.un.org/record/474711

US House of Representatives, 1948, *Hearings Regarding Communist Espionage in the United States Government*, Public Law 601 (Washington, DC: Government Printing Office).

US House of Representatives Committee on Un-American Activities, 1951, *Hearings Regarding Communist Espionage, First and Second Sessions* (Washington, DC: Government Printing Office).

US State Department, Office of the Historian, "Foreign relations of the United States, conference at Quebec, 1944," document 181, https://history.state.gov/historicaldocuments/frus1944Quebec/d181

US State Department, Office of the Historian, "261, 'Memorandum of the division of territorial studies,' CAC-302, December 28, 1944," https://history.state.gov/historicaldocuments/frus1945Malta/d261

US State Department, Office of the Historian, "173. Telegram from the Embassy in Japan to the Department of State, Tokyo, June 10, 1960," https://history.state.gov/historicaldocuments/frus1958–60v18/d173

US State Department, Office of the Historian, "174. Telegram from the Department of State to the Embassy in Japan, Washington, June 10, 1960," https://history.state.gov/historicaldocuments/frus1958–60v18/d174

VENONA, "KGB interviews GRU agent and net controller name ALES 30 March (Release 3)," 30 March 1945, https://media.defense.gov/2021/Aug/01/2002818545/-1/-1/0/30MAR_KGB_INTERVIEWS_GRU_AGENT.PDF

Vespa, Amleto, 1938, *Secret Agent of Japan: A Handbook to Japanese Imperialism* (London: Victor Gollancz).

Walton, Calder and Christopher Andrew, 2020, "What spies really think about John le Carré," *Foreign Policy*, 26, December, https://foreignpolicy.com/2020/12/26/what-spies-really-think-about-john-le-carre/

Watabe Kyōji, 2010, *Kurofune Zenya: Roshia, Ainu, Nihon no Sangokushi* [*Eve of the Black Ships: Annals of the Three Kingdoms of Russia, the Ainu, and Japan*] (Tōkyō: Yōsensha).

Weiner, Tim, 2007, *Legacy of Ashes: The History of the CIA* (New York: Doubleday).

Weinstein, Allen, 2013, *Perjury: The Hiss-Chambers Case* (Stanford: Hoover Institution Press).

Weinstein, Allen and Alexander Vassiliev, 1999, *The Haunted Wood: Soviet Espionage in America—The Stalin Era* (New York: Random House).

Wells, David, 2004, *Russian Views of Japan, 1792–1913: An Anthology of Travel Writing* (London: Routledge).

Wells, David, 2019, *The Russian Discovery of Japan* (London: Routledge).

Whymant, Robert, 1996, *Stalin's Spy: Richard Sorge and the Tokyo Espionage Ring* (New York: St Martin's Press).

Wilce, Matt, n.d., "Journalist, gymnast, schoolboy, spy," *ASIJ Stories*, https://www.asij.ac.jp/asij-stories/journalist-gymnast-schoolboy-spy

Williams, Brad, 2021, *Japanese Foreign Intelligence and Grand Strategy: From the Cold War to the Abe Era* (Washington, DC: Georgetown University Press).

Willoughby, Charles A., 1952, *Shanghai Conspiracy: The Sorge Spy Ring* (New York: EP Dutton).

Wilson Center Digital Archive, "Yalta Conference Agreement," 11 February 1945.

Wright, Peter, 1987, *Spycatcher: The Candid Autobiography of a Senior Intelligence Officer* (New York: Viking).

Yamaguchi Kōji, 2000, "Popurizumu toshite no shinbun (2): Akiyama Teisuke to 'Niroku Shinpō'" ["A newspaper as populism (2): Akiyama Teisuke and 'Niroku Shinpō'"], *Hyōron Shakaikagaku*, 62, pp. 125–53.

Yamanouchi Akito, 2006, "Katayama Sen, zai Ro nihonjin Kyōsan shugi-sha to shoki kominterun" ["Katayama Sen, Japanese communists in Russia and the Comintern's early days"], *Journal of Ōhara Institute for Social Research*, 566, pp. 29–53.

INDEX

Note: Page numbers followed by "*n*" refer to notes.